D1083294

VERBATIM:
VOLUMES III & IV

A VERBATIM BOOK

VERBATIM Books are distributed
to libraries by
Gale Research Company
Detroit, Michigan 48226

© Copyright 1976, 1977, 1978, 1981 by
VERBATIM®. All rights reserved. No part of
this book may be reproduced in any way without permission in writing from the publisher.

VERBATIM®, The Language Quarterly
Essex, Connecticut 06426, U.S.A.
Market House, Aylesbury, Bucks., England

ISBN: 0–930454–12–X

Printed in the United States of America

VERBATIM

THE LANGUAGE QUARTERLY

Vol. III, No. 1   May 1976

EDITOR: LAURENCE URDANG

"Ouch!" he said in Japanese

Axel Hornos
Pittsford, New York

Of all the areas covered by comparative linguistics, interjections and onomatopoeic words are perhaps the richest in surprises.

Take "Ouch!", a word whose brief, plaintive urgency is vocalized pain itself; a cry straight from the heart. It is so instinctive that many English-speaking people would confidently maintain, upon questioning, that it must be common to the entire human race regardless of country, language, or skin color.

We know this is far from true. Step on the toes of a Spaniard, an Italian or a Frenchman, and he'll cry out an anguished "Ay!" Pinch hard a Scandinavian, German or Dutch, and he'll respond with a hoarse "Au!" Poke an inadvertent finger into an Indonesian's eyeball and he'll cry "Adú!" A Japanese will say "Aíta!", a Greek and Russian "Okh!", a Portuguese "Uí!"

Or consider "Phooey!", that potpourri of dashed hopes, irritation, and demurral. Yet "Phooey!" would be meaningless to a Spanish-speaking person, who will say "Ufa!" instead. An Italian will growl "Uff!", a Frenchman "Zut!", a Chinese "Che!"

On the other hand our explosive "Hurray!" sounds very much alike in all European and Latin American countries, except to the Italians, who chant "Evviva!" instead.

Another Italian word, "Bravo!", has proved so decisive when one wants to express his admiration for a particularly good bit of opera singing, that it has been adopted by most European and American countries. But in Asia, where Italian opera is not so popular, they think differently. "Bravo!", in the sense of "Well done!", becomes "Bagús!" in Indonesia, "Hau!" in China.

In Spain you don't call a friend with a "Hey, John!" You say, "Oye, Juan!" In Italy, it's "Olà, Giovanni!" in Russia, "Ey, Ivan!" In France, "Eh, Jean!" In Holland, "Sech, Jan!" In Greece, "Aye, Ioannis!" In Germany, "Hallo, Hans!" In Argentina, "Che, Juan!" (The latter explains the "Che" in Che Guevara: Argentine-born, Guevara frequently used this expression when addressing his Cuban friends. Hence the nickname.)

"Wow!" is another interesting ejaculation, thick with tongue-tying wonder. However meaningful the expression may be to a speaker of American English, the Portuguese shout "Oba!", the Danes "Orv!", the Germans "Toll!", the Italians a tame "O!", the Turks "Ya!", the Japanese and Chinese "Wah!", the Indonesians "Ajaib!" As to the French, they have that beautifully eloquent expression which only a Frenchman could have begotten, "Oh! là là!"

Put an American, an Italian, a Frenchman, a Spaniard, a German, a Greek and a Russian in a circle, make each swallow a spoonful of cod liver oil, then listen to their reactions. You'll hear, respectively, the following sounds, "Ugh!", "Pooh!", "Pouah!", "Poof!", "Hoo!", "Oof!", and "Phoo!" Now ask them to squash a big bug underfoot, and they'll snarl "Pooh!" (or "Yakh!"), "Poh!", "Bah!", "Bah!", "Pah!", "Poof!" and "Phoo!"

Animal cries as heard by people around the world are another source of surprises. Take "Bow-wow," our uncontested version of a dog's bark. But it's "Oua! Oua!" or "Gnaf! Gnaf!" to the French, "Wau-wau" to the Germans, "Han-han" or "Wan-wan" to the Japanese, "Au-au" to the

Greeks and Portuguese, "Am-am" to the Russians, "Wang-wang" to the Chinese, "Vov-vov" to Scandinavians, "Hav-hav" to the Turks.

Our "Cock-a-doodle-do" is something else. Frankly, to me it sounds more like some fancy word out of a musical rather than a rooster's crowing. The French and Portuguese hear it as "Cocorico" (the Japanese as "Koke-koko"), the Germans, Spanish-speaking, Italians, Russians, Turks, and Scandinavians, with slight variations, as "Kiki-rikí." Nobody will deny that these sounds are much closer to the rooster's defiant cry than our unconvincing "Cock-a-doodle-do."

Pat a cat, and it purrs. But it "ronronne" in France, "ronronea" in Spain and Latin America, "fusa" in Italy, "schnurrt" in Germany.

To our ears a dove coos, but to the French it "roucoule," to the Germans it "gurrt," to the Spanish-speaking it "arrulla," to the Italians it "tuba," to the Japanese it "popo." A chacun son coo.

Whoever coined the word "twitter" must have combined love for birds with a fine ear. To the French, birds "gazouille"; one almost hears a bevy of birds sweetly chattering on a tree. The Italians say "cinguetta," the Spanish-speaking "gorjea," the Germans "switschert."

On the other hand, a cat's "meow" sounds very much alike in most languages, as does a cow's "moo." (In Japan it is, interestingly, "niao" and "moh." This is perhaps because the cat's and the cow's calls—and to a large extent the rooster's—are more easily imitated by the human voice than, say, a dog's bark or a bird's twitter.

There is still another group of onomatopoeic words, those that imitate man-made and natural sounds and those that suggest motion. Here are a few in their English, German, French, Spanish and Italian equivalents:

English	German	French	Spanish	Italian
rumble	*rumpeln*	*gronder*	*retumbar*	*rimbombare*
sizzle	*zischen*	*grésiller*	*sisear*	*friggere*
sniff	*schnuppern*	*reniffler*	*husmear*	*fiutare*
clang	*klirren*	*résonner*	*resonar*	*squillare*
bubble	*sprudeln*	*bouillonner*	*burbujear*	*bollire*
spurt	*spritzen*	*jaillir*	*surgir*	*spruzzare*
swish	*sausen*	*cingler*	*silbar*	*sferzare*
buzz	*summen*	*vrombir*	*zumbar*	*ronzare*

rustle	rascheln	froufrouter	crujir	frusciare
shriek	kreischen	hurler	chillar	strillare
snore	schnarchen	ronfler	roncar	russare
splash	planschen	éclabousser	salpicar	schizzare

How can one account for such wide discrepancies?

According to most linguists, onomatopoeic words vary from language to language as the phonologies of the languages vary. Once the sounds become established, they are conventionalized. In a way this is regrettable. If everybody used only the sound words that are closest to one's way of hearing them—I, for one, swear that barks sound more like "Woof-woof" than "Bow-wow"—languages would be the richer even though communication might go—well, to the dogs.

Can We Write This Wrong?

A. S. Flaumenhaft
Lawrence, New York

We're on speaking terms with the phrase "on the double,"
But say "on the single," and, boy, you're in trouble.

Take "nevertheless"—we hear it galore,
Yet nary a murmur of "neverthemore."

Note this: "in the long run"—unless it's a race;
Why not, "in the long walk" to slacken the pace?

If "good for what ails you" does not turn the trick,
"What's bad for your ailment" could very well click.

Of course "notwithstanding," but, no, it's unfitting
Wherever you're standing to say "notwithsitting."

The list of "well-heeled' is often unrolled,
Yet never unrolled is a list of "well-soled."

If facts are "forthcoming," we'd feel better knowing
That sooner or later they will be "forthgoing."

In brief, if "the odds are good," tell me, my lad,
Why we don't allow that "the evens are bad."

Mrs. Malaprop's Bicentennial

James D. White
Mill Valley, Calif.

F ew Americans are likely to be in better trim for the commemorative exertions of 1976 than the residents of Northern California, where in 1975 a sort of warm-up bicentennial was observed—unwittingly, it's true, but with a vigor worthy of the chief figure in the original event.

The beneficiary of all this unconscious memorializing was Mrs. Malaprop, the British comedy character who swept the London stage in 1775 with certain contributions to the ruination of the English language. The Mrs. Malaprop role in Richard Brinsley Sheridan's play, *The Rivals,* was that of a busybody intent upon marrying off her young niece to a wealthy aristocrat. In her eagerness to impress, she persisted in using words and phrases beyond her assured vocabulary, and the havoc she wrought with the mother tongue is recalled today in *malapropism* as an accepted term for misused or mismatched expressions.

Mrs. Malaprop's bicentennial, at least hereabouts, actually was the latest in a series of vintage years. This can be reported with some confidence because of the tape recorder, a relentless device for such jobs as preserving and spotting on playback the bungled expression which ordinarily might go unnoticed or unverified.

This merciless gadget, when plugged into the public dialogue via radio or television, also reveals the formidable dimensions of the Malaprop tradition. Sheridan presumably contrived many of Mrs. Malaprop's lapses, but almost without exception the modern examples cited below appear to have been created with anything but deliberation, in the heat of argument and under the pressure of electronic communication. The casualties probably never realized what they'd said.

All this became apparent over the last several years, during playback sessions with taped newscasts, broadcast interviews and talk shows in the San Francisco Bay area. Although the monitoring was done to check public opinion trends on unrelated subjects, the Malaprop spin-off was unmistakable. Some samples had to be run through more than once to be believed. There can be little doubt—the spirit of Mrs. Malaprop lives, as in these samples from notes excerpted from tape transcripts:

"The use of drugs [among the young] is on the upcrease," a San Francisco police officer assures a newscaster.[1] As a new word, *upcrease* may face a dubious future, but its meaning is clear, which wouldn't be true of the corollary, *inswing*.

From Seaside, down the coast, a local official turns up in basic agreement with our San Francisco word-coiner, but mixes metaphors instead of words. He says that the problems of dealing with the young do indeed take us "along an upstream trail."[2] Again, this may be preferable, as compared with an uphill swim.

Such scrambling of vaguely similar expressions is only slightly more common than the supercharged effort to get a point across, as exemplified by the retired Marine Corps general who was complaining about the arguments he encountered on national defense. ". . . And they usually invariably say . . . ," he fumed.[3]

These misadventures took place during telephone interviews. It is the talk show, however, that features the misfit metaphor and the delightfully wrong word at both ends of the line.

"Too many people have been sold down the drain," laments one caller.[4]

"If the circumstances were on the other foot," argues another.[5]

"I don't pull any bones about it," declares still another on a talk show which regrettably went unrecorded but is not easily forgotten.

"You're talking around the bush," complained one listener to a talk show jockey.[6] Unfortunately the appropriate answer came from quite a different jockey to an entirely different listener. "You," he said, "are out of your rocker."[7]

One jockey, probably deliberately, boggled a caller with this reproof: "You have just used two words that set my hair on edge."[8] No hint as to whether his teeth were on end, and in any case the listener gave no indication of finding anything unusual about it.

On another occasion a listener flabbergasted his talk show guru by declaring: "I think we need to get down to the brass roots of the problem."[9] Silence, with the man at the mike presumably sorting out brass roots from grass tacks.

Those are specimens from fast-moving exchanges, but people with more time to think also contribute.

"The nutshell of it is . . . ," explained a locally famous trial lawyer.[10]

"I believe they are cut out of the same mold," said one San Francisco mayoral candidate of two rivals.[11]

And a radio commentator gave this reply during a law-and-order panel discussion: ". . . If he had actually broken a crime or could be accused of breaking a crime. . . ."[12]

But the talk-show jock is the old dependable. One, defending the objectivity of the press in general, said it "bends overboard to be fair."[13] If the information media find this awkward, they could, of course, go over backward.

The newscast contains an occasional gem, but none gathered in this sampling quite matched the inevitable traffic accident report which described a victim as "killed fatally."[14]

The advertising copy writer also contributes now and then, as in the public service announcement which asserted that "fatigue is a major cause of automobile safety."[15] Or the finance company plug with an announcer intoning: "It's Christmas, and you're socked under with bills . . ."[16] Or another finance company barker who urged the listener to "discuss this in the confidence of your home."[17]

Nor is the printed ad innocent. There was the New York department store, touting a high-priced gown in *The New York Times* with this coy demurrer: "Far be it for us to say" just where and when this unique creation should be worn.[18]

Harried newspaper copy desks still produce, as in the

feature attributed to the *Sacramento Union* wherein a local citizen was described as a kindly soul "who will lend an ear to anyone who wants to listen."[19]

Lest one be deluded into thinking that the mighty, if fallen, are immune, out of the past is Richard M. Nixon's quoted comment, long before the distractions of Watergate, on the death of Adlai Stevenson:

"In eloquence of expression, he had no peers and very few equals."

It seems clear that the Malaprop effect, identified 200 years ago and long confined to the uninformed and the careless, now occurs throughout a much broader population because of the increased pressures and volume of modern communications.

---

[1] Inspector Carrigan, telephone interview, KCBS. [2] Unidentified, KNBC. [3] Lt. Gen. Lewis Walt, taped segment, network newscast. [4] Caller to Robin King, KNEW. [5] Caller to Joe Dolan, KNEW. [6] Caller to Harv Morgan, KCBS. [7] Fred Wilcox, KCBS. [8] Jim Eason, KCBS. [9] Caller to Bob Murphy, KNEW. [10] George T. Davis, radio interview. [11] Jack Morrison, radio interview. [12] Bob Murphy, KNEW. [13] Hilly Rose, KCBS. [14] News item, KCBS. [15] KCBS. [16] Pacific Finance Co. commercial, KGO. [17] Pat Michaels, KNEW. [18] Bergdorf Goodman ad, *The New York Times.* [19] Quoted by Herb Caen, *San Francisco Chronicle.*

EPISTOLAE

In response to Norman Shapiro [II, 4], I interpret *I could care less* as elliptical: add ... *but it would be difficult!*

In response to Sol Rosenfeld [II, 4] and his claim that English *s* is never pronounced "sh," I'd reply, as G. B. Shaw did, by asking "Are you sure?" (G.B.S., himself, when stopped and asked "Are you Shaw?", replied "Positive!" and strode on.)

Roger W. Wescott
Drew University

[This second point was also brought to our attention by Louis A. Leslie, Scarsdale, New York. In all fairness, it should be pointed out that Mr. Rosenfeld was quoting—and, perhaps, had been misled by—Peter Farb's book, *Word Play.*   —*Editor.*]

Ellipsis . . . Faulty and Otherwise

G. A. Cevasco
Associate Professor of English
St. John's University, New York

"Would you like to join me in a cup of coffee? asks the straight man. "No thank you," quips the comedian. "I don't think there's room enough in there for both of us." Granted, such a weary bit of humor can be trying, but it does serve as a pointed example of what grammarians call "faulty ellipsis."

Everyone who listens carefully to the speech of others has heard countless examples of sentences that omit words necessary for effective communication. A short while ago one of my neighbors shocked me momentarily when he announced: "When properly stewed, I really enjoy apricots." It didn't take me long to realize, of course, that he had omitted the words *they are* after the first word of his confession.

I had a few lingering doubts, though, because shortly thereafter he informed me rather solemnly that he wanted to get some work done around his house. "I plan to mow the lawn with my wife," was the way he put it. Not being especially fond of his wife, I mumbled to myself, "Go right ahead." But I was forced to conclude that he must have meant that he planned to mow his lawn with his *wife's help*. Yet I was still perplexed. Why had he not said, "I plan to have my wife help me mow the lawn"?

Faulty ellipsis may be contagious. Whether my neighbor infected his wife or she contracted it from him is difficult to determine. One day I overheard her say to their young daughter: "Mommy will put your pajamas on." That would be quite a sight, I thought. Another time I heard her complain to her husband when he was trying a bit too hard to feed their child: "Osberta can eat herself."

Lest it be thought that my neighbors are the only ones I know addicted to such peculiar expressions, here are a few more examples of faulty ellipsis that I recently heard from friends, acquaintances, and students:

They painted themselves.
Do you feel like ice cream?

We had Mr. Colso for dinner.
A boy scout can cook himself.
Wash your face in the morning and neck at night.
A gentleman never crumbles his bread or rolls in his
    soup.

I was really taken up short one day when I heard someone state that he could not recommend a certain Captain Scott. The ostensible reason: "He has little Air Force experience and no navel." [Surely, he meant *naval experience.*]

Ellipsis, as defined by grammarians, is usually taken to mean 'the deliberate omission of a word or words necessary for complete syntactical construction but not required for meaning readily implied by the context of a sentence.' More simply put, ellipsis is saying what we mean but not using all the words we could to say it. The mismanagement of ellipsis is easy, however, and rather common. "This privilege of making words work for us *in absentia,*" Wilson Follett once remarked, "entails, like all privileges, responsibilities and risks."

Much of the strength of English depends upon economy, and ellipsis can be an excellent means of attaining an economy of expression. Economy of expression keeps monosyllables at the core of language, curtails the overuse of particles, tends to regularize verbs and to reduce inflectional forms. The wrong kind of economy, however, can be either a source of humor or outright confusion.

Eighteenth-century grammarians were especially troubled by "improper" ellipsis. Robert Lowth, for example, in his *Short Introduction to English Grammar* (1769) was particularly concerned with the omission of particles. Robert Baker, the author of *Remarks on the English Language* (1770), agreed with Lowth. He judged the use of *government* for *the government* to be "an expression of great barbarity." He also insisted upon the preposition before the pronoun in phrases like "write [to] me."

In his *English Grammar* (1785), J. Mennye cited and condemned many examples of elliptic sentences from the King James Bible, from the poetry of Pope, from the prose of Hobbes, and from other prominent writers. Hugh Blair in his *Lectures in Rhetoric and Belles Lettres* (1793) maintained that such expressions as "the man I loved" and "the dominions we possessed" were faulty. "Though this elliptical style be intelligible and is allowable in conversation and epistolary writing," he dogmatized, "in all writing of a serious or dignified kind, it is ungraceful."

Virtually all eighteenth-century grammarians were overly concerned with "improper ellipsis." In the nineteenth century, however, Carlyle wisely recommended that literary men ought to be paid by the quantity they did not write.

Can we of the twentieth century object to such everyday elliptical expressions as:

I'll light my [tobacco and smoke my] *pipe.*
[This] *House to* [be] *let* [for dwelling].
Georgene is [at] *home.*
Margreet did not want to go, but she had to [go].
The hostess will make the card party and [the]
    tea [*serving*] *a success.*
Though [it is] *possible, it is not probable.*
[The] *First* [to] *come* [will be the] *first* [to be] *served.*

The above examples of acceptable ellipsis could easily be multiplied a hundredfold. Faulty ellipsis is not so common.

Words, of course, should never be omitted unless the intended meaning is clear without them. Except where word omission interferes with the sense content of a verbal construction, ellipsis ordinarily must be deemed acceptable. With all we have to say it is well we can omit a few words now and then.

EPISTOLAE

Doctor Jewett [II, 4] says (perhaps facetiously?), "During the French Revolution, a member of the royalty, imprisoned in the Bastille. . . ." I would be amazed to know that he really thought that such a thing could happen, so I assume that he is "pulling our leg." The mob tore down the Bastille, quite literally, on the first day of the Revolution and found only one old man in the prison.

Dr. Jewett's final paragraph makes it clear that this is a spoof, but I think I might have been happier if the verse had been tossed out of the window of the Concièrgerie! Or from the tumbril.

Louis A. Leslie
Scarsdale, New York

Grass Roots

A. S. Flaumenhaft
Lawrence, New York

There's a species of grass named *corkscrew*; there's another named *drunk*—that's right, *drunk grass* (however, no grass is called *sober*).

And how many other differently named kinds of grass would the man in the street (or even the student of English) guess there are—a dozen? a hundred? . . . There are over a thousand!

Several nights ago I heard a politician use the term *grass roots*, and it suddenly struck me, a retired high school English teacher, that I was ignorant of its derivation, even though I did know the expression denoted people and places "far from the madding crowd's ignoble strife." I flipped the pages of my unabridged dictionary to *grass*, then I turned the page in quest of *grass roots*, only to discover another full page of *grass*, and on the page after, more *grass*.

"Walt Whitman," I mused, "could not have envisioned this variegated vastness of verdure when he described grass as the handkerchief of the Lord,' or even Carl Sandburg when he empathized, 'I am the grass, I cover all.' "

At a glance I saw that my semantic curiosity about *grass roots* must bide a wee, while I traversed these fields of grass.

The first entries in the ten-column list were *adlay, African cane, African millet,* and *alang-alang* (which means 'alang grass' which in turn means '*Imperata cylindrica*. E. Tr. As. Af. 3.').

The last entries were *zacate limon, zacaton, zebra grass,* and *zinyamunga* (which meant 'elephant grass, though it sounded like a college yell).

I started browsing in the veldt and brightened at *bird* and *bull grass, lemon* and *lime grass, pony* and *poor cat grass, rattlesnake grass,* and, praise be, *rescue grass.* Now properly hooked, I grabbed pencil and paper and began copying and columnizing and commenting.

Extant are: *wire, wood,* and *wool grass; sand, silk,* and *satin grass; paper grass, wind grass, water grass.*

For the birds are: *fowl, goose, canary, cockatoo, pigeon* and *penguin grass.* And the good provider has supplied *chicken corn.* Also *turkey foot* ('In North America, a species of Andropogon.') I was about to sniff, "fiddle-sticks," but "drumsticks" seemed more appropriate.

As a matter of taste: *vanilla, chocolate corn, ginger, sweet* and *sour, candy, molasses,* and *sugar grass.* And, as might be expected after this binge of confection, *toothache grass.*

Of and about the animal kingdom are: *deer* and *camel grass, elephant* and *tiger grass, kangaroo grass, fox* and *dog grass, cattail, rattail, mouse* and *mousetail grass,* and, just for luck, *rabbit foot.*

Puzzling it is that our country, the United States, has nary a blade of grass named for it. *Arabian millet* there is, and *Australian love grass, Canada long grass,* and *Bermuda* and *Cuba grass, Egyptian finger grass, English blue grass, French rye grass, Italian reed, Japanese barnyard, Korean lawn, Mexican whisk . . .* even *Himalayan barley.* Countries the world round have grasses bearing their tags, but the U. S., withal its *horn of plenty,* is nominally barren soil grass-wise. Is it not time that those concerned with making America the beautiful do a little name-dropping in their peregrinations about the land: "I hereby brand thee *United States Whatsis grass* or *U. S. Tag-You're-It grass.*"

Whereas the nation has no grass bearing its label, some of its states do. For instance, *California, Kentucky, Nevada* have their *bluegrass, Dakota* and *Texas* their *millet,* disproving the axiom that the whole is greater than any of its parts.

Now, breathe deeply for *scented* and *lavender grass,* and hold your nose for *stink* and *stinking grass.*

The religious will thank the Lord that grass is *sacred* and *holy,* and that not a single blade is dubbed "profane."

Those of us who espouse the finer things in life may read significance into the fact that there is *love grass,* but no *hate grass.*

To make one shudder, or at least wince, are: *Job's tears, devil, witch, centipede, spider, cheat, coxcomb, smut,* and *cutthroat grass.*

Yet, there are *silk* and *satin* fields to wander, with *spring* behind and *summer dew,* in grasses *black* and *blue* and *silver,* and even *white* and *pink,* certainly variegated enough to snap a *gardener's garters.*

As evidence that there is a method in this mad*mess,* I cite: *lady grass* (two words), *mangrass* (one word); *sun, star grass; fog, fountain grass;* grass that's *hard,* grass that's *quick*, and grass that's *bent; beach grass, blowout grass; prickle grass, chess grass; poverty grass* ("Paradox of Poverty Amid Plenty"?) And in conclusion, *creeping panic*, followed by *panic* unqualified.

Which raises the question: Is grass by any other name just as green?

Having closed my unabridged dictionary on *grass*, I idly opened my desk encyclopedia to the same subject, and was flabbergasted to learn that I had barely grazed the surface, for there I read that there are "several thousand members of the grass family." And to think that I'd started out to get to the bottom of "grass roots". . . .

EPISTOLAE

One of the finest breeders of Irish bulls is the weather reporter in Seattle who announces "a 100 per cent possibility of rain, with showers" and "If we have rain today, it will be snow."

Barbara Marsh
San Diego, California

"I'm writing a letter to your client," the man said, "but I'm carboning and duplicate-sampling you."

This happened to me today. It is the first time I've been *carboned*, I think. Definitely the first time I've been *duplicate-sampled*.

As a fugitive from Madison Avenue, I frequently wince when I hear such living language sprigs laid at the door of that fair street. This baby was dumped on me by a salesman for an industrial organization in the Midwest.

I write in the hope of reaching enough keepers of the lexicographic zoo to alert our wordherds to an apparently heretofore unsuspected source of outrageous philological waifs.

Let's not blame all the lumpy newies on Madison Avenue, hey guys?

Joe Ecclesine
Rye, New York

The Mysterious Origin of the Tarot

E. E. Rehmus
San Francisco, California

One of the most exasperating puzzles confronting the student of the occult is the ultimate origin of the Tarot (French *tarault*, German *Tarock*) and it has been variously attributed to such far-ranging peoples as the Egyptians, the Hindus, the Chinese, the Gypsies, and just about every other race. We now see it as containing many Kabbalistic elements and recognize it solely as an object of occult research and as a device for telling fortunes.

But it arose with a curiously full-blown suddenness amongst the upper class Italians in the 14th century as the "tarocchi" (plural of *tarocco*) 'a game played with 78 cards painted with suns, moons, devils and monks.' The deck was composed of 56 cards of the ordinary Italian suits (*coppe, spade, bastoni,* and *denari*) plus 21 *tarocchi* or trumps, and an additional card, 'the fool' (*il matto*). The latter is the source of the modern Joker. So popular did this game instantly become—how could it fail, with monks next to devils in the pack?—that by 1415 the illustrious Marziano had painted a deck worth 1500 gold crowns!

It is at once obvious to anyone who has studied the history of these fascinating cards that they cannot have been the sudden and unique invention of some clever gamester alone, but must have a more ancient tradition lying behind them. Since we are immediately halted in our investigations at the 14th century, however, the real source of the Tarot can only be guessed by an intuitive kind of comparative philology. As an amateur etymologist perhaps I may be allowed somewhat more latitude for speculation than the academician.

The first possibility that comes to mind—one that we may quickly discount—is the possibility that the word *tarocchi* arose by analogy with *malocchio*, the infamous Italian 'evil-eye,' although the Tarot was long considered by God-fearing Christians as "the devil's picturebook." We can equally reject the notion that it derived from some such imagined word as *ter-occhio*, suggesting the wondrous Tibetan "third-eye" of mystic and vatic power.

Many speculators have suggested that the Latin word *rota* 'wheel' is the Tarot's origin. When the word is written in a circle, the final T disappears. *Taro*, then, could easily be made into Latin anagrams or magic squares in early occult practice, such as:

A T O R	R O T A
T O R A	O T A R
O R A T	T A R O
R A T O	A R O T

Perhaps the words in these squares are supposed to form sentences. But if so, they do not translate well: 'Hathor speaks in thought through the Torah'? 'The Tarot wheel is the plough of Otar'? Most scholars now feel that it is more likely to be a variation of the word *Torah* than of *rota*.

The Tarot's beginnings, however, may well have been deliberately obscured. Although we can readily find far-fetched coincidences such as Eskimo *târk* (meaning "obscure'?), Mandarin *tsarng* ('to hide'), English *tarn* (originally, a lake without an outlet, hence 'one that is hidden'?), as well as *dark* itself—ultimately from Old High German *tarni* ('*secret, dark*'). They are all fanciful comparisons, to say the least.

But what if we head in another direction in our search to shed some light on these "dark" origins? Old High German has another word related to *tarni*, viz. *tarchanjan* ('to hide'), which at an oblique angle leads us to the Finnish *tark-astus* ('examination, scrutiny') and *tul-kki* ('an interpreter'). But here the trail ends in a maze of possibilities.

If we choose to limit our discussion to card-playing alone, we can blaze still another trail—southward, this time. Since *l* and *r* alternate among many languages (e.g., English *title* and French *titre*), we are permitted to equate the Finnic *t-l* with *t-r*, and we might just be tempted to compare the latter with Arabic *tarha* ('discard') or *taraha* ('throw down').

But a far more enlightening path can be taken if we progress from *tulkki* and *tarchanjan* back down to Armenian *tarkmanel* ('to translate'), which is the Greek *dragoumanos* ('an interpreter') or our word *dragoman*. From this we proceed to Arabic *tarjuman*, Hebrew *turgman, m'thurgman* ('interpreter') and finally to the Chaldee *targum* ('an interpretation'). From TAR-G to TAR-C or TAROC is but a step.

But *g* may equal *h* and here at last we confront ourselves with the Hebrew *T-Ṛ-H*, meaning 'to warn, forewarn,' or even *ter-etz* 'answer, solve,' as examples of the many things the Tarot is expected to do for us. From there we may even go once again all the way down to the ancient Assyrian word *adr-u* ('dark') or up the other way to Basque *adir-azi* ('to interpret'). From *t-r-h*, however, we also derive *Torah*, the Judaic Law, and Tarot-Kabbalistic connections have long been established by Hebrew scholars. Indeed, one of the cards, The High Priestess, actually bears the scroll of the Torah in her arms.

Yet there is an even sharper, more convincing source than the word *Torah* for the satisfaction of our intuition. It is too much of a coincidence that the Hebrew *tera-ph-im* (hieroglyphs used in ancient Judaic divination) were originally old Hebrew gods, perhaps corresponding to the points in the Kabbalistic "Sepher Yetzirah" (or "Book of Creative Emanations"), 22 in number, which is the exact number of the Tarot trumps if we include The Fool. We must remember that in Hebrew spelling the vowels were omitted: *taro(t)*, *tora(h)* and *tera(phim)* could all be the single root *t-r-a-°* (final "a" in Hebrew having the breath sound of "h"). This prototype would have all the multiple meanings listed above.

We may therefore say that the Tarot has a Hebrew origin and that it surely must have been discovered in the Italian *ghetto* (an Italian word, by the way, from *borghetto*, a borough or section of a city) which, as we know, was the traditional Jewish quarter, as in Rome. From there it was brought out into 14th century Italian society as the card game. The Tarot, as we have often suspected, was apparently a secret device for studying the *Kabbalah*, possibly assisted by the symbolic *teraphim*, in the dark days of medieval Jewish persecution.

°This actually *is* a word ('blow of a trumpet'), but I'm postulating an earlier root.

A Bicentennial Pair: George & Patsy

Arthur J. Morgan
New York, New York

Everyone knows that George Washington's wife was named Martha—many people know that her maiden name was Dandridge and her married name, after her first marriage, was Custis. But not many people are aware that George didn't call his wife Martha. He called her Patsy.

Furthermore Martha Dandridge Custis had a daughter whose name was also Martha. Now here was a good chance to distinguish between the two Marthas at home, but by stubborn custom the daughter was also known as Patsy.

First of all, to substantiate the nickname or pet name by which the Father of his Country called his wife, here is a quotation from a letter he wrote to inform his wife that he had just been called to the highest post in the American Revolutionary Army:

> "My Dearest: . . .
> "You may believe me, my dear Patsy, when I assure you, in the most solemn manner, that so far from seeking this appointment, I have used every endeavor in my power to avoid it. . . ."

And the letter ends:

> ". . . and to assure you that I am, with the most unfeigned regard, my dear Patsy,
>
> > Your affectionate
> > George Washington."[*]

And how did this all come about? Well actually in the 18th and 19th centuries the name Martha, which was quite popular, gave rise to the nickname Matty, then Patty, then Patsy. These nicknames are reminiscent of the nicknames for Margaret: Meg, Peg and Peggy. However, although Peg and Peggy are still recognizably derived from Margaret, Patty and Patsy no longer are recognizable as being related to Martha.

The reason, of course, is the rise in popularity of the name Patricia, to which these nicknames are now closely attached. (Witness Pat Nixon and Patty Hearst.)

The interesting and rather touching letter to "Patsy" Washington was dated Philadelphia, 18th June, 1775.

Ladies of the White House, Laura C. Holloway, Bradley & Co., Philadelphia, 1882, pages 46-7.

EX CATHEDRA

The recent appointment of Father Ambroise-Marie Carré to the Académie Française provides an opportunity for a few observations on that august body in particular and on the legislation of language in general. The Académie, which consists of 40 lay and clerical functionaries, was founded in 1635 by Cardinal Richelieu as a "brain trust" for King Louis XIII. But its chief function during the past 100 years or so has been the "protection" of the French language from the contamination by words of other languages. Several years ago, this erupted in a concerted campaign against Franglais, the corruption of the French language as a result of its miscegenation with English. Although the Académie continues its valiant, though bootless efforts—even to the extreme of condoning, if not inspiring the government's warning to advertisers that a fine would be levied against those who use the interdicted loanwords. It publishes an official dictionary, the latest edition of which appeared in 1905, and a grammar, the eighth edition of which was published in 1935.

The history of the Académie is an interesting one, but a little too involved to recount here. It must be remembered that, literacy being what it was in those days (a condition it seems we are rapidly approaching once again, which, in itself, ought to be a warning to those who yearn for "the good old days"), the nonreading public was more likely to be exposed to any semblance of literature by attending performances at the theater, probably in much the same way in which our functional illiterates establish their relationships with the face of the TV tube. In those days, the government felt compelled to intervene, not to save the people, you understand, but to preserve that extraordinary vehicle—*la langue Française*—which, as the property of the state, was falling into the hands of aliens, seditionists, and corrupt influences like Molière, Racine, La Rochefoucauld, and other assorted hoodlums. Among its first accomplishments was a criticism of *Le Cid*, by Corneille, and it would appear to have gone to greater heights from then on.

With the exception of two minor lacunae, one occasioned by the suppression of all Académies from 1793 to 1803, during the aftermath of a local fracas, the other resulting from the 1940-45 inconvenience, the Académie has continued to flourish.

In addition to its watchdog activities, the Académie dispenses literary prizes, presumably to those authors whose works are free of linguistic transgressions. Generally, the efforts of the Académie have had little or no effect on improving the purity of French and cannot be said to have done very much for its body or flavor, either.

In America, we may deplore the grammar, the rhetoric, the vocabulary, and the lack of expressiveness of governmental officials, of journalists, of entertainers, and of others who may be considered as having some influence on English, if only because they seem to have a dominating control over our media of mass communication. But only a very few of us are purists, and it can be demonstrated that when you scratch a purist you find a liberal. Surely, it would ill suit any speaker of English to forbid any but English root words into the language: the result would be stultifying, throttling. Fully half (if not more) of the current word stock of English has its origins in the Romance languages; another substantial portion comes from almost every other language under the sun.

When the English speaker borrows a word like *succotash* or *kimono*, when he coins one like *transistor* or *telephone*, and when he adapts one like *zeppelin* or *pizzeria*, he does so consciously, trying in certain instances (*transistor*, *telephone*) to be highly denotative and in others (*succotash*, *kimono*, *zeppelin*, *pizzeria*) to be connotative, as well. English speakers seem to like that exercise, for it is a practice that has become a habit since the Danes, the Angles, and the Saxons got together more than eleven centuries ago.

There is an arbiter neither elegantiarum nor grammaticorum in America. Aside from the futility of it all, perhaps there is something about the idea that interferes with our notions of freedom of speech. As we have noted, though some of us may deplore the inability of others to express themselves in articulate, elegant, "grammatical" style, we must acknowledge that problem as traceable to a lowered standard of education and not to the admittance into the language of foreign contaminants.* Some may lament the absence of an Academy devoted to the legislation of English vocabulary, grammar, and syntax, but, judging from the effectiveness of the Académie Française, it seems to us that the archaic senility of such an activity could be exceeded only by the discovery, somewhere in the outskirts of Paris, of a thriving industry in buggy whips, obsidian knives, and flint arrowheads.

---

*As we go to press, we note, for instance, that the New York State Board of Regents has voted, unanimously, to accept a 9th-grade proficiency in English and mathematics as satisfactory for fulfilling the requirements for a high-school diploma.

EPISTOLAE

In your review of the revised edition of *The Random House College Dictionary* [VERBATIM II, 3], you admit that "Baseball is one of our weakest points" while discussing the definition of *designated hitter*. While the points you raise are valid, there are two points you make which I feel I must correct.

Pitchers of neither team "resort to a designated hitter." Rather, a team's manager decides whether or not to "resort to" using a *dh*.

In your version of the definition you start with the words "pinch hitter." *Designated hitter* and *pinch hitter* are not synonymous. A *ph* (or 'substitute batter,' to use the term in the official rules) can pinch-hit only once in a game and then must either take the field in the next half-inning (in which case he is no longer a *ph* because he is batting for himself) or be replaced by a regular fielder. A *dh*, however, stays in for the entire game. If, on the other hand, a *ph* substitutes for a *dh*, the *ph* then becomes the *dh* for the rest of the game. See?

David M. Glagovsky
Arlington, Virginia

Yes. We made the error of using pinch hitter *in the generic sense of 'any batter who substitutes for another,' ignoring the fact that it is a very specific, denotative term in baseball.* —Editor

Prepositions and Other Words Not to End a Sentence With

With dismay, perplexity, irony, consternation, and as great a variety of emotions as there are attitudes about language, enough readers have pointed to our occasional use of a preposition at the end of a sentence to warrant our commenting on the subject.

To those who maintain that *preposition* means 'in place before,' we reply that although that's what it might have meant, etymologically, in Latin, it doesn't necessarily mean that in English, where it is the name of a grammatical class of words.

To those who cite a "rule" enjoining the ending of a sentence with a preposition, our reply must be a little more complicated. First of all, Who formulated such a rule? As far as we can determine, its origins can be traced to the 17th-century stylists—Dryden, chief among his contemporaries—who modeled their English on Latin in the vain hope of attaining a "classical" style. They ignored an important fact or two, the most important of which is that English, notwithstanding its huge stock of Romance vocabulary, is of Germanic, not of Latin origin. Languages are classified by their structure, not by their lexicon. Yet, once that has been recognized, can anyone imagine imposing German word order on English? For that matter, normal word order in Latin—with notable exceptions for purposes of style—requires the verb to appear at the end of the sentence; a rule of that kind imposed on English would result in utter chaos.

The fact is that in Latin, the preposition was almost invariably placed before the word it modified. But it is pointless to impose that practice on English.

While we're at it, we might as well give to the "split-infinitive" rule its quietus: the simple fact is that if one insists on modeling his syntactic style on Latin, one must avoid splitting an infinitive because in Latin the infinitive is a single word, composed of a root (like *ama-* 'love') plus an inflected ending (like the infinitive marker *-re*). Placing something between them is akin to defying a law of physics, let alone of Latin grammar.

There is yet another point to be made about so-called "prepositions." Contrary to popular belief, many of the words in English so categorized are actually adverbial particles. For instance, the *in* in *take in* 'deceive,' the *up with* in *put up with*, the *off* in *take off* 'depart,' behave more like adverbs than like prepositions. How would those who object to ending sentences with prepositions handle perfectly good English utterances like *Come in, Charley was easily taken in, His behavior is difficult to put up with, I want to go out, Do you mind if I look on* [*while you repair that watch*]?, *The doctor is ready to see you: you may go in*, and thousands of others, including, *That's something I don't wish to comment (up)on, I don't know what you're talking about, That remark is uncalled for,* and [II, 4] "... acceptability and unacceptability vary with ... the degree of 'perfection' ... the purist is capable of insisting upon."

Style and emphasis favor *You'd be so nice to come home to* over "It'd be so nice to come home to you," poetic license notwithstanding

After all, all speakers of every language have at least one artistic talent in common—creating language—and, as we well know, ideas of artistry, creativity, and elegance vary widely. VERBATIM hereby bestows on each and every one of you a Poetic License, irrevocable for as long as you live, no fees or renewals required.

An Epilogue to "Apostrophes"

A few sharp-eyed readers have pointed out what they took to be an improper use of the apostrophe in our article on that very subject [II, 4]. In the second paragraph appeared the following:

"... we recall that a friend of our parents' gave ..."

and the objection was to the apostrophe after *parents*.

This is what is generally known as the double genitive (or double possessive), and has a history going back to Old English. Its most common reflex is seen in such constructions as *a friend of mine, that remark of his*. But when a noun is substituted for the pronoun, the construction persists: *a friend of my mother's*. Similarly, *a friend of our parents'*. We find *a play of Shakespeare* alternating with *a play of Shakespeare's*, the distinction being, perhaps, a matter of style. We happen to prefer the style with the apostrophe.

A Grammar of the English Language, Vol. III, *Syntax*, George O. Curme, D. C. Heath and Co., 1931, p. 77:

> The double genitive and the *of*-genitive are often used side by side without any differentiation of meaning: *a play of Shakespeare's* (or *of Shakespeare*). But the forms are gradually becoming differentiated. The double genitive is associated with a liveliness of feeling, expressing the idea of approbation, praise, censure, pleasure, displeasure.

Some 40-odd years after that was written, we are not at all sure that we agree with the connotative description, but we are firm in our conviction that the double genitive is an active fact in the English language.

EPISTOLAE

Professor Fowkes in "Talking Turkey" [VERBATIM II, 3] mentions the fact that a word used for turkey in Hindi is *perū*. He fails to note, however, that that is the Portuguese for turkey and that the Portuguese navigators and explorers (followed by traders) doubtless brought both the word and the bird to the subcontinent.

In Peru, while it would be delightful if the bird were called '*hindi*,' it is actually called *pavo*. This makes it a sort of minor league peacock, since the latter is either *pavón* or *pavo real*. However, there is also another word for the turkey in South America which sounds as though it might be a native word: *guanajo*.

Fowkes suggests that the Italian word for turkey, *tacchino* is a derivative of *tacco*, ". . . but which *tacco*?" Well, I don't know what he means by that; *tacco* is usually 'heel,' so *tacchino* would be 'little heel.' This doesn't appear very likely, but the Italian lexicographer Migliorini could think of nothing better than "forse voce onomatopeica," 'possibly onomatopoeic.' (It is an endearing thought that Italian turkeys cry "Tacchino!" just as the ax falls.)

Arthur J. Morgan
New York, New York

Giving Up the Ghost

Mabel C. Donnelly
University of Connecticut, Hartford

In the 20th century the major surviving meaning of *ghost* is, according to the *OED*, "the soul of a deceased person . . . appearing in visible form." This is the meaning associated with Halloween.

Ghost meaning 'soul or spirit, the principle of life' survives only in the colloquialism *to give up the ghost* and in the liturgical *Holy Ghost*. At the present time, even the liturgical expression is giving way to *Holy Spirit*.

Early English uses of *spirit*, according to *OED*, are derived from "passages in the Vulgate in which *spiritus* is employed to render Greek *pneuma*," ['breath,' whence *pneumatic tire*, *pneumonia*, etc.]. The translation of *pneuma* by *spirit*, the *OED* goes on, "is common to all versions in the Bible from Wyclif onward."

But examination of the Gospel according to St. Mark, i, King James version, shows verse 8, "baptizing with the Holy *Ghost*," whereas verse 10 refers to "a *spirit*, like a dove, descending." In King James, then, as in references during the Middle Ages, *Cursor Mundi* and others, both *ghost* and *spirit* were used without constraint, often interchangeably.

Only recently has the Catholic church expressed a preference for *Holy Spirit* rather than *Holy Ghost*. A *Catholic Dictionary*, D. Attwater, ed., 3rd ed., 1958, cites "a tendency nowadays to prefer Holy Spirit" because of the "common meaning" of the word *ghost* referring to "apparitions or illusions." *Ghost*, says the *Dictionary* is certainly archaic."

So it seems that in mid-20th century *ghost* has been put in the prison of Halloween.

BIBLIOGRAPHIA

SLIPS OF SPEECH, by John H. Bechtel, The Penn Publishing Company, 1901, 217 pp. Republished by Gale Research Company, 1974. $12.00

> Rarely use a foreign term when your meaning can be as well expressed in English. Instead of *blasè* [*sic*], use surfeited or wearied; for *cortège* use procession; for *couleur de rose*, rose-color; for *déjeuner*, breakfast; for *employé*, employee; for *en route*, on the way; for *entre nous*, between ourselves; for *fait accompli*, an accomplished fact; for *in toto*, wholly, entirely; for *penchant*, inclination; for *raison d'être*, reason for existence; for *recherché*, choice, refined; for *rôle*, part; for *soirée dansante*, an evening dancing party; for *sub rosa*, secretly, etc.

The selection quoted above and this book are important, for they illustrate how style and even meaning in language have changed during a brief 75 years. Of the items listed, today's speakers of English would probably consider only *couleur de rose, déjeuner, employé*, and the archaic *soirée dansante* (replaced by the later, but now also archaic *thé dansant*) as affected. But the rest—11 out of 15—are readily encountered in common speech and writing. These deal less with the question of fashion in language than with language itself. One, *recherché*, has a more common sense today as 'arcane, recondite, obscure' than as 'choice, refined,' though dictionaries still list the older sense, chiefly because it may well be encountered in writings more than 50 years old.

Language fashions change, too: under "Trite Expressions," we can find such unfamiliar "stereotypes" as *counterfeit presentment, the hymeneal altar, the rose upon the cheek, the debt of nature, the bourne whence no traveler returns, the devouring element, a brow of alabaster.*

Under "Very Vulgar Vulgarisms," we find (among regionalisms and eye-dialectalisms) *fooling you, lots of, teeny.* Included is a list of "objectionable expressions' that was prepared by William Cullent Bryant for his staff when he was editor of *The Evening Post*. Among them are many that we continue to find in poor style today: *gents, (to) decease, darkey.* But a major portion of the items on the list are quite standard today: of specific words to avoid, we know of no modern injunctions against *bogus, collided, compete, donate,* and many others; of substitutions, we find quaint such interdictions as *casket* (for *coffin*), *jubilant* (for *rejoicing*), *official* (for *officer*), *pants* (for *pantaloons*), *reliable* (for *trustworthy*), and *quite* (when prefixed to *good, large,* etc.).

Perhaps a little expensive for the average book buyer, this small volume is nonetheless recommended for libraries whose users are interested in the development of the English language and in the contemporary history of its usage.

📖

THE LANGUAGE OF MEDICINE, John D. Dirckx, M.D., Harper & Row, 1976, 170 pp. $4.95

As the subtitle of this curious but intriguing little paperbook informs us, Dr. Dirckx has written a book that deals with the evolution, structure and dynamics of words used in the medical profession. The author, Medical Director of the Student Health Center at the University of Dayton, makes it quite clear that he is writing especially for members of the medical profession—but trusts that nonphysicians will find his book both instructive and entertaining.

A few years ago this reviewer foolishly thought that he knew a little bit about the English language, but after 16 years as a professional medical writer and editor, including five years spent as a medical lexicographer (with sidetracks into the murky depths of general lexicography), it can truthfully be said that the mind not only boggles but nearly collapses under the weight and complexity of the information Dirckx offers.

This book will be of interest to many readers of VERBATIM—not just as persons involved in language and the magic of words generally, but as potential or actual patients who want to learn more about the jargon that is sometimes necessary in medicine (together with the concealment of ignorance, which is not).

At first glance, this book appears to contain about 5,000 pages. This is a deception of reading time. Each page is closely packed with words, words, words—key entries in italics (fully indexed) with snap comments about their etymologies and current standings. The book is fairly loosely structured. It contains seven chapters, dealing with everything from medical slang, jargon, and gibberish to modern coinages, abbreviations, and trade names.

In spite of the fact that the author points out errors of usage and lack of clarity in medical writing, he attempts to justify the use of much medical jargon by claiming that only medical writers and journal editors care about accuracy and that physicians understand well enough the logical absurdities involved. He comments that a patient might talk of a "shiner" whereas a doctor (holy of holies) would speak of a "periorbital ecchymosis," which is true only if you could imagine a doctor referring to cephalalgia instead of a headache or odontalgia instead of a toothache. It just isn't done in practice, except for papers submitted to medical journals; and the editors of such journals will soon set the author straight.

Occasionally, Dirckx steps into a nicely planned trap of his own design. He claims that "several physicians have a regrettable habit of inventing, or at least misapplying, terms to cover their inability to arrive at a diagnosis. There must be several million people who have been told by their physicians that they have *low blood pressure*, a condition unknown to writers of textbooks of medicine." On that point one must question the author about his medical qualifications, especially since he makes such a big point of this so-called error. The fact happens to be that every major medical textbook in the world lists low blood pressure (under the medical heading *hypotension*). The only technical point to be conceded is that low blood pressure is not a disease entity but a feature of some primary disorders (Addison's disease being the best known). Of course, low pressure is also a fact in acute shock (circulatory collapse) and other conditions, such as myocardial infarction, orthostatic hypotension, and hemorrhagic fever. One leading medical textbook (Harrison's *Principles of Internal Medicine*, p. 225) even mentions that chronic low blood pressure may be a feature in "malnutrition, cachexia, chronic bed rest, and a variety of neurologic disorders . . . especially in the standing position."

It is no fun to pick on errors, simple or complex. The

fact is that this book is quite useful and makes extremely interesting reading.

Dirckx occasionally pokes fun at his fellow physicians. He mentions that, "Though they readily stretch the meanings of words, physicians show little imagination or initiative in the fabrication of new words in medicalese. Exceptions are *retrospectoscope*, a mythical instrument with which the pathologist is reputed to achieve 20/20 hindsight in identifying the errors and omissions of the clinician, and the acronymic *Gok's disease* (God only knows)."

American doctors have traditionally been looked upon by their patients as nearly mystical and gòdlike superbeings. It is refreshing to see a book that attempts to prick the bubble of this illusion, even though the primary audience may not find it altogether amusing. Much of the magic of medical jargon is exploded. Technical terms are revealed as smokescreens for ignorance or insecurity in many cases. The play must go on. As the author tells us, "Besides the special jargon that physicians use when they speak to patients about technical matters, there is yet another *patois* in which doctors converse among themselves about these matters when they must do so in the presence of the patient. The former idiom is intended to make complex ideas intelligible, the latter to make simple ideas opaque."

Edward R. Brace
Fellow, American Medical Writers Association
Aylesbury, Bucks., England

EPISTOLAE

"They Don't Write English Like They Used To" [VERBATIM II, 3] suggests that they don't write French or German like they used to either. The pâté-mad Alsatians mentioned, if French-speaking, spell the name of their city *Strasbourg*. Those who are German-speaking spell it *Strassburg*. "Strassbourg" must be the Freutschais spelling.

Henriette Berger
Oberlin, Ohio

College Slang 1975

Slang, the area of language that allows the linguist to show himself human, reveals much of the humor and ingenuity of language makers. Most of us have coined a phrase or word at one time, and all have used or not used a term, thereby helping to decide its fate. All of us, therefore, make language.

The following are some current slang expressions collected on the campus of Clemson University, Clemson, South Carolina.

ace, *v.* to do very well on a test. Also, **blitz.**

bean up, *v.* to take drugs in order to study all night.

bitch building, a sorority dormitory.

blitz, *v.* See **ace.**

bomb, *v.* to do very poorly on a test. Also, **flag.**

Bugs Zoo, an introductory course in entomology.

dude ranch, a fraternity dormitory.

Flick Lit., an introductory course in film.

flag, *v.* See **bomb.**

gaper, *n.* a conspicuous fraternity pledge.

get jacked, to become enthusiastic about a game, course, weekend, etc.

goob, *n.* a large pimple. Also, **pointer, zit.**

gorp, *n.* "if he were the last male on earth you'd be reluctant to date him."

Grit Lit., a course in southern literature.

grub, *v.* to pet.

hunk, *n.* a handsome, well-built male.

Land of the Midnight Sun, the architecture building, as a rule, where projects continue day and night.

lavaliered, *adj.* pre-engaged.

library, *n.* the bathroom, largely because in the dormitory it is the only quiet place to study.

lunch lip, a voracious lip.

munchies, *n.pl.* snacks.

mystery meat, suspicious cold cuts.

nerd, *n.* a conceited gorp.

Pimple Lit., a course in adolescent literature.

Po, *n.* affectionate term for the post office.

pointer, *n.* See **goob.**

poop file, a fraternity file of old tests.

pork it, what a lunch lip does best.

query, *n.* a test.

rack, *n.* the female chest.

rack monster, one inordinately fond of his bed.

scope, *v.* to look over at a classmate's test paper.

shoot some hoops, to play an informal game of basketball.

sleeze, *n.* a loose woman. Also, **slooze.**

smoker, *n.* a fraternity party held to recruit pledges.

spaced, *adj.* wigged, freaked, or otherwise slightly removed from reality.

submarine races, the, a favorite necking spot.

suckin' wind, in danger of failing.

turkey, *n.* an undesirable. Also **zero.**

zit, *n.* See **goob.**

Sterling Eisiminger
Clemson University

EPISTOLAE

Shortly after reading "You Know What" [VERBATIM II, 3], I caught myself writing, in a letter to a friend, "His health has had its ups and its you-know-whats," and it occurred to me that there is a motive for using this substitution formula that Professor Read did not mention in his enjoyable article. I think that it is not an uncommon tactic to employ the formula in order to say to one's hearer or reader, in effect, "I am using a tired old expression, but I want you to know that I am well aware of doing so." To say, "He is living in a fool's you-know-what," is narrowly to skirt banality, and this, you will agree, is to be avoided like the you-know-what.

Stanley M. Holberg
St. Lawrence University

Constant Rider's comments on baseball Spanglish [VERBATIM II, 3] invite comparison with French-Canadian baseball terminology. Obviously more linguistically chauvinistic than our neighbors to the south—being more linguistically vulnerable—the Canadians have developed a complete native vocabulary. Some terms—*le but, la manche, la chandelle*—have been borrowed from other sports. Most, however, have been manufactured out of whole cloth by sportswriters and announcers and officially adopted after frequently lengthy deliberations.

Thus, in Canadian parlance, a *frappeur* 'batter' will come up to the *marbre* 'plate' (lit. 'marble'), face the *lanceur* 'pitcher' on the *monticule* 'mound' who, in turn, *lance la balle* 'pitches the ball' to the *receveur* 'catcher.' The pitch may be a *rapide* 'fast ball,' a *courbe* 'curve,' even a *tirebouchon* 'screwball' (lit. 'corkscrew'). If the batter *s'élance dans le vide* 'swings and misses' (lit. 'lurches out into space') or lets a good pitch get by, he is penalized with a *prise* 'strike,' the third of which—result of a bad swing or a *décision de l'arbitre* 'called strike' (lit. 'umpire's judgment')—produces a *retrait sur prises* 'strikeout' (lit. 'withdrawal on strikes'). Four balls, on the other hand, put him on base with a *but sur balles* 'base on balls.' He may, of course, *frapper un coup sûr* 'get a hit' (lit. 'hit a safe shot'), from a *simple* 'single' to a *circuit* 'home run,' or a *fausse balle* 'foul ball,' or a *ballon au champ extérieur* 'outfield fly,' or a *flèche* 'line drive' (lit. 'arrow'), or a *roulant* 'ground ball' (lit. 'roller'), etc.

A *chandelle* 'pop-up' (lit. 'candle') may be caught by the *arrêt-court* 'shortstop,' who, if he is fast enough, may *doubler les coureurs sur les pistes* 'double up the runners on the base paths' and *terminer la manche* 'end the inning.'

Suffice it to say that while the foregoing terms—and dozens more—are ostensibly French, few Frenchmen would have the vaguest notion of the scenario they describe. Proof that, in the sports realm at least, France and French Canada, like the England and America of Churchill's famous comment, continue to be two countries separated by the same language.

Norman R. Shapiro
Wesleyan University

Even the best writers (novelists, historians, columnists, etc.) seem to have trouble with contractions of what I always thought to be *spirit and image*. We get *spitting image, spit 'n' image*, and a few other variations. It seems to me that the only correct contraction should be *spi't 'n' image*.

Regarding Norman Shapiro's wonderment about *I could care less* [VERBATIM II, 4], it is my opinion that it's just plain sloppy talk by people who couldn't care less about what they are uttering. It sounds O.K. to their careless ears. These same people would never say "I could agree more."

H. N. Meng
Bethesda, Maryland

⊠

Jon Mills asks [II, 4] for other words besides *facetious* which use vowels in sequence. Besides the well-known *abstemious,* one can find *parecious, arsenious, acheilous, acheirous, bacterious, arterious, affectious, fracedinous, acleistous* and *annelidous* in *Webster's Second.* Is it possible to find a word with vowels in order that does not end in *-ous*? I haven't found one in *Webster's,* but *cacheticorum* and *arteriosum* are in *Dorland's Illustrated Medical Dictionary,* and *conus arteriosus* is in *Webster's Third.*

The November 1968 and February 1970 issues of WORD WAYS, the Journal of Recreational Linguistics, generalized the AEIOU problem by asking for Websterian examples of words containing each of the 120 different possible orderings of the vowels. Examples for 109 were eventually located—all but AEIUO, AUIEO, EAIUO, IAEUO, IAUEO, IEAUO, IUEOA, OAIEU, OAUEI, OEIAU and UIAEO), and the word *Milquetoast* (in *Webster's Third*) was subsequently found to fill one of these holes.

Short well-known eight-letter words with the vowels each represented once are *dialogue* and *euphoria.* Two seven-letter examples besides *sequoia,* are *moineau* and *miaoued.* The French language has a fine six-letter example, *oiseau.*

Mr. Mills also mentions the vowel-replacement problem, exemplified by *pack-peck-pick-pock-puck.* Examples of these are so easy to find that WORD WAYS readers introduced the additional constraint of Y as a vowel. In the August 1975 issue, Darryl Francis proposed *math-meth-mith-moth-muth-myth: meth* is in *A Dictionary of New English* (1973), and the others are in *Webster's Third.* In the November 1975 issue, several readers pointed out the examples *Dane-dene-dine-done-dune-dyne* (all in the *Penguin Dictionary of English*) and *pale-Pele-pile-*

283

pole-pule-pyle (all in the *Funk &Wagnalls College Dictionary*). *Mana-mane-mani-mano-Manu-many* can all be found in *Webster's Third*. In the February 1976 issue, Dmitri Borgmann gives examples of from three to eight letters in length, but he must use obsolete words from the *Oxford English Dictionary* in the longer examples.

A. Ross Eckler
Morristown, New Jersey

[A general round of applause (one hand clapping) to those readers who sent in *abstemious*. As for the vowel-sequence problem, it might be solved most neatly by a fast chorus of *Old MacDonald Had a Farm!* This gives us the opportunity to call our readers' attention to the excellent quarterly periodical, WORD WAYS, published by Mr. Eckler. WW is filled with word games, articles on some of the more recondite anomalies of language, and a great deal of linguistic acrobatics. A sample issue is $2.00; a year's subscription, $8.00. Address WORD WAYS, Spring Valley Road, Morristown, NJ 07960, and send remittance in full with your order.   —*Editor*]

Although Bruce D. Price is quite correct that Noun-speak [VERBATIM II, 4] has become endemic in the language, he cites only one lengthy example, *U.S. Air Force aircraft fuel systems equipment mechanics course*. This is fair specimen. But General Electric has issued an *earth resources technology satellite data collection platform field installation, operation and maintenance manual,* and the University of Michigan has produced a *shore erosion engineering demonstration project post-construction season progress interim report*. Many, many more examples could be cited from the world of science and technology.

My own interest is the expression that consists of an adjective followed by two nouns. This construction, which is innocent of hyphens, I term the Lulu. It is especially poignant in the names of occupations. Thus we see want-ads for a *vibrating equipment manager*, a *buried pipeline designer*, and a *destructive lab technician*. When a dangerous de-fusing job is to be done, we call on an *unexploded bomb expert*. There is a girl in the business office of a midwestern University whose official title is *Dishonored Check Collector*. Occasionally a super-Lulu appears, as in the ad in the Wall Street Journal for a *frozen ethnic food manufacturer.* Luluized groups are not uncommon: NASA has an *Energetic Particle Team,* and the governor of California can call on a *7-person mudslide advisory panel* (7-person mudslides are something like 4-person bobsleds, I assume). The students at Caltech can partake of meals like an *interstellar molecular sack lunch seminar,* and those at the University of Kansas can eat at a *home cooked family owned restaurant.*

It is clear that mixing in a few adjectives with Nounspeak greatly increases its range and flexibility. I'd like to comment further on this, but you'll have to excuse me. Lulu just called. I have an appointment at the Contaminated Soil Removal Facility.

Robert L. Bates
Columbus, Ohio

In reference to Russell Slocum's article, "A Quick Brown Fox Jumps Over the Cwm Fjord-Bank Glyph Biz" [VERBATIM II, 4], let me suggest that now is the time for all good men to come to the aid of holo-alphabetic precision.

Slocum's apocryphal story of the World War I cryptoanalyist to the contrary notwithstanding, the sentence offered as an illustration of typical holo-alphabetical brevity (at 34 letters) is just not holo-alphabetic. He may offer, and VERBATIM may publish, his example, *Pack my bag with five dozen liquor jugs,* but this does not make the sentence fit the basic definition, since it contains no *x,* thereby invalidating it either for intellectual exercise or cryptoanalysis.

The correct version, of course, is *Pack my box with five dozen liquor jugs.* Slocum perhaps can take comfort in the fact the sentence is often misquoted as *Pack my bag with six dozen liquor jugs,* presumably for the sake of a more euphonious rhythm; this version, alack, lacks the *v.*

Let me now progress from this quick quibble to a more civil cavil. Slocum began by identifying *A quick brown fox . . .* as a "grammar school writing exercise" incorporatin' all 26 letters of the alphabet in a 33-letter sentence. This suggests that in Reading, Pa., or elsewhere, pupils still are being taught penmanship, something that will be news to parents and educators of most communities.

Be that as it may, I submit that Slocum's example,

again, is more representative of cerebral wishing among those who are obsessed with brevity as a desideratum than it is of actual usage. The standard version of this sentence is *The quick brown fox jumped over the lazy dog's back,* as everyone knows who has tried out a new typewriter on a merchant's display. The important attribute of this sentence is that, when combined with the numerals, it tests the full set of typewriter keys and also just fills a single line across standard 8½" x 11" typing paper with this neat pica display:

The quick brown fox jumped over the lazy dog's back
1234567890.

Also, unmentioned by Slocum is the use of "The fox" (and not "A fox")—sentence and numerals—as the standard automatic tape-driven test for teletype function, known to generations of telegraphers, telephone long-lines trouble-shooters, and wire-service newsmen. This invariable, longer version has the additional advantage that on repetitive lines the letters and numerals are displayed in vertical columns, plainly revealing what particular combination of electrical symbols is at fault, as well as providing· a neat all-over pattern charting the fox's track as he pursues his carefree track across and down the page, as well as over the lazy dog's back.

Harold F. Osborne
Bethesda, Maryland

According to your May issue [VERBATIM II, 1], *Sanka* brings five cups of coffee in Canada. My friend R. L. D. claims that when he orders a *dry martini* in Berlin, they bring him three. . . .

Douglas T. Henderson
Philadelphia, Pennsylvania

Spanish author Pío Baroja said there existed a store-house of verbal adornments, popular words and phrases commonly known and employed. He declared that he tried to avoid the place.

I once decided to stop requisitioning the hackneyed adj.-adv. *pretty.* I shortly discovered a formidable professional element among the pro-*prettys* arrayed against me.

From that very day's newspapers, the *Wall Street*

Journal had "*pretty* well-known fact" (quoting a Radcliffe sophomore); the same paper's book reviewer's column had "*pretty* impressive personalities"; *The Christian Science Monitor*'s Editor's column had "*pretty* obvious"; the *Los Angeles Times* had "*pretty* petty" (quoting the Mayor at a press conference), and a TV newscaster added "*pretty* quickly."

Edwin Newman's *Strictly Speaking* devotes several paragraphs to *pretty good.*

Tracing the usage back to Shakespeare's time ("A pretty while these pretty creatures stand . . ." *Lucrece,* 1.1233) and beyond only adds to the seeming indispensability of the practice.

The *Dictionary of American Slang* shows how humorist James Thurber handled the situation by carrying the usage to its ultimate foolishness. He described a building as ". . . a little big and pretty ugly."

A. W. Reichel
Los Angeles, California

Are any business executives, I wonder, losing sleep over how to dictate letters to their feminist secretaries?

Years ago, in secretarial school, I was taught that the proper salutation in a letter addressed generally to a business firm was "Gentlemen:". Does the considerate boss of today start his dictation with "Gentlepersons:"?

And what will become of "Dear Sir:"? There are alternatives that have been used in the past—and may still be in use for all I know—but they have slightly comic overtones. "Dear Sir or Madame:", for instance, carries the implication that there is some uncertainty in the writer's mind as to the sexual leanings of the person addressed. There is no such vacillation in "Dear Sir/Madame:". Here, the writer has clearly made up his mind that he is addressing an out-and-out hermaphrodite. "Dear Person:" has a somewhat disparaging air to it and might be useful for irate letters to banks or credit departments about their alleged computer breakdowns. However, it wouldn't do for companies or customers whose good will is sought.

One solution might be to omit the salutation entirely in impersonal letters of this kind, in which case the closing "Yours very truly," would be superfluous. Could the result be called a letter of any sort? The unthinking courtesy of most business letters may be phoney—after all,

I know the bank manager isn't truly mine or even respectfully mine, nor does he hold me particularly dear—but there is a kind of Dickensian charm about it that I like.

Gloria Dawkins
Unionville, Ontario, Canada

I enjoyed very much the article "Where the Harts Wear Pants" by Sister Mary Terese Donze [VERBATIM II, 4].

I recall that in my fourth grade experience it was not the hymns that puzzled me, but Church History. The "Diet of Worms" I firmly believed to be a bad name for Martin Luther. It seemed a bit revolting, but fairly appropriate. Not until the seventh grade did I learn that *diet* was the name of a legislative assembly, and *Worms* was the name of a German city. Now in a good ecumenical spirit we sing hymns written by Martin Luther. May he rest in peace!

Mary M. Roche
Meriden, Connecticut

Anent the Gratuitous Negative [VERBATIM II, 2], when I arrived in Central Ohio circa 1929, it was common in rural parts to hear, *I doubt he'll not be here tonight.*

The inverse of the Gratuitous Negative: *Thanks a lot* really means 'No thanks for that left-handed compliment'; while *Thanks a million* still conveys a great thanks.

Shame on W. M. Woods [II, 4] and his search re *cowbird, Molothrus ater.* In 1828, in *American Orthnic Biography,* Audubon wrote, "From the resemblance of its notes to that of the word 'cow-cow', this cuckoo is named Cowbird in nearly every part of the union."

Edwin H. Hammock
Columbus, Ohio

Until sixty years or so ago when Kentuckians began filtering into our east central Indiana farm community populated by descendants of local pioneers, there wasn't a *creek* in the whole township. We had *spring branches*—whether the "spring" was because they flowed from springs or flowed mainly in spring and tended to dry up come summer might be something to look into—but when they

flowed they flowed into *cricks* where we swam and caught
shiners and crawdads and tadpoles; and also hellgrammites
for bait for bigger fish in bigger *cricks* and the *river*.

We also have a *brook* now. A few years ago a trans-
planted New England couple built a house above our *Fall
Crick*. They are trying but have not qualified yet for their
naturalization papers. They keep forgetting that their
brook is a *crick*, and they still bring up water in a *pail*,
which hitherto hereabouts had been only what Jack and
Jill went up the hill with.

Our neighbors from back east take *paper bags* along
on mushroom hunts; those from Kentucky take *pokes;* and
we natives take *sacks*.

Though *Webster's* was the only dictionary in our early
farm library, we went along with *Oxford preferred* when
we *greazed* our wagon wheels with axle *grease*, getting our
hands *greazy*, too.

And more on Dr. Kurath's *Mary*. New neighbors
from Kentucky who moved to a farm up the road a piece
from us had a daughter *Murray*, same as our last name.
They spelled it *M-a-r-y*.

Candace Murray Huddleston
Connersville, Indiana

This refers to the note of Philip E. Hager [VERBA-
TIM II, 4].

I had never before heard of his *ditch and delve*. The
counting rhyme, as I remember it from my childhood,
goes: *Eleven, twelve, dig and delve*.

Dig and *delve* are more nearly synonyms than are his
ditch and *delve*. And the assonance is more effective. The
tongue attacks the next syllable from the position it was
left in by the preceding syllable without any need for
silent repositioning.

If Hager really wants to get into what he calls
"specific binomials," he should examine the language of
the law, of lawyers: *aid and abet, cease and desist, to wit
and in particular, find and discover, disclose and admit,*
ad nauseam.

I wish to comment on the expression *any more*. My
comments may have some pertinence to dialect geography.
Bergen Evans and Cornelia Evans in their *Dictionary of
Contemporary American Usage* (Random House, New
York, 1957) give the examples *He doesn't come here any
more* and *We go there often any more*, and state that in

the examples *any more* means simply 'now.'

I believe the linguistic situation is more complicated. I believe that in the negative usage *He doesn't come here any more* the term means 'He used to come here [perhaps habitually], but he doesn't come here now.' In my experience, the negative usage would be so understood over most of the United States and perhaps in most of Canada.

My first acquaintance with the affirmative usage of *any more* was in middle-eastern Illinois and contiguous parts of Indiana—Robinson, Palestine, Olney, Illinois and Vincennes, Dugger, Bloomington, perhaps Indianapolis, Indiana. In that region, at least, the statement *We go there often any more* means 'We used to go there often, then we stopped going there for some time, but now we go there often again.' A specific example from my own experience is *Did you know the Ten Cent Store has those jelly orange candy slices any more?* [Note to Bruce D. Price: Not only scientists abuse the noun-adjective, or run-on noun; farmers do it too.] This meant that the Ten Cent Store once sold the candy routinely, then stopped selling it, is now doing it again.

In that region, the use of *any more*, either affirmative or negative, is often prefatory, as *Any more, I go to bed before ten,* or *Any more, I can't remember anything.* These mean, respectively, 'I used to stay up past ten, but now I go to bed before ten,' and 'I used to remember most things, but now I can't remember anything.' You will notice that the prefatory use of *any more* conforms to the Evanses interpretation of the affirmative use, meaning simply 'now.' The final placement of the affirmative *any more* has a different meaning, a more complicated meaning.

W. M. Woods
Oak Ridge, Tennessee

For years I have been an avid reader of advertisements; the Madison Avenue boys would find me the perfect target for their endless nonsense. I have reveled in the puns, errors, idiotic claims and materialistic appeals of these creative writers. Ernest Dichter's *The Strategy of Desire* (Doubleday and Company, Inc., 1960) became my laugh-inducing Bible for years.

Who would have thought that, with all this background in commercial falderal, I would find the most outrageous advertising claim right here in Pomona? A sign in a local jewelry store states the following:

Ears pierced FREE—While you wait!

VERBATIM is wonderful! Keep it coming!

James Dunne
Pomona, California

Since two recent issues of VERBATIM have contained lists of unusual names, perhaps you would be willing to add my collection:

Belle Gravey Hellfat   *Seneca M. Gamble*
Sleeth Heffelfinger Wilkie   *Melborne Moose*
Marcy Tinkle   *Slaughter Linthicum*
Herome L. Opie   *Urban Shirk*
Oscar A. Doob   *Ardella Sweek*
Laurie Doughty Dorr   *Delight Diefenderfer*
Griffin M. Lovelace   *J. Hayden Twiss*
Ovid Fiveash   *Senta Hella Poock*
Hyacinth Ringrose   *Ingo A. Esch*
H. Milton Flitcraft   *J. Blan Van Urk*
Burton Bunch   *Alphabet John Duntz*
Leat Woolheater   *Iduma Self*

Luther Orange Lemon, who was on Ms. Brown's list [VERBATIM II, 2], was also on mine, because he was a man I knew in business.

Kenneth Godfrey
Orient, New York

Here are a few from our collection:

Lois Achue   *Ted Bear*
Norma Tweedle Ballew   *Harold Belcher*
Basil Bibby   *Clement Bourgeois, Jr.*
Avis Crowe   *Dr. Paul Cutright*
Ormly Gumfudgin   *Mildred B. Dey*
A. Tilden Cree   *Anthony Albino*
Ann Tilley   *Kelly Green*

Editor

To the American example *right down* [I, 1] might be added W. S. Gilbert, *The Gondoliers,* finale of Act I: *a right-down regular Royal Queen.*

There is a good example of the "Gratuitous Negative" [II, 2] in Sterne's *Life and Opinions of Tristram Shandy* (1760 ff.), Book V, Chapter VII, which runs: "He is certainly dead.—So am not I, said the foolish scullion."

Professor Fowkes gives words for *turkey* in many languages [II, 3], but he does not mention that the Portuguese for it is *peru*. I wonder if the Hindi can by any chance be derived from this. Incidentally, in Spanish *un Perú* means 'a fortune.' According to Corominas, the Spaniards used *pavo* (from Latin) for peacock until the turkey came along, whereupon they transferred this word to it and called the peacock *pavo real* (where *real* means 'true, real,' and not 'royal,' as might be thought). Italian *tacchino* is onomatopoeic, according to Olivieri's etymological dictionary. He compares Serbian *tuka* 'turkey' and Turkish *tavuk* 'hen.'

Mr. Sharp [II, 3] seems to be indulging in folk-etymology. ... [The] obvious connotation of the name *Smerdyakov* is *smerdet'*, 'to stink,' which is cognate with *merde*. *Smert'* 'death' is from a different root and is cognate with Latin *mors:* the reason for the Slav prefix *s-* is an interesting one. English *smart* is not connected with either of the above but perhaps with Latin *mordeo* 'to bite.' For authorities see the etymological dictionaries of Russian, Latin and English by Vasmer, Walde and Onions, respectively.

Paul S. Falla
Bromley, Kent, England

I am amazed that your commentators upon the subject have failed to connect *Smerdyakov* with the word which surely is the immediate association for any Russian: *smerd'*. It is an old Slavic word denoting 'evil emanation, odor.' Equally evocative is the verb *smerdet'*. Its meaning: 'to stink.'

But Dostoevski drew upon more than one associative source: the word *smerd* (without the "soft sign") is an ancient and pejorative one for 'serf, vassal.'

Thus one need not reach farther than the actual first syllable of the character's name. Dostoevski obviously wished less to suggest 'death,' as has been put forward, than—Dickens-like—the qualities of this man.

Valentina Litvinoff
New York, New York

[*Which is what we said at the very outset!* [II, 2]
—*Editor*]

In the 1930's the editors of the AMERICAN SPEC-TATOR—Eugene O'Neill, Theodore Dreiser, George Jean Nathan, Branch Cabell, Charles Angoff—raised hell with the newspapers for the spellings (still prevalent) *kidnaper* and *kidnaping*. Would they complain about your *diagraming* [II, 3]?

Turkeys do have a native name, *guajolote*, in Mexico; I was surprised that Fowkes [II, 3] didn't mention it. But he also neglected the Spanish *pavo*, even though the species name of the wild turkey is *gallopavo*. A young domestic turkey is called *cocono* or *coconito*. Santamaria, *Diccionario de Mejicanismos*, also records the more local names *cihuatotolin, conche, mulito, pipila*, and *totol*.

Ronald K. DeFord
Austin, Texas

[On *diagraming*, etc.: The "rules" of American English spelling, notwithstanding O'Neill, et al., provide that the terminal consonant of an unstressed final syllable should not be doubled when an ending is added. British practice differs. Hence:

AMERICAN	BRITISH
diagraming	*diagramming*
labeling	*labelling*
paneling	*panelling*
programing (concert)	*programming* (from *programme*)
programming (computer)	*programming* (from U.S. usage)

Practice in America varies to some extent, but variations are considered departures from the "rule."

We have always considered the prevalent practice in America to spell *programming* (computer) with two *m*'s as attributable to the unavoidable conclusion that computer specialists are simply bad spellers. In school, we were taught to spell *kidnaper* and *kidnaping* with single *p*'s.

—*Editor*]

Referring to Constants Rider's letter on Spanglish [II, 3], the examples could be augmented by hundreds more from Ricardo J. Alfaro's *Diccionario de anglicismos* (2nd ed., Madrid, 1964). which is a whole 480-page dictionary full of them.

The form *keks* 'cakes'—I don't deny that it exists—is certainly un-Spanish-looking. Spanish orthography would normally call for *queques*. In fact, the form *panqueques* (sometimes *panquequas*) is fairly common in parts of Latin America.

A few corrections: Accent marks are needed on *béisbol, fútbol* and *vólibol*. Also:

sueter	should be *suéter*
champu	should be *champú*
mitín	should be *mitin*
lider	should be *líder*
folklorico	should be *folklórico*

Concerning the question, Where did the *n* come from, instead of *m*, in *jonrón* 'home run'?, the answer is simply that Spanish phonology does not permit an *m* at the end of a syllable when followed by *r*, nor, for that matter, at the end of a word (with the exception of a few Latinisms, e.g., *álbum, máximum, mínimum*).

Another Spanish phonological taboo: words beginning with *st-* or *sp-* require an initial vowel, e.g., *estudiar, español*. That's why the wine named *Spañada* may be O.K. as wine, but its name is phoney Spanish. English, of course, has analogous taboos: we have no words beginning with *sb-* or *sg-* or *sd-*, though they are common in Italian.

Woodruff W. Byrne
Sarasota, Florida

I have always shared your reviewer's delight in the hodge-podge of colorful information in *Brewer's Dictionary of Phrase & Fable* [II, 3]. But to judge by an example trustingly cited in the review, this information can be conspicuously inaccurate.

"Cupid's golden arrow is virtuous love," we are told, with *Midsummer Night's Dream* cited in support. Ovid's tale of Apollo and Daphne is given as evidence that "Cupid's leaden arrow is sensual passion."

Not so. According to Ovid, when Apollo spoke scornfully of Cupid as a bowman, Cupid in revenge shot a golden arrow into Apollo, which inflamed him with love for Daphne. But Cupid pierced Daphne with a leaden arrow, which made her desperately flee Apollo's love and develop an aversion to the very word *lover*.

Curiously enough, *Brewer* conveniently prints accurately in Latin the key passage from Ovid, but both the *Brewer* editor and your reviewer must not have read it or noticed the crucial word *fugat*.

Midsummer Night's Dream is equally unsupportive in the matter of virtue. Along with swearing by Cupid's golden arrow, Hermia swears "by the fire which burn'd the Carthage Queen." In the case of Dido as in that of Apollo, it is quite evidently the intensity and irresistibility of the love caused by Cupid's golden arrow that counts, and not any distinction between the sensual and the virtuous.

Robert Gorham Davis
Columbia University

VERBATIM

THE LANGUAGE QUARTERLY

Vol. III, No. 2   September 1976

EDITOR: LAURENCE URDANG

Grammar: The Terms Betray the Bias

Donald A. Sears
California State University, Fullerton

Those of us over fifty have learned our grammar several times over, struggling each time with shifting terminology. From the Latin-based grammar of Wooley with its nominatives, genitives, and accusatives through the dos and don'ts of early Hodges (*The Harbrace Handbook*), we boxed ourselves into the structural approaches of the fifties, and drew Calder-like mobiles of branching trees as we pursued Chomsky's transformational logic. With an occasional wistful glance at the traditionalist Longs (*The System of English Grammar*), we confounded ourselves in Fillmore's cases and Lamb's stratifications. For the changes have been rapid; and to our confusion, each new school of grammar has developed its own taxonomy. With each development we have been asked to learn a fresh array of terms, always with the claim of greater "scientific" precision.

Closer examination of these terms, however, reveals

less science than poetry, less precision than metaphor, less innovation than acceptance of the latest intellectual fad. To each age, its dominant world view; with each shift, a compulsion to substitute new terms in the old disciplines, be they of history, criticism, science, or in this case language study. The following is an initial attempt to bring order to taxonomic chaos, to suggest categories in the development of grammatical terminology.

1. THE NORMATIVE

Now two centuries old is the familiar terminology that started in the eighteenth century, grounded in its belief in universal norms and raised by the moral nineteenth century to overtones of ethical values. Compounds were labeled *impure* and *improper* when their morphemes were drawn from more than one language. Suffixes were accused of *tainting*; words *contaminated* one another. Paradigms were found to be *defective* in Modern English. And semantic change was analyzed in terms of *amelioration* and *pejoration, elevation* and *degradation.* Grammar itself was *right* or *wrong.* To mishandle the semicolon was to stray from the paths of rectitude and commit a *comma fault.* From religion itself came terms such as *hierarchy, canonical forms,* and *relics.* But a new breeze of Darwinian evolution was in the air even as the normative terms were pouring forth.

2. THE EVOLUTIONARY

While the great debate of religion versus evolution echoed among scholars, the normative terms of grammar with their religious moralism were under attack by the new. Words were now seen as *native* or *alien;* they became *naturalized* and *domesticated,* underwent *diffusion* and *migration.* In the process of *acclimatization,* they became *conditioned* by *environment.* The results might be a *mutation* or *adaptation.*

As the age wore on, Darwinian terms broadened into biomedical terminology applied as metaphor to language. The *pedigree* theory traced the *family tree* and *branches* of the Indo-European languages. We read of *word-crossing, linking,* and *liaison.* Some suggestive verbs became known as *copulative;* nouns and pronouns might be *epicene;* constructions might be *pregnant.* Words were studied *root* and *stem,* and were caught in acts of *nesting* and *symbiosis.* Some were found to undergo semantic *rejuvenation.* But biological determinism was going down before physical determinism and a new fad of naming was a-borning.

3. THE PHYSICAL SCIENTIFIC

The drive to make linguistics scientific flooded the literature with jawbreaking terms derived with new affixes of *-ival*, *-eme*, and *allo-* (*adjectivals*, *phonemes* and *morphemes*, *allomorphs* and *allosemes*). The search for natural "laws" identified *centrifugal* and *centripetal* forces. "Root" was replaced with *element* and *nucleus*, leading to *residue* forms and *residual* phonemes. *Amalgams* and *agglomerations* were identified from *components*, *constituents*, and *segments*. *Diachronic* versus *synchronic* approaches vied with *endocentric* versus *exocentric* to confound the neophyte. From geology came terms like *drift*, *matrix* and *embedding*, *attrition*, and *petrification*. Gradually, however, some newer sciences—closer in subject matter to linguistics —were emerging.

4. THE COMMUNICATIONIST

From the Bell Telephone Laboratory came communication theory, from MIT came cybernetics, and from IBM the application of mathematics to computer science. The linguists snuffed the change of air and spoke of *sets* and *subsets*, of *encoding* and *decoding* messages, of *code switching* and *feedback*, of *frame* and *base*, of *senders* and *receivers* and semantic *noise*. Language now was seen in terms of *input* to generate an *output*. The *efficiency* of the *code* could be measured in terms of its *productivity*.

What the next intellectual wave will contain of scientific detritus and terms to torment the tyro the eighties will tell. We can at least be sure that future linguists will continue to respond to the trends, to lend their discipline the aura of scientific exactitude by adapting and adopting the latest fashion. Happily for those of us more humanistically inclined, there are still those linguists who have drawn their metaphors from general fields. From music come *allegro* and *lento* forms; from industry, *constructions*, sentence-*building*, and *modification;* from banking, *borrowing* and *loan* words. More generally still, consonants may be *broad* or *slender*; and vowels, *dark* or *light*. Words may be *full* or *empty*, and morphemes appear as *bound* or *free*. Words may be *telescoped*, *clipped*, or *coined*; some remain as *stumps*, stand *forlorn*, get packed into a *portmanteau*.

We await the next development whether it come from rocketry and outer space (boosters? capsules? orbits?) or oceanography (the deeps? submerged?) or environmental science (ecology? semantic smog?)—whatever. Come it will, as future linguists proclaim their newness with borrowed metaphors of the trendiest intellectual development of the future. Their terms will betray their bias.

EPISTOLAE

It distresses me to note [II, 3] your contributors so flagrantly ignoring the existence of Portuguese as one of the major Romance Languages. Indeed, statistically it is the second most widely-spoken Romance tongue, preceded only by Spanish and in front of French and Italian by tens of millions of speakers.

Although it bears a superficial resemblance to Spanish, Portuguese is really quite a different language with grammar, cadence, and tonal quality all its own.

In "Talking Turkey," Professor Fowkes credits Hindi for geographying our "turkey" as "perū." The proper Portuguese word for that succulent bird is "peru"; it should not require immense research to trace the word back beyond the Hindi Curtain to the Portuguese sailors and merchants who, in the 15th and 16th centuries dropped seeds of their language and culture around the globe.

And in "Conjugal Oddities," Axel Hornos has short-change himself and family by confining his fascinating game to Spanish, French, and Italian. Had he window-shopped Portuguese, he would have discovered such gems as:

meia 'stocking'/*meio* 'half'
pá 'shovel'/*pó* 'dust'/*pão* 'bread'/*pé* 'foot'
leite 'milk'/*leito* 'bed' (of a river, road)
pia 'sink'/*pio* 'chirp'/*pião* 'top' (toy)
doca 'dock'/*doce* 'candy'
lixa 'sandpaper'/*lixo* 'rubbish'
mão 'hand'/*mau* 'evil'

I am not a professional student of language but simply (to quote the advertisement which originally enticed me into subscribing to VERBATIM) someone who "loves words." And so I find it especially gratifying that the Portuguese-speaking world does not load pejorative connotations into their word for *amateur*. Their single word *amador* means both 'non-professional' and 'lover.'

Harry Oster
São Paulo, Brazil

299

Esrever Hsilgne

Robert A. Fowkes
New York University

L ong before the hucksters told us that *Serutan* spelled backwards was "nature's"—implying apparently that the product was the opposite of natural—I acquired the habit, or psychological affliction, of reading words and signs backwards. It was an attendant phenomenon on another puerile stunt, that of reading a page upside down. Before the age of ten I could do this almost as fast as reading right side up. I was a slow reader. Possibly the only practical value that subsequently accrued from this aberration from normal human behavior was an ability to handle with relative facility scripts reading from right to left.

It was fascinating to me to imagine a meaning to *Gnikoms On!*, and I pictured to myself some sort of gas mask or anti-emphysematic device to be put over our juvenile faces. Exactly what kind of pots *lluf pots* were, escaped me. One day, as I waited for a bus to take me to school and to the tender mercies of a ferocious substitute, Miss Luke, which was clearly in the days before the substitute was at the mercies of the pupils, I read her name and title on the approaching *Loohcs Sub*. Much later came the realization that the opposite of *University* is, approximately, *it is revenue*, something that various deans have been telling me for years, while assuming the *alumni* to be *in mula*.

A store in a town where I lived as a child was called *Garton's*, and since I once bought a handkerchief there in an emergency, *snotrag* seemed an appropriate reversal of the name. A Chinese neighbor in the same town once ordered *klim* in the grocery store, and I assumed with childish delight that he was saying *milk* backwards, until he added, "extra heavy." Years later a dried milk product was actually called *Klim*.

That pornographic danger could lurk in simple names of products was obvious when *Tums* read alphabackwardly as *Smut*. That *animal* is the reverse of *lamina* struck me while I was doing a crossword puzzle, a blow from which I soon recovered. Long before commercial diaper services tended to fundamental infantile needs I perceived that a *diaper* was *repaid,* but I was not exactly sure how, or to whom.

Our neighbors' tough son *Dennis* seemed to merit the backward condemnation *sinned,* but his rather pious *sister* seemed to have difficulty in reading *resist.* Why a *decal* should be *laced* or a *dessert tressed;* why a *peek* should *keep,* or the *dew* be *wed*—not wet?—or *Camus* become *sumac,* or a *gnat* have a reverse *tang,* or a *tuba abut,* or a *trap* be a *part,* was no clearer than the *room* on a *moor,* or *Emil* in *lime,* or *grub* in a *burg* (possibly a *hamburg: grub mah!*). A *keel* could spring a leak, but hardly a *leek.* Were some *kinfolk* named *Klofnik? Fidelio* is *oiled if*—if what? If the singers are in good voice? A *reward* could come backwards out of a *drawer,* and an *Yliad* was a distorted *daily* epic. Did we *retap* the *pater* as a source of supplemental allowance?

Many fragments of reverse English look as if they could or should mean something: *dradnats* for *standard* (reminiscent of a mangled dreadnought?), *red now* for *wonder* (ex-fascist, perhaps), *Kroy wen* (cry when it hurts?) for *New York, yawbus* (not mine!) for *subway, set a ropave* for *evaporates, rewolf* for a *flower, torrac* for a backward *carrot.* The *state·* turns into a plural in reverse French, while *united* is almost detained in the same language, and *muni-mula,* whatever that is, is forthcoming—or backcoming, from *aluminum.*

A non-existent New York University student named *Duarf* finished second in the race for some class office one year; he was a not too backward *fraud,* as were those who had entered his name. *Sreknoy* for *Yonkers* suggests a new and imminent horror (*Schreckneu-Neuschreck?* I have often read the street sign *Yonkers Ave.* as *Eva Sreknoy,* imagining vaguely some frightening Valkyrie).

The *devil lived,* but waxed *livid* when called *divil;* but *evil* is not *live,* and *denim* is not *mined. Aborigines* may possibly back out of a place called *Senigiroba,* why not?

But *radar, kayak, gag, poop, peep,* and *noon* are on a frustratingly complete *level* of palindromicity, not a city in which this reverse English thrives.

A Roman schoolboy supposedly read the Latin name of his city (of course Latin; what else?—well, maybe some antecedent of Latin) backwards and thus rendered affably effable the ineffable name *amor: Roma.*

The title *Erewhon* baffled me in high school, for I didn't get "nowhere" reading the utopian designation backwards (despite Leumas Reltub's possible justification in treating *wh* as a unit, and despite later temptation to render *Geritol* as *Low Tiger*, or *English* as *shingle*).

In school we used to try the reverse trick on our own names (for, unfortunately, I was not alone in the madness). We cheated in one respect: we retained the order of first and last names. Thus, the procedure that produced *gnikoms on* was not followed (the product would have been, rather *on gnikoms, presumably an exhortation to a team of some extraterrestrial origin). Nevertheless, *Trebor Sekwof* looked and sounded like a conceivable reverse of *Robert Fowkes*; schoolmates branded it an improvement, in fact. *Mij Snave* even worked for *Jim Evans*, as did *Dranreb Efeeko*, more or less, for *Bernard O'Keefe*, or *Ekim Navillus* for *Mike Sullivan*. But *Ztirf Ztluhcs* did wretchedly for *Fritz Schultz*, while *Nan Tibbit* had a rough time indeed in shifting into reverse.

Well, even the *Forverts* is read *rikverts*.

But shun Dylan's *Llareggub*; it's imperative.

ᘓᘓᘓᘓ

I am interested in enlarging my collection of English words in which a hyphen is necessary to distinguish one word from another, otherwise identically spelled. I solicit help to expand the following list:

| *dis-ease* | *re-creation* | *draw-er* |
| *pray-er* | *re-present* | *re-form* |

I would be particularly interested in forms without *re-* or *-er* and in forms that are less likely to be assimilation followed by back-formation.

Gene Chase
Asst. Prof. of Mathematics
Messiah College
Grantham, Pennsylvania 17027

ᘓᘓᘓᘓ

Duo for Voice & Percussion

We were discussing Alfred Noyes.
Howells said he'd never heard the sound
But volunteer'd: "Once I heard Saul Bellow
I didn't mind hearing Ezra Pound."

E. O. Staley
Maplewood, New Jersey

Tom Sawyer Whitewashed

Nancy LaRoche
Hartford, Connecticut

How wonderful to be weaned on the likes of *The Wind in the Willows*, I thought, as I scanned the pages of a large, library anthology of children's literature, chock full of nursery rhymes, fairy tales, excerpts from the "classics." There he was again, the incorrigible Toad, tricking his would-be reformers, evading the Law which forever tries to restrain his natural, lovable recklessness.

But it was primarily Grahame's language that gave me pause—the delight in words, their marvelous creative and evocative power, the music and magic in the lines that lure the child into his fictional world. The genius of Grahame lies in his refusal to talk down to his audience, to adapt his style and diction to the "limited" verbal world of children. Rather he stretches their linguistic horizons; part of the fascinating new world to which they are introduced and to which they respond is an awareness of new sounds and words, a sensitivity to the *how* of expression. Little does it matter that the structural patterns are often unfamiliar and the words themselves likely to trip the tongue, not to mention the understanding, of many an adult—*wonted, paroxysm, habiliments, squandering, contemptuously, languid, artful*. But mood and meaning are clear to the child, who drinks in all his vessel can hold, all the while being subtly affected by the excess mysterious verbal waters swirling and splashing about him.

I'm getting carried away with words myself, I know. As I was saying, I was riffling the pages of a children's anthology when I was seized with these musings. I next happened upon a passage from *Tom Sawyer*—the whitewashing episode, of course. It had been carefully whitewashed itself, apparently in preparation for oral reading by a teacher or librarian or whoever else might be engaged in introducing children to the delights of literature. (It seems unlikely that a parent would have been responsible for the excisions and substitutions I found.)

I studied the perversions of the text, attempting to discover a motivation or method in the madness. It appears to me that this is what happened to Poor Tom. (Parentheses indicate excisions, *italics* substitutions.)

Unfamiliar words or words deemed difficult had been omitted entirely or replaced by "simpler" ones: the (locust) trees; a Delectable Land, dreamy, (reposeful) *restful,* and inviting; he passed his brush along the topmost (plank) *part*; he went (tranquilly) to work; Tom (contemplated the boy) *thought* a bit; the (balmy) summer air. In not one instance cited here, nor in the many instances not cited, would the original wording have prevented a young listener from grasping the idea.

What was evidently considered "improper" English and some regionalisms were also cut: Jim never got back with a bucket of water (under) *in less than* an hour; Ben Rogers (hove) *came* in sight. Similar treatment was given allusions or other references to the unfamiliar. The listeners were deprived of seeing and hearing Ben Rogers "personate" a steamboat. And "Tom planned the slaughter of more innocents" becomes "of more innocent boys," while "part of a jew's harp" is verbally purloined from his catalogue of worldly wealth by this contemporary Bowdler.

The last excision, however, may have been motivated instead by whatever led this custodian of children to shield them from all references to race or slavery: (White, mulatto, and Negro) boys and girls gathered round the town pump; soon the (free) boys would come tripping along. And in this version a young Black boy addresses a White boy by his name only—the deferential, respectful "Marse" is abandoned for the naked "Tom."

Passages that do not advance plot or contain dialogue but rather describe moods and attitudes or present ideas are blocked out completely: (There was a song in every heart; and if the heart was young the music issued at the lips); (A deep melancholy settled down upon his spirit); (Life to him seemed hollow, and existence but a burden). The famous distinction between work—"whatever a body is obliged to do"—and play—"whatever a body is not obliged to do"—was prevented by pencil from falling on the ears of the young listeners, many of whom were probably at work that very moment.

This horror story ends with the most unkindest cuts of all—those apparently made for "moral" purposes. While others worked and Tom watched, he "had a nice, good, (idle) time." Evidently idleness and goodness are mutually exclusive terms for the sacred snipper. Tom's essentially immoral behavior must not be reinforced. So the youthful audience subjected to this truncated version is left with Aunt Polly's admonition that she'll "tan him" if Tom stays out too long at play and doesn't return for more assigned chores. They are deprived of Twain's beautifully ironic ending to the incident: Aunt Polly rewards Tom for his labors by bestowing upon him a choice apple while he at the same time, in the current vernacular, manages to "rip off" a doughnut as well.

"I know the taste of the watermelon which has been honestly come by, and I know the taste of the watermelon which has been acquired by art. Both taste good, but the experienced know which tastes best," said Twain. And those kids would be among the experienced. Wouldn't they love the apple and the doughnut and the delicious payment for work not done? Wouldn't we all? But they mustn't be allowed to savor, even vicariously, the delights of stolen and unearned pleasure. And they mustn't be allowed to see authority successfully and unknowingly thwarted!

Well, I may be making much ado about nothing or a mountain out of a molehill (depending on your respective literary and metaphorical lights). But I don't think so. True, this is an isolated instance whose circumstances are unknown. My inferences are pure conjecture.

Yet no matter the agent of or reason for *Tom Sawyer's* mutilation, its validity as a symptom of the sickness that afflicts too many young readers remains. Uncomfortable with the unfamiliar, if not openly hostile to it, they rebel at extending the boundaries of their linguistic and literary worlds. They are ignorant of the fact that to do so is to expand the horizons of their *real* world. This hacked-up version of *Tom Sawyer* illustrates their unformed tastes to perfection—no "hard" words, no unfamiliar references, no descriptive passages, no controversial subjects. And were Tom's theft and deceit of Aunt Polly included, not a few would feel compelled to sit in judgment on him, their assessment of his moral guilt or innocence constituting their sole, supreme response to the work.

Who is robbing them of the richness that is language, that is literature? The culprit is the mentality that takes the locust from the trees, the balmy from the air; that reduces reality to fact and action, destroying mood and meditation; that erases the unpleasant past of our "peculiar institution" rather than seizing upon it as part of our present; that fears and hence censors the foibles and faults of humanity.

Gullah: A Historical Note and Quiz

Sterling Eisiminger
Clemson University

Thomas Pyles called it the great exception to the homogenity of American speech. But while Gullah has long recognized as a difficult dialect, its origins have been disputed. Prior to the work of Lorenzo D. Turner, a Negro linguist familiar with the West African languages, who spent over twenty years researching the origins of Gullah, scholars mistakenly assumed during the first forty years of this century that the dialect was illiterate English acquired and modified by black slaves who lost their native tongue and learned a second language from their white overseers. Turner's painstaking fieldwork has shown that over six thousand words (four fifths are personal names) in Gullah are of African origin. The parent tongues include some thirty West African languages among which are Efik, Hausa, Wolof, Malinka, Kongo, Yoruba, and Ibo which are spoken in countries in and between Senegal and Angola. (The term *Gullah* itself is either a shortened form of *Angola* or a form of *Gola*, the name of a tribe in Liberia.)

Turner notes that because of the relatively low duty charged for African slaves and the African reputation for meekness (as opposed to West Indian slaves), some 100,000 Africans were brought to the tidewater regions and sea islands of South Carolina, Georgia, and Northeastern Florida between 1708 and 1808; although import was illegal after that, many were still brought in. Isolated historically and geographically, the Gullah blacks retained much of their African linguistic inheritance, and probably through the interplay of black and white children, as Mitford Mathews suggests, some Africanisms such as *voodoo, juke, jazz, banjo, samba, tote, buckra, cooter, okra, gumbo,* and *chigger* crept into English. Of course, the slaves adopted and altered many modern and obsolescent English terms too, including: *watermillion* 'watermelon,' *drap* 'drop,' *gwine* 'going,' *larn* 'learn,' *sarpint* 'serpent,' *pizen* 'poison,' and *puppus* 'purpose.' Employing an African intonation and featuring an absence of inflection (*e* replaces *he, she,* and *it*), this amalgam or pidgin called Gullah is spoken today with a rapid, crackling, musical delivery by perhaps 250,000 people.

The literary uses of Gullah have been modest. In the early nineteenth century at least three white literary artists, Caroline Gilman, Edgar Allan Poe, and William Gilmore Simms, made varying use of the Gullah culture. After the Civil War and well into the twentieth century, local colorists made somewhat wider use of the dialect. These writers include Joel Chandler Harris, who is better known for his use of up-country dialect, Ambrose E. Gonzales, who compiled an extensive glossary of Gullah in his collection of Gullah tales *The Black Boarder*, and DuBose Heyward, author of *Porgy*.

The following matching quiz has been compiled from the terms collected by Ambrose Gonzales, Lorenzo Turner, Ann Haskell, Reed Smith, and myself. Try to match the standard English term on the right with the appropriate Gullah equivalent on the left.

—— 1. tittuh	A. remnant
—— 2. tetch	B. sister
—— 3. goober	C. peanut
—— 4. geechy	D. to question
—— 5. to quizzit	E. Gullah
—— 6. shut-mout'	F. to speak
—— 7. she-she talk	G. to exaggerate
—— 8. a shout	H. dawn
—— 9. to crack (one's) teeth	I. feminine gossip
—— 10. day clean	J. a wife
—— 11. lawfully lady	K. a shrew
—— 12. clap-hat bitch	L. secretive
—— 13. to cut de green calabash	M. a religious dance marked by ecstatic motion
—— 14. free issue	N. married man's girl, not his wife
—— 15. a settin' up	O. to harrass
—— 16. side-gal	P. flattery
—— 17. sweetmouth	Q. covetous
—— 18. bad mouth	R. collection plate passed to pay for the funeral
—— 19. big eye	S. curse
—— 20. burial saucer	T. a wake
—— 21. to tarrigate	U. child of white mother and black father

Answers: 1B, 2A, 3C, 4E, 5D, 6L, 7I, 8M, 9F, 10H, 11J, 12K, 13G, 14U, 15T, 16N, 17P, 18S, 19Q, 20R, 21O.

Addenda

The language of the eastern mountain regions of the US—the Appalachian region—has a number of interesting colloquialisms. *Ary* and *nary* (or *airy* and *nairy*) are used quite naturally and unaffectedly by persons native to this region to mean 'any' and 'not any,' or 'none.' They tend to use these colloquial expressions, in preference to the more generally used terms, as emphatics. (I suspect that there is a linguistic rule here. The older term is preferred when the intent is quite serious, when the emotions are deeply involved, when ingrained values and standards are at stake. Notice the use of Biblical—really Elizabethan—language in matters of religion.)

The word *gravel*, which in General American is a collective noun, has here both a singular and plural form. For example, *He picked up a handful of gravels and threw a gravel against the window to wake Tom up.*

Molasses is frequently used as a plural, particularly by the less educated: *These molasses was made in Cade's Cove.*

Lens is sometimes used as if it were plural. *Both lens of my safety glasses were so scratched up they had to give me new ones.*

I ran into a colloquial term, old around here, but new to me, just the other day by eavesdropping on one end of a conversation on the phone between Johnny Loy and Greg Mansfield, both of whom work at Oak Ridge National Laboratory where I, too, am employed. Johnny is the general factotum who sees to it that the plumbing works, the doors open and close, the lights burn, and so on, in Buildings 4500N, 4501, and 4505. Johnny is a myth and tradition in his own time. There is a genre called Johnny Loy stories around here. These stories go back to the very birth of atomic energy.

Greg is a very scholarly fellow, a translator of six or seven languages in the Information & Reports Division (Library). Greg comes from up northeast, somewhere.

Johnny is strictly local, of mountain heritage.

As I eavesdropped on one end of the conversation, it became apparent that the talk was about a pretty little secretary who was getting married to a craftsman at the Lab. I didn't know either of them, but apparently both Johnny and Greg did.

Johnny said into the phone, "Greg, I feel awful sorry for that little girl. I feel real sorry for her. Greg, that son-of-a-bitch is a bank-walker if I ever saw one. I saw him once in the old change-room in 3950, and the son-of-a-bitch is a real bank-walker, if I ever saw one."

Apparently, Greg, on the unheard end of the line, wondered, as I did, what a "bank-walker" might be.

"Why, Greg," said Johnny, "you remember when we were kids, and we went down to the swimming hole to skinny-dip; boys built like you and me, we got our clothes off and got in the water as quick as we could, to avoid embarrassment. But up on the bank was that *bank-walker*, striding around and showing off. He usually didn't have much brains, and usually he was skinny and knock-kneed—or bowlegged—and he generally didn't have much to be proud of, but he had something to brag about, and he bragged about it by bank-walking."'

W. M. Woods
Oak Ridge, Tennessee

ꟿꟿꟿ

From time to time, we are moved to comment on the questionable literacy of "educated" people, but no one, as far as we know, has yet offered any comment on professionals' use of their own language. We find it just as disconcerting to read a menu on which words are misspelled as we should to learn that our doctor doesn't know how to spell *penicillin, pneumothorectomy,* or *staphylacoccus.* To be sure, there are fields in which the professional or trade jargon is mainly oral, but the restaurant business isn't one of them, notwithstanding the nature of the business.

A restaurant in Essex, Connecticut, offers a dish trimmed with "Mandarian" oranges; the same place lists a "roast beef sandwich with au jus," and, when we queried the waitress for an explanation, it was explained that "the au jus is on the side." Another restaurant, in nearby Ivoryton, offers the hybrid dish, "medalions de veal."

While we're on the subject of restaurants, readers may be interested to learn of a (very good) homestyle restaurant in Chester, Connecticut, called *Otto's Restaurant.* Several years ago, Otto sold the place, and the new owner's name is Walter. Not wishing to change the name of the restaurant ("good will" being worth $1.00), the new owner now has a large sign outside that reads: "OTTO'S RESTAURANT—Otto's Name Is Walter."

BIBLIOGRAPHIA

THE INTERPRETATION OF LANGUAGE. VOLUME II: UNDERSTANDING THE UNCONSCIOUS MEANING OF LANGUAGE, by Theodore Thass-Thienemann, Jason Aronson, Inc., 1968, 437 pp., reprinted 1973. $12.50.

Once, following dominant fads, I conceived of linguistics as something approaching an exact science. Once I believed that etymology held the key to vast stretches of language change. Then, while giving a seminar report on Plato's *Kratylos*, with its optimistic implication that the etymon would lead us to the "real meaning" of a word, I exclaimed, with a flash of insight, "He obviously didn't mean it! This is satire!" Whether that insight (of 40 years ago) was genuine or spurious, the cynicism engendered remains. Paradoxically, my fascination with etymology has never waned.

The present volume[1] with its curious sub-title (who or what is "unconscious"?) shows a similar fascination with etymology and is also reminiscent of the idea espoused—or rejected—by Plato, that etymology gets us to the "real" meanings. The author favors the word *properly*: Old English *an-lic* 'only' "properly" meant 'one-body'; Hungarian *lóhere* 'shamrock' "properly" means 'horse testicle,' etc. Present-day meanings are evidently "improper." Sometimes, however, the author overlooks earlier meanings himself. In treating the "polarization (not a freezing process) of milk and meat" (pp. 38-39) he apparently equates meat with animal flesh. But the biblical passage quoted (Hebrews 5.13-14) has *stereà trophē* 'solid food,' which could be vegetarian, and the polarization is not milk vs. meat but liquid vs. solid.

Sarko-phágos "flesh-eater" for 'coffin,' traditionally explained (as early as Pliny, and before) as referring to the limestone that consumed the corpse, is regarded as meaning rather the return into the "swallowing womb" of the mother (*Terra Mater*), pp. 39; 303. This would, granted, shed light on Job 1.21: "Naked came I out of my mother's womb and naked shall I return thither." That "returning thither" had me worried a bit as a boy in Sunday School, where a mass of terrifying lore was dispensed. (I also shared Nicodemus' bewilderment at the admonition, "Ye must be born again.") If we say that the return is to Mother Earth, the riddle is at least half-solved. One recalls

Faust's, "The Mothers! Mothers! It sounds so strange."[2] Recent semantic developments make *mother* sound still stranger.

Highly alarming is the assertion that *education*, Latin *educatio* (like the German calque *Erziehung*) was not "originally" ("properly"?) a drawing-out (of the best in a pupil? from barbarism to cultivation?) but has a more sinister reference to cattle-breeding and denotes castration, cf. "From Castration to Education" (pp. 114-117). The word *wanton*, we are told, indicates the opposite of this baneful educated state, meaning "not pulled out," therefore intact in vital respects and gloriously *lewd*; ignorance was indeed bliss.

The author's theory states that language (= vocabulary) has been transformed by repressive anxiety over three "focal points of organic existence". (p. 11): the beginning (birth), the end (death), and the act of creating new life (sexual union). Three main sections of the book partially reflect that division, with considerable overlapping and interpenetration: "Separation and Reunification" (13-42); "Oedipus—Identity and Knowledge" (43-117); and "The Return—Childhood Lost" (119-226). There follow addenda, notes, bibliography, and indexes (with Old English curiously put under "Index of Foreign Words").

Thass-Thienemann bases his interpretation on child psychiatry, developmental psychology, and dream interpretation. He explores subconscious verbal fantasies by following the "long, wide way of language" (p. 1). He tells us that modern English bears messages sent in a remote past (to whom?); there is a hint that post-hypnotic suggestion is actualized in the fantasies of the disturbed. If so, this must be by the remotest of controls, even cutting across ancestral lines. It seems that only a population of "ethnic purity" from very ancient times until the present could assure the kind of message-transmittal assumed here. The author is, admittedly, aware that language is not handed on through the genes, but he does call ancient speakers "our ancestors." Would not "predecessors" be better? What about speakers of English (perhaps monoglots) whose ancestors were Ugrian or Basque or what-not? Furthermore, are we now sending messages to distant generations in the future? What are we trying to tell them? Despite this carping criticism, there is something intriguing in the contemplation of the long course of language transmission and the obvious connection (via breath and psyche) with remote predecessors, whether relatives or not.

The book abounds with fascinating lore and is really engrossing reading. I have more confidence in the psychological portions, about which I know little—hence the childlike trust—than in those bordering on linguistics. I would disagree with some etymologies, which are usually not the author's own, but admit that even "false" etymology plays a role throughout the ages. There are more than a few errors of detail; some words are assigned to the wrong language (Irish, Sanskrit); others are nonexistent, although they no doubt were found in the author's sources. He cannot know all the languages cited, hence the room for error of evaluation. Transcriptions are sometimes unfortunate (for Sanskrit, Hebrew, Gothic), but these too follow others (although the absence of diacritics may be an original feature). Linguistic works cited are, while substantial, mostly old.

The author evidently became enamored of the term "phonemic" at some time. But his use of the term violates the phonemic principle. Whether the "phoneme is dead" or is alive and well, it has meant to those using it a significant unit within the sound-system of one language; it is thus meaningless to apply it across language boundaries as does our author (pp. 34, 35, 91, 101, 108 *et passim*).

Once or twice he is surely pulling our leg(s). The sons of Austrian and Hungarian nobles, we are told, were called, like the eldest son of the King of France, *dauphin*. Schoolbooks were prepared *ad usum delphini* 'for the use of the dolphin (dauphin).' This is compared by the author (p. 16) with English "school of fish." One needs to head for the *Elephant and Castle* for a strong drink.

Most of the disagreements above are petty in nature —not all. Even errors in detail and terminology will not vitiate a valid central thesis. But one or two implications are hard to accept. For example: vocabulary change is best observable in aberrations of the disturbed; their speech reflects more accurately an ancient stage than does the speech of the "normal" speakers. The afflicted are in the favored position of being able to make profound revelations of a broad cultural nature, sometimes approaching the universal (this contrasts with Freud's treatment of speech aberrations as an individual phenomenon). In his rational moments, the patient apparently has no such magic touch with pristine language. How, though, can he recapture an ancient semantic level when there are no inter-mediate steps? *Men darf zayn meschugeh*? Perhaps it helps.

The volume appears to be extremely useful (with ob-servation of the necessary caveats) for those concerned with language, folklore, comparative literature, Biblical studies, etc., in addition to the author's own major field. It would also perhaps prove fruitful to us in languages and linguistics to turn to some of the publications in the bibli-ography that are no doubt important sources hitherto over-looked by most of us.

Robert A. Fowkes
New York University

1 I confess to not having read volume I, which doubtless disqualifies me as a reviewer, although this is evidently a complete and separate work in itself.

2 Goethe, *Faust*, Part II, line 6217: *Die Mütter! Mütter! 's klingt so wunderlich*.

📖

THE GUINNESS BOOK OF NAMES, Leslie Dunkling, Guinness Superlatives Limited, Enfield, Middlesex, Eng-land, 1974, 256 pp. £3.20.

No book in onomastics comparable to this one has been published in the United States. Frankly, it is doubt-ful that a publisher here would have accepted it. Perhaps only in England, where the professional and the amateur faculties of an author can still tie the subtle knot that as-sociates sensibility, can the disrhythmic quidnunc, the gouty antiquarian, or the purely innocent be granted space. Although the text qualifies as an astounding success, it con-tributes little that is substantially new to a specialist. In that way it is like a one-volume edition of Mencken's *The American Language*—compendious, encyclopedic, stylisti-cally distinctive, and informed. Sounds impossible and slightly tipsy!

The book is truly attractive in format and layout, with relevant photographs and illustrations throughout. For in-stance, a photograph of the musical scores of "Louise," "Michelle," and "Tip Toe Through the Tulips" is used to point up the associational influences that may cause par-ents to name their child because of the current popularity of a song. *Tulip* is, of course, the name given by the singer Tiny Tim to his daughter. Dunkling coins *nameograph* as the descriptive term for identifiable sketches of famous persons, such as Washington, Lincoln, or Churchill. A free-style drawing of Charlie Chaplin illustrates *Chaplin*. The book jacket, a montage of pictures, shows a cut of the upper half of a nubile girl wearing a Princeton University T-shirt, the mainmast of the sailing vessel *Cutty Sark*, a birth registration sheet for 1883, a geological survey map of the island of Hawaii, a platter of cheese wedges (brands named), cheesecake (Miss England of 1970 reigning in near-undress), the Drunken Duck, and rogues' gallery shot of Leslie Dunkling, full-face and right profile, No. 1199062. The jacket exudes a sprouting sensuality that must not go unnoticed.

With this falderol out of the way, we can slip between the covers. Dunkling has the audacity to title the first two chapters, "What's In a Name?" This dampens the enthusiasm of anyone knowledgeable with the name game. Yet, both short chapters are carried off with a flamboyance not seen in any books on names that I know. He even quotes the "infamous" lines from Shakespeare's *Romeo and Juliet* at the very beginning, a commencement hardly promising. It is here, however, that we are confronted with a critical mind. The passage is worth quoting:

> Juliet's beautiful speech, which in context is a passionate plea for what is known to be a lost cause, is often misinterpreted. Juliet does not believe what she says even as she says it, and Shakespeare certainly did not believe it. He gives quite a different answer to his own question many times in his plays and poems. With his usual genius, however, he makes Juliet ask herself a timeless question which has an infinity of answers. The innumerable sub-editors who have echoed the question at the head of a thousand columns simply acknowledge the fact. We must also acknowledge it, and attempt to find some answers.

In control here is a brash and daring commentator who uses a trite approach to introduce something quite serious and important.

After this comes a short, too short, glossary of name terms, and then sections on a name's meaning, origin, and density. The highly complicated concept of the "name-print" theory is described enough to make us wish he had developed it further. According to this, all of us have "an onomastic finger-print"; that is, we react in personal ways to names on a list, something that will reveal both our general and our specialized knowledge. It is a kind of name association test, only more limited, though probably no less revealing. Other sections include commentary on duplication and transfer, names as vocabulary, personal name substitutes, modifiers, love names, hate names, and the psychological problem of "one's own good name."

He classifies names in "at least four ways": By their linguistic status; by their formal characteristics; by type of origin; and by the nomenclature to which they belong. In each section, the author subtly and unpretentiously inserts linguistic and psychological interpretations. Names are discussed synchronically and diachronically; for instance, *Belcher* probably had the ameliorative meaning of "pretty face," from *bel chiere*, but its English form and present meaning can leave the owner "sadly exposed." He is especially concerned with his own name, a concern that extends to all of us who have "strange" names. Schoolboys taunted him with "Does dung cling?" Some persons insist on hearing *Dumpling*, either through actually being hard-of-hearing or through maliciousness. The name is easily derived through analyses of sound changes in English dialects that connect surnames like *Dunkley* with place names of *Dinkling* and *Dinckly* in Lancashire. Such commentaries permeate the text.

In a sense, the book is an introduction to both the theory and practice of names and naming. No extensive treatment of any category of names occurs, although the encapsulating is so sophisticated as to obviate any necessity to list examples for the sake of listing or proliferating. The categories, then, are not exhaustive, but they indeed cover major areas and types: Names of pubs, houses, streets, trades, magazines, flowers, ships, apples, railways, lorries, on to "No End of Names." With some casting around, we could find omissions, one notably being names in sports, except for a mention of names of racehorses. So encompassing is the coverage that Dunkling's supposition that we may have more names in our vocabulary than we do "ordinary language" must be taken seriously.

Mr. Dunkling has produced a book that deserves shelf space anywhere that good books are found and reading time by anyone who pretends to fluency in English. If the owner's reading ability is skewered to the bell bottom, then the book can serve well as a coffee-table adornment, a martini-klatsch conversation piece, or for a roach pinch-out. It is a breezy, salty, and substantial book from across the sea.

Kelsie B. Harder
*The State University College
at Potsdam, New York*

To Cave

The word *cave* is listed only as a noun in Webster's, but I have long known it as a verb. *To cave* or *to go caving* primarily means 'to explore a cave.' Ah, to go caving! And whoever goes is a *caver*.

Now oddly enough, I do find the words *spelunker*, n. and *spelunk*, v.i. in Webster's. I have been a caver for more than twenty years, and I have known a thousand, two thousand cavers. Never, ever, have I heard anyone speak of himself as a "spelunker," and the thought that someone might be about to *spelunk* is droll. I *have* on occasion known cavers to use the words in print to insult somebody.

Cavers go caving, but there are some very nice things that caves themselves do that most noncavers do not know about, although they instantly understand when they hear. Caves *go* or they *pinch out. Going cave* is a cave or cave passage that gives no indication of pinching out. Such cave is *virgin cave*. It is a big thrill to explore virgin cave. And to find *big cave* is a special treat. *Live cave* shows a lot of promise; *dead cave* does not. In a cave, cavers *look for cave*, searching for those small holes that may lead to wonders. I think that is about all. I'm all caved out. Now I wish you all could listen to a record of "The Caving Mother Blues."

Red Watson
Cave Research Foundation
University City, Missouri

ᔐᔕᔐᔕ

Trite 'n' True

There is a special version of the linguistic binomials that fascinates me which is found in the area of advertising. I can remember when, in the not-too-distant past, products advertised for sale were rather simply and directly named. One readily understood what was meant by *Old Dutch Cleanser* or *Dutch Masters*, by *Ry-Krisp* or *Rice Crispies*, by *Quaker State Oil* or *Quaker's Rolled Oats*.

Not so these days when product designations tend toward slogans, aphorisms and expository phrases. *Hard as Nails, True to Life, Hour after Hour* and *Twice as Nice*—all in the cosmetic field—are examples of this genre.

One specific trend currently is what might be termed the double-barreled or conjunctional approach. This is not an entirely new phenomenon, as witness such venerable commodities as *Sea & Ski* (rhyme), *Spic 'n Span* (tradition) and *Head & Shoulders* (geography).

What is so alarming is the overkill that is being practiced. For instance, *Shake 'n Bake* are seasoned bread crumbs, *Break 'n Bake* are pizzas, and *Bake & Take* are reusable aluminum pans. *Thick 'n Creamy, Cool 'n Creamy,* and *Warm 'n Creamy,* refer, respectively, to salad dressing, pudding, and a beauty cream warmer.

In the next-to-Godliness category we find *Soft 'n Clean, Groom and Clean,* and *Squirt-N-Kleen,* the last an oral hygiene device. Covering the moisture spectrum pretty well are such items as *Wash and Care, Spray 'n Wash, Wash 'n Dri, Tote 'n Dry,* and *Soft & Dri,* mostly in the "beautifying" business.

There are *Bathe 'n Glow* (baby lotion), *Mop & Glo* (floor cleaner), *Sweet 'n Low* (artificial sweetener) and *Punch 'n Gro* (garden product). There are *Gloss 'n Toss, Toss 'n Serve, Brown N Serve, Stir N Serv, Mix 'n Drink, Heat 'n Eat, Whip & Chill, Wipe 'n Dipe, Cut 'n Clean, Kleen 'n Shine; Stretch 'n Seal* and *Scratch & Sniff* (the last a notebook). Then, too, we must remember: *Lean & Lively, Long & Silky, Silk 'n Hold* and *Silk 'n Silver.* Finally, let us not forget *Tuf 'n Ready* and *Crisp 'n Tender; Spray 'n Wash* and *Spray N Vac; Thick & Frosty* and *Fit & Frosty; Rich 'n Easy, Nice & Easy, Nice 'n Soft* and *Soft 'n Pretty* . . . and *So-on 'n So-forth.*

As you can see, the list is *Long 'n Endless.* However, the outlook isn't as bleak as it appears. Fashions in advertising, like fashions in clothes, change quickly and we shall soon be on a *New 'n Different* kick.   Harry Cimring
Hollywood, California

EPISTOLAE

In addition to "A Bicentennial Pair: George & Patsy" [III, 1], there was a "Tom & Patsy"—The Jeffersons. Both Mrs. Jefferson and the daughter were Marthas, called Patsy.

And further, I too am Martha, and have been called Patsy all my life.

Martha (Patsy) White
San Rafael, California

BIBLIOGRAPHIA

KEYWORDS, A Vocabulary of Culture and Society, by Raymond Williams, Oxford University Press, 1976, 286 pp. $10.95 cloth; $3.50 paper.

We assume that one of the highest compliments to be paid a book is an expression of envy at not having been the author of it. Unhesitatingly, unabashedly, we submit that we regret not having written this book. In all honesty, though, we must add that we regret, too, being incapable of having written so lucid yet so erudite a descriptive analysis of semantic change taking place in that odd place described as being before our very eyes, under our very noses.

The author has selected 155 English words (like *aesthetic, alienation, art, behaviour, bourgeois, bureaucracy, capitalism, career,* . . . *creative,* . . . *culture,* . . . *democracy,* . . . *equality,* . . . *family,* etc.) that he considers to be key words in modern culture. Through detailed discussion of their etymologies, their cognates, their synonyms and antonyms, and their general historical and contemporary behavior, he traces the development of each from its purely formal origin through its semantic development as illustrated by the political, philosophical, and critical writings in which it has been employed. The discussions vary in length from less than a page to several pages, and each carries a list of cross references (at the end) to related Keywords in the book. Monolingual lexicographers are traditionally accused of carrying on some sort of verbal incest because they attempt to define the words of a language using the words of the language itself. If not precisely incestuous, it must be acknowledged that the practice of monolingual lexicography is, indeed, an exercise in circularity, unlike bilingual or multilingual lexicography, which, at least, offers the salve of being able to use a metalanguage. Williams sidesteps this problem rather neatly: by virtue of dealing with so few words, he can, in effect, use the rest of the language as a metalanguage and no circularity is apparent.

Though admittedly a small niggle, it might be necessary to point out that nothing would be gained from arguing that some of these Keywords ought to be replaced by other Keywords of our own choosing; but that would prove a bootless argument, indeed, for we should soon become mired in the philosophical questions of Williams' choices rather than in the genuine enjoyment and admiration of his treatment of those he has selected. No one can gainsay the importance of these 155: at worst, he can but lament that there aren't 1550 or 15,500 or 155,000 treated in like manner.

For here is what lexicography is all about.

Witness these cuttings, presented entirely out of context:

> **Equality** has been in regular use in English since [early 15th Cent.], from . . . [OF] *équalité* . . . [L] *aequalitatem*, . . . r[oot] w[ord] [L] *aequus*-level, even, just.

> [**Medium**] . . . **Media** became widely used when broadcasting as well as the press had become important in COMMUNICATIONS (q.v.); it was then the necessary general word. MASS (q.v.) **media, media people, media agencies, media studies** followed.

> [**Liberal**] . . . But **liberal** as a pejorative term has also been widely used by socialists and especially Marxists. This use shares the conservative sense of lack of rigour and of weak and sentimental beliefs. Thus far it is interpreted by **liberals** as a familiar complaint. . . .

> [**Literature**] . . . Where Johnson had used **literature** in the sense of being highly literate in his *Life of Milton*, in his *Life of Cowley* he wrote, in the newly objective sense: 'an author whose pregnancy of imagination and elegance of language have deservedly set him high in the ranks of literature.'

As can be seen from even this small sample, it is almost impossible to deal with language without encountering controversy, and we do not mean to imply, in our earnest recommendation of this book, that the reader will necessarily agree with all of the views expressed. Yet, views cogently expressed are in short supply this season, and especially in the cheaper (albeit impermanent) paperback edition, this book can be guaranteed to engender thought and stimulate discussion. It is required reading for all who moan that we don't use English the way we used to.

If we allowed ourselves a niggle, above, perhaps we may be permitted a quibble here: the typographic style gets a bit cumbersome at times. For instance, once a cross reference to another entry has been indicated by setting a given word in small capitals, it is unnecessary to supply the redundant '(q.v.)' following. The editors would have done better to have followed *OED* (or VERBATIM) style. As far as the style of the writing goes, the author would have been well advised to have avoided such phrases as "- - - is a complex word" and "- - - is a difficult word," one of which appears in almost every entry. Neither is required for the formulaic approach to his subject, which he has managed to avoid without sacrificing a measure of useful uniformity among the entries.

〽〽〽

Proverbially Speaking. Don't minimize the man who maxim-izes.

A. S. Flaumenhaft
Lawrence, New York

ETYMOLOGICA OBSCURA

hermaphrodite to *bulldagger*

Etymologically the most interesting word in the English language is probably *dike*, referring to a lesbian, with all its variations such as *Diesel-dike* 'a fat lesbian who walks like a Mack truck,' etc. What is so interesting and unusual about *dike* is that all the intermediate forms of this term, from its etymological original, which is *hermaphrodite*, to its most evolved derivative, *bulldagger*, are all in simultaneous existence at the present time and have been at least since the 1930s; and I have at one time or another heard them all in actual use: *hermaphrodite, morphodite, morphodike, dike, diker, bull-diked,* and *bulldagger.* The "bull—" element in these last two of course refers to largeness or maleness.

G. Legman
France

Ahless Havad

Where did the ahs in Havad go?
Who managed this sly maneuver?
Some Irish Yankees put one each
On the ends of Chiner and Cuber.

E. O. Staley
Maplewood, New Jersey

320

BIBLIOGRAPHIA

PLACENAMES OF GEORGIA, Essays of John H. Goff, Edited by Francis Lee Utley and Marion R. Hemperley, University of Georgia Press, 1975, xxxviii + 495 pp. $16.00.

John Goff had as many trades as fingers: he was a scholar, teacher, dean, economist, transportation director for TVA, consultant for TVA in Alabama and for Bonneville Power Company in Oregon, chief economist and director of research for FDR's Transportation Board of Investigation and research, writer, and self-appointed inspector of Georgia placenames. During the last 17 years of his life, Goff made hundreds of observations on Georgia placenames, but he published most of these in the *Georgia Mineral Newletter*. Marion R. Hemperley of the Georgia Surveyor General Department and Francis Lee Utley, late of the Ohio State University, have edited 135 of these essays to give both the general reader and the specialist in onomastics a thoroughly delightful volume. This book is a handsome, entertaining, and informative collection—a significant contribution to the study of linguistics, history, geography, and folklore which are the domain of placename study.

Like Thoreau, Goff was no theorist. He loved a meandering road, and, because he was not on another man's errand, the inspector took the time to go his own way. He began his work tracing the course of the Old Federal Road in North Georgia; in the years that followed, he studied the names of creeks and crossroads—and all the terrain and settlements in between—with the same loving attention that Thoreau gave to the ice, woods, and chickadees around Concord.

As a result, Goff's work has the effect of a sprawling epic catalogue of Georgia placenames, more than 1500 of which are indexed by the editors. The range of his scholarship and the deftness of his intuition, however, are bound in an engaging prose style that makes a reader grateful to be shet for a while of the orthodox taxonomist:

No Business Creek is one of those distinctive names of Georgia and for a long time the writer thought it was the only such moniker in the country until he found a North Business Creek listed in Henry Gannett's *Gazetteer of Virginia*. This discovery led to some searching which turned up a second No Business Creek in Morgan

County, Alabama, northwest of. Hartselle. This find in turn raised a question about Gannett's North Business Creek; perhaps he had made a slip by interpreting No as No., an abbreviation for north. Apparently there was such an error, because a reliable Virginia map disclosed that the correct designation is No Business and not North Business Creek. Further study may show the name is also employed in other sections. But be that as it may, usage of the expression in such widely separated areas as Virginia, Georgia, and Alabama implies that old-timers were generally familiar with the appelation. (p. 150)

Gopher Town, or "Go' Town" as the place is sometimes called, is a crossroads on Georgia 39, below Donalsonville in central Seminole County. According to a good informant, the name was derived from the fact that an enormous gopher was once killed in the vicinity and its dried shell hung over the door of the community store. The term gopher in this case does not refer to any of the various species of western rodents, but to a burrowing land turtle (*Xerobates polyphemus*), which can be found on the lower Coastal plain. The creatures are sometimes caught and their flesh used as food. (p. 128)

The exact site of the town of Eastertoy is not known but most likely it centered about present Dillard, which is located on a fine rise that overlooks the beautiful bottoms along Betty Creek and the Little Tennessee. Old people around Dillard used to say that they had always heard that Indians were living at the site when the first white people arrived to take up properties they had won in land lotteries. Further evidence that the place was at Dillard can be found in the fact that Mud Creek which is also known as *Estatoah*, or as *Estatoah Falls Creek*, enters the right side of the Little Tennessee on the northeast side of Dillard. (p. 279)

It might be of interest to add that the crossroads at Plains of Dura was the intersecting point for two early traces. One of these routes, Bond's Trail, led southward from old Traveller's Rest, below Montezuma on Flint River via Ellaville, Quebec (on Georgia 153 in Schley County), Concord Crossroads, Plains of Dura, Plains, and Paradox Church Crossroads in the southwest corner of Sumter. From there it crossed into extreme northwest Lee County and joined what is now the Edwards Station-Bodsford Road, just to the east of Chokeeligee Creek. This last route, a former Indian path, ran along the eastside of Kinchafoonee Creek. To the south of its juncture with Bond's Trail, at a point about two miles northwest of today's Neyami in Lee County, it forked with one branch leading southeastward through Neyami at the site of old Starkville, thence eastward to Pindertown, a noted Indian crossing point on the Flint River. The other prong continued south alone Kinchafoonee Creek to Kennards Settlement and Cowpen, at the present bridge on Georgia 32. (p. 36)

Even with the eight footnotes deleted here, the historical and geographical value of the work seems apparent even in these representative passages. The discussions of placenames are equally rich with information for the linguistic geographer and the folklorist. Besides the regional words, *cowpen* /képĕn/, *gopher*, and *pinder*, mentioned above, subregional words are also documented in local designations, e.g., *Redbug Road* would be *Chigger Road* in North Georgia and the village of *Red Bud* northwest of Atlanta wouldn't appear in South Georgia. *Bonny Clabber Bluff* would be *Thick Milk Bluff* if the area had been dominated by Germans instead of Irish, and *Blue John Creek* would be *Skimmed Milk Creek* if a modern urban namemaker felt obliged to use a dairyman's pejorative. The political folklorist will surely find significance in the fact that Jimmy Carter's hometown of Plains is a fairly recent abbreviation of *Plains of Dura*, the site of Nebuchednezzar's great golden image that led to the fiery furnace for Shadrach, Meshach, and Abednego.

In three essays on the phonology of Georgia placenames, Goff discusses local pronunciation of nearly 100 local designations, recording divided usage, illustrating variation with a fairly consistent and successful nontechnical description, and clarifying accentuation when needed. Outlanders are given the preferred native pronunciations of *Albany* ["All′ benny"], *Aragon* ["Arrow′gun" or "Arrer′-gun"], *Schley* ["Sly′"], and *Taliaferro/Bolivar* (which make a perfect rhyme in Georgia). Even Georgians will learn from this book; how many of us would pass a pronunciation quiz that includes *Gardi* ("Guard-eye"), *Philamee* ("Flimee"), *Schlatterville* ("Slaughterville"), *Sowhatchie* ("Syehatchie"), and *Towaliga* ("Tyelye′gee")? There is some comfort, however, to find even the natives of Screven County rhyming it with *Stephen, seven,* or *driven.*

The good life and hard traveling of Georgia's people are reflected across every page of this fine book, from *Social Circle* and *Fancy Hill* to *Scrougetown, Scufflele Bluff,* and *Lordamercy Cove.* Even without an *Amsterdam, Athens, Berlin, Bremen, Canton, Cairo, Damascus,* two *Dublins, Egypt, Geneva, Lisbon, Madras, Mecca, Natal, Rome,*

Scotland, Turin, Tunis, and Vienna on the map of his
favorite state, Goff could have concluded his work as Man
Walking and with no apology to Thoreau:

> If with fancy unfurled
>   You leave your abode,
> You may go round the world
>   By the Old Federal Road.

Lee Pederson
Emory University

"—but this Thesaurus!"

I

A dictionary is a word-society
Recording next of kin—and doubtful heirs;
To know a word one must concede co-action
And recognize both genes and variants:

Consider *gens*, host to appendages
That he fulfills, becoming with their aid
Degeneration, gentry, and *benign,*
Congenial, generous, and *genteel*;
Through limpet affixes he can expand
Yet in himself remain intact.

To know a word—to wonder how it lapsed:
Why did stout *toad-head* yield its place to *tadpole*?
And Roman *little mouse* retreat to *muscle,*
Then later in sea-armor mask as *mussel*?
Did *mob* from *mobile vulgus* wax pernicious?
And *bus* from *omnibus* decrease in content?
And when did *quelque chose*, deprived of birthright
By artless tongue, descend to mocking *kickshaws*?
What lack of energy reduced the pace
Of quick *s'aventurer* to leisured *saunter*?
What weariness betrayed the jovial *surfeit*
To such vicissitudes as end in *sad*?

So in that ordered word-society
Is every member diagramed for sound
Maintaining each his use and proper place.

II

But this Thesaurus! Challenging your thought
To find the mediant word to give it flesh!

This teeming source that quickens or confines
Displaying for your choice its lavish store,
To ground your thought or kite it through the sky.

Kaleidoscopic words of shifting forms;
And blustering, leaping, turbulent words that rage;
Words straight as shot-purveyors of precision—
And undecided fluttering words on planes
Of almost-meaning—weightless butterflies;
Cargoes of samplings from the tongues of Time
(The very words poetic thought found sound.)

This Mardigras of words where thought is king.
These unrelated members own no rule
Except to serve—to shape the inherent arc
That launches thought into transcendency.

S. C. Joughin
Hackettstown, N. J.

◊◊◊◊

Spell-Bound. A movie about a screen siren who casts her charms on men should be *hex*-rated.

A. S. Flaumenhaft
Lawrence, New York

◊◊◊◊

Unusual names [II, 2] can be delightful: *Larry Derryberry.* . . .

Reinhold Aman
Milwaukee, Wisconsin

. . . embarrassing: *Siflis; Hartupee; **Marcy Tinkle;** Edward L. Wiwi.* . . .

Jack Grieshaber
Cincinnati, Ohio

. . . irresistible: **Tordis Isselthwaite.** . . .
. . . contradictory: **John Senior, Jr.** . . .

Constance Finkel
University City, Missouri

BIBLIOGRAPHIA

WORDS AND WOMEN, by Casey Miller and Kate Swift, Anchor Press/Doubleday, 1976, 197 pp. $7.95.

Prejudice is the name for the animosity between or among people on the basis of religion, color, nationality, sexual proclivity, language, wealth, health, employment, intelligence, taste, hirsuteness, education, height, weight, age, behavior, opinions, and, as we all now know, sex. In other words, any of the multitudinous, multifarious elements that serve to distinguish us from one another can serve as a basis for our prejudices.

Propaganda is the name for the process of persuading people to behave in a certain way. The authors of this book discuss one kind of prejudice only—sexist—and hold that the English language itself, by its very grammar, serves as a self-perpetuating medium for sexist propaganda. True, other, cultural factors—particularly such practices as a woman's loss of her name upon marrying—are mentioned; but the focus is on language.

The argument is irrefutable, though it is sometimes a little difficult to separate Miller/Swift's purely descriptive approach from a surely destructive reproach. For example, they cite the treatment of *manly/manful/mannish* vs. *womanly/womanlike/womanish* in *The Random House Dictionary*. At first, the reader is put off by the authors' comment: "The broad range of positive characteristics used to define males could be used to define females, too, of course, but they are not. The characteristic of women—weakness is among the most frequently cited—are something apart." [p. 59] Put off because one assumes that it is the lexicographers who are being taken to task. But on the following page appears this: "Lexicographers do not make up definitions out of thin air. Their task is to record how words are used, it is not to say how they should be used." Thus, it emerges that Miller/Swift have it in for the language, not for the lexicographers.

That's a great relief, for no lexicographer ought to tangle with these two ladies, whose argument is all the more telling for the volume of evidence they adduce from all kinds of writing. Who can doubt that English—though not, to be sure, English alone—reflects still the traditional anti-female biases of its speakers' culture. Even those who object to the awkward, often silly distortions and contortions resorted to in an attempt to achieve "equality in language" will be compelled to admit, upon closing this book, that the language is rife with constructions, syntax, grammar, and lexicon that, even if not any longer deliberately anti-female, certainly perpetuates an inequality, willy-nilly, that women have fought to correct with considerable success. The problem that emerges and that is central to Miller/Swift's argument is that notwithstanding the advances made in the liberation of women, the very language they must use tends to propagandize against their freedom and purpose.

In ranging far and wide for good and bad examples with which to support their cause, Miller/Swift sometimes slip, as when they praise the *American Heritage School Dictionary* for defining *sage* as " 'A very wise person, usually old and highly respected,' in contrast to the 'mature or venerable man sound in judgment' of a widely used college dictionary." The college dictionary happens to be right and the *AHSD* wrong in this instance, for, while there is no reason why a *sage* must be male, the unassailable fact is that all sages have always been male, and we would defy Alma Graham or anyone else to unearth evidence (outside of science fiction) that the word has ever been used to refer to a female.

There is some consolation for all of us (Miller/Swift, too): language does change and that for that reason alone we may look forward to a future of diminished prejudice. However, it must be emphasized that by that very token people should stop using etymologies of modern English words in order to "prove" that their "real" meaning is the original one. Etymologies are interesting and can be useful in determining the linguistic and semantic changes that a word has undergone, but it is as ridiculous to fasten on an obsolete meaning as the "true" meaning of a word as it may be to fasten on its current meaning: words are *symbols*; they are not things they symbolize.

It may seem that because of the sensitivity of the subject, any adverse remarks in a review of a book on sexism in language will be construed as an attack on feminism itself, notwithstanding protests to the contrary (especially by a male reviewer). But the only possible criticism that this reviewer might offer is about the authors' intensity, which frequently results in nothing more than a switching in the order of explanations and arguments. One must therefore be careful to read to the end of each analysis in order to find the authors' mitigation of their criticisms, which are usually directed at the medium rather than the message.

To the best of our knowledge, no comparable study—certainly, no comparably responsible, sober, comprehensive study—has been done by anyone else, and this work is welcome particularly because it should serve to lay to rest, once and for all, the facetious inanities perpetrated on us by those who, under the guise of humor, create linguistic absurdities that tend to perpetuate vicious sexist propaganda.

EPISTOLAE

Bravo to Bruce Price for his insightful and witty article on Nounspeak [II, 4]. He may be a little too categorical, however, in stating that, unlike Germanic, "the Romance languages virtually forbid it." True, the practice is not indigenous to Romance, nor is it as versatile. (That is, with the debatable exception of Esperanto—of largely Romance lexicon but generally Germanic syntax—in which one can agglutinate nouns almost ad lib. E.g., the nouns *pluvo* 'rain,' *mantelo* 'coat,' *fabriko* 'factory,' and *loko* 'location' are easily combined to form a perfectly comprehensible chain: *pluvmantelfabrikloko*. But such a process is typical of the language and leads neither to obfuscation nor affectation.) French has been quite hospitable to noun pairs for some time—with or without hyphens, often capriciously—and is becoming even more so as the language suffers from the spread of its own equivalent of Newspeak, ironically dubbed *Hexagonal*. Except for some chic Anglo-American calques like *auto-école* 'driving school,' such pairs differ from the Germanic variety in that the qualifying noun always follows the qualified, not vice-versa. Hence *homme* 'man' + *grenouille* 'frog' for 'frogman.' They can be broken down into (at least) three types:

1. True appositions, in which the second (qualifying) noun plays the role of a predicate adjective; as in *soldat citoyen* 'citizen soldier,' *homme orchestre* 'one-man band,' et al.

2. Metaphorical appositions, as in *homme grenouille, guerre éclair* 'lightning war,' i.e. 'Blitzkrieg,' *roman fleuve* 'saga,' lit. 'river novel,' *homme sandwich* 'sandwich man,' i.e. in the ambulatory, publicity sense, et al.

3. Syntactical ellipses, in which simple juxtaposition replaces anything from a preposition to an entire phrase. Thus, *café-concert* (for a *café* where one can also hear a *concert* of sorts), *bloc-notes* 'note-pad,' *coiffeur hommes* 'men's barber,' *pause café* 'coffee break,' the slang *arrêt pipi* 'rest stop,' et al. One even hears (and reads) nowadays such innovations as *trajet-bureau* 'office distance,' i.e. 'travel time from office to home.'

Another favorite ellipsis is of relatively recent vintage, namely the omission of the preposition *de* in such expressions as *la question salaire* 'the salary question' for *la question du salaire,* etc. As a result, three-noun chains are now quite possible in French, however much they may make purists cringe. One may well hear office workers discussing the *question pause café,* or historians analyzing the *concept guerre éclair,* for instance.

Given the fundamental difference between this type of chain and the Germanic, it is hard, offhand, to envision any four-noun examples. But who knows what wonders of verbal shorthand may yet lurk over *Hexagonal's* horizon?

Norman R. Shapiro
Wesleyan University

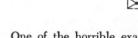

One of the horrible examples that illustrate and enliven your brief note about apostrophes [II, 4] invites a small quibble that leads directly to a somewhat more extensive tangential comment to supplement your summary—not to disagree with it. Certainly the punctuation mark in *Drink with the Urdang's* is a catostrophe; and the one in *Ham 'n Eggs* is a prepostrophe unless balanced by an a[fter]postrophe to mark the omission of the *d.* (Perhaps the best way to avoid the smell of "n" you rightly deprecate in the logical *Ham 'n' Eggs* would be *Ham-n-Eggs,* in which the two hyphens announce that the compound has been manufactured for the occasion and the absence of apostrophes implies that the process of contraction has been completed so the omitted *a* and *d* are no longer missed.)

My quibble is to deny the need to add an *'s* in *St. Paul United Methodist Church* (despite its Florida address), though the addition would undeniably be legitimate. The apostle is not thought of as possessing the church in any literal sense, but the use of *St. Paul's* here would be just as correct as the use of *Shakespeare's picture* in reference to a recent print that could never have belonged to the playwright. The possessive, expressed either by an *'s* or by an *of*, has less literal implication of ownership than our grade school teachers may have led us to assume. Conversely, it is legitimate to speak of the *Adams mansion* (without an apostrophe) whether the Adamses own it now or not; the house is associated with the Adams family in other ways too. Such adjectival use of a noun—either a common or a proper one—is firmly established in English.

This freedom to either use or omit the *'s* is quite common, though the degree of freedom varies widely from one situation to another. At one extreme, St. Paul's municipal auditorium (if there is one in the Minnesota city) could be called the *St. Paul Municipal Auditorium* but hardly *St. Paul's M. A.* At the other, one could not speak of *Mr. St. Peter's wife* without an apostrophe, though a number of *St. Peter wives* (or, with a slightly different sense, St. Peters' wives) might be met at a family gathering. But an association of teachers can equally well be called a Teachers' Association (because the association belongs to those who belong to it) or a Teacher Association (in which *Teacher* is used as an adjective telling what the Association consists of or is for the benefit of); probably the choice in this case is based less often on logic than on the degree of aversion to punctuation marks. None of this, of course, is any defense for the traveler who reports having visited *St. Peters* while in Rome.

Incidentally, the cowbird letter by W. M. Woods [II, 4, 16] contains a misstatement, though this does not affect his argument. The cowbird is not "a relative of the European coocoo, or cuckoo, or whatever"—regardless of its egg-laying habits—though "some immigrant, probably of German origin" might well have been misled as indicated. The cowbird is one of the blackbirds and hence is an icterid, along with the meadowlarks and orioles. My own speculation, offered as a less amusing and less imaginative competitor to that of Woods, is that the association between cowbirds and cows may have been much closer in the days before spraying reduced the tick population on the latter.

Francis E. Throw
Wheaton, Illinois

The linguistic term Mr. Cimring is fishing for [II, 4] is

presumably *clipping.* (In usage manuals, such as Fowler or Treble & Vallins, the broader rubric *curtailed words* is used.) The most thorough treatment of English clipping (to this writer's knowledge) is in Hans Marchand, *The Categories and Types of Present-Day Word-Formation* (Ch. IX).

Even the term "curtailed words" does not cover all types of familiar designation, since some also *add* (affective) elements instead of subtracting, or subtract and add at the same time (cf. *Johnny* and *John-Boy*; *Joe* and *Joey*, for Joseph; and *Chevvy* and *Chev* for Chevrolet).

Cimring's felicitous phrase, "over-familiarity with language," is particularly applicable in the case of many popular place-name forms. Note, for example, the preciosity of the tourist who feels he must refer to Las Vegas as *Vegas*, as though this made him a member of some sort of in-group. *Frisco* (or sometimes, in writing, " 'Frisco") is also a favorite of the pseudo-sophisticate (San Franciscans themselves cannot abide the appellation).

Not all local folk are upset by the pop name for their town, however—sometimes, indeed, it is known only in the immediate area (*Pally*, for example, for Palo Alto, California). In other cases the derived name has all but replaced the official one. *L.A.* has been in free alternation with "Los Angeles" for decades now, to no one's distress (and in blissful unawareness, certainly, of the settlement's name at the time of founding—"El Pueblo de Nuestra Señora la Reina de los Angeles de Porciúncula").

To anyone who wants to carry on with it I offer here the beginnings of a list of Western Canadian place-names that have undergone surgery, for better or worse:

British Columbia has, of course, *Van* for Vancouver, and, in a less-than-inspired wordplay, *O.K. Falls* for Okanagan Falls (to add to the complexity, the falls are no longer there). Prince Albert, Saskatchewan, famed for John Diefenbaker and its federal penitentiary, is (not surprisingly) *P.A.* Winnipeg, Manitoba, fulcrum of the nation, is called *The Peg* (reinforced, perhaps, by another Manitoba place-name, *The Pas* [°oe pa]?). And in Alberta, whence I write, there are *The Hat* (Medicine Hat); *The Bridge* (Lethbridge); *Rocky* or *Rocky Mountain* (for Rocky Mountain House); and *Pincher* (Pincher Creek).

To return to clippings proper, and to keep VER-BATIM readers up to the minute, I close with the following note: Rhodesians, according to a recent news dispatch,

331

now have one they could do without, namely, *the Terrs* (general for 'the terrorists').

B. H. Smeaton
The University of Calgary, Alberta, Canada

⊠

The discussion of Nounspeak [III, 1] prompted me to retrieve a choice collection of occupational titles which have long languished in my files, gleaned from the packing-house industry.

Certain employes in that industry are, among other classifications, known by such job titles as *catch basin skimmer, expeller operator, tallow washer, melter operator, deodorizer, evaporator man, glue bone residue man, inedible renderer, smoker, expeller, lard draw off man, dry sausage handler, temperature man, receive and feed man, put in tongue protector, cheek and temple chiseler, neck boner, beef shackle remover, burry sheep facer, jaw bone chiseler, cold calves splitter* and *bell puller.*

Please do not ask me what any of these job titles mean.

Stanley H. Brams
Labor Trends
Southfield, Michigan

⊠

I was glad to see that someone like A. Ross Eckler submitted [III, 1] a good many more examples of words with the five vowels in sequence. This does not, however, exhaust the list. I can add *larcenious* (for the more usual *larcenous*), *aerious* (which the 17th century used for *aerial*), and *caesious.* Of course these and the others can be made to contain *six* vowels in order by adding the adverbial suffix *-ly.*

As to the shortest words with the five vowels used only once, another seven-letter example is *eunomia,* listed in the *Oxford English Dictionary Supplement.* Without resorting to the French *oiseau,* I can even supply a six-letter example that English took over from Greek: *eunoia* 'alertness of mind,' listed in *Webster's New Twentieth Century Dictionary.*

In his discussion of the Gratuitous Negative [II, 4], Norman Shapiro went seriously astray in citing as an instance *I can't stay but a minute* for *I can stay but a minute.* Both sentences are entirely correct, *but* being used in its meaning of *except* in the former and of *only* in the latter. What is of particular interest is that the latter usage descends from a stage of English when the *but* (for *except*) was combined with a negative *ne* or *n'* before the verb, e.g. *He n' is but a boy.* Thus we find John Lydgate writing in the early 15th century, *They nentende nyght nor day/But vnto merthe,* and William Caxton, later in the century, penning, *I ne entende but onely to reduce thauncient rhyme to prose.* Eventually the lightly-pronounced *n* vanished, and the negation was subsumed in the *but,* which thus came to mean *only* as well as *except.*

Bruce Price, in his article "Noun Overuse' [II, 4], committed a howler in referring to "Sir Quiller-Couch." The titles "Sir" and "Dame" must be immediately followed by the given name (with or without the family name). "Lord Olivier" is correct, but it has to be "Sir Laurence" and not "Sir Olivier."

Robert St. Clair's book review [II, 4] erred in saying, "What is important about this *historic* account. . . ." He ought to have said *historical*—the two adjectives are no more synonymous than *classic* and *classical.*

Finally, Axel Hornos [III, 1] might like to know that for "Ouch!" the Japanese are just as likely to exclaim "Itai!" as "Aita!" Both interjections make use of the same ideograph.

Caldwell Titcomb
Brandeis University

✉

In light of a statement by John J. Ruster [II, 3] that "it is a peculiarly Celtic trait [to reckon] people and things in sets of twenty," I think it worthwhile to note modern Danish ordinal numbers, which have an obvious historical root in a base-20 system. These numbers are: *ti* (10), *tyve* (20), *tredive* (30), *fyrre* (40), *halvtreds* (50), *tres* (60), *halvfjerds* (70), *firs* (80), *halvfems* (90), and *hundrede* (100). Until very recent decades, 50 through 90 were rendered with the suffix *-sindstyve. Halvtredsindstyve,* for example, yields a morpheme-by-morpheme translation as *half* (*halv*), *three* (*tre*), *times* (*sinds*), *twenty* (*tyve*). "Half-three" is equivalent to 2½, so what we have in the number is an equation, $2\frac{1}{2} \times 20$ ($=50$). The western-oriented Swedes, who speak a very similar language, dispensed with this system, substituting for 50, for example, *femti,* or *five-ten,* which yields another equation, 5×10 ($=50$). The Norwegians have followed suit, and I suppose it is only a matter of time before the Danes do likewise.

Frank Willard Riggs
Orem, Utah

Ed Fitzgerald, Radio Station WOR, New York:

> Question: "What do you call transposing initials, Ed? It isn't Bowdlerism, is it?"
> Ed: "No, that's cutting down."
> [of certain mocking writers]: "They were bitten by the Mencken-Nathan syndrome."

Pegeen Fitzgerald, WOR, New York:

> "[I once saw] a statue of a female woman in the park."
> "[He] had an ear and an eye for the light touch."
> "The midi didn't catch on but the long coat kinda semi got a foothold."
> ". . . the astrological sign you were born over."
> "That organization is largely, completely self-supporting."

Jack O'Brian, WOR, New York:

> "Ed [Sullivan] had little forensic talent."
> "He creates the best roast beef."
> ". . . the enormity of the probity of 'Sherlock Holmes.'"

John W. P. O'Brien
Flushing, New York

If James D. White had been in San Francisco on election night, June 8, he might have added one more splendid specimen to his collection of malapropisms in California. This came from a TV commentator who assured his voters that "California voters have today dipped their toe into a very mixed bag."

James J. Kilpatrick
Woodville, Virginia

While I'm not sure that all Mr. White's examples are precisely what I think of as "malapropisms"—some are simply scrambled metaphors, while others sound rather bullish (in the Irish sense)--I submit two further examples of inventive speech, both from the same high school student of mine in Dexter, Maine: "That really hits the nail on the spot" and "No, not by a long short."

T. E. D. Klein
New York, New York

The mistress of modern malapropisms was, of course, the late Jane Ace, who, with her writer-husband, Goodman

Ace, co-starred in the 1930s and 1940s on the radio program, Easy Aces. Such gems as You could have knocked me over with a fender, Don't just sit there like a bum on a log, *and* I've worked my head to the bone trying to think of her name *readily demonstrate the malapropinquity of the Aces. There is no doubt that Jane had that certain Je ne sais pas.*   *Editor*

⊠

It is true that the *Authorized King James Version* of the Bible uses both *ghost* and *spirit*, and that modern English usage prefers the latter (except in the phrase "to give up the ghost"), as noted by Mabel C. Donnelly [III, 1]. But the biblical vocabulary for psychic, spiritual, mental, and emotional states is vastly more complicated, and rich, than a single citation (Mark 1:8, 10) can suggest.

Biblical dictionaries on the subject can be exasperating, and concordances soon reveal the complexities involved. Hebrew uses at least two "spirit" words (*ruach* and *nephesh*), while Greek has three (*pneuma, psyche,* and *nous*). But the use of these words in the Bible often seems arbitrary, and so translation into English can be confusing. In addition to *spirit* and *ghost*, we can have *wind, life, breath, soul, mind,* etc. Try this text on your aeolian harp: "You shall love the Lord your God with all your heart, and with all your soul, and with all your strength, and with all your mind . . ." (Luke 10:27).

Just to add further to the verbal maze, the biblical view of personality was psychosomatic (and distinct from Platonic dualism—"the body is the prison-house of the soul"). So in both the Hebrew and Christian Scriptures, what we would call psychic or spiritual states are freely ascribed to physical organs and other parts of the human anatomy. Blood, heart, head, hands, feet, eyes, breast, mouth, reins (kidneys), liver, bowels, etc. are all invoked as ways for expressing mental, spiritual, and emotional states. Here the *Authorized King James Version,* in my view, is much to be preferred to the more pallid modern English translations. I list some examples:

Authorized King James	*American Revised Standard*
Examine me, O Lord, and prove me; try my reins and my heart. (*Psalm* 26:2)	Prove me, O Lord, and try me; test my heart and my mind.
My beloved put in his hand by the hole of the door, and	My beloved put his hand to the latch, and my heart was

my bowels were moved for him. (*Song of Songs* 5:4)	thrilled within me.
Mine eyes do fail with tears, my bowels are troubled, my liver is poured upon the earth. . . . (*Lam.* 2:11)	My eyes are spent with weeping; my soul is in tumult; my heart is poured out in grief.
Put on therefore, as the elect of God, holy and beloved, bowels of mercies, kindness, humbleness of mind, meekness, longsuffering. (*Col.* 3: 12)	Put on then, as God's chosen ones, holy and beloved, compassion, kindness, lowliness, meekness, and patience.

Two minor matters: (1) *Holy Ghost* is still preferred (to *Holy Spirit*) among many in the so-called Holiness churches, including—so I'm told—the serpent-handlers of West Virginia. Perhaps in this instance we have the association of snake-bite as the testing of faith (and victory over death) with *ghost* as the accepted word for 'the soul of a deceased person' (*OED*). (2) *Giving up the ghost* must be related to common expression of concern when someone sneezes. *God bless you!* and *Gesundheit!* are holdovers from the primitive belief that a person's vital breath (spirit, wind, life, soul, ghost) is expelled during a sneeze.

Hugh T. Kerr, Editor
THEOLOGY TODAY

I do not know what church, if any, Ms. Mabel C. Donnelly of the University of Connecticut at Hartford, author of "Giving Up the Ghost" [VERBATIM III, 1], attends, but, in the Anglican Communion throughout the English-speaking world as well as in many other Protestant denominations, the liturgy continues in the great tradition of both the King James version of the Bible and the *Book of Common Prayer* and uses the term "Holy Ghost," as in "Praise Father, Son and Holy Ghost."

Ms. Donnelly is correct in that the Roman Catholic liturgy expresses a preference for *Holy Spirit* rather than *Holy Ghost*, but the very existence of a Roman liturgy in the English language is a contemporary development. The *Book of Common Prayer*, according to the best reference work on Christianity, *The Oxford Dictionary of the Christian Church*, "has remained practically unchanged ever since" 1662.

Kenneth Seeman Giniger
New York, New York

Re: "The Enigmatic Eggplant" [II, 4]. Actually there are three English names, the third being *Guinea squash*. This may be a disparagement of the Italian farmers who just cultivated the eggplant commercially in the United States, or perhaps (I guess at this) a reference to the West African region whence it was transmitted to Spain by Arab traders.

[I cannot find *Guinea squash* in any of the dictionaries I have consulted but it is noted in *Hortus II* as is *Pekin eggplant*.]

Aubergine may have entered French through Catalan as the Catalonian pronunciation of *al berginia* is a bit nearer the French than the Spanish *al berenjena*. *Aubergine* has been used for the name of an artist's color and was a popular color of cut French velvet at the turn of the century.

A distinctive type of eggplant grows in China and has been raised there since antiquity. China may have been the place of its first cultivation.

Among the Japanese there is an old saying: "He who sees an eggplant, a hawk, and Fujisan on New Year's Day is blessed forever."

M. R. Paskow
Sonoma, California

⊠

Might I suggest that if *aubergine* [II, 4] derives ultimately from Arabic *al-badhinjan* we take a second look at the Hindi *bharta* and consider the possibility that it could be an even more ultimate source for the Arabic word itself? What is the exact breakdown of *al-badhainjan*? Is it 'the indian egg'? The Arabic for 'egg' is *bayda* (*badha*?). I don't know the Arabic for 'plant' but even if it is something like *injan* or *hinjan* the entire Arabic word could still be folk etymology for a word borrowed from the Hindus, perhaps even from Sanskrit. There are many examples of Afro-Indian correspondences (e.g., Sanskrit *simha*/Bantu *simba*: "lion").

Price's "Noun Overuse Phenomenon Article" [II, 4] is both welcome and telling. Perhaps its appeal is primarily to the poet, but everyone could profit from it. There are some who might say that it is not nouns so much which are at fault as the failure to use more evocative ones, but that is skirting this issue.

Noun overuse is the result of several invidious modern trends. One is the direct result of teaching adjective avoidance in our English classes. Another is that NOT

337

stringing nouns together takes time, that modern commodity which is so poorly rationed. Good writing calls us to go back over what we have written, crossing out the dross, replacing it with a more acceptable style.

Perhaps we use fewer verbs because we do less. Sitting in an office all day and before a TV set all evening is scarcely conducive to thinking in terms of dynamically active verbs. But of course it is the use of verbs that is the allopathic antidote to excessive noun usage. Our overemphasis on commerce and technology slides us into dreary non-creativity. Even to use adjectives properly requires training in English usage. It's easier to run nouns together than to worry about choosing between difficult alternatives such as, say, *continuous* and *continual*.

For it isn't only more verbs and adjectives that we crave. We should sweat more over grammar. We should explore more carefully all the other parts of speech and we should cease to neglect our idioms.

If only we were to connect the noun strings with hyphens that would be a start. Our writing might not suddenly become clearer, but it would draw attention to noun overuse with an end to facilitating its excision.

Good sentences thrum to an inner rhythm. They don't just galumph along any old way. They describe real processes. They don't list unwieldy impedimenta over which we stumble as over a marine's obstacle course. As Price points out, that is what makes sentences go clunk-clunk. We should remember Poe's "Unity of effect" which means that the writer chooses only words that contribute to his whole thought, that enhance that thought or at least that do not distract us from its purpose.

This, however, requires discernment and word-sense, so maybe not everyone should be entitled to call himself a writer simply because he can link words to one another the way a monkey might string bunches of grotesquely unmatched beads together.

As usual, *poeta nascitur non fit*. Why not put all our starving poets to work rewriting the garbage turned out by the whole politics-advertising-Academia-technology-military-industry-institution-corpus?

Ed Rehmus
San Francisco, California

Perhaps we look too hard for an explanation and become uncharitable.

Those who first said *I could care less* are misguided, but their motives are pure. Through faulty perception, they see *less* as a negative. Coupling it with *couldn't,* they reason, would be to utter a (shudder!) double negative.

I would not dismiss them as H. N. Meng did: "people who couldn't care less about what they are uttering." They care, but their care is misguided. They worship in the same pew with those who ask, "Whom shall I say is calling?"

True, their error is picked up and perpetuated at the expense of correctness, but who is to say how many more errors would be made and perpetuated if they did not try to be super-correct?

Dick Creed
Winston-Salem Journal

⊠

The little boy whose parents used to read him a story each night at bedtime complained about the stories saying: "Why do you always bring that book which I don't like to be read to out of up for?"

Robert Sinnott
Norwell, Massachusetts

⊠

E. E. Rehmus, in "The Mysterious Origin of the Tarot" [III, 1], gives "Mandarin *tsarng*" as *fitting the formula t-r-.*

Apparently he does not know that the *-r-* merely encodes the second Mandarin tone according to the ingenious system of National Romanization devised by novelist Lin Yutang and linguist Y. R. Chao.

(The full four-tone set is: *tsang, tsarng, tsaang, tsanq.*)

Grant Sharman
Hollywood, California

⊠

I am collecting citations to trace the demise of the strictly intransitive verb. I am not ready to pin it down yet, but I think the tendency to find a transitive use for previously intransitive verbs—to make up a transitive form, if necessary—has been going on from the very beginning of English.

Our Germanic-based language is a little uncomfortable with the strictly intransitive verb, the verb without a direct object. German itself treats as a reflexive or insists on a direct object for verbs that in English are intransitive. In English, we can say, "Sit down." In German we must say, "Seat yourself." I could give hundreds of other examples in other "tonguages" to show the general aversion to verbs without a direct object, at least in our branches of languages.

I cite the following: *Function. The firing pin functions the primer, the primer functions the igniter, the igniter functions the booster, the booster functions the main charge.* (From Army TM's of WW II.) *Respond. Respond an ambulance to this location.* (The Captain on the TV program *Emergency,* speaking on his radio.)

I solicit from your readers other examples of hitherto strictly intransitive verbs bent around into transitive shape. I need proper citations, source, author, date, etc., pinned down.

W. M. Woods
Oak Ridge, Tennessee

꿨꿨꿨

VERBATIM

THE LANGUAGE QUARTERLY

Vol. III, No. 3   December 1976

EDITOR: LAURENCE URDANG

That Dirty Bird

Steven R. Hicks
University of Missouri at Kansas City

The elation the pioneers must have felt in their New World Eden was seldom expressed in the unimaginative names of their first settlements. But if Plymouth and New London represented outposts of Christian European culture, the fact remained that much of God's handiwork in America—topography, plants, and animals—lacked names in "civilized" tongues. Of those names bestowed on American species by latter-day Adams, at least one must stand as an example of our ancestors' earthy exuberance. Charlton Laird, in his *Language in America*, provides the best short explanation of the origin of *shitepoke*.

> Some animals were named for notable conduct, among them the shitepokes, heron-like creatures of several varieties, who, when frightened, behave like the soldiers in *The Naked and the Dead*; they have difficulty maintaining what Norman Mailer calls a tight cincture. According to legend, a fleeing shitepoke could evacuate for half a mile; the latter part of his name means *bag*. (pp. 245–6)

Having been raised in a family where *shitepoke* was a term of endearment for a baby—as apt as that usage may have been, in view of the word's literal meaning—my curiosity was aroused.

The *OED* confirmed Laird's derivation of the word, defining it as "The small green heron of North America." The single citation was dated "c 1850."

Following the first component of *shitepoke* to its more familiar form, however, revealed the compound *shit-sack*, paralleling in structure and meaning the name of the American heron. *Shit-sack* was defined as "an opprobrious name applied to non-conformists." Two citations, both from English works, were dated 1769 and 1785. The latter, Grose' *Dictionary of the Vulgar Tongue*, noted that the term was applied to "a dastardly fellow."

But if *shit-sack* pointed away from the avian world, the entry following *shitepoke* brought me back. *Shiterow*, compounded of the now-familiar first element and a second that "may be a corrupt form of *Heron*," was defined as the latter bird. As early as the 14th century, a scribe translated the Norman French "un beuee de herouns" into English as "a hep of schitrowys." A second citation attested that around 1827 the people of County Wexford, Ireland, were using *shederow* to mean both "heron" and "a thin weakly person."

Craigie and Hurlbert's *A Dictionary of American English on Historical Principles* led me in an interesting new direction. Again defined as the green heron, *shitepoke* was noted to have an unknown origin. The earliest citation, however, predated that given by *OED*, being from an 1832 history of Maine. This citation provided a new clue, for it read, "The Skouk . . . is vulgarly called a 'shite-poke.'" Craigie and Hurlbert also referred me to their *Poke* n.⁴.

Skouk, of "uncertain" origin, was said to be "possibly the same word as *Skoke*¹ or *Skoke*²: note the parallel relationship between *Poke* n.⁴ and *Poke* n.³." The earliest citation for *Skouk* itself was Morse's *American Geography* of 1974, in which *poke* and *skouk* were listed as names of the green bittern. *Skoke*¹ and *Skoke*² proved to be disappointments. The former, from a Massachuset Indian word, referred to *Poke* (-weed) n.³; the latter, probably derived from a Delaware Indian term, was a name for skunkweed. The entries for *Poke*, however, did reveal the promised parallel relationship noted previously. *Poke* n.⁴, with or without *shite-*, denoted the 'green heron' or 'American bittern' (an aquatic bird of habits similar to the heron's); and *Poke* n.[3] 'pokeweed.' *Poke* n.[4] and *Poke* n.[3] thus showed a connection like that of *Skouk* 'green heron' to *Skoke*[1] 'pokeweed.' Nevertheless, I considered myself little wiser for knowing that *shitepoke, poke,* and *skouk* were synonyms, and that one dated to 1794. At this point, unrelated research revived my enthusiasm with the discovery of a use of *shitepoke*—for a person!—predating the citations in all the reference works consulted.

Carl Holliday's *The Wit and Humor of Colonial Days,* in tracing the colonists' satiric mood as the Revolution approached, quotes from a series of pamphlets printed in 1774–5, *"The First Book of the American Chronicles of the Times."* In this parody an anonymous patriot author mimicked the Biblical style in his description of the arrival of General Gage's army in rebellious Boston.

> "36. Now it came to pass, while the Gageites abode in the land of the Bostonites, they day by day committed iniquity; they made great clattering with their sackbuts, their psalteries, their dulcimers, bands of music, and vain parade.
> "37. And they drummed with their drums, and piped with their pipes, making mock fights, and running to and fro like shitepokes on the muddy shore."
> (Holliday, pp. 95–6)

The rebel author obviously refers to a creature of aquatic habits. Equally obvious is the fact that we cannot know at this late date if the author intended his readers to understand that the excretory habits of the British soldiery were similar to those of the shitepoke. In the context, however, it seems unlikely that the comparison was meant to be flattering. If our patriot satirist was any kind of a student of etymology, he may have been making veiled allusion to the then-current English slang term *shit-sack,* above. Such insults, in the form "sack of shit," remain in modern usage. At any rate, it is apparent that even at the date of this first recorded printed use of *shitepoke* the word's possibilities as a derogatory epithet were already being explored.

A published inquiry on the current uses of *shitepoke* produced thirty-six replies. Twenty informants (56%) knew the term solely as one for a bird. Sixteen persons named the heron, bittern, or similar waterfowl, but one-half of that number cited a printed reference for the identification. Other birds named included the buzzard (Ohio),

Northern raven (New York), and road-runner (!: western Nebraska). Five people mentioned the defecating behavior of the bird as the source of its name. A delightful letter from Mr. John H. Pomeroy of Maryland explained the shitepoke's appellation as being "from the bird's habit of defecating when flushed."

Eleven informants (30%) applied *shitepoke* solely to a person, and five (14%) used the term for both a person and a bird. The latter group disagreed, however, as to what characteristic of the bird was implied by the application of *shitepoke* to a person. A lady in Michigan inferred that "long-legged awkwardness" was intended. A Missouri man considered a "shankpoke" to be one who *poked* his nose into affairs in the manner of a heron searching for aquatic food. The Nebraska lady who used *shitepoke* for the road-runner derived the word's use as an epithet from that bird's "senseless over-activity."

Those informants applying *shitepoke* solely to a person reported only two entirely positive definitions. One of these, from a lady in southern New York state, was as "a term of endearment for a baby," exactly as my mother used the term in Missouri.

Outright folk-etymologies, on the other hand, were invariably derogatory. A Pennsylvania man wrote that a *shitepoke* is like a *slowpoke*, with the difference that the former malingers by going to the bathroom. (This definition uses Craigie and Hurlbert's *Poke* n.[7], "a lazy or slow person; a stupid person.") A Florida woman found the explanation of the term in the behavior of the glutton to whom she applied it, defecating, "poking more food in his mouth," defecating, etc.

But a woman in Montana, who learned *shitepoke* from German parents, may have been near etymological roots in her definition "gossips, lawyer shysters . . . a cheat or unsavory person." Partridge's *Origins: A Short Etymological Dictionary of Modern English* notes (*Shoot*[5]) that *shyster* seems to be derived from such roots as the German *Scheisser* 'defecator' and so is closely akin to *shitepoke* and *shitehawk* (*Shoot*[6]). The same author's *A Dictionary of Slang and Unconventional English* yielded *shit-pot*, "a thorough or worthless humbug (person): a sneak . . . mid-C. 19–20; ob.," a possible connection suggested by a Delaware informant who defined *shitepoke* in similarly unattractive terms. An intriguing letter from Will County, Illinois, reported that *shitepoke* denoted a crane, but mentioned local use of the bird name "yellowhammer" for "dirty and disreputable . . . not necessarily poor" natives.

My informants gave nine different spellings of *shitepoke*, and reported six synonyms, including "shit stork" (California) and the cryptic "baloop-da-doop" (North Dakota). Definitions and application, as we have seen, differed widely. But, like the authorities consulted, my informants overwhelmingly agreed that *shitepoke* and its variants remain thinly-veiled and contemptuous epithets.

"*Giving the English language to the Americans is like giving sex to small children: they know it's important, but they don't know what the hell to do with it.*"

—Morton Cooper
Author of *The Queen*

"Don't Say it!"

Hear Finish Before (Pause) You?

Ruth Brown
New York Society for the Deaf, New York City

No longer does a person need to be deaf in order to enjoy using sign language. Thanks largely to the perseverance of deaf adults and their hearing offspring, the past decade has witnessed a flowering of sign language systems—American Sign Language or Ameslan, Signed English, Signing Exact English, sign-mime, and cued speech—in this country.

Of these, Ameslan is the most useful for communicating with most deaf people and the most fascinating from a linguistic viewpoint. To begin with, in an obvious departure from formal English usage, it lacks articles, and plurals and verb tenses are supplied either through context or by the addition of the word "finish." The Ameslan title of this article thus translates into English as: "Have you ever heard of this before?"

For fullest communication, facial expression and body language must also be used when signing in lieu of aural inflection cues. "Think funny (pause) you?" translates from Ameslan into English either as: "Isn't he funny?" or "So you think he's funny, do you?" depending on whether the signer wears a smiling facial expression and relaxed posture, or a grim facial expression and threatening posture.

Strike your right fist down on top of your left fist twice. Then flick your right index finger twice quickly away from the side of your forehead. You have just signed "Work-work, for-for" in Ameslan. This translates into English as "What are we working so hard for," and again your face and body must supply the correct punctuation and depth of feeling appropriate to the utterance of the sentiment.

Are you surprised to find yourself using Ameslan so easily? Then tap the side of your forehead twice with your right index finger, curl and "freeze" the fingers of both hands in mid-air, and point to your chest. You have just signed "Think freeze me!" in Ameslan, or in English, "I was so surprised I couldn't think!"

Perhaps you wish to express a quizzical attitude by stroking your chest lightly, quickly and upward, with the middle fingers of both hands, then bringing the tips of thumbs and fingers of both hands together twice. You've just said in Ameslan, "Exciting, more?" or in English, "What else is new and exciting?"

Straddling your left index finger between your right index and middle fingers, then rocking the latter two fingers slightly and pointing to your chest indicate "Undecided me" in Ameslan or "I haven't decided yet" in English.

Or instead you may want to flick your right index finger upward next to your forehead, then form an "O" in mid-air with your cupped hand before pointing to yourself. That would convey in Ameslan, "Understand zero me!" or in English, "I don't understand a single thing!"

Another way to sign what you mean is to run your right middle finger vertically across your open left palm upward in the direction of your chin. Hold the tip of your tongue against your upper front teeth and let a sly expression creep into your eyes. You have just said in English, "I'm going to take advantage of this!"

If you want to use an Ameslaner's favorite phrase, it can be best expressed by the erect index and little fingers, open palm, outstretched thumb and upright forearm simultaneously spelling out "I-L-Y," the Ameslan acronym for "I love you."

Conversely, if you think Ameslan's just a lot of hogwash, you could vent your feelings by wrapping the fingers of your left hand loosely around your upright right thumb, then jerking the thumb downward with an emphatic movement. This sign happens to be a graphic description of a physiological function.

Often there is a pictorial similarity between the sign and the concrete thing it represents, which is sometimes reinforced by also using the initial letter of the word. To cite only two examples here suffices: The word "tree" is signed by having the left hand, palm down, support the right elbow, while the right fingers remain outstretched and the right forearm turns from side to side. The word "water" is signed with the sign for "w"—the outstretched index, middle and ring fingers of one hand—tapping against the chin.

All signs are classified according to *position* in relation to the head or upper torso, *shape* of the fingers or hands, and *motion* in relation to the rest of the body. In this connection, it is interesting to note that nouns indicating the human male—man, father, husband—are signed above the nose; those belonging to the human female—aunt, daughter, grandmother—below the nose. Long ago someone must have decided men have minds while women have mouths. While today liberated women would scorn such a connotation, it cannot be denied that such a gestural distinction is helpful in practice.

Like all other living languages, Ameslan changes and thrives, thanks to the input and encouragement it receives from the National Association of the Deaf, teachers of the deaf in total-communication school programs, various meetings and sports events run by and for deaf people, institutions like Gallaudet College, the National Technical Institute for the Deaf, California State University at Northridge and New York University's Deafness Research & Training Center, the Registry of Interpreters for the Deaf and the National Theatre of the Deaf. Television coverage of deaf people, such as of the recently crowned Miss Deaf America 1976-1978, on a captioned news program also makes more people aware of sign language.

Anyone can obtain a basic knowledge of Ameslan by enrolling in one of the many sign-language classes offered by adult education programs, churches and colleges throughout the country and by studying any of several textbooks available. After a beginner masters the one-handed manual alphabet and a basic vocabulary of perhaps five hundred signs, he is ready to enjoy the peculiar logic, economy, and beauty inherent in Ameslan.

"Take advantage of"   *"I Love you"*

"Understand"

"Freeze"

"Water"

"Tree"

Photographs by Ruth Brown

ΩΩΩΩΩ

Since nobody has (as yet) pointed out my gaffe, let me be the first to correct myself. In my letter on French Canadian baseball terminology (III,1), I attributed to Winston Churchill the observation that England and America are two countries separated by the same language. Now, while Churchill more than likely subscribed to it, and may well have repeated it, the original quote should, of course, be credited to G. B. Shaw.

Norman R. Shapiro
Wesleyan University

Menu Barbarisms

John G. Caffrey, Ph.D.
Suffern, NY

For some years I have collected specimens of mangled language from printed menus. Some of them are the result of carelessness or an attempt to spell phonetically, while others represent real ignorance or misunderstanding. I except the "difference of opinion" classics such as *sherbert* or *Welsh rarebit*.

The following are more or less self-explanatory.

Soup du Jour of the Day	*Duck Al Lorange*
Beef Dipped in Au Jus	*Coy au Vine*
Table Dhote Special	*Frogs Legs Paovencle*
Cold Slaw Vinegarette	

A subclass exhibits the "dropped d" which reflects colloquial usage:

Old Fashion [*cocktail*]	*Chop Sirloin* (or *Sir Lion*)
Pickle Beets	*Southern Fry Chicken*
Stuffed Stripe Bass	

Some are merely pretentious:

Roast Rib of Prized Beef	*Egg Omalit*
Twisted Egg Dough Roll	

Others are merely unfortunate:

Bowel of Soup	*Socutash*
Homemade Deserts	*Chilli*

When I pointed out *Swish Cheese* to a waitress, she was helpful: "You know, with the holes."

Liver with Smothered Onions, frequently encountered, must derive from the older "Liver smothered with onions," but I have found waiterpersons who explained that smothering must be a cooking prcoess.

When I first began to teach English in 1946 there was a local campaign to stamp out FOOD AT IT'S BEST on a local restaurant's roof. Dozens of hot letters from students finally produced an effect: the apostrophe was taken out, but the space was left. This motto now appears on menus and appears to be impossible to stamp out. But an art form which can spawn *Chopped Suey* must be forgiven its little weaknesses.

BIBLIOGRAPHIA

THE PLIGHT OF ENGLISH, by Basil Cottle, Arlington House, 1975, 159 pp. $7.95 [A VERBATIM Book Club Selection]

ON WRITING WELL, by William Zinsser, Harper & Row, 1976, viii + 157 pp. $6.95

The subtitle of *Plight* reads, "Ambiguities, Cacophonies, and Other Violations of Our Language"; that of *Writing*, "An Informal Guide to Writing Nonfiction." Here are two books about the use of English, one by an experienced practitioner of the craft of nonfiction, author of nine books (plus *Writing*) and of an enormous number of articles in national periodicals, who teaches at Yale, the other by a scholar at Bristol University in England, author of a dictionary of surnames and of *The Triumph of English: 1350–1400.*

Zinsser's book falls into the style of a text quite early, when he makes his straightforward plea for simplicity. Consequently, his book reads like an English handbook; notwithstanding the author's demurrals, despite his urging that the details of his exposition be searched out in grammar books, the reader comes away with the definite impression that he is being taught. There is nothing wrong with being taught, but it is hardly as engaging as being exposed to learning. *On Writing Well* is a serious book and not really very entertaining.

Cottle, on the other hand, exhibits the sly cynicism one comes to associate with editorial writers in *The Times* —people like Philip Howard and Bernard Levin. There is no doubt that *Plight* is the more learned of two books, but its erudition is clothed in a combination of practical advice and detached humor. Cottle also makes his plea for simplicity of expression:

> One of the first casualties in the search for affectation is the verb *to be:* opposing the idea that men wear beards out of another kind of affectation, someone sensibly wrote, 'Surely the affectation is in the removal of facial hair, not in its retention'; few writers would leave it at that—*is in* would be varied to *is found in, rests in, dwells in, lies in, stands in, shows in, stems from, issues from, proceeds from, belongs to, originates in, is discernible in, is ascribable to, is symptomatised by,* and thus the value of the good old plain word *is* is further cheapened.

Cottle's book has more humor than Zinsser's; but that may not be an adverse criticism for those who prefer to keep learning and entertainment separate. Cottle's book has more information about the history of the language, and it seems very apt where it appears; but the absence of such information in Zinsser's book will be no loss to those who want to get on with the business at hand. Cottle's book, by rough estimate, contains about ten per cent less text than Zinsser's yet costs more than 16 per cent more (at retail); but such differences are trivial. Cottle's style, though entertaining in content, is less informal than Zinsser's.

The authors appear to have set out with the same ends in view, to enlighten readers in the difficult business of writing well—at least well enough to communicate. Both directed their books to people of education who wish to improve their techniques with language, not learn them from scratch. In their approaches to these purposes, the authors differ markedly: for acquiring techniques, Zinsser's book must be recommended over Cottle's; for enjoyment, Cottle's takes the honors

EPISTOLAE

I have been udderly delected by the assay on Malatropisms in the currant VERBOTIN and am confidential that such articulates would do much to accrease the cirularity of your readership. In any K's, I am unclothesing my check to cover a year's sumstription.

Donald W. Lee
Galveston, Texas

As a new subscriber to VERBATIM I wish to tell you how much I enjoyed my first issue, that of May 1976. I particularly enjoyed *Mrs. Malaprop's Bicentennial* by James D. White, the theme of which coincides with my thinking.

I would like to pass on to you my contribution for a more hilarious language. My former employer used to say, "This corporation has set up rules of conduct for the employees and we expect you to live up to them sacrilegiously."

W. N. Loos
Pittsburgh, Pennsylvania

Dear Mom
I love
you
Do you
love me

The note reproduced above was found on the door-step of a couple whose children are grown. Speculation about who had written it, why, and under what circum-stances lead the imagination into the empyrean at one ex-treme and innumerable culs de sac at the other. The note speaks volumes about modern society, family, mores, per-sonality, and communication (in its broadest senses). It serves as a point of departure for some random comments on the word *mother* and its congeners.

Mother, as most communications experts will be quick to offer, is a "loaded" word. Like *God, country, sex, C.I.A.* (replacing the *F.B.I.?*), it can be regarded—in western cul-ture, at least—as a lexical element pregnant with connota-tion, teeming with psychological overtones. To the modern observer of slang, *mother* is referred to facetiously as a half a word, frequently (in eye dialect) spelt *muthah.*

It is interesting to note that *ma* and *maw*, which may be regarded by some as family language, reappears as *Ma Barker*, the notorious leader of a murderous gang, whose ironic nickname makes her renowned cruelty seem all the more heinous.

The *ma* of ". . . And your ma is good-lookin' " (*Sum-mertime*) is the same as the one in Shopright Supermarkets' "Hey Ma! What's for dinner?" and in *Ma and Pa Kettle*— all folksy and bucolic.

Momma (spelt that way) evokes the "red-hot momma" notion; spelt *mama*, but pronounced the same way, the word reverts to familial status. But we must not ignore the warmth of the epithet in combinations like *Mama Cass*, whose ample proportions seem to have won her this sobri-quet as much as her personality did. *Mamma Leone's*, a restaurant in New York City, evokes the image of a moth-erly Italian lady presiding over pots of steaming spaghetti and tomato sauce. Certainly, "Momma Leone's" would never do. Also in New York City is the more formal *Mother Bertolotti's*; not lacking in warmth entirely, this name evokes images of matriarchal domination.

The "Last of the Red-hot Mommas" (Sophie Tucker) evokes an image of ample sexiness, chiefly because we can recall the person herself. This is not the *mama* of "Mah mama don' tol' me" (*Blues in the Night*) or of *I Remember Mama* (can you imagine, "I Remember Momma"?). It is the *momma* of "Come to Momma, come to Momma, Do!" (*Embraceable You*).

Among the musical groups are *The Mamas and the Papas*, and references to *Momma* appear, now and then, in song lyrics: "Hey, sweet Momma, tree-top tall, Won't you kindly turn your temper down," ". . . Momma's going to buy you a . . .," and so on. The most famous is probably *Mammy*, which is so evocative of a large, black, motherly woman as to be virtually denotative.

Mum, which is more common in England than in the U.S., emerges as an affectionate term of address and as a designation with the same connotations: *His mum is having a dinner party for his fiancee* leaves the listener (or reader) with the impression that the son's relationship with his mother appears to have changed little since he was a small boy, an impression that might be based on fact or might be intentionally humorous. *Mater*, surely, is a term associated, in Americans' minds, with the sort of formal, Victorian relationship expected between an upperclass Englishman (of almost any age) and his mother.

Mom, with all its simplicity and warmth, is chiefly a term of address rather than of reference, but can be found in contexts like *Mom and Pop Store*, referring to a family-run retail business that carries the connotation of being only marginally profitable, and in "More Parks' sausages, Mom!"

Coming full circle back to *mother*, recalling the songs of yesteryear, we have such sentimental classics as "Just Break the News to Mother," "M is for the Million Things She Gave Me," "Mother Macree," and so on.

Mother also has its unpleasant senses, especially as a term for the whitish bacteria found on the surface of fermenting liquids (also called *mother of vinegar*), *mother's* (or *mama's*) *boy*, and *mother yaw*, a rather revolting pathological term. It serves as a kind of folk-word denoting 'source' in *mother liquor, mother lode, mother-of-pearl,* and *mother tongue*. Its other connotations can be seen in *mother-naked* ('original'), *motherland* ('original'; compare *fatherland*), *mother superior* and *mother church* ('maternal'), and *mother wit* ('innate'). *Mother Goose* remains a unique referent; *Mother Carey's chicken*, a petrel, received its name from one knows where.

These casual observations probably leave a great deal unsaid, particularly about words like *mother-in-law*, but that might be just as well.

EPISTOLAE

A few remarks on the myriad delights of VERBATIM III,1:

I wish that Axel Hornos had distinguished between the two kinds of interjections: those that are mere sounds—the "ouch" and "phooey" variety—and those that are actual words used exclamatively. When an Italian shouts *bravo*, for example, he isn't just voicing indiscriminate onomatopoeia; he is using a bona fide adjective. (Hence the feminine, *brava*, to a deserving diva.) Likewise the German *toll* 'fantastic, smashing,' and the Indonesian *bagus* 'beautiful' and *adjaib* 'wonderful.' Similarly, several of Mr. Hornos's examples are verb forms. The Spanish *oye* is an imperative of *oír* 'hear'; the Dutch *zeg*—note the spelling, though pronounced "zeCH"—is an imperative of *zeggen* 'say,' as in the English 'Say there'; and even the Italian *evviva*, thinly disguised, is fundamentally a verb: the hortatory subjunctive of *vivere*, plus an exclamatory *e*, and meaning, roughly, 'Long (may you) live!' Numerous current American monstrosities could be cited as interesting hybrids of the two types of interjection, generally expansible: e.g., 'like wow!', 'like I mean wow!', 'like man I mean wow!'

H. N. Meng's suggestion that the *spit* of *spit and image* is a deformation of *spirit* delights my etymo-logic, but unfortunately I think it misses the mark. While *OED* documents this use of *spit* no earlier than the 1800s, Partridge (*Dictionary of Slang and Unconventional English*) gives analogous usages from two centuries before. That we are dealing here with honest-to-goodness *spit* and not *spirit* (or even *spi't*) would seem to be corroborated by a similar French phrase, attested as early as the 15th century. A child who is the image of his father is commonly said to be *son père tout craché*, freely translated as 'the very spit of his father.' The *Nouveau Dictionnaire Etymologique du Français* (Hachette-Tchou, 1971) offers as an explanation the analogy between the act of spitting and the act of procreation which, if accurate, is rather a far cry from the realm of the spirit.

In passing, Candace Murray Huddleston's reference to the Kentuckian use of *poke* for *sack* or *bag* calls to mind the origin of the expression *to buy a pig in a poke*. The term is, of course, cognate with the French *poche* 'pocket.' Interestingly enough, the French buy cats in theirs, not pigs, as in the expression *acheter chat en poche. . . .*

And lastly, as for your comments on sentence-ending prepositions, I couldn't agree more. Especially with the observation that they are often really verbal particles . . .

Still, logic and linguistic histroy notwithstanding, a certain aversion to ending a sentence (or clause) with a preposition has ingrained itself into the instinct of would-be discriminating speakers over the years since the 18th century grammarians imposed their spurious rule. (That is, in relative clauses, and where the preposition is a real one and not a verbal particle.) In defense of the purists it should be admitted that it is, in fact, a convenient rule to have when we want to tailor our speech to the audience and the occasion. Circumstances will tell me whether to say "the guys I work with" or "the gentlemen with whom I work." It's one of those differentiations, however illegitimate their origin, that English is richer for holding onto. (Or "onto which English is richer for holding"?)

Norman R. Shapiro
Wesleyan University

VERBATIM [II, 4] second column: In the review of Mencken's *The American Language*, it is stated that "*Yankee* is apparently derived from the Dutch *Jan Kees* (John Cheese)." The translation in parenthesis is wrong: *Kees* is a proper name (short for Cornelis = Cornelius) and in no way related to the Dutch word for cheese. The same mistake is made by Mario Pei in *The Story of the English Language* (1960), page 107.

[III, 1]: Axel Hornos offers *Sech, Jan!* as a Dutch equivalent for *Hey, John!* However, the word *sech* does not exist in the contemporary Dutch language;

356

at best, it could be construed as a phonetic rendering of a certain dialectical mispronunciation of *zeg*. But then, *Zeg Jan!* would be a rather poor translation of *Hey, John!*

The other examples given in this article could also have been enriched with Dutch equivalents. In Holland, the cod-liver-oil drinker would say *jasses* or *jakkes* or *ajakkes*, the bug squasher *bah*. As to animals' sounds, it's *wau wau* or *woef woef* for dogs, *kukeleku* for roosters. Cats *spinnen*, doves *koeren* or *kirren*, birds *kwetteren* or *tjilpen*, and cats (again) *miauwen*.

Harry Cohen
Brussels, Belgium

Regarding Robert Fowkes's "Esrever Hsilgne" in the latest VERBATIM:

Let us not forget poor Hazel Shade:

. . . She twisted words: pot, top,
Spider, redips. And 'powder' was 'red wop.'
She called you a didactic katydid.

(*Pale Fire*, Nabokov)

Emily P. Brady
Lexington, Massachusetts

Lately I have noticed a minor, lopsided flirtation with the word "former." A guest on a quiz show, while discussing his new book, mentioned the "Nixon family's former dog." How did this pet manage to change species, I wonder.

And then I heard an athlete described as "a former graduate" of a certain university. Once a graduate, aren't you always a graduate. It sounded as if he had to give back his diploma.

Lastly, did everyone notice the wonderful, but unconscious (I think), pun uttered by a congressman in the midst of the Legionnaire disease controversy? He chided President Ford for "injecting" politics into the immunization plans!

Cathy Butler
Seattle, Washington

The Cape Cod Reader

Henry Morgan
Truro, Massachusetts

On Lower Cape Cod, specifically in the village of Truro, a common English word that started life as a noun has become a verb, adverb, gerund, participle, conjunction, interjection and practically every other part of speech. In fact some of the parts are elusive and therefore it seems best just to give instances of usage and the reader can make up his own mind.

> *Bullshit.* A simple declarative, usually taken to mean 'I have reason to doubt the veracity of what you just said.'
>
> *I was bullshit.* In effect, 'very very angry . . . upset . . . terrified.' It's necessary to consider the context of what has been under discussion and to observe the speaker's manner. Sometimes the phrase follows a fairly simple announcement—e.g.: "I just got my electric bill and I was b."
>
> *My wife was b. with the kid.* 'The kid has done something it shouldn't have done. The wife hit it.'
>
> *He lives in that b. house near you.* The speaker in this instance is a plumber who is being called much too often by the owner of the house to do repair work. The plumbing was installed by his chief competitor.
>
> *This year my gahden went b. on me.* 'Weeds. Also, rabbits, chipmunks, corn borers, raccoons, etc.
>
> *The weather turned b.* [Fisherman] was out in his illegal trawler and got caught in fog.'
>
> *The harbormaster went b.* 'He also got caught by the harbormaster.'
>
> *This here chowdah is b.* 'Canned.'
>
> *The way I have to start my cah, I have to b. it for a while.* 'Old car. It has a manual choke and it has to be "babied" a bit.'
>
> *The wind blew b. last night.* 'The anemometer registered gusts over seventy mph—not uncommon.'

Another multi-faceted word in our town is "unreal." About half the goings on, especially during the tourist season, are thus described. "The way he was driving—it was unreal." "She burned the corn. Unreal." And so forth.

What may be of interest to students of the genre is the not-all-that-rare combination (I've heard it three times in the last month) viz: "Unreal bullshit." While there is no accurate way of translating this into something more meaningful, still, it serves its purpose.

Charmed and Other Quarks

August A. Imholtz, Jr.
College Park, Maryland

The U.S. Energy Research and Development Administration (ERDA) announced on June 8, 1976, that a group of physicists working at Stanford and the University of California thought they had discovered a new subatomic particle believed to be the long sought "charmed" quark. "The new particle," according to the ERDA news release "appears to be made up of a combination of a 'charmed' quark and another non-'charmed' constitutent. If this discovery is confirmed, physicists will have established the existence of 'charm' and gained a much deeper understanding of the world of subatomic particles."

The existence of quarks was first proposed by the American physicist Murray Gell-Mann as the basis of all matter. He hypothesized three elementary quarks, quark ρ, η, and λ, which through their various combinations explain the properties of all other subatomic particles. Had Gell-Mann been a Lewis Carroll enthusiast, he might have named his hypothetical particles snarks; but instead he borrowed the word *quark* from James Joyce's *Finnegans Wake*. *Quark* occurs in the first line of the poem (p. 383) recited by gulls and other birds to King Mark of Cornwall:

Three quarks for Muster Mark.

But what is a quark? The Trieste scholar Steilo Crise, in an article published in the *James Joyce Quarterly*, correctly observed that *quark* does not exist as a substantive in English. There is a rare English verb to *quark* which is probably of imitative origin and was first used by J. F. Campbell in his *Popular Tales of the West Highlands* in 1860: "The gurgling and quarking of spring frogs in a pond." In the slang of the American West the verb was used as a synonym for murder. Since birds do not gurgle, even in a quarkly way, nor commit murder, the meaning of Joyce's "quark," like so many of his other recondite words, must be sought outside English.

Quark is a common German word for a rather bland variety of cottage cheese. The modern German word is derived from Middle High German *twarc* which in turn was derived from the West Slavic (Wendish) word *twarog* sometime before the 14th century. *Twarog* is cognate with Czech *tvarog*, Polish *twaróg*, Bulgarian *tvarog*, and Russian *tvorg*, all of which mean 'curds or soft cheese.' The Slavic words appear to be related to Greek τυρος, meaning 'cheese,' and Avestan *tūiri-* meaning 'milk that has become cheese.' Karl Lokotsch, however, believes that the Slavic words are derived from the Turkish *turat*, a word meaning 'curdled milk or cheese.'

Helmut W. Bonheim, in his *Lexicon of the German in Finnegans Wake*, offers the following definition: *quark:* curd, rubbish, trifle. 'Curd' is correct but 'rubbish' is, at best, a misleading gloss. *Quark*, from its orgiinal meaning of 'cheese,' came to be applied to any cheeselike substance, especially human or other animal excrement. Hence the proverb quoted by Jacob and Wilhelm Grimm:

> *Getretner quark*
> *Wird breit nicht stark.*

Finally, the third meaning of *quark* is, as Bonheim points out, a 'trifle, a little nothing unworthy of consideration.' In *Finnegans Wake*, the second and third senses seem more appropriate than does the primary meaning of 'cottage cheese.' The assumption that one or more of the German meanings of *quark* should be understood in the song of the gulls and curlews is supported by the context of both direct and disguised references to the myth of Tristram and Isolde and by the fact that "Muster," the first substantive after *quark*, is the German word for 'model, ideal, or type,' which refers to Mark and H. C. Earwicker, the hero of *Finnegans Wake*.

Whatever Joycean sense *quark* assumes, one may still speculate whether matter, according to the Quark Theory, is really composed of green (for color, like strangeness, is a property of quarks) cheese, crap, or, in the end, nothing really worthwhile.

EPISTOLAE

While not able to supply Robert Fowkes with a palindromic English city name [VERBATIM III, 2], a double palindromic Wisconsin Indian river name might be of interest: *Kinnickinnic*.

As to Old Trebor, *peek ti pu & yats llew*!

Reinhold Aman
Milwaukee, Wisconsin

ETYMOLOGICA OBSCURA

That Ubiquitous Cockroach!

Enter any building in which these depressing creatures thrive and you will be told at once that they were not there before ("in the good, old days") but that they were "brought in." Likewise, when you cross the border into a foreign country the language of the country will tell you the same story. Everyone knows that the English word derives from the Spanish *cucaracha*; the spelling "cockroach" is due to popular etymology. It has nothing to do with roosters or even that carplike fish known as "roach" (Old French *roche*), although the slang for a marijuana butt, *roach*, seems to derive from the Mexican song, "La Cucaracha," judging by the lyrics: "Ya no puede caminar porque . . . le falta marijuana que fumar." In other words, the cockroach was "brought in" by the Spaniards. But there is also a Latvian word *kukaraca*—and which country got it from which? Incidentally, the Basques call all beetles *karrakaldo* and the Australian aborigines of Melville Island called any insect *kărakàringa*. But no one in his right mind would hazard any connection between them—or would he?

Even if we break the Spanish word down we don't get much closer to its origins. The Spanish *cuca, cuco* is merely a kind of caterpillar. And just to show that Latvian & Spanish have more than one (accidental?) form in common, for *cuca* there is the Latvian word for 'insect,' *kukainis*, which is puzzlingly similar also to the Japanese word for 'insect,' *konchu*. Again, is this merely more of my mania for juxtaposing "impossible" relationships or is there something we don't know?

Cucaracha, however, has even more interesting relatives. Among these is the Greek *kantharis*, or blister-fly, a kind of beetle from which we get cantharides or Spanish fly, quite wrongly believed to be an aphrodisiac—unless you are a bull or if you *like* burning & blisters! Another relative (not so "impossible" this time!) is the sacred beetle, or *scarab* of Egypt: h-p-r (cf. Malayalam *parra*, 'cockroach') or *chepera*. In German this word falls from grace as *Schwabe* 'cockroach' which the Germans believe comes from Swabia—just as we believe our pests came from Spain. Its real origin, however, is not Swabia, but the Lithuanian *vabalas* (cognate of English *weevil*) or *beetle* via Czech *svab* 'cockroach.'

I believe, in contradiction to most etymologists, that

the Egyptian scarab, *chepera*, is our word *chafer*, French *cafard*, and possibly Italian *scarafaggio*. In Sanskrit the *r* becomes an *l* and the elements are transposed resulting in *pulaka* 'insect.' The Aztec word *chapul* 'grasshopper' as in the fashionable Mexico City district, *Chapultepec* or 'Grasshopper Hill' is another odd similarity. But *pulaka*, rather than *fugio* or some such root, as many would have us believe, is most likely to be the origin of Latin *pulex*, English *flea*. This is despite the fact that many old textbooks use a blanket term for all nocturnal pests, *lucifugia* 'light-fleers' even to the inclusion of rodents.

If we substitute *b* for *p* in *pulaka* we get the Latin word for cockroach, *blatta*. Although that is not a cognate of English *beetle* (< OE *bitula*, 'a biter'), *blatta* could conceivably be a relative of Old English *budda*—not any friend, however, of Gautama—as *scearn-budda* is only a dung-beetle. *Weevil* could also be another relative and the latter is almost certain to be part of the same ugly family as Portuguese *barata* 'cockroach' and Albanian *brumbull* 'beetle.'

Thus, for the meaning 'cockroach' we find any number of alternate senses: 'insect,' 'beetle,' 'grasshopper,' etc. Since all of these creatures are first of all insects and secondly pests, the Egyptians sought to incorporate all of these meanings in the one sense of *scarab* which then represented therefore a creature of persistence and reincarnation or immortality. The identification of the scarab with the dung-rolling beetle was purely visual and secondary. Don Marquis may or may not have been aware of all that when he made Archy, the cockroach who used his typewriter by night, a reincarnated being descended all the way from the Egyptian pharaohs, but the fact is the cockroach is the hardiest and most ancient of all insect scourges.

As for its geographical origin, it seems mysteriously & gradually to have appeared from all sides and no matter how much one culture may try to blame another, the fact is it is impossible to determine where it ultimately came from. Aside from *cockroach* the native English term would seem to be *wood louse*, except that a wood louse is a sow bug or a termite and only has the meaning of 'cockroach' in a metaphorical sense.

I hasten to add that there are none of these awfuls in *my* house, which is probably just luck—but please *don't* knock on wood(work) because you never can tell!

E. E. Rehmus
San Francisco, California

BIBLIOGRAPHIA

THE PHRASE-DROPPER'S HANDBOOK, by John T. Beaudouin and Everett Mattlin, Doubleday & Company, Inc. 1976, x + 115 pp. $5.95

From the jacket copy it is difficult to tell whether this little book is supposed to be serious—until one reads in the Introduction that it is "meant as a guide to the game, a game of tongue-in-cheek badinage and verbal bluffery." A shorter description would be "A Manual of One-upmanship for Cocktail Party Conversation."

The authors provide a guide to befuddlement of the pompous by leading the reader over a course of study in which he is exhorted to learn and use jargon (*developmental lag, hypoactive, behavioral objectives*), irrelevant historical events ("Not since the Gadsden Purchase have we seen such a flagrant disregard of the public interest"), a collection of choice items from French, German, Yiddish, Latin, and English, and, of course, phrase-dropping ("Revenons à moutons," "Timeo Danaos et dona ferentes").

If you consider deception to be fun, you will enjoy reading this book and even using it. Its main premise is that no one really knows what he's talking about anyway, so you might as well get aboard the bandwagon. Woe be unto you if you encounter any who have their wits about them and take as much delight in flushing out the phonies as they may take in bamboozling the pretentious.

A WHIMSEY ANTHOLOGY, Carolyn Wells, compiler. New York: Charles Scribner's Sons, 1906. Republished by Gale Research Co., Detroit, 1976. xiv + 221 pp. $8.00. [Available only from the publisher.]

THE LITTLE STAR

SCINTILLATE scintillate, globule orific,
Fain would I fathom thy nature's specific.
Loftily poised in ether capacious,
Strongly resembling a gem carbonaceous.

When torrid Phœbus refuses his presence
And ceases to lamp with fierce incandescence,
Then you illumine the regions supernal,
Scintillate, scintillate, semper nocturnal.

Then the victim of hospiceless peregrination
Gratefully hails your minute coruscation.
He could not determine his journey's direction
But for your bright scintillating protection.

Anonymous.

ON THE STREET

He bought a little block of stock
    The day he went to town;
And in the nature of such things,
                    That
                    Stock
                    Went
                    Right
                    Straight
                    Down!

    ❂   ❂   ❂   ❂

He sold a little block of stock:
    Now sorrow fills his cup,
For from the moment that he did,
                    Up.
                    Right
                    Went
                    Thing
                    Blamed
                    The

    ❂   ❂   ❂   ❂

He bought a little block of stock,
    Expecting he would taste of bliss;
He can't let go and can't hang on,

Anonymous.

WHAT HIAWATHA PROBABLY DID

HE slew the noble Mudjekeewis,
    With his skin he made him mittens;
    Made them with the fur side inside;

Made them with the skin-side outside;
He, to keep the warm side inside,
Put the cold side, skin-side outside;
He, to keep the cold side outside,
Put the warm side, fur-side, inside:—
That's why he put the cold side outside,
Why he put the warm side inside,
Why he turned them inside outside.

Anonymous.

300 whimseys [*sic*] by Anonymous, Lear, Addison, Kipling, Poe, Herrick, Burgess, Carroll, Hood, Swinburne, Dickens, Southey, Holmes, Gilbert, Cosmo Monkhouse, and lesser-known poets, collected by the lady who gave us *The Anthology of Nonsense Verse.* A necessity to any library that aspires to a collection reflecting fun with language in verse.

OBITER DICTA

We note that more and more companies and institutions include in their employment advertising and, in many cases, on their letterheads the slogan, "An equal opportunity/affirmative action employer." The "equal opportunity" part of the slogan seems forthright and sufficiently unassailable not to merit comment, unless one might be allowed the cynical observation that if you have to advertise your equality, honesty, or whatever, the obvious inference is that it might have once been suspect.

But the second part doesn't yield quite so readily to acceptance. Is "affirmative" to be construed in the sense, 'positive; assertive'? If so, then one could be led to assume that any job applicant had the right to expect *affirmative* action on a work application: that is, the affirmative action employer would have to say "Yes" to any applicant. What is probably intended is the sense of *assertive* action; in other words, "We don't shilly-shally when asked for a decision on an application." That's all well and good, but in these days when the cop on the beat (and on TV) can no longer utter a simple "Yes" or "No" to a question but replies with an "Affirmative" or "Negative," we wonder why companies persist in a meaning that could be easily misunderstood and doesn't reflect the more commonly accepted sense of the word.

A Plea for Plain Talk

Douglas R. Woodworth
Judge, Superior Court
San Diego County

As some practitioners are cognizant, I harbor a personal idiosyncratic affinity for sesquipedalian words, and would invite you to indulge your own polysyllabic propensities, if you feel ineluctably constrained to do so, in expounding recondite legal propositions in my courtroom.

But talking to witnesses and jurors is another thing. Plain English is a must. I don't mean you should talk down to them, but you are hurting your cause if you cloak your thoughts in strange garments. You may have seen that this second paragraph is made up mostly of everyday Anglo-Saxon words; yet you can tell what I mean, I hope, just as well as you could in the first paragraph.

Time and again I have observed lawyers evoke their hostility or bafflement by unnecessarily using fancy words instead of plain ones. Here are some recurrent samples:

Actual Usage	Plain Usage
subsequent to	*after*
prior to, antecedent to	*before*
rationale	*reason(s)*
conjecture, speculate	*guess*
converse	*talk*
interrogate	*question*
hypothesize	*suppose, let's say*
in the vicinity of	*near(by)*
approximately	*about, around*
audible	*aloud, out loud*
perceptible, visible	*in (plain) sight, noticeable*
negligent	*careless*
preponderance	*greater weight*
stipulate, acquiesce, concur	*agree, go along with*
emphasize	*stress*
(substantially) contemporaneous	*about the same time*
equitable	*fair*
aggregate of, totality of	*all*
totality of circumstances	*whole picture*
employment	*work*
(earned) compensation	*pay*
participate	*take part*
voluntary	*willing*
intentional, deliberate	*on purpose*

intend to	*mean to*
supersede	*replace*

You can no doubt think of dozens of other examples. This vice, which I might label "ornamental opacity," probably results from years of saturation with professional jargon in college and law school. We lawyers are supposed to be masters of the art of communication. So let's escape from the shackles of academic obscurantism, and assume a special responsibility for plain talk and lucid writing.

The first goal should be to weed out these roundabout—Oops, I almost said "periphrastic"—ways of putting simple thoughts into words.

This article first appeared in the *California State Bar Journal*, from which it is reprinted by permission.

୧୦୧୦୧

Mr. Ted Bear, Historian, Air Force Flight Test Center, Edwards, California, wrote to enquire whether *an* or *a* is to be used in a parenthetical construction like ". . . an (unspecified) number of years ago." We've been perplexed about this problem too, but a long time ago we decided that because the construction is what might be called a "visual colloquial" form, *an* would be preferred to *a*. Similarly, "a (new) auditorium." In such cases, the parentheses around the word or expression are "weak" and are intended only for visual effect.   *Editor*

୧୦୧୦୧

Any of you people putting out VERBATIM or any readers have ideas about the extraordinary use of the word *signifying* as a synonym for "seriously discussing"?

In court one day I heard a black man tell the court that after a shot was fired in the vicinity of a bowling alley all the parking-lot people gathered about and were "signifying." I asked other blacks what that word meant to them and they agreed that it means to gather worriedly and discuss an event. The judge said he didn't know what the word meant; said he had never heard of such a meaning for that word.

My dictionaries are of no help. Is it a Southern meaning? Mid-western?

Pete Chappars
Oxford, Ohio

Irish Bulls—Second Series

Robert A. Fowkes
New York University

A short time ago our little article on so-called "Irish Bulls (*VERBATIM* II, 1) provoked a surprising amount of correspondence. Since one or two readers were incautiously kind enough to ask for more, we are rashly reacting to that suggestion with "another debut," a term I have from a neighbor who was forced to retire and referred to his appearance at the usual farewell party as "my final debut." He bullishly added, "I'm starting the eventide of life with a terrible feeling of the morning after the night before," whereupon a friend said, "Well, the heyday of your career took place mainly at night." He attended night school and alleged that he excelled in those subjects that he never took. Although he did well enough in life, he was once severely rebuked by his wife for having signed "an oral contract," which, as everybody knows, "isn't worth the paper it's written on."

As a boy in Europe he began in the apprentice system: "I started with zero pay, but they were so pleased with my work that they doubled it every year." He became active in a union and recalled with pride his part in negotiations: "We once tried to put through a demand for no working between meals, but we figured some lazy guys would cheat." The factory had a yearly trip and "Everybody without exception left town for the annual outing once a year, but the ones that stayed behind wrecked the place."

At the retirement party mentioned above, Mr. Selfmademan said, among other things, that if he could begin his life over again, he would not start to work at such an early age, even if he lived to be a hundred!

He was no more materialistic than the next fellow but admitted that, "The sweetest sound to my eyes was the lovely metallic clang of a five-pound note." Some mornings, in order to save time, he would dry himself before taking his shower. But when his wife tried to serve him a new brand of instant coffee, he protested, "I can't drink this stuff! I'm allergic to all the things they've taken out of it."

He subscribed to a house organ and was told that it was gratis. He asked whether there was a special rate for bulk orders. He became a great sports fan and contributed several gems like, "Those sturdy hands have kicked the greatest number of field goals in the county." He was loyal to the home team and boasted, "We invariably win, though not always." After one tremendous international soccer match he related, "As we all rose for the singing of our national anthem, there wasn't an empty seat in the stadium."

Some of his pronouncements were rivaled by "sports-casters" during the last world series. One said, "Those skillful hands of Pete Rose surely cover a lot of ground in the air." He also pontificated, "The Reds are favored to win, and, as we all know, everybody hates a favorite." Then came the irrefutable logic, "If you can't stay close to Cincinnati in the scoring column, they'll beat ya."

Another athletic bull came from the incomparable Paavo Nurmi or a slanderer of his. When asked the magic formula for setting a world record in the mile (then about 4 mins. 12 secs.), Nurmi supposedly replied with a Finnish bull (or reindeer?), "You start out at full speed, gradually increasing pace."

When a loudly bawling child was asked, "What are you crying for, little fellow?" he answered, "Boo-hoo! Dennis kicked me in the belly when my back was turned." That Dennis chap took piano lessons, to the dismay of the neighborhood, and his proud, tone-deaf but not entirely dumb father said, "I must admit that Dennis seemed hopeless at first, but he's been improving with each preceding lesson." In school, however, Dennis majored in mayhem, and one teacher showed him the door with the old-fashioned verbiage, "I'll never allow you in class again; that'll teach you!"

When Dennis was born, an event from which the town ultimately recovered—but slowly—his grandfather learned what the child's name was to be and asked the father, "Whatta ya calling him Dennis for? Every Tom, Dick, and Harry is called Dennis." At the christening, Dennis was the only one present to take water. Among the countless toasts proposed was one by Dennis's father: "May all our children get rich parents!"

One guest asked another, "Did you come by car?" and received the sarcastic reply, "No, by camel." "Ah, that's a horse of a different color!"

Other bulls have been heard recently on radio and television, and one or two have probably been heard that were not said—a sort of bullish situation in itself. These were new to me: "You've got to give that man credit; he always pays cash!" "Many things occur to me, but nothing ever happens." "Those who stir up trouble among nations are no friends of peace." One of more ancient vintage recently heard again is: "After they got rid of capital punishment, they had to hang twice as many people as before."

A colleague came up (or down) with this rewording of an ancient slur: "Those who can, do; those who can't, teach; all others become linguists." Oh, well, they philological gap.

My friend who retired concluded his autobiographical remarks with a sigh and the following suprapontic bull: "But that's all water over the bridge."

Finally, the following would have been funnier in a less tragic era, but it is still funny as an instance of the bovine stupidity of man: "Wanted: man and woman to care for two cows, both Protestant"—a possibly fictitious ad (possibly not!) in an Ulster newspaper, quoted in Seán McCann, *The Wit of the Irish* (London: Leslie Frewin, 1968), p. 74. What do you mean, "it's no bull"? At your service.

EPISTOLAE

In Jon Miller's letter about quotation marks, he asks why advertisers use quotation marks around such phrases as "Tastes Great!" "The use of quotation marks," he says, "must have a predictable motivational effect. I would like to know what it is."

In journalism, quotation marks are used to set aside an important factor in a story. The quotation marks immediately call attention to any sentence on a printed page. When they are used on such phrases as "New! Improved!," "Home-made Taste," etc., they have even greater effect because of their closeness to each other.

Consumers are more likely to believe a direct quote if it is attributed to Mrs. Amanda Housewife of Anytown than if the same phrase comes from an advertising agency, so quotation marks help lend credibility to the claims.

Besides that, quotation marks bear the same relationship to words that advertising does to products: they are used to attract attention. Because of this, it seems only natural for quotation marks to be used around advertising claims.

Steven Short
Long Beach, California

More About the Name *Cowbird* for *Molothrus ater ater*

W. M. Woods
Oak Ridge, Tennessee

In a letter [II, 4] I conjectured that *Molothrus ater ater*, the Eastern Cowbird of North America, got its vernacular name because of the similarity of its habits to those of the European cuckoo *Cuculus canorus*, that immigrants called the bird the *kuh-kuh-bird*, then by abbreviation the *kuh-bird*, and finally by improper translation from the German *cowbird*.

Mr. Edwin H. Hammock of Columbus, Ohio [III, 1] cast shame on me because he imagined I had overlooked a remark by Audubon in an *American Orthnic Biography* (1828): "From the resemblance of its notes to that word [cow-cow], this Cuckoo is named Cow Bird in every part of the union."

In fact, this citation is given in the *OED*, and I was quite aware of it. I rejected Audubon's explanation for two reasons. No cowbird ever said anything resembling "cow-cow" when I was around, and no other ornithological work I have come across reports any such sound as "cow-cow" although many of them go into considerable detail in reporting the voices of this bird. Then, Audubon himself apparently revised his opinion in a later revision of the cited work. His *Birds of America* [Vol. 4, p. 20, 1840–44 Edition] contains the following: "This species derives its name from the circumstance of its frequenting cow-pens." And. "It has no song properly so called, but utters a low muttering sort of chuckle. . . ." Further, "On inspecting it, however, I at once felt convinced that it was nothing else than a young Cow-pen-bird, scarcely fledged. . . ." [Ibid., pp. 20–21].

For other descriptions of the voice of *M. ater ater* see *Field Guide to the Birds* by Roger Tory Peterson [2nd Ed., p. 216] and *Natural History of AMERICAN BIRDS of Eastern & Central North America* by Edward Howe Forbush & John Richard May [Bramhall House, NY, p. 477].

If further refutation of the "cow-cow" hypothesis is needed, I have an unpublished private communication from Mr. J. B. Owen, a well-known ornithologist who writes a bird column for the Knoxville News-Sentinel—and to whom

I am indebted for several references cited in this article—which states, "As for my own observations, I agree that the cowbird does not have any call or song that could resemble its name."

One of the authors of Forbush & May [loc. cit., p. 478] gives a first-hand account of an observation that may have bearing on the question. "One spring day I observed a male [cowbird] on the ridgepole of a house, attitudinizing for the benefit of his consorts. His attempts at song were peculiar and probably unusual. With each swelling of his throat he produced a soft rather musical sound in two syllables like that of the cuckoo of Europe, but with the accent on the last syllable thus—*cook-oo'*, but several seconds elapsed between the calls."

This observation, if anything, strengthens my general conjecture, for habits aside, such a call would directly suggest a relationship with the European cuckoo, or coo-coo, and thus *kuh-kuh-bird, kuh-bird, cowbird*. Indeed, with the stressed last syllable of its voice, the bird might well have been termed the *coo-bird* to begin with, which eliminates the need for the postulated abbreviation, even for any association with the Old World bird. Only an imagined translation from the German is now needed.

For completeness, and in fairness to the objective question involved, I ought now to briefly cite other references given to me by Mr. Owen, or turned up by me, whether these support my conjecture or not.

Words for Birds by Edward S. Gruson, p. 254 (1972): "Cowbird is a contraction of Catesby's 'Cowpenbird' of which he says, 'They delight much to feed in the pens of cattle, which has given them their name.'" [Catesby lived a century ahead of Audubon (1682–1749) and wrote on the *Natural History of Carolina, Florida, and the Bahama Islands.*]

Life Histories of North American Blackbirds, Orioles, Tanagers, and Allies by A. C. Bent (1958): "It deserves the common name cowbird and its former name, buffalo-bird, for its well-known attachment to these domestic and wild cattle." [The name *buffalo-bird* would support the "association with cattle" hypothesis since it suggests that the symbiosis of bird with bovine was well-established and well-known before the introduction of domestic live stock. Still, if this be so, one wonders what happened to Amerind words for the buffalo-bird.]

Mr. J. B. Owen, referred to above, gives the following notes. [I do not have these references.]: Alexander Wilson, who was slightly ahead of Audubon, called the bird the cow bunting. The National Geographic's *Song & Garden Birds* says that cowbirds "snatch insects stirred up by hoofs and alight on the backs of the animals to pick off ticks and other pests." A highly respected volume, *Birds of the World*, by Oliver L. Auston, Jr. says "except for the giant cowbird of Central and South America . . . . . . cowbirds seldom alight on cattle, but flock around to feed on the insects disturbed by their feet."

At this point, I think we can very fairly reject the "*cow-cow* call" hypothesis, without any shame whatever. We are then left to choose between the orthodox etymology "association with cows" hypothesis, and my heretical "*kuh-kuh-bird* → *kuh-bird* → *cow-bird*" conjecture.

It will require further, deeper research and quantitative empirical observation of this interesting bird to settle the matter. [I often think that etymologists muse too much over musty manuscripts and neglect the evidence of the real-time world, shining bright and informative all about them.] Of course, if the cowbird has changed its habits since the introduction of chemical sprays reduced the tick population on cattle, as Francis E. Throw of Wheaton, Illinois, opines [III, 2], the question may remain moot. In etymological matters, it is seldom possible to discharge every possible or plausible objection or counterexample.

Readers of VERBATIM ought, by now, to be developing some affection for the cowbird. *We are perplexed, however, by the high degree of acoustic refinement exhibited by bird-listeners that permits them to be so firm in their convictions that* cowbirds *say "cuckoo" and not "cow-cow." Is it possible that we are dealing with dialect differences among* cowbirds? [*That isn't as far-fetched as it sounds: ornithologists do report regional variations in the songs of the same species.*] *Perhaps someone has encountered a* cowbird (*or a whole family of* cowbirds) *with a speech defect? And why should only German immigrants have been listening to his bird's song (if "kuh-kuh" can be said to be a song)? To us, a "coo-bird" is a pigeon or a dove: they're the ones that say "coo." And how could the* Eastern

Cowbird *be confused with the* Buffalo-Bird, *which, if it frequented buffaloes, would have had trouble finding them in eastern North America? As to the question of whether chemical sprays might have reduced the tick population, it suggests that the entire matter may be entomological rather than etymological.*

EPISTOLAE

The following interesting incident may have escaped your notice.

As Fred, a Benedict, emerged from behind the Arras to enter his Brougham waiting on the Macadam, he was wearing Jodhpurs and a Cardigan. No Beau Brummel, his Burnsides had been untouched by Occam's razor. Wearing a Panama instead of his usual Balmoral, he munched a Bologna Sandwich, drinking his Java from fine China. His faithful Boswell was a Maverick who had recently escaped the Guillotine, having been pursued by a Lynch mob who tried to Shanghai him. He was smoking a Havana while holding a half-eaten Napoleon. Just then an Amazon clad in a Bikini and accompanied by her Abigail Meandered over in her Landau drawn by a Clydesdale instead of her regular Berlin with its matched team of an Arabian and a Percheron. She said, "It's Hobson's choice, Fred. Put your John Hancock right here. Then we're going to the Mausoleum if a Bobby doesn't stop us." Fred said "No, I won't be a Vandal. I'll Boycott such a Neanderthal notion. Besides, I'm going to the cattle show on an Annie Oakley. I'm to be the Solomon deciding between a Guernsey and a Jersey. I've just got time to pick up my Prince Albert, my Havelock, and a bottle of Cognac, but first I've got to stop at the Crapper; there may not be a John on the Pullman." Just then the third Bohemian in a Dolly Varden pulled up in a Hackney. "My Zeppelin did a Corrigan so I had to take a Sedan instead" she explained, eating a Hamburger which she had warmed on an Etna. At this point your correspondent, feeling like a Frankenstein, left to file his story.

Nominally,
David H. Scull
Annandale, Virginia

Animal-Like Adjectives

Lynne Tieslau Jewell
Assistant Director, News Bureau
University of Southern California

As an amateur wordster, my personal lexicon contains lengthy lists of various types of words. I have columns, for example, of words derived from famous people's names, like *martinet, Ferris Wheel* and *Stroganoff*. I even have a women-only column, brief as it may be at this point, with such entries as *maudlin* and *bloomer*. Not all the categories focus on people. Portmanteaus, acronyms and spoonerisms are additionally itemized.

But to date the list that has been a particularly exhilarating experience has been my collection of animal-like words. I am fascinated with *-ine* (Middle English, 'pertaining to') ending words that relate to the animal kingdom. Some are obvious, like *bovine* 'cowlike,' *canine* 'doglike,' *feline* 'catlike,' *elephantine* 'elephantlike' and *equine* 'horselike.' Others are not as familiar, *anserine* 'gooselike,' *ranine* 'froglike' and *caprine* 'goatlike.'

My search for animal-like adjectives began several years ago. A newspaper article described the announcer at a Playboy Bunny of the Year Contest as a "porcine" ('piglike') emcee. I thought what a perfectly polite way to depict a fat slob; there must be more like this. Since then I have zeroed in on other journalistic uses of the words. For instance, in May 1975, the Associated Press ran a story, accompanied with a sketch, on "bovine" brassieres. (And, incidentally, the bovine bras come in four sizes to support sagging udders.)

Vulpine 'foxlike' starlet and *aquiline* 'eaglelike' nose are *Timese* favorites. In *People* (13 Oct. '75), the caption over a picture-story of the bearded actor Peter Ustinov read, "Leonine Ustinov." "Clown Emmett Kelly Jr. has a small but elephantine wedding," was a kicker in the table of contents of *People* (2 Aug. '76). Nuptials for the 51-year-old Kelly and his waitress-girlfriend were conducted atop a circus pachyderm.

Related to this particular list are words ending in *-ian*, meaning characteristic or resembling. Examples are *apian* 'beelike,' *simian* 'apelike' and *vermian* 'wormlike.' Then there are words like *swine* and *ermine*. Although they end in *-ine*, they are not included in the list, as they are not adjectives describing a certain creature.

The following is a glossary of my collection of animal *-ine* adjectives that pertain to, resemble or are characteristic of an animal:

accipitrine 'hawklike'
anguine 'snakelike'
anserine 'gooselike'
aquiline 'eaglelike'
asinine 'asslike'
bovine 'cowlike'
canine 'doglike'
caprine 'goatlike'
cervine 'deerlike'
colubrine 'kingsnakelike' or 'gartersnakelike'
elephantine 'elephantlike'
equine 'horselike'
feline 'catlike'
herpestine 'mongooselike'
hircine 'goatlike,' especially in strong odor or lustfulness
lacertine or *lacertilian* 'lizardlike'
lemurine 'lemurlike'
leonine 'lionlike'
lupine 'wolflike'
lutrine 'otterlike'
murine 'mouselike'
oscine 'songbirdlike'
ovine 'sheeplike'
passerine 'perching-songbirdlike'
pavonine 'peacocklike'
piscine 'fishlike'
porcine 'piglike or 'swinelike'
ranine 'froglike'
serpentine 'serpentlike'
suilline 'hoglike'
suine 'swinelike'
taurine 'bull-like'
ursine 'bearlike'
viperine 'viperlike'
vulpine 'foxlike'

EPISTOLAE

At my suggestion, VERBATIM is circulated around our editorial department. I was interested in the latest issue to see someone's contribution of strange names, because whenever I use the phone book I have one eye open for possible additions to my list of "collectables."

I thought you'd be interested to know that the following can be found in the 1976 Toronto phone directory:

People

Roman Flicker, Bunny Shoom, Jerry Journey, Homer Tremble, Dewey D. Bloom, F. B. Titball, Tyrone Nurse, Cyril Coveyduck, and Roger Ruttgaizer.

Businesses

Joy Auto Collision, Jubilant Sales Ltd., Elegant Jobbers, Tajmahal Auto Body, High Class Billiards, and High Tension Clothier.

Catherine McVicar
Copp Clark Publishing
Toronto, Ontario, Canada

EX CATHEDRA

Those who have not been so fortunate as to have been exposed to that paragon of British publishing known as *The Times* cannot be aware of the treasures to be found in a national newspaper that summarizes the contemporary history and culture of a country in about 20 pages daily, some percentage of which is devoted to advertising. Within memory, the front page of *The Times* was dedicated to the (in)famous "Personals," now relegated to the back page. In place of the Personals appears news, or what might generally pass for news. In a random *Times* picked up as typical [Monday, October 18, 1976], one might have been misled into believing that the drought of last summer had occasioned a postponement of the Silly Season: the revaluation of the German mark was announced after a surprise meeting of the "snake"; "Uncompromising show of police strength keeps football hooligans under control"; "Mao 'almost nagged to death by his wife' "; the death of Carlo Gambino in New York may lead to a "struggle for 'Godfather' succession"; and "Bagpipes sound [in St. Peter's Square, Rome] for new Scottish Saint." The featured photograph meriting page one coverage is of "Ramu, a three and a half ton killer whale, being winched from its pool at Windsor Safari Park before being flown to an aquarium in California. It had become too big for the pool."

One observation of some usefulness is that *The Times*, which has no stated policy in the "ears" alongside its name on page one, seems to cleave to the tenet that unimportant but interesting news merits coverage, but in only a limited space. Contrariwise, important but not always interesting news receives succinct but by no means sparse treatment. *The New York Times*, on the other hand, sports its heart in its ear: "All the news that's fit to print," a slogan that has often been reinterpreted as, "All the news that fits we print," and not without some justification. The *NY Times* fancies itself the documentalist of events of the world, though one is often given to wonder how a reader can be expected to wade through the morass of verbiage in which a *NY Times* story is almost invariably embedded. It was (at least) once observed that *The New York Daily News* was one of the best edited newspapers in America. Not the best written, you understand; for what was referred to was the ability of the *News's* editors to distill into one brief paragraph the same information that *The NY Times* needed three columns to describe.

To one who is familiar with the style of *The NY Times*, it is amusing to speculate to what lengths it would go to treat such items as the following, reproduced in their terse entirety from *The Times* [of London]:

Purge in Pakistan
Rawalpindi, Oct. 17.—In a big purge of the Pakistan Administration, more than 500 of senior ranks in Government and autonomous departments have been dismissed.

Whisky vats explode
Sao Paulo, Brazil, Oct. 17.—Nine vats exploded at a distillery in Sao Paulo state, causing a fire that destroyed more than 500,000 gallons of cane whisky.

China nuclear blast
Hongkong, Oct. 17.—China today successfully conducted another nuclear test.

The "Letters to the Editor" page of *The Times* [of London] is far more revealing of the character of its readers than is the parallel page of *The NY Times*. After several weeks of to-ing and fro-ing about Scots' eating their porridge while walking about, on October 18 readers finally got down to business with contributions like these:

Sir, It is with horror that I read in *VAT News No 11* that "it has been decided that gallop fees which are charged by a landowner for granting permission to gallop horses over his land are liable to VAT at the standard rate with effect from 1 July, 1976."
Do we now have galloping inflation?
Yours truly,
Clifford Prowse,
St. Fillans,
Ray Mead Road,
Maidenhead,
Berkshire.
October 14.

Sir, In your Special Report today (October 13) on business travel, the last item in the table of contents reads "What to pack; taking your wife." This is particularly gratifying to me: fairly flexible, of small dimensions and weighing only 84 lb, I could be accommodated in a travelling bag of quite moderate size.

Yours faithfully,
Gwyneth M. Ohlsen,
31 Hill Rise,
Woodhouse Eaves,
Loughborough,

Leicestershire.

October 13.

Needless to say, other correspondence deals with matters of greater import, but one can always find the light touch among the more ponderous. Perhaps *The NY Times* takes itself too seriously.

Certainly, one cannot despair that *The Times* [London, again] has lost its touch if one can fight off the lugubrious prospects of sinking sterling with headlines like, "Keeping the bounce in synthetic rubber," "Parris brings downfall of Trojan fortress" [M. J. Parris, playing for Slough, scored the winning goal against the Trojans in the National Club Hockey Championship], "Mr. Ford looks like boring his way back to the White House."

And what depths of Holmesian intrigue are conjured up by the cryptic advert in the Announcements column: "C. M. Please ring 77557. Move in 2 weeks. P. T." Had the initials been different, we might have speculated about the Prime Minister's anticipation of a quick defeat by Mrs. Thatcher's Tories in a surprise vote-of-confidence election.

EPISTOLAE

I regret that in your "Noun Overuse Phenomenon Article" by Mr. Bruce Price [II, 4] you failed to include the newspaper headline, "Jones Hits Fish Sale Ban Repealer," although the omission is understandable, since it never got in the paper.

As the former head of the copydesk of *The Baltimore Evening Sun* (in the 1930's), I have been waiting for an article about *literally*. "The American destroyer was literally disemboweled" was a sentence in an Associated Press dispatch during World War II. A recent book of mine cites "The Packers Literally Exploded in the Fourth Quarter." Even more bloody was a politician's boast, "I literally tore that fellow apart, eh?"

In television news recently towns have been *literally* erased from the map, the English language has been *literally* murdered (could it truly be?), and spectators at a hockey game *literally* tore the place to shreds.

Keen Rafferty
Emeritus Professor of Journalism
The University of New Mexico

BIBLIOGRAPHIA

HOW REAL IS REAL?, by Paul Watzlawick, Random House, 1976, xiv + 266 pp. $10.00.

It is impossible, in the few pages of a journal like VERBATIM, to present and describe, let alone discuss, the myriad aspects of language—its history, development, use (and misuse), its style, variety, poetry, its grammar, syntax, vocabulary, pronunciation, its learning, teaching, its curiosities, its relevance, its metaphoricity. If the truth be known, not all the professional journals nor all the books published in every conceivable language, ancient or modern, are sufficient to contain all that can be said on the subject. It is partly for that reason that we review books in VERBATIM, for we hope to introduce to the reader sources of knowledge and an ever-increasing wealth of information about language than it would be feasible for us to attempt to cover in a thousand lifetimes and in ten thousand pages. Whether the reader considers the foregoing an excuse for our inadequacies or a rationalization for the shortcomings of VERBATIM is irrelevant, for its purpose is to introduce him to some of the facets of language that may have failed to catch his imagination.

Notable among writings dealing with the ways in which man's view of his universe are tempered by the language he speaks is the classic "Four Articles on Metalinguistics," by Benjamin Lee Whorf, originally published by the U. S. Department of State, now available in a collection, *The Collected Writings of B. L. Whorf*, MIT Press. We shall review that collection at some other time; for the present purpose, we mention it because it deals with language and reality, the subject of Dr. Watzlawick's book, and comes readily to mind not for comparative or contrastive reasons but purely for associative ones.

There is little originality in *How Real Is Real?*, but we can recommend the author highly as an excellent and, as far as we know, accurate reporter of a broad variety of matters relating to language. The central theme of the book is that communication (manifest as language in one form or another) tempers and controls our concepts of reality. Although the accuracy of the book's flap copy is questionable in its statement, "The connection between communication and reality is a relatively new idea," we suppose that its author could cavil with the weasel-word *relatively*, for the notion is at least as old as the Allegory of the Cave in Plato. Nonetheless, the book itself reveals, in an easy-to-read style, much interesting information on communication between man and beast and among men.

The first two parts of the book, "Confusion" and "Disinformation" are less concerned with language, per se, than with behavior. That is understandable in light of Dr. Watzlawick's professional association with the Mental Research Institute in Palo Alto and the Department of Psychiatry at Stanford University. But the behavior discussed is behavior resulting from information, most of it conveyed by language.

Those unfamiliar with research that has been under way for many years in cross-species communication will be interested in the author's excellent, though brief, descriptions of recent and current experiments with chimpanzees and dolphins.

From Confusion to Disinformation among human beings to Communication with chimpanzees and dolphins to extraterrestrial communication may be leaps far too enormous to describe in the small compass of 266 pages, and, to be sure, the author cannot dwell on any of his topics for very long. But the reporting is clear, the sequence is logical, and the entire book is readable, entertaining, informative, and interesting. Dr. Watzlawick offers little in the way of editorial comment, unless one wishes to impute to the pattern of his inclusions and exclusions a sinister purpose. A sufficient bibliography and an index round out the book, which we are delighted to recommend.

EPISTOLAE

Just to "nit-pick" a bit—Bruce Price's article on noun overuse is a bit simplistic in its criticism of military or scientific gobbledygook. Much of this scientific noun overuse had its origin during World War Two, when it was necessary to train inexperienced and in some cases uneducated people to use very sophisticated and complex equipment.

Having been active in the aerospace field, I would say that the term "spaceship" was never used to describe a vehicle in our space program, and if someone were to actually use the phrase, he would be laughed out of the lab or shop and be accused of reading too many space comics.

So, *booster rocket, ignition system,* with commas, means exactly that—the ignition system for the booster rocket (*rocket* is another obnoxious word—they are engines, not fireworks), not the ignition system for the staging rockets which might be called *first stage, ignition system* and so on.

I am the first to groan loudly at most of the gobbledygook used by scientists and the military, but not all of it is "noun overuse" and does have its place in communicating one to the other.

R. Roy Williams
Malibu, California

Dr. Kerr's excellent letter concerning certain words for some Biblical concepts raised once again an old speculation of mine that the unuttered (by the ancient Hebrews) four-character word which is anglicized as *YHWH* is an onomatopoetic word based also on breath or wind. To try to pronounce it without vowels gives it a zephyr sound.

Thus the word, avoided by using *Lord* in some versions and *Yahweh* in others, may have similarities to *ruach* and *nephesh,* the "wind"-words for *spirit.* These two also give the sound of breath and moving air when pronounced.

Referring to Dr. Kerr's last line, it may be something to be sneezed at.

Frederick W. Cropp
Santa Barbara, California

Axel Hornos' fine and interesting article, "Ouch! he said in Japanese," is marred by an error in one of the Greek examples that he offers.

"Hey, John!" is rendered in Greek as "Aye, Ioannis!" This is an impossible construction because Greek is an inflected language and requires that *Ioannis* be in the vocative case instead of the nominative, as given by Hornos. However, *Ioannis* is the form of the name which is used in the formal (katharevousa) language only; it is never used in the spoken language, especially in speech as familiar as

"Hey, John!" The spoken form is *Yiannis* for the nominative and *Yianni* for the vocative. This error, however, is doubly compounded by the appearance of *Aye* for "hey," a word, which, as far as I am able to determine, does not even exist in modern Greek. "Hey" in Greek is simply *e*, as the "e" in get. Hornos' example, then, should read, "E, Yianni!"

Thomas Daniel
Warren, Ohio

⊠

Professor G. A. Cevasco's article, "Ellipsis . . . Faulty and Otherwise," [III, 1] inspired me to write down ellipses I am fond of. Until reading his article, I had been making only mental notes.

Immediately I recorded those Rhode Island elliptical expressions which had first jarred my ear but now, nine years after moving to this state, sound normal: "graduate college," "live home."

I then remembered, and recorded, an Ohio expression of mine to which a Chicago-born friend objects: "My hair needs cut."

I found ellipses not only from the past, but in conversations of the present. Speaking of job opportunities, a colleague said, "The field is saturated, from what I've heard." A Providence newscaster said one Friday, "Have a great weekend from all of us." And, as I left for vacation this summer, someone wished this upon me: "If I don't see you, have a nice vacation."

The upshot of my recording ellipses is my realization one day that the ubiquitous "hopefully" is used elliptically —an explanation most welcome to me, since I have not understood why I disliked that word. Even so, ellipses will always be with us, [I say] hopefully.

Judy Scarfpin
Assistant Dean of Students and
Assistant Professor of English
University of Rhode Island
⊠

"Ellipsis . . . Faulty and Otherwise" by G. A. Cevasco [III, 1] made me reach for a list that I have been compiling these last few months. Why, I have been asking myself, do writers tend to omit that. most necessary verb form?
1. ". . . the author doesn't have to create her. For the

family already has."
2. "I did not attend Stanford, but after visiting the campus recently, I sincerely wish that I had."
3. "Nobody calls after her, though the Colonel would have liked to."
4. "There is a mystique that surrounds Grace and has from the beginning."
5. "He writes beautifully and always has."
6. ". . . but what I want most to do is write a book for children. Actually I have."

(Items 1, 5, and 6 are from THE WRITER magazine. Item 2, from HARVARD MAGAZINE; item 3, from a student's term paper. Item 4 is from the L. A. TIMES.)

William H. Ready
English Department
St. Vincent's Seminary, Montebello, California

It is interesting to note that British usage varies: in each of the above examples, the word done *would follow the auxiliaries* have *and* has *to stand as surrogate for the ellipticized verb.* Editor

When I was a student at the Sorbonne in Paris an (unspecified) number of years ago, a friend of mine told me of an experience in a taxicab there.

An acquaintance of his riding with him thought he noticed that they were passing a building for the second time. Possibly forgetting that many buildings in Paris look alike, he concluded that the taxidriver was going around and around the block in order to run up the fare. Though he had no reason to believe that the driver was a philosopher, he asked him belligerently, "Quelle est la grand idée?"

Ted Bear
Edwards, California

VERBATIM

THE LANGUAGE QUARTERLY

Vol. III, No. 4   February 1977

EDITOR: LAURENCE URDANG

Mail Lib

Clair Schulz
Clinton, Wisconsin

Several years ago Johnny Cash recorded a song that lamented the plight of a boy who suffered ridicule because his father had chosen to name him Sue. If I correctly interpreted the amused expressions of those I observed listening to the song, people regarded it as a novelty record designed to create laughter in the same manner that the boy's name brought giggles from his peers. I found little in the story to smile about for it sounded all too personal to be taken as mere whimsy.

From the first grade through graduate school there has been a conspiracy to change my sex. In grade school teachers needed three weeks each year before they stopped lining me up with the girls. During the first roll calls in high school I had to wave the teachers' eyes away from the girls' side of the room when they called my name (except in physical education; that teacher thought the computer had made a mistake). My classmates, ever sensitive to the adolescent sense of masculine identity, called me

"Ernie," a name that even some of the teachers picked up. However, in college I discovered that nicknames as well as swords have two edges: two friends dubbed me with the name of a famous hair coloring product. And I cannot recall a single professor to whom I was a stranger failing to begin a semester by searching the room for a "Miss Schulz."

But stereotyping by name is not limited to education. Nowhere does it stick deeper or grow with more pernicious root than in the incorrectly labeled mail I have received over the years.

At one time the malady was not so obvious. While I was in high school I occasionally received written inducements from secretarial and beautician schools. The offers themselves were much easier to toss aside than my sister's requests for me to restyle her hair or type letters for her.

Going to college seemed to expand the possibility of my name reaching more mailing lists. I began to attract catalogs from dress manufacturers and cosmetic companies. Offers to subscribe to women's magazines filled my mailbox. Semiannually I received a large envelope that was explicitly directed to "today's modern coed." These envelopes contained coupons for products that could remove my blemishes and unwanted hair, improve my figure, lengthen my eyelashes, replace my baggy pantyhose, and eliminate my personal hygiene problems. I decided it was time to take action.

I tried placing *Mr.* in front of my name in the return address. People apparently discarded or discounted the envelope. Then I began signing my entire name to letters, but that was also futile. *Clair Alan Schulz* came back *Clair Ellen Schulz*. Once I wrote to the most persistent offenders and simply stated, "Please remove my name from your mailing list." The letters continued to arrive. I wrote again and changed the emphasis: "Please remove my mail from your naming list." This also had no effect. I am now considering sending them a letter containing a fictitious change of address for the nonexistent person they have created.

I have rejected my friends' suggestions to use initials for I have no desire to be called *C. Alan* or *C.A.* or even *Al*. Initials depersonalize; consider how sterile authors would appear if they hid behind abridgments like E. Waugh or J. Cary. My name is distinctive and I wish to retain it. What I wish to eliminate is the liberties that strangers take with it.

I suppose I owe it to the efforts of Gloria, Betty, Kate, Bella, et al., that I am now receiving mail addressed to *Ms. Clair Schulz*. It is comforting to know that even though my winged assailants are not certain as to whether I am married, single, or divorced they at least seem convinced of my sex.

Some would encourage me to file complaints of blatant sexism against the disciples of preconceived notions, but I have not reached the breaking point yet. I'm waiting for something I can turn into a cause celèbre like the receipt of a brochure from an abortion clinic or a catalog from Frederick's of Hollywood. Then I will seek an act named sue.

Author's Query

For a project, entitled *Materials for a History of American Translation*, supported by preliminary grants from the American P.E.N. Translation Committee and from the Translation Center of the School of the Arts, Columbia University, and to consist of

    (1) Register of Translators & Areas of Competence/ Preference,

    (2) Index of Translators & Their Translations,

    (3) Descriptive Bibliography of Critical Writing on Translation, and

    (4) Translation Courses & Programs in Academic Institutions,

I shall be grateful for all data and information pertaining to (1) individual translators and their body of work— bibliographies of work completed during their careers and of works in progress, and (2) data on critical writing by translators and on translation (books, articles, essays, reviews, prefaces, introductions, treatises, commentaries, etc.), especially in areas relatively neglected or little translated into English.

Copies of (1) the project outline, (2) questionnaires for each category, and (3) projected cross-indexed entries are available on request.

Stefan Congrat-Butlar
Translation Index
175 West 87 Street (#24A)
New York, N. Y. 10024

Aunt Minnie's Chicken Talk

William Bancroft Mellor
New York, New York

I t is reasonably certain that my Aunt Minnie never saw a cock-fight in her life, and it can be stated with equal certainty that she is completely unaware that about 150,000 American zealots this weekend—and every weekend during the cocking season—will be busily engaged in pursuing or watching this sub rosa activity at hundreds of pits scattered about the country from coast to coast.

Yet, like most others in the United States who are equally unaware of a subterranean sport which finds its outlet alike in plush pits on Long Island estates and in makeshift arenas covertly operated in the Tennessee hills, or deep in the New Jersey pine barrens, gentle little Aunt Minnie's speech is liberally and habitually salted with pungent phrases that stem directly from the cockpit.

"Well!" she will exclaim when her favorite grand-nephew outruns his playfellows. "He certainly showed *them* a clean pair of heels!"

Like most of the rest of us, Aunt Minnie is ignorant not only of the origin of the phrase but of its real meaning as well. She would be highly indignant if she were told that she was actually calling the boy a coward—but that is what the phrase orginally meant.

Gamecocks have fought since the days of ancient Rome in metal spurs, which cockers call *heels*, and the bird which did not fight, which kept its heels unbloodied and ran away from the other rooster, was said to have shown his opponent *a clean pair of heels*.

Although the cockpit is as remote from the lives of most of us as a brontosaurus wallow, our language has been richly endowed by The Sod, and few of us get through a single day without recourse to at least one phrase from the lexicon of cocking.

Even Aunt Minnie would recognize the origin of some of these frequently used phrases—the word *cockpit* itself, commonly employed in connection with boats or airplanes; *cocky*, meaning 'brash' or 'conceited'; *cock-sure* 'over-confident'; *pit against* 'to set someone against an adversary'; and *game*, 'courageous.'

Stand the gaff, an expression used to denote the

ability to bear up bravely in the face of adversity, is another which most people would spot as referring to the spurs or *gaffs* worn by a cock during a fight, and when we advise a belligerent friend not to *get his hackles up*, we are dimly aware that the expression is associated with the great feathered ruff which stands out on a gamecock's neck when he spots another male fowl in his vicinity.

Show the white feather, a phrase denoting cowardice, is another which some will recognize as stemming from the cockpit, though few know its exact meaning. It refers to the white fluff found at the base of the tail in many strains of game fowl, particularly those descended from the breeds which found their way here 100 years ago from the North of England—the Whitehackles. When the tail of one of these birds is drooped during a fight, and the cock thus acknowledges defeat, the white fluff, normally covered by the saddle and tail feathers, shows plainly.

Less easily recognized by Aunt Minnie and others unfamiliar with the parlance of the pit are the origins of such expressions as *coming up to scratch* 'to measure up to a standard,' and the slang expression, *in the bag*, both of which, however, are in everyday use. In the cockpit, the *scratch* is a line drawn by the referee in the dirt of the pit floor, behind which the cock is placed at the beginning of the fight. If he fails to rush eagerly up to the mark to meet his adversary, he is said not to *come up to scratch*: he is an inferior chicken, fit only to be consigned to the stewpot. Although not one in a thousand users of the expression realizes it, *in the bag* also comes from the exciting world of cocking. Until comparatively recent years, it was common to transport game chickens to the scene of battle in cloth bags rather than in the comfortable and elaborate carrying cases now in vogue, and the roosters were not removed until the fight was about to begin. A cocker, confident of the prowess of his feathered warrior, would say that victory was *in the bag* for him.

Similarly, *he died kicking* does not, as might be supposed, refer to the muscular spasms frequently suffered by creatures which succumb to sudden and violent death; it, too, comes from the pit. It referred originally to the gamecock which continued to fight, kicking out with his steel-shod heels, even as he was expiring under his enemy's death-dealing blows.

The prize ring also owes many of its expressions to the cockpit: the *count* was used in the pit hundreds of

years before it became the method of determining the outcome of boxing bouts; *referees* and *handlers* exercise the
same function in both sports, though cocking is the older,
and the practice of sponging a tired fighter's head was
common in the cockpit long before the lowly fist fight became a formalized sport.

The word *cocktail* also stems from the cocking world,
although some lexicographers would have us believe it was
first applied to a drink invented by a Colonial New England barmaid, who stirred it with a cock's tail feather. It is
much more likely that the word is a corruption of the
phrase *cock-ale*, a noisome brew used by handlers as far
back as the reign of Henry VIII to strengthen and stimulate a gamecock when he was being conditioned for battle.
This "cock-ale" contained soft gruel, stale beer, port wine,
chopped oysters, and other assorted ingredients which were
supposed to make the rooster a raging tornado in the pit.
Tempted by the alcoholic content of the brew, in spite of
its less attractive elements, the conditioners of that day
used to sneak a nip for themselves now and then, and by
all contemporary accounts, the beverage was no less potent
than a ten-to-one vodka Martini is today.

The list of cockers' terms currently in use is large:
*running out on a fight, flying the coop, cutting a wing,
dead game*, and many others all stemmed from the same
source. And then there is *cock of the walk*, referring to one
who is supremely confident of himself and who dominates
all of those around him. This relates to the ancient, and
still common, practice of putting game cocks out on country "walks" where there are no other roosters, in order to
harden them physically and to stimulate the development
of their egos to the point that they will not tolerate the
presence of any other male fowl.

The combative instinct is so highly developed in game
fowl that cocks, once they have attained maturity, cannot
be reared together in flocks like common chickens but must
be separated and placed either in individual pens or on
farm "walks" where they are allowed to roam free with a
small flock of hens, unchallenged by any male competition.
Hence, *cock of the walk*.

He blew up a storm, a phrase common in the West
and Middle West to describe a man who has achieved a
sudden and spectacular success in business or other activities, also comes from the pit. It describes the cock
which fights with a spectacular, wing-flapping style that

blows up a small hurricane of dust from the pit floor.

And the expression, *keep your pecker up* (be of good courage) doesn't merit an X rating, as one might suppose: it refers to the gamecock's bill, which, when the bird is tired and near defeat, keeps sinking lower and lower toward the ground.

All ready for the fights now, Aunt Minnie?

It's no trick to fix wicks or mix wax;
I'm sick of thick chicks in slick slacks;
   For kicks, I stack sticks,
   Pick flax, or pack bricks,
Sack tacks, or ax ticks, or track yaks.

William Alsop
North Granby, Connecticut

Prurient Prudes

Laurence Urdang
Editor, VERBATIM

It is curious how people who may otherwise give the outward appearance of sanity and common sense are often found to be totally unaware of the difference between cause and effect. This phenomenon can be observed among organizations more frequently than in individuals, perhaps because most individuals have to think for themselves, whereas organizations seem to be dominated by the same individuals functioning as a committee. The result is no different from that seen in mob psychology, where individuals will collectively undertake the most stupid, destructive activities that no single individual would condone, let alone engage in.

History can point to many examples: the Inquisition; the Salem witch-burnings; the political witch-hunts of the 1950s; the police behavior in Chicago during the Democratic National Convention in 1968; the Kent State riots, and so on.

Sophistication and education are not barriers to such actions. Those who deplored the Nazi book-burnings of the 1930s engage in figurative book-burnings of their own:

> A . . . conservative women's group, the Austin Awareness League, has picked a . . . target for criticism: the sexual slang they found in the *Random House Dictionary* proposed for high school use.
>
> The Anchorage, Alaska, School Board has voted to remove 1975 editions of the *American Heritage Dictionary* from all elementary schools in the municipality on the grounds that it contains definitions of "vulgar, slang words" that are "better left in the gutter." The board's action drew strong criticism from the city assembly, which after a unanimous vote sent off a stern letter opposing the ban.
> But board members complained that city fathers should stick to fiscal matters and not interfere with the board's "right to set school policy . . . and make philosophical decisions." The board had, incidentally, rejected a school administration recommendation not to ban the dictionaries entirely but merely to more closely supervise their use by youngsters.
> [from *Library Journal*]

It seems ridiculous to have to point out to these "protectors" that the words they object to seeing in the pages of these dictionaries:

(1) were not invented by lexicographers;
(2) were undoubtedly well known to the students;
(3) represent records of the speech and writing of many speakers of English;
(4) were unlikely to be found by the two groups unless they were looking for them (hence, knew where to look);
(5) and wouldn't be found by students unless either:
   (a) they knew the words and knew where to look; or
   (b) they just happened to be reading through the dictionary one day and found them.

The last possibility strikes any reasonably intelligent person who knows kids as extremely unlikely. Of the other possibilities, numbers (1), (2), (3), (4), and (5a) are well-known *facts*. So what has gone wrong? Aren't we contending with groups of prurient prudes who go around looking up filthy words in dictionaries and then complain when they find them?

Let us examine the only other possibility, notwithstanding how remote it may be: A youngster sees word X scrawled on a wall (probably in the schoolyard!). He doesn't know what it means and goes to the dictionary. There he finds that X is a word for some part of the body or a bodily function and that it bears the label *"Taboo,"* *"Obscene,"* *"Vulgar,"* or some other, similar label. This alerts him to the fact that X is a word that shouldn't be used in polite society. He is then faced with the choice of not using it or of using it. If he doesn't use it, no one will say anything. If he does use it, say to a teacher, he will rapidly learn that he should have paid attention to the label in the dictionary. It is very doubtful that he will be asked where he learned the word, for no teacher could possibly be so naive as to ask such a question: anyone who did so would be drummed out of the corps, for, as everyone knows, such words are learned in the "street," not from dictionaries.

Dictionaries may be used to fulfill a variety of functions, including doorstop, paperweight, and kindling. The language makes the dictionary, not vice versa. The dictionary provides accurate information about the pronunciations, meanings, etymologies, spellings, and, in most cases, appropriate usage levels of the words listed in it. It is not infallible and can reflect only the best and most accurate judgment of the scholars who prepared it. They don't create the language, they describe it, with as much detachment as they can summon. Moreover, because of the way dictionaries are arranged, the user must know the word about which he is seeking information before he can find it. As far as is known, no general dictionary offers a special section where the taboo words are listed together, as a sort of a vocabulary-building device for extending the user's mastery of obscenities.

What the prurient prudes may be objecting to is the notion that if the objectionable words appear in print, that gives them a patina of acceptability or respectability. What arrant nonsense! The daily newspapers and TV are filled with reports of murder, incest, arson, torture, theft, treason, genocide, prostitution, sexual deviation, deceit, treachery, rape—all possible manifestations of crime and moral turpitude—yet students are encouraged to be informed about "current events," and would find it difficult to avoid learning about them. Surely, a hard-to-find dirty word in a dictionary is the last source of information that is likely to corrupt a student.

It all boils down to one thing: style. According to some moralists, style in language and style in behavior are not unrelated, and they are probably right: being polite has its virtues. But eliminating the word *murder* from the language will have no effect on those bent on murder, and whether you call an act sexual intercourse, copulation, cohabiting, coitus, sexual union, the reproductive process or by any other name, it's still the same activity. The real question is, Which term is appropriate to the given social context? and with all the mincing, puritanical Board members around, their children will never be able to learn that from the one most simple, innocuous, impersonal, accurate, authoritative source—the dictionary.

Clerihew

Said Lady Mary Wortley Montagu,
When rebuked for omitting an *accent aigu*,
"I leave diacritics
To Continentals and Semitics."

J. Bryan, III
Richmond, Virginia

Ooglification in American English Slang

Roger W. Wescott
Drew University

The coinage *ooglification* is my expansion of the American slang term *oogly*, meaning either 'extremely attractive' or 'extremely unattractive.' The reason for the paradoxical meaning of this adjective is that it is in reality two adjectives. The first of them, which has an alterantive form *ogley*, is derived from the verb *ogle* and means 'worth ogling' or 'deserving of being stared at.' The second is a deformation of the adjective *ugly*. In each case, the stressed vowel or vowel sequence of the standard form has been converted to *oo*, as in *boohoo*. This process is one which structural linguists call replacive infixation: it is familiarly illustrated by the substitution of *e* for *a* in the plural of the noun *man* or by the substitution of *i* for *o* in the past tense of the verb *do*.

As it happens, almost any English vowel or vowel sequence may be converted into *oo* as one way of "slangifying" the word in which it occurs. Examples follow:

vowel(s)	common form	slang variant
short a	*skedaddle*	*skidoodle*
e	*cigarette*	*cigaroot*[1]
i	*diddle*	*doodle*
o	*goggle(s)*	*google(s)*
u	*guzzle*	*goozle*
long a	*Scandinavian*	*Scandinoovian*[2]
e	*sleaze*[3]	*slooze*
i	*divine*	*divoon*
o	*oaf*	*oof(us)*
short oo	*push*	*"poosh"*
ow or ou	*anyhow*	*anyhoo*

Not all vowels are equally susceptible to ooglification. Those that seem most susceptible are: short o (as in *noodle* for *noddle*), short u (as in *poof* for *puff*), long o (as in *gool* for *goal*), and ou = ow (as in *snoot* for *snout*).

Sometimes even "blurred" vowels in unaccented syllables are subject to ooglification. An example is *bazooms*[4]

395

for *bosom*(s). Here the stress has shifted from the first to the second syllable. A plausible explanation may be that, when *-oo* occurs as a slang suffix rather than an infix (as in *superoo* for *super* or *smasheroo* for *smash(er)*), the primary stress of the word shifts from the first syllable to the last.

The burlesquing effect of replacive -oo- may help explain some otherwise puzzling pronunciations. A number of foreign languages contain proper names spelled with -u- and prounced with short -oo-, such as *Buddha* or *Guggenheim*. Because of the doubled consonants following the stressed vowels in these names, one would expect them to be pronounced with short vowels in English, as in *pudding* or *snuggle*. Instead, however, they are nearly always pronounced with the long -oo- of *boo* or *goo*. It may be that such unexpected pronunciations represent a less than subtle derision of alien families and titles.

In any case, American slang seems to me not just oogly but ooglific. If any *Verbatim* readers share my feeling and wish to share ooglified forms with me and with other readers, I hope they will pass them along.

1 *Cigaroot* may also be explained as a blend of *cigarette* with *cheroot*.

2 *Scandinoovian* may also have the form *Scandihoovian*. (Compare *hoodoo* for *voodoo*.)

3 *Sleaze* is itself campus slang for "loose woman." The form *slooze* may be influenced by *flooz(e)y*, "prostitute."

4 Here the *ba-* may have been reinterpreted as a slang prefix. Compare *bazoo*, "mouth," in relation to *zooed*, "drugged."

EPISTOLAE

Another item for your collection of malapropisms:

It was reported on our local radio station that someone was arrested for driving while intoxicated and for "driving in an erotic manner."

Not in the same category, but interesting:

The unit of female beauty is the milli-helen, which is defined as the amount of beauty required to launch one ship.

W. K. Viertel
Canton, New York

Permission, Admission, Remission and the Missionaries

Laurence Urdang
Editor, VERBATIM

Aristides, editorial writer for the venerable, respectable, learned, occasionally stuffy, always erudite AMERICAN SCHOLAR, joins the funeral procession (chief mourners: Ted Bernstein, Edwin Newman) for the English language: the Winter 1976/77 issue contains a rehash of the same old drivel. Safely ensconced in the cowardly concealment of his pseudonymity, Aristides contributes his comments on the language in much the same way that a Mad Bomber makes anonymous phone calls and the classic kidnapers leave messages composed of pasted-up letters cut from magazines and newspapers.

His polemic against the current decline in expressiveness in the language is prompted, in this specific instance, by *6,000 Words*, published by G. & C. Merriam Company as a supplement to *Webster's Third*, but from the tone of his article, it would appear that the subject has been rankling in his intestines for many moons. Since, for such ax-grinders for the "purity" of English, the past holds more than the present or future, his point of departure is the respectable Mencken. But one is given to wonder whether Aristides would have been quite as enthusiastic had he reached his present state of old-fashioned respectability contemporaneously with the publication of Mencken's works on language, in the early 1930s.

Reflecting incredible naivete for one who writes, albeit pseudonymously, with such learnedness, Aristides moans:

> I should prefer a more prescriptive dictionary, one that notes, where called for, that an entry is a "cant" word, to use the term Dr. Johnson used in his *Dictionary*. I prefer this not out grundyism, but because I doubt if a language can long survive in health under a policy of (to use another new entry from *6,000 Words*) "open admissions." *6,000 Words*, then, is nearly useless as a guide but excellent as a record. Like the period it indirectly chronicles, it is itself a curate's egg.

Aristides' writing, too, is a curate's egg. To pick a few nits: (1), *grundyism*, in the sense used, should have been capitalized; (2), a dictionary, being in alphabetical order, can hardly be said to *chronicle* anything, directly or indirectly; and (3), a dictionary is, by definition—since Aristides is so fanatic about precision—a *record*: its use as a guide to levels of usage is a secondary function, imputed to it largely by its users and abusers.

Dictionaries today tend to be somewhat encyclopedic, if not by virtue of entries that, for some unknown reason, many scholars consider nonlexical (e.g., proper names), then because they contain information about the lexicon that is felt to be encyclopedic (e.g., usage notes, synonym and antonym lists, synonym discriminations, illustrations, etc.). Johnson's *Dictionary* contained no illustrations. Shouldn't modern dictionaries be criticized for having them?

Aristides continues by speculating on the opinion of our culture that a future historian would have if he were to depend on *6,000 Words* as his sole evidence. To begin with, the straw man being set up, like most straw men, is utterly without substance. Why not acknowledge that *6,000 Words* is merely a supplement and include the main work, *Webster's Third*, as well? The main work "suffers" from the same descriptivism as its supplement. If only modern historians had available to them a "Webster's Third" and a "6,000 Words" for Etruria and for ancient Egypt, Babylonia, India, China, Arabia, the Americas, Anatolia, Europe, and Palestine! What incredible wealth would be found in those pages!

Even with the relative paucity of documents available to modern historians of ancient cultures, linguists have little difficulty in sifting, given a sufficient quantity of evidence, the level of usage, the slang, the colloquial, the taboo, the scatalogical. The wealth of information that could be gleaned about those cultures by the discovery of a large dictionary, intact, would be immeasurable. It would be impossible to have concocted more timely evidence than that presented in *The New York Times* on December 30, 1976:

> Then a colleague, Dr. Giovanni Pettinato, who is a
> language expert, found what amounted to a dictionary
> of the new language, called Eblait[e], that defined
> each word in Sumerian, a language that is known to
> archeologists. When this key was used, the tablets

revealed that the palace was not just a minor seat of government but the center of a huge empire. . . .
["Ruins Show Urban Life Rivaling Egypt's"]

Webster's Third and *6,000 Words* are by no means perfect examples of the art of lexicography, for they contain inanities and infelicities that resulted, apparently, from their editors' slavish attention to a philosophy of defining that could have improved from re-evaluaton as the work progressed. But that is a subject for another article. The only subject germane to this argument is that pertaining to the basic principle of descriptivism, which modern lexicographers have accepted as a tenet. The skill with which they execute their art is irrelevant to this discussion.

Aristides writes, in his closing remarks:

> In writing about language, in considering the state of the lingo, there is always a tendency to assume a prelapsarian time—a linguistic Eden where language was once clear and crisp and fitted exactly its function. Bad language has, of course, always been with us: language meant to obscure, to deceive, to defraud.

These statements belie the lamentable lamentations that precede them. Worse than that, the second comment has little, if anything, to do either with the first or with the rest of the article, for, if the truth be acknowledged, "language meant to obscure, to deceive, to defraud" is very rarely "bad" language, even in the ambiguously implied senses of *bad* employed in the general tone of the article: on the contrary, "language meant to obscure . . ." is most often the language of Nixons, Hitlers, and others who couch their nefarious thoughts in the very sort of eloquence Aristides probably admires. Moreover, the first sentence of the above quotation belongs in *this* article, not Aristides'.

What can be concluded from his farrago of fuzzy logophobia? The learned Aristides, like many lesser critics, falls into the trap of trying to exorcise the language—admittedly a fashionable position these days—and the lexicographers who honestly record its fortes and foibles in their methodical, scholarly way. Instead, his target ought to be, more properly, the speakers of the language and their practice of the art of its use. Lexicographers, for the millionth time, don't *make* the language, they *report* on it. The shortcomings of their attitudes and abilities are one thing; the language is another. Aristides' attitude is reminiscent of that of the (erstwhile) dictionary editor, long since attracted to a career outside lexicography, who rejected *basket case* as an entry for *The Random House (Unabridged) Dictionary* on the grounds that he found the metaphor "disgusting."

It is *style*, Aristides, that you rail at, not the words of the language themselves. Infelicitous, ungrammatical, solecistic, unsemantic, unskillful, and just plain bad style in the use of language is what drives all of us to distraction. It isn't the words but how they are chosen and put together that constitute deathless prose (or poetry). Some of us are better at choosing and putting together than others.

It is entirely likely, too, that those who are responsible for the coinages so severely criticized by Aristides have a different view of the world from that which traditionalists have set forth—though their view, in turn, probably differs substantially from that of their forebears. An example may be seen in the use of the word *like*—not the *like* of *Do like I do* but the *like* that occurs in utterances like *(like) man, I was (like) walking down the street and suddenly (like) there was this cat I hadn't seen for (like) two whole years.* In such contexts, it is possible that *like* serves two functions, one, a simple syntactic one to replace *er* or *um*, the other a semantic one to express the speaker's hesitancy at expressing what might be construed as an incontrovertible fact without the "disclaimer." Such insecurity, if, indeed, that is what it is, may stem from a felt lack of education, or, because it is so characteristic of a certain level of speech, from a desire to be with an in-group, or merely from habit. Other examples of a more lexical and less complex nature may be attributable to a different metaphoric view of life that, just because it is unconventional and unfamiliar, becomes subject to the darts of fuddy-duddyism.

Language, like time and the river, changes continuously, and we can never use it in exactly the same way twice. As such, it can be only approximation as a "medium of expression,' for not only does it change, but we and our emotions and everything we use language to describe change. The wonder of it is that we can understand each other at all. *Plus ça change, plus c'est autre chose.*

Of one thing we can be sure: just as today's older generation of English speakers condemns the speech of its youth, today's youth, when they become tomorrow's older generation, will condemn their offspring's speech. And, for another prediction, we shall always have those among us who, like Aristides, have their gaze fixed firmly on the past.

———————

Who is Aristides? Why did he select such a nom de plume? Does he aspire to identification with Aristides the Just (d. 468 B.C.)? Hardly, for that Aristides was a statesman. With Aristides of Bithynia (b. 129? A.D.)? Unlikely, for that Aristides, a sophist, was known to be exceedingly vain about his eloquence, comparing himself to Demosthenes. With Aristides of Athens (fl. 150 A.D.)? Not likely, for that Aristides, author of an apology for the Christians, bequeathed us nothing of value. With Aristides of Miletus (fl. 150 B.C.)? Less than likely, for that Aristides wrote fiction, and ours would have us treat his writings as fact. With Aristides of Thebes (fl. 350 B.C.)? Probably not, for that Aristides was a painter. With Aristides Quintilianus (fl. 150 A.D.)? Scarcely, for that Aristides is the author of a valuable treatise, "On Music," and ours appears deaf to the music of the spheres.

The Citation File

In an article in *The Sunday Times* [London], October 10, 1976, appeared an article, "Dowagers and the black Governor," by Jillian Robertson. It dealt with the appointment of the first black (native Australian), Sir Doug Nicholls, to a high governmental position, as Governor of the State of South Australia. What interested us were the Australianisms it contained, given here with their glosses:

abo an informal term for aborigine.

aborigine a native of Australia before the arrival of white settlers.

Cumeroogunga district where the Yoti Yoti tribe lives.

fair dinkum the real thing.

goanna any of several large monitor lizards.

indiginee new name given to *aborigines*, presumably to help avoid the stigmas associated with the older term.

poor fella condescending term for an aborigine.

real beaut very satisfactory; most acceptable.

wichetty grubs larvae resembling long, fat, white caterpillars without legs, regarded as a delicacy by the aborigines.

Yoti Yoti a tribe of aborigines.

BIBLIOGRAPHIA

*CRAZY TALK, STUPID TALK, How We Defeat Our-
selves by the Way We Talk—and What To Do About It,*
by Neil Postman, Delacorte Press, 1976, xviii + 269 pp.
$8.95.

It is uncertain whether anything is to be gained in de-
voting space to a review of this book, but a couple of man-
hours have been spent reading it and thinking about it, so
it might merit a few man-minutes to writing the review
and some more to reading it.

It may be assumed that the title is intended to shock,
and it does. The shock wears off with each repetition of
each phrase in the text, and the reader is left with the feeling that this is a work that the author, who has made many
serious and worthwhile contributions to the study of language, dictated into a portable tape recorder while running
from one classroom to another. The style is breathless,
headlong. If it were possible to determine such a condition
from a written document, one might venture to assume
that the author had written it while under the influence of
a heavy dose of "speed."

The main theme seems to be the importance of rec-
ognizing and maintaining "semantic environment." This is
nothing more than "appropriateness": in other words, when
you are at the embassy, murmuring "Good evening, Mr.
Ambassador" when you move down the receiving line, you
don't follow the greeting, in the same tone of voice and
with a smile on your face, with "Your fly is open" or "My
grandfather was hanged for horsestealing." Either (or both)
may be true, but both are inappropriate to the occasion.
With myriad examples interspersed with mediocre jokes
and occasional inanities, it takes the very articulate author
xviii + 91 pp. to get the point across.

Postman sees nothing wrong with mixed metaphors or
with clichés; he is seeking a higher good: proper semantic
environment. Inappropriate metaphors, however, are another matter: ". . . a metaphor whose configuration nowhere coincides with the realities of any actual situation
in which he finds himself. The technical name for such a
process is paranoia." Is that the linguist's view of the true
nature of paranoia? a misapplication of a rhetorical device?
Such a warped simplification may come as a surprise to
linguists and psychiatrists alike.

The author seems to suffer from a modern ailment common among those who have discovered that a glib approach will gain listeners and readers: as long as you set forth your ideas with authority, it matters little what you say, for people will believe you, and you will acquire disciples and acolytes.

For this reason, though not this reason alone, *Crazy Talk* is a dangerous book. As the reader progresses (if "progress" is not misapplied here—the feeling is more like that of a nightmarish plunge over a cliff), he is ineluctably drawn to the conclusion that the crazy, stupid talk of the title isn't what the author is writing *about* but what he is *writing*. Examples of silliness abound: " 'I love you' is a very important sentence and is probably spoken a thousand times everyday in California alone" (p. 155); ". . . what about the *Miss* in *Miss Jones* (what exactly is Jones missing?)" (p. 65); "If fanaticism is falling in love with an irrefutable answer, then a neurosis is falling in love with an unanswerable question" (p. 145). "And so we have here a sort of paradox. On the one hand, we must naturally assume that others are using words to mean what we would, and that such meanings have some stability. But on the other hand, we must remember that this is only an assumption, that at any given moment a coin of the realm may not be worth quite what we imagined. And, naturally, our purposes will be short-changed."

This is linguistic philosophy couched in the language of the stand-up comedian. The writing style is a good example of the kind of inappropriateness scored by the author.

ON BEING BLUE, by William Gass, David R. Godine, 1976, 91 pp. $8.95 hardcover; $20 slipcased, signed edition (limited to 200).

I often wonder why publishers and editors, with only rare exceptions, are usually ignored. The rare exceptions are Alfred Knopf, Bennett Cerf, and Maxwell Perkins. It is as often the publishers and editors who are responsible for good books being made available as it is the authors who wrote them. It takes some talent and not much money to design and manufacture a book 'artistically, one that provides as much aesthetic pleasure visually and tactilely as it does in its reading.

On Being Blue is such a rare combination, though, at $8.95 for a 91-page book, one must be prepared to back up his sybaritism with cold, hard cash. Without further ado, let me give the publisher his proper kudos for a book featly done.

On Being Blue, subtitled *A Philosophical Inquiry*, could, without distortion, have been subtitled "A Philological Inquiry" (in the etymological sense of *philological*); it is a sensitive aesthetic experience that, had it been typeset with ragged right lines, would have been construed as free verse. It is a paean, an encomium to the color blue in its infinite shadings, spectral and moral, emollient and painful, serious and facetious. As the reader of this review must surmise, *On Being Blue* has an inspiring, almost hypnotic effect.

> The blue lucy is a healing plant. Blue John is skim milk. Blue backs are Confederate bills. Blue bellies are Yankee boys. . . .
>
> Children collect nouns, bugs, bottlecaps, seashells, verbs: What's that? What's it doing now? Who's this? and with the greed that rushes through them like rain down gulleys, they immediately grasp the prepositions of belonging and the pronouns of possession. But how often do they ask how cold it is, what color, how loud, rare, warm, responsive, kind, how soft, how wet, how noxious, loving, indiscreet, how sour?

The book abounds in four-letter words (besides *blue*). It is a sensuous, erotic book that seems to say "Color me blue." It ranges from Democritus to Demosthenes to Henri Bergson to Henry Miller to Henry James.

> . . . while there is time and you are able, because when blue has left the edges of its objects as if the world were bleached of it, when the wide blue eye has shut down for the season, when there's nothing left but language. . . .

A CIVIL TONGUE, Edwin Newman, Bobbs-Merrill, 1976, 207 pp. $8.95.

Mr. Newman's new book is presented by the publisher as "high comedy in a serious cause." The cause—an effort to warn against "a smog of jargon" that is settling on our land—is indeed a serious one, as those of us who care about such things will without doubt agree. Comedy, on the other hand, is more subjective. Often there are some who will laugh at the joke itself, while others may find the manner of its delivery amusing.

Wisely, Mr. Newman undertakes to formulate at the very beginning a summary of the point he is bent on making. "A civil tongue," he writes, "means to me a language that is not bogged down in jargon, not puffed up with false dignity, not studded with trick phrases that have lost their meaning. It is not falsely exciting, it is not patronizing, does not conceal the smallness and triteness of ideas by clothing them in language ever more grandiose, does not seek out increasingly complicated constructions, does not weigh us down with the gelatinous verbiage of Washington and the social sciences. It treats errors in spelling and usage with a decent tolerance but does not take them lightly."

There you have it in a nutshell. To speak with a civil tongue means to say what you mean, openly, clearly and with due regard for the beauty and the integrity of the language.

Why are so few of us able to do that?

The author, who ruefully refers to criticisms of numerous departures from perfection in the use of the language in his earlier work, *Strictly Speaking*, has clearly been more careful this time around. One wishes, however, that he had not followed the above definition of purpose with a comment about "a stream of sound that disk jockeys produce," not because it might be difficult for all disk jockeys to produce a single stream of sound but rather because the statement will lead inevitably to Congressional *bloks*, *ad hok* meetings and music that is out of *synk*. These things are highly contagious, as Mr. Newman is the first to point out.

A Civil Tongue, rather than adding new types of smog to the basic pollutants studied in *Strictly Speaking*, expands the list of ingredients in the old one. We are now regaled with the overuse of the word "major" in the *New York Times* (*major tests, major enemy categories, major social implications, major states, major rail lines ad infinitum*) as well as 650 *major* items in a single energy message from Gerald Ford. And we find it difficult not to laugh at *compositionwise, environmentalwise, economywise, energywise, inferiorize, rigidize, overstrategize* and *parameterize*, among other epidemics.

What appears to be involved here is a major job of

collectionizing for the purpose of shocking us publication-wise into remedial action. And it must be admitted that the net result, funny or not, does, at the very least, make us aware that English is rapidly becoming an endangered species.

In terms of cause and comedy, there is reason to feel that Mr. Newman on occasion sacrifices the former for the latter. It is one thing to attack the media, the bureaucracy, the professions, etc., for their mindless proliferation of dumbspeak. The guilty ones in these realms do, or at least should, know better if only for the reason that their callings demand it. But when he devotes a whole chapter to the grammatical errors, malapropisms and vocabulary deficiencies of sports figures, we must believe he is holding them up to ridicule for our amusement. This can border on the cruel, so we shall limit ourselves here to a single example for illustrative purpose: ". . . said the (fight) manager: 'It's problemental.'" Criticism in the chapter on Howard Cosell and the like is another matter.

And speaking of the media, Mr. Newman declares at one point: "My vendetta against the term media arises not only for the reasons already given but because it implies a go-between, one who takes orders and carries messages, one who is employed by others for their purposes." This declaration almost qualifies the utterer for inclusion in the sports chapter, not only, to use Mr. Newman's phrase, "because the word *media* is plural and could hardly imply *a* go-between," but because when one is employed by others it would hardly be for other than their own purposes.

Because *A Civil Tongue* will be read by many who without it might be unaware of the peril to which the English language is being exposed, the book provides a valuable addition to the current lists. And it cannot be denied that it is easy to read and to enjoy.

Martin Panzer
New York, New York

THE MAMMOTH BOOK OF WORD GAMES, by Richard B. Manchester, Hart Publishing Company, New York, 1976. $6.95 (U.S.), $7.95 (Canada) paper.

Walter Raleigh, not the one who spread his cloak in the mud for Queen Elizabeth to step on, but the one who didn't, once remarked:

> I wish I loved the Human Race;
> I wish I loved its silly face;
> I wish I liked the way it walks;
> I wish I liked the way it talks;
> And when I'm introduced to one
> I wish I thought What Jolly Fun.

I feel the same way about most word games. The real reason, of course, is that I am no good at them; I can't show off by doing a London *Times* crossword puzzle in four minutes flat. But just in case you are one who *does* like word games, you should have Richard B. Manchester's *The Mammoth Book of Word Games* in your library, or at least in that of your children. The whole family will find it Jolly Fun (there are answers in back, too). Mr. Manchester has accumulated enough challenges to keep you sharpening your pencil for hours; the front cover does not exaggerate when it notifies you that the 510 lubberly pages (8½" x 11") provide "OVER A FULL YEAR'S ENTERTAINMENT."

The first entry is perhaps a bit simpler than most, but it gives you the idea. You are asked to find equivalents containing the word "light" for a list of twenty-five expressions. "*A tower having warning beacon for ships at sea,*" for instance, is a . . . Ah! You are already catching on. At another point, you are asked to reduce big words to little maxims: "Aberration is the hallmark of *homo sapiens* while longanimous placability and condonation are the indicia of a supramundane omniscience" turns into . . . but there! I won't give Mr. Manchester away. There are Word Mazes, consisting of vocabulary puzzles that I am reluctant to penetrate for fear of running into a Minotaur somewhere inside. There are Threezies, where you list all the words you can think of containing certain three-letter sequences. (Mr. Manchester says that at least nine words contain the sequence OTO. I could not get beyond *motor.*) There are enough cryptograms to fill a crypt. (I plan to create an insoluble cryptogram some day by substituting two other letters for what I contend to be the shortest verse in English—well, half in English. The wife of the British Ambassador is hostess to the wife of the Spanish Ambassador, and their conversation runs as follows:

"T?"
"C."

It should make a great cryptogram, but I haven't got around to it yet, and neither, I gather, has Mr. Manchester.)

Cryptograms lead on to Jumbles—emigrants, one assumes, from the lands where the Jumblies live; these are anagrams on various themes. There follow Quizzes, which test background knowledge (I didn't dare try them); Picture Quizzes, where you are wrong if you put *porcupine* under the picture of an anteater; Crossword Puzzles, clearly not edited by Will Weng; Across-tics (the pun is self-explanatory); Blankies, which seem to be Jumbles sitting around the fire telling stories; and Initialettes, which in an earlier day were called Categories or Guggenheims. There is more besides.

Word games are an excellent introduction to the delights of English. If you have offspring still on the morning side of pubescence, I hope they will have an opportunity to savor this book before intenser drives supervene. Indeed, whatever your own level of verbal sophistication, you cannot lose by thumbing through these word games; for,

You may be introduced to one
That makes you think What Jolly Fun.

Willard R. Espy
Author, An Almanac of Words at Play

A DICTIONARY OF AMERICAN IDIOMS, by Maxine Tull Boatner and John Edward Gates. Revised Edition edited by Adam Makkai. Barron's Educational Series, 1975, xiii + 392 pp. $4.50 (paper).

This book was first published in 1966 under the title *A Dictionary of Idioms for the Deaf*. The present edition has been provided with a preface by Professor Makkai, who has also "added more than 250 modern idiomatic phrases to the collection." It is difficult to guess exactly what the publishers had in mind when they chose for the cover a crude cartoon drawing of a bald eagle dressed in checked cap and trousers. The allusion is, one supposes, to the American-ness of the idioms, although most of the phrases in the book are probably not exclusively American, either in use or by origin. The cover does serve to tell the reader something about the book, however. Balloons issuing from the eagle's beak claim that this dictionary contains over 4000 common idiomatic expressions, including slang, proverbs, and clichés, and that everything is completely up-to-date, excellent for foreign speakers, and valuable to students of American English. The last two claims are ambitious. If one has set out to produce a dictionary for foreign learners and serious students of the language, one has assumed responsibilities that are not lightly discharged, especially if the subject is such an uneasy and ill-defined one as idioms. A really useful dictionary for foreign learners of English would certainly require a much more scrupulous and systematic editorial effort than has gone into this rather casual compilation.

Professor Makkai's preface makes some basic points about idioms. "An idiom . . . is the assigning of a new meaning to a group of words which already have their own meaning." Some examples are *to blow one's stack, to fly off the handle, what's more, of course, to get up, like a breeze, time off, this is it.* He distinguishes two types of idiom. The *lexemic idiom,* like *hammer and tongs* ('violently') can easily be identified with one of the familiar parts of speech (*hammer and tongs* = adverb). Longer idioms, like *to be caught between the devil and the deep blue sea,* "do not readily correlate with a given grammatical part of speech"; these he terms *phraseological idioms.* The main characteristic of both types (and, obviously, of proverbs and sayings, which constitute a third type) is their grammatical rigidity. "Their form is set and only a limited number of them can be said or written in any other way without destroying the meaning of the idiom." That is, idioms do not permit certain simple operations—the pluralization of nouns, the inflection of verbs, the insertion of an adverb before a verb, etc.—which can be carried out on ordinary literal phrases.

Thus, transitive verbs in idiomatic expressions frequently will not passivize (*the cowboy kicked the bucket,* but not **the bucket was kicked by the cowboy*). In this case, as with many phraseological idioms, the passive transformation destroys the idiom by literalizing it (*the bucket was struck by the cowboy's boot*). One wishes the Professor Makkai had had more space in the preface to devote to this feature of grammatical defectiveness and the invariance and variability of idioms, because these matters are not adequately covered in the individual dictionary entries.

The body of the dictionary is well laid out, with useful run-on entries (e.g., *fence-sitter* under *sit on the fence*), "compare" and "contrast" references that draw attention to related expressions (*get lost*, compare *drop dead*; *give up*, contrast *hold on to*), register labels for *slang, informal, formal*, and *literary*, and usage notes that give information about the context in which the idiom is used (as a command, to show surprise, to express disapproval, etc.). In the usage-note category—certainly the most helpful feature for foreign students of English—the editors have seen fit to label some phrases "clichés," some "trite phrases," and some "hackneyed phrases." One wonders why *get down to brass tacks, one foot in the grave, smell a rat, slip through one's fingers,* and *shot in the arm* are clichés, while *sleep a wink* is trite and *pay the piper* hackneyed. One wonders also whether any of the three labels, even if they had been clearly differentiated, do much more than express a subjective judgment. As someone has said, "A cliché is an idiom which I do not like." How much more useful is the kind of usage note one finds at *on end*—"Used with plural nouns of time." It is typical of the casual editorial approach that this note is a half-truth—one cannot say "I've been waiting for you for seconds on end." Still, it is this attempt to supply information about context and use that is essential when one is defining idioms. A major shortcoming of this dictionary is its failure to do so consistently and in sufficient detail.

An alarming amount of space in the dictionary has been given to paraphrases of the illustrative sentences. The sentences themselves are appropriately colloquial and simple embodiments of the preceding definitions. The paraphrases are at best needlessly repetitive and too often approach absurdity. For example, at the entry *on one's chest*, with this peculiar second-person definition—

> Hidden in your thoughts or feelings and bothering you; making you feel worried or upset; that is something you want to talk to someone about . . .

the illustrative sentence and paraphrase read:

> *"Well, Dave," said the coach, "You look sad—what's on your chest?"*
> (The coach asked Dave what was making him disturbed. Did he want to talk it over?)

The paraphrase is pointless, but the illustration is worse since its probable effect is to conjure up an image of the athletic Dave's hairy chest. (This is, of course, an elementary lexicographical blunder—to put a metaphorical phrase in a literalizing context. It is a pastime of lexicographers to invent such monsters, e.g. *When she went on vacation she packed absolutely everything. She even took a megaphone, for crying out loud!)*

The illustrative sentences and paraphrases develop a different sort of nonsense when they occur, as they unfailingly do, after definitions of straightforward terms or names for tangible material things. For example:

> *credit card . . . Mr. Smith used his credit card to buy gasoline.*
> (Mr. Smith bought gasoline and showed the man a card with his name.)
> *panel truck . . . The flowers were delivered in a panel truck.*
> (The flowers were brought in a closed truck.)
> *parish house . . . The ladies served a spaghetti supper in the parish house.*
> (The ladies had a spaghetti supper in the church social building.)

One doubts that these entries—and there are an enormous number of the same type—really qualify as idioms according to Professor Makkai's definition (they are simply names for particular kinds of cards, trucks, and houses); perhaps that is why these illustrations and paraphrases seem almost comically futile.

These few objections to details are related to much more serious questions about the character and purpose of this book. One is not told how this collection of idioms was assembled. Were the entries selected on the basis of a citation-reading program? What sources were used? Were the idioms selected according to some judgment of frequency? Were the invented illustrative sentences based on citations? The book was originally compiled for the deaf (and for that original purpose perhaps the illustrative sentences and paraphrases had a real pedagogical value); why was it not rethought and restructured for a more general readership—or at least for a specific readership—before it was published in its present form? One doesn't have the answers to these questions, but it is hard to avoid the suspicion that they would help to explain why there is so little evidence of editorial responsibility in this dictionary.

Thomas Hill Long
Aylesbury, Buckinghamshire

411

The Seating of Zotz

Walter C. Kidney
Essex, Connecticut

Read widely and you end up with a magnificent but not totally useful vocabulary. For my part, I find no application for such words as:

gumphion: death's-head banner displayed at funerals;
ergastulum: house of correction for Roman slaves;
dob-dob: member of the hoodlum element in a lamasery;
verbunkos: dance performed to persuade people to enlist in the Hungarian army.

What a waste. And I regret any chance to drop into my conversation the months of the Maya year, just for their Dunsanian sound. The Maya had 18 twenty-day months, plus five or six official days of bad luck. The year began with *Pop*, which fell between the *Nameless Days* and *Uo*. *Uo* fell between *Pop* and *Zip*, and so on. Even more Dunsanian, suggesting a play for grades 6 to 8, was *The Seating of Zotz*, the correct name for what otherwise would have been *20 Zip*.

Some 15 years ago I worked on a job ideal for collecting such glittering trash, the *Random House Dictionary* project. Much of my time was spent in technology, and my working day was a shower bath of *bruzzes, brobs, froofs, snaths, downrights, chime hoops, larry cars, equation kidneys, cullin stones, crizzle glazes, glost fires, muffle furnaces, blue billy, sugar of lead, butter of arsenic,* and *Victoria Green Mother Liquor*. The sea yielded *futtock shrouds, euphroes, baggywrinkles,* and *paravane skegs*. Lists of standard paint colors included *Cream Dream, Pewke,* and *U.S. Army Pansy*. My Japanese sword mounts won satirical attention from John Ciardi. Heraldry was mine too, a whole private language. I learned not to use *or* 'gold' in definition examples because my colleagues would always fire them back with penciled "Or what?" 's. But I did enter the various ways of describing a disk. Depending on the tincture, a disk is a *bezant, plate, torteau, hurt, gulp, guze, ogress, pellet, gunstone,* or *fountain.* Crosses can be—among other things—*crosslet, potent, avellan, moline, paty, formy, fitchy* or *paty or formy fitchy at the foot.* An *escutcheon semé of cross-crosslets* is *crusily,* and if the cross-crosslets are *fitchy* it is *crusily fitchy.* An escutheon is sometimes divided by *dancetty, urdy, undy, embattled,* or *embattled grady* lines, and can be *barry, bendy, paly, barry-bendy, paly-bendy, paly-wavy, lozengy, chequy,* etc. The sun is in its *splendor,* the moon is in her *complement* or *detriment,* the pelican is in her *piety,* the lion is *gardant passant* and *ducally gorged,* and royalty is represented by *opinci, yales,* and *enfields,* one of which has *swivel-mounted horns.* How the Scottish dragon with flames issuing from *both* ends is blazoned I never did discover.

Meanwhile a friend in biology was encountering the *sarcastic fringehead,* the *confused flour beetle,* and the *free-living flatworm.*

Some of these things did get into the dictionary, but in most cases there was nothing to do but pause, admire, and dismiss them gently.

Traveler's Credo

Mary E. Gross
St. Petersburg, Florida

I believe in Bolivia
and in Lago Titicaca
in Oraru
in Potusi
and also in Chuquisaca.

Tombouctu I can take on trust
Saskatchewan I rely on
prize Ararat
laud Zanzibar
sing praise to ancient Isfahan.

Now you, my bold Bolivian
may name your fancy loud and clear
Sopchoppy town
fair Chincoteague
Oshkosh Dime Box or Rensselaer.

Dash It All

Ethel Grodzins Romm
Harcourt Brace Jovanovich

For centuries we've labored over hyphenation by historic principles, as in any traditional dic·tion·ar·y. We're now coping with the new hyphenation by breathing principles, as in a dic·tio·na·ry improved by modern linguists. Their work, however, flowers in bound volumes only. On the pages of the smaller dailies across the land we are enjoying hyphenation by computer according to *Hatai!* principles. A recent morning offered *dau-ghter* in our local daily.

My hometown newspaper in Middletown, N. Y., was the first daily in the world to be printed cold-type on off-set presses. That printing innovation of 1956, since adopted by more than half of America's papers, has led to the widespread use of computers for scanning typewritten copy and setting type. Computer typesetting is never monitored by live editors. Without them, hyphenation may return to the pre-linotyping, anything-goes, days of yore.

When the computer was an infant, it could do only simple things, such as separate the *-ly* in adverbs: *mad-ly, glad-ly*. Naturally it also wrote *butterf-ly*, but that was understandable and altogether forgivable; why burden it with an instruction required only rarely: "Divide at *ly* except *-fly*"?

Having passed kindergarten, the computer secretly promoted itself to junior high. The first clue was the morning it wrote *dau-ghter*, although it had been taught to divide *-er*, like *-ly*. The new choice was the subject of much breakfast discussion. We reasoned that *daughter* is a long word to shoeborn into the end of a narrow newspaper column, that at *-er* the word still wouldn't fit, and the computer must have used—in doing its best to fill the line—what appeared to be an arcane magnetic principle not immediately apparent. We felt we might be watching the birth of inanimate intelligence.

I must report that the *Times Herald Record* computer has grown smarter. It has dispensed with most historic as well as inhalation principles and does largely what

it knows best: it counts; then very matter of factly it chops
off the word, *Hatai!* Here are three examples:

> [Ann Landers] Dear Glad: So am I. I hope so-
> mebody out there listens.

> Witnesses said the violence was sparked off when a
> group of blacks tried to set fire to a Zulu boardingh-
> ouse and the tribesmen retaliated.

> Nixon's intended gifts of his San Clemente home could
> give him a big tax deduction for six years. Sort of a "s-
> queezing citizens" home.

The computer counts so well that very few words are
now hyphenated in the paper, a great saving of space.
And the new syllabication has enlivened the news, sometimes turning it into far-out poetry.

But for certain readers, it's not good news. Pulling
apart words into their syllables may be the most efficient
way for poor readers to figure out printed matter. There
are hordes of marginal readers today who, for many other
reasons, have already given up reading newspapers. Dash-
ing the language any which way is, for them, no joke.

In a front-page article in *The Wall Street Journal*
[Nov. 9, 1976] about "Winners & Sinners," the *N. Y. Times*
house organ dealing with grammatical and stylistic goodies
and baddies in *The Times,* the information appears that
The Philadelphia Bulletin has a similar bulletin. To quote
the *WSJ*: " 'The big problem is finding the time to sustain
it,' says Sam Boyle, the Bulletin's assistant managing editor
responsible for Second Guessing [the title of the house or-
gan]. 'It may not look like it's hard to put out, but believe
me, it is.' "

We'll take you at your word, Sam.

BIBLIOGRAPHIA

A DISCURSIVE DICTIONARY OF HEALTH CARE,
U. S. Government Printing Office, Washington, 1976, 182
pp. $2.40

This is a truly staggering book, which—as the title
page proudly announces—was "Prepared by the Staff/for
the use of the/Subcommittee on Health and the Environ-
ment/of the/Committee on Interstate and Foreign Com-
merce/U.S. House of Representatives." Truly. And the
chairman of the CIFC is Harley O. Staggers of West Virginia.

The dictionary is a serious work designed to help
untangle the jargon and technical terms associated with
the national health program and national health insurance,
currently still under debate. It is an immediate joy to see
that the compilers have a sense of humor in what otherwise would be a dry work indeed. One first notices this
in the Contents list, for page 169, "Abbreviations and
acronyms (alphabet soup expanded)." In an otherwise
straightforward Introduction, we are disarmed momentarily
by being told that,

> The definitions which have been prepared are not
> in any sense official or final. They are not necessarily
> the definitions which the Committee will give to
> these terms when they are used in the actual
> writing of national health insurance law. Nor is
> any part of the dictionary completely exhaustive:
> available time and energy have necessarily
> limited the effort.

For this information we have to thank Paul G. Rogers,
the chairman of the Subcommitee on Health and the
Environment.

In spite of the fact that presumably none of the members of the "professional staff" chosen to prepare this dictionary have had prior experience in lexicography, they
have done an admirable job in their attempts to give ex-
pansive information on the fleeting meanings of terms
used by the medical, legal and insurance professions—as
they relate to the congressional debates on national health
insurance. Approximately one thousand headwords and
over one hundred abbreviations and acronyms are defined.

416

(There is some amusing padding, such as the entry *dictionary*—an attributed quote from Ambrose Bierce's *The Devil's Dictionary:* "a malevolent literary device for cramping the growth of language. This dictionary, however, is a most useful work.") The text is enhanced by numerous anatomical illustrations taken from woodcuts originally prepared for two 16th-century books by Andreas Vesalius (*De Humani Corporis Fabrica* and an *Epitome,* both published in 1543).

For the most part, the definitions tend to reflect the jargon and ostensible confusion of the primary sources of the headwords themselves. (H. W. Fowler and Sir Ernest Gowers, where are you now that they really need you!) For example, the definition of *prior determination* is "similar to prior authorization but less restrictive in that payment will be made if prior authorization is not sought, provided that it would have approved the service as needed." Within the same letter, we discovered that *ping-ponging* is "the practice of passing a patient from one physician to another in a health program for unnecessary cursory examinations so that the program can charge the patient's third-party for a physician visit to each physician. The practice and term originated and is most common in *Medicaid mills.*" Some entries are invaluable cross-references: *"poor* See *poverty."*

Some "naughties" are revealed, as we learn from the entry *kiting:* "increasing the quantity of a drug ordered by a prescription. Either the patient or pharmacist may kite the quantity of the original prescription, for example, by adding zeros to the number shown on a prescription. When done by a pharmacist, he then provides the patient with the quantity originally prescribed but bills a third party, such as Medicaid, for the larger quantity."

Just one more. The entry *elephant policy* refers us quickly to *trolley car policy:* "a facetious name for an insurance policy which is so hard to collect benefits upon that it is as though it provided benefits only for injuries resulting from being hit by a trolley car. Typically used by mail order insurance."

If this dictionary had not already been written it would be virtually impossible to invent it. Nevertheless, sorting out jargon is a respectable occupation. In all fairness, quite a few entries are lucid and valuable to a better understanding of inevitable bureaucratic opacities. But one cannot escape the lingering impression that this is a classical (and possibly unique) example of jargon breeding jargon. Thus the introductory disclaimer, already quoted, perhaps implies a nervous lack of faith and justification in what has been accomplished.

The compilers certainly must be given generous credit for telling it like it is. But what it is is frightening.

Edward R. Brace
Aylesbury, Buckinghamshire

Little Error Spells Big Mistake

1. "The Crime of the Ancient Mariner" (Coleridge) . . . . .
2. "Wife of Samuel Johnson" (Boswell) . . . . .
3. "The Glisteners" (De la Mare) . . . . .
4. "The Pickwick Capers (Dickens) . . . . .
5. "With Rue My Art Is Laden" (Housman) . . . . .
6. "The Old Lady Shows Her Metals" (Barrie) . . . . .
7. "I Wandered Lovely As a Cloud" (Wordsworth) . . . . .
8. "Home Thoughts from a Broad" (Browning) . . . . .
9. "In the Time of the Braking of Nations" (Hardy) . . . . .
10. "When I Was One—Ann, Twenty" (Housman) . . . . .
11. "Richard Gory" (Robinson) . . . . .
12. "A Noiseless Patient Spied Her" (Whitman) . . . . .
13. "Death of the Tired Man" (Frost) . . . . .
14. "Abraham Lincoln Balks at Midnight" (Lindsay) . . . . .
15. "I Have a Rendzvous with Beth" (Seeger) . . . . .
16. "God's Whirled" (Millay) . . . . .
17. "A Belle for Adano" (Hersey) . . . . .
18. "A Table for Critics" (Lowell) . . . . .
19. "Fanny and Zooey" (Salinger) . . . . .
20. "Critique of Pure Treason" (Kant) . . . . .

A. S. Flaumenhaft
Lawrence, New York

(Answers are on page 420.)

EPISTOLAE

Below are some examples of one of our more recent (i.e., unlisted in Wentworth and Flexner's *Dictionary of American Slang*) derivational morphemes in action (all are from the *Detroit Free Press*):

Maybe Her Mom's a Clothesaholic [1/25/76, title of Ann Landers' column]

Mom-to-Be's a Candyholic [2/12/76]

So who cares if the majority of the telephone calls we indulge in are non-essential and time-wasters? . . . "It's someone to talk to, isn't it?" I was once told by another phonoholic. [columnist Bob Talbert, 3/11/76]

Anyone, but especially impulse buyers, can become a credit-cardaholic. [7/11/76]

Fasting also may be the answer for foodaholics who find one forkful of food too much, a thousand not enough. [medical columnist Lindsay Curtis, M.D., 7/15/76]

Should the process become truly productive, I propose the label *aholicism*, 'The irresistible impulse to use the suffix *(a)holic* to describe irresistible impulses.'

Alan M. Perlman
Wayne State University

The "person" versus "man" hysteria continues apace.

Ellen Cooperman of Babylon, Long Island, plans to carry her campaign to change her name to Ellen Cooperperson all the way to the Supreme Court, despite the opposition of Justice John Scileppi. "I would like my name to reflect my humanitarian beliefs," explained Ms. Cooperperson, divorcee, mother of a 9-year old son, and owner of Feminist Productions, a film company.

Firstly, shouldn't that be "hu-person-itarian" beliefs?

Secondly, she likes to use the term "herstory" in place of *history*, a cutesy, but highly illogical neologism: the feminine possessive pronoun, *her*, is from Middle English; the masculine possessive pronoun, *his*, is from the Old English; *history* is from Latin and Greek (*historia*), further derived from *histor* or *istor* 'knowing or learning.' The personal pronoun *his*, which was never present in *history*, further disappears in the form *istor*.

Thirdly, if she will, let Ms. Ellen C. play around with the word *hysteria*, from the Greek *hystera* 'womb.' I hope she is not about to alter that to "hersteria." After all, what is more feminine than womb, no matter what word the Greeks had for it?

Harry Cimring
Los Angeles, California

"Wow!", or perhaps "Oba!", "Orv!", "Ya!", or even "Ajaib!!" My first two issues of *Verbatim* contain delights beyond imagining, to be savored and cherished, and reducing me to a state which can be described accurately only by the earthy phrase "off my gourd."

I must argue, though, with Mr. Hornos' *"Ouch! he said in Japanese* [III, 1]. Human languages may be familiar but little is known, really, of foreign animal talk. It is vital to know, therefore, if Mr. Hornos' animal sounds are phonetic—which seems unlikely—and if not, just how are these foreign animal sounds pronounced? Unlikely, because, in the case of Greek dogs, a non-Greek-speaker could only wonder if Greek dogs say "ow ow" as in the German "auf," or "oh oh" as in French "aux." Greeks pronounce the letters alpha upsilon, or au, as "aff" or "av." But in fact what Greek dogs actually "say" is gamma alpha upsilon, or "γαυ γαυ"—phonetically "grraff grraff," a more accurate representation of "bow wow" than exists in other languages. (Greeks somehow do manage to roll their gammas, producing a sound similar to the "gr" in the French word "grand.") But, please, help! If "popo" is not phonetic, how will I ever know the sound of a Japanese

❦❦❦

Little Error—Answers (from page 418)

1. Rime 2. Life 3. Listeners 4. Papers 5. Heart 6. Medals 7. Lonely 8. Abroad 9. Breaking 10. One-and-Twenty 11. Cory 12. Spider 13. Hired 14. Walks 15. Death 16. World 17. Bell 18. Fable 19. Franny 20. Reason

dove? For that matter, how *would* one say "Ajaib!" to an Indonesian?

Mr. White ("Mrs. Malaprop's Bicentennial") [II, 1], would have enjoyed a recent TV interview with a New England Patriot player who claimed they had won their game by keeping right on top of their P's and Q's.

I'd also like to acquaint you with a local landmark. Upon entering the original building of the Boston Public Library, newcomers are transfixed by the baffling message "TIXE NA TON" painted on the glass of the inner door. Obviously this would not merit a second glance by Mr. Fowkes ("Esrever Hsilgne") [III, 2]; others remain mystified until leaving the building when the sign miraculously rights itself.

I have the pleasure of looking forward to a chunk of solid pleasure four times a year when *Verbatim* is delivered. THANK YOU for it—in every language.

Claire W. Belyea
Cambridge, Massachusetts

Reading the latest issue sends my mind on many trails. My all-time favorite was a listing in the San Diego phone book for *Augusta's Topsoil Hair Products Manufacturing Co.* By its address, I judged that it was a hair-straightener. I dialed the number, said that I had seen the listing, and was curious about the product. A voice replied, "Well, ma'am, we thinks we has a ve'y fine product fo' the hair and scalp, and we wanted a nice-soundin' name fo' it— y'know, lak 'Wildroot.' So we named it *Topsoil.*"

Many years as a proofreader left me wondering why restaurateurs never bothered to learn the French they consistently misused; why an extra "r" always crept into *sherbet*; why *avocado* could assume so many guises, the commonest being "avocoda"; why *chili* was so often "chile"; why *au beurre* was "au burr"; why *béarnaise* was "bernaise."

The one that set me back most, however, was an advertisement for a language school that promised, "You will be able to parse any irregular verb in three weeks." Thinking it was just a slip of the tongue, I changed *parse* to *conjugate*. It came back to be corrected—*parse* was what

421

they wanted! (That is one language school I shall never attend.)

Elections seem to do strange things to commentators—"It is apparently going to be close if they do not succeed at all," and to candidates—"Help us begin to put a stop to the end of spending."

Barbara Marsh
San Diego, California

. . . .*And why is it that restauràteurs can't even spell the name of their occupation? It appears as "restauranteur" more often than not!* —*Editor*

Your request for comments [III,2] about professionals and their use (misuse) of their language strikes a familiar chord with me. As a stenotype court and convention reporter, I often reported in technical areas where it soon became apparent to me that I knew more about the day-to-day vocabularies of many people than they themselves knew. Almost all doctors mispronounce *gynecology*—so often now that many American dictionaries show the "doctors' choice" as an alternate.

Here's an old medical anecdote which may be new to this generation:

Q   Describe the injury as you saw it.
A   He had an extravasation of serous fluid into the soft tissues of the optic region causing extensive discoloration.
Q   Do you mean he had a black eye?
A   Yes.

Engineers do very well with *sine*, but usually fall flat on *cosine*.

Edwin H. Hammock
Columbus, Ohio

On "The Enigmatic Eggplant" [Etymologica Obscura, II, 4], the modern Greek encyclopaedia and dictionaries offer the following:

1.   μελιντζανα (*melintzána*) derives from the Italian *melenzana*. (Ref.: John Stamatakos, *Dictionary of the Modern Greek Language*.)
2.   μελιζανα (*melizána*) or μελιντζανα (as in 1.) is the

colloquial for τρυχνος η μελιζανα *(trychnos e melizána)*, which in Latin is *solanum melongena.*

I think that we modern Greeks owe our μελιντζανα to *al-badhinjan* of the Arabs.

On "Talking Turkey" [II,3], in modern Greek your turkey is our γαλλος *(yállos)*, which means, 'the French bird' or διανος *(thiános)*, which means 'the Indian bird.'

Nick Raptis
Athens, Greece

You may have already noted that the Dodge dealer in nearby Old Saybrook, Connecticut, has what at first blush would appear to be an unfortunate name for someone in his trade: *Risko*, which he uses instead of dodging the issue by using "Seaport Motors" or some other evasion. However, "Esrever Hsilgne" would spot the advantages of word of mouth advertising when he drives in the lot to see the owner's 1937 cream convertible Bentley with his vanity plates spelling his name backwards.

Your "roast beef reporter" could only have seen this week a placard in Newport's finest Greek cafe, Odyssey, that proclaims theirs is "ah just."

Vincent Smith
Newport, Rhode Island

Professor Fowkes might consider mixing Sucrets with his Tums and spelling both backwards.

Aaron M. Fine
Philadelphia, Pennsylvania

It takes quite a time for your magazine to reach me so if my remarks seem to refer to several past numbers, I hope at least they are still pertinent.

I doubt very much that the expressions of "spitting image" meaning "likeness" comes from "spirit and image" as Mr. Meng suggested in his letter in III,1. Even the

French have the same expression for similarity, e.g., "C'est son père tout craché." More likely the origin is to be found in "spit" meaning an ejection from the mouth combined with primitive belief that progeny of the gods were born through the mouth [e.g., Zeus and his brothers were all first swallowed and then spit out again by their father, Kronos]. It was also believed, in primitive cultures, that certain birds were impregnated through their mouths. One of the *Panchatantra* tales, I can't check it here in Greece on my barren island, tells of a bird—peahen? magpie?—who informed on her master's wife when she had intercourse with a lover (or failed to inform?). In any case, this bird was cursed ever afterwards to being impregnated only through the mouth as punishment.

For that matter, all creation came symbolically through the mouth: "In the beginning was the Word and the Word was God. . . ."

Betty Anthony
Hydra, Greece

As Robert A Fowkes points out in his delightful article [III,2], reading backwards can be fun. By sheer good luck, I happened to marry a man whose name spelled backwards is *Snikwad*, a name he immortalized (for our children) in a series of cartoons depicting the adventures of the Snikwad family. One of these same children, by the way, was so charmed with the discovery that *Lipton's* spelled backwards is *Snotlip*, that none of us to this day has had the heart to point out the mistake.

Anagrams are fun, too. A year or two ago we got hooked on Arthur Swan's Wit Twisters in *Saturday Review* and began making up our own for inter-family amusement. An early example is:

"I can't be ― ― ― ― ― ― ―," his mother stated,
"For all the ― ― ― ― ― ― ― he's created.
I'd ne'er have ― ― ― ― ― ― the little guy
If that randy ram hadn't ― ― ― ― ― ― by."

Unfortunately, as time went on, our messages began to get rude and coarse—possibly a sign of waning interest. In an effort to liven things up, I have lately been trying to combine the limerick form with the original idea. This has proved more difficult than I had anticipated and, so far, all I have been able to come up with are these feeble efforts:

There was an old — — — — from **Duluth**
Who drank vastly of — — — — and vermouth.
She — — — — quite a fuss,
When kicked off the bus
And her gestures were grossly uncouth.

An ugly old — — — — named **McDwight**
Trained his — — — — to attack me on sight,
So I've hired some nuns
To hurl stale currant buns
At his hounds as they — — — — out at **night**.

Perhaps your readers can come up with something more electrifying—chances are I've been dragged down by the low standards of the Snikwad side of the family.

Gloria Dawkins
Unionville, Ontario, Canada

I am surprised that the learned author of *Esrever Hsilgne* [III,2] didn't know (or note) that Kay Boyle once wrote a short story entitled *Kroy Wen*. But he might be interested in knowing that the craze he writes of serves still another purpose: creating delightful euphemisms. Thus, I have a friend who berates his children if they should *traf* in public. And, speaking of *Serutan*, this same friend tells me that its manufacturers are about to market a soft drink, *Sip*.

John B. Newman
Queens College, New York

In reference to a letter from Hugh T. Kerr [III, 2], he certainly picked examples that show just the opposite of what he wanted to prove: that the King James version of the Bible is preferable to modern translations:

My beloved put in his hand by the hole of the door, and my bowels were moved for him.	*My beloved put his hand to the latch, and my heart was thrilled within me.*

As they say in the Army: you do, and you'll mop it up!

It has been painfully obvious for a long time that the King James version was out of date and long overdue for rewriting. It is fashionable nowadays to say that the King James version is still the best, but I submit that this is just snobbishness. I suppose every religion has to have a book that most people do not understand and must be explained to them by an elite, but the King James Bible had gotten to the point where even the elite could not make sense out of it.

On the subject of *ghost*, the Catholic Church did one sensible thing this century when it replaced *Holy Ghost* with *Holy Spirit*. The word *ghost* has so many silly and laughable connotations that this change was centuries overdue. As always, this sensible change was balanced by the sudden idea that we have been misspelling for years the name of the man who built the Ark. Now it is spelled *Noe*, not *Noah*. All I can conclude is that maybe the Church is trying to convert over to Spanish.

Jerry Mendel
Plainfield, New Jersey

In the September issue Hugh T. Kerr writes of "ghost and spirit" pointing out that one wishes a person who sneezes "God bless you" or "Gesundheit" as a matter of concern that he might be "giving up the ghost" or that his soul or breath of life might be departing his body.

It is also likely that the association of sudden death with a sneeze had its origin when, prior to improved medical therapy, many people went on to the last stages of syphilis acquiring thereby a weakened aorta. A sudden surge of increased blood pressure accompanying a sneeze often caused that great vessel to burst, and death followed quickly.

Thus the person who said "God bless you" had good reason to fear that the sneezer might suddenly lose his spirit and his life even though he did not know why.

Lester Saferstein, M.D.
Kansas City, Missouri

B. H. Smeaton's letter on clipping inspires me to offer my list of Australian diminutives [spellings improvised]. *Aussie* is familiar to Ameriacns, but that mainlanders go on holiday to *Tassie* may not be. (Both are pronounced with a *z*, by the way, as is *mossies* for mosquitoes.) While teaching, I learned about *bickies* at morning tea (biscuits, our cookies), was asked if I had taken a *sickie* after a one-day absence, and discussed the girls' *cozzies* at the Swimming Carnival. (Has anyone ever figured out why Americans wear bathing suits to go swimming and some other nationalities wear swimming costumes for bathing?)

On a camping tour I heard references to the *littlies* and *oldies* in the group. We stopped at a *Leaguie* 'Leagues Club' and played the *pokies* 'poker machines.' One of the teenagers was from *Sainty* 'St. Mary, N.S.W.,' whose football team is well known—the *Sainties* in her speech. Reveille took the form of the leaders going around the tents calling "Wakey, wakey," in the same abominably cheerful voice that accompanies "Rise and shine."

Some of those sounded fine to me; others caused a mild shudder. But I never got used to *Chrissy* and *pressy*. I would wait, muscles stiffened to receive the blow, for a user of either to mention a *Chrissy pressy*. It never happened.

I should add about *sickie* that it isn't a straightforward synonym for *sick day*. One takes the latter to nurse a cold, the former to go to a ball game, and an absence of less than two days, preferably three, will be interpreted, even on the administrative level, as a *sickie*.

Katherine Adamson
Columbus, Ohio

How did Harry Cimring in "Trite 'n' True" [Vol. III, No. 2] ever miss *Light 'n' Lively?*

Phylis Feinstein
Silver Burdett Company
Morristown, New Jersey

Apropos of malapropisms: on the menu of the Back Door restaurant of Dalton, Pennsylvania, are lamb chops "cooked to your likeness."

B. R. Mullin, M.D.
Rockville, Maryland

Archie Bunker in the Classroom

Teachers of vocabulary may have more reason to thank Norman Lear's Archie Bunker than criticize him and his abuses of the language. Most errors made by this popular television character can be categorized as malapropisms though he is occasionally guilty of a spoonerism (e.g. "hard-pore cornography"). A collection of Mr. Bunker's slips of the tongue can form the core of an entertaining and informative vocabulary class.

My own procedure has been to distribute the sentences and then ask what was the word the character should properly have used; what does the proper word mean, and, if necessary, what does the word which the character used mean?

Here are a few you might try:

"I've been *impudent* ever since I got laid off."
[To a Jewish visitor:] *"Shaboom!"*
[To a policeman:] "You can't get no *judasprudence* these days."
"You've got to control your *carnival* instincts, Gloria."
"Edith's *mental pause* is causing her dizziness."
"I gave the [accident victim] mouth-to-mouth *restitution.*"
"Don't go out in the rain; you'll catch *utopia.*"
"Listen, Meathead, don't take things out of *contest.*"
"It ain't *German* to this conversation."
"I've never used a *lollipop* in my speech in my life."

Skip Eisiminger
Clemson University

VERBATIM

THE LANGUAGE QUARTERLY

Vol. IV, No. 1   May 1977

EDITOR: LAURENCE URDANG

Deciphering *The* Four-letter Word in a Medieval Manuscript's Satire on Friars

Carter Revard
St. Louis, Missouri

The English may now reclaim from the Scots the honor, if such it be, of being the first to put the popular quadriliteral into writing. As one might expect, however, they used a bastard form of the word, and they wrote it only in cipher: thus, even though the poem containing this coded occurrence has been in print for a hundred and forty years, the Victorian scholar who printed it with full knowledge of what he was printing, but who left it to his readers to decipher the medieval scribe's code, could certainly have felt that the public would not be corrupted by the word, and it was left to D. H. Lawrence and others to curl the aspidistra permanently.

As for the Scots claim to primacy in this matter, it rests on the shoulders of William Dunbar, whose poem of ca. 1502 was the first instance which the editors of the OED's *Revised Supplement*, Vol. I. (1972), could find of a written use of the word. However, a British Museum manuscript, Harley 3362, contains among its many jokes, proverbs, riddles, and pious poems a group, on folio 24r (old number ing p. 47), which vigorously vituperate friars. Certain lines of this invective are written in a cipher or code, and when deciphered one word among these is *fuccant*, which in context is indubitably our word, though it has been given a mock-Latin form (with participial *-ant*) in keeping with the macaronic language of the lines in which it occurs.[1]

These lines were first printed in 1845 by Thomas Wright, in his *Reliquiae Antiquae* (Vol. I, pp. 91-92). Since they have not been reprinted, I shall present them here, before discussing their contents, date, and some problems concerning them.

1   fflen flyys and freris / populum domini male caedunt,
        þustlis and breris / crescentia gramina ledunt.
        Xriste, nolens guerras, / sed cuncta pace tueris,
        Destrue per terras / breris flen fly3es & freris.
5   fflen fly3es and freris / Foul falle hem þys fyften 3eris,
        ffor'non þat her ys / louit flen fly3es ne freris.
        Fratres carmeli / nauigant in a both apud Eli;
        Non sunt in celi / quia gxddbov xxkxx3t pg ifmk—
        Omnes drencherunt / quia sterisman non habuerunt.
10   ffratres cum knyuys / goþ about and txxkx3v
          nfookt xx3xkt.
        Ex Eli veniens presenti / sede locatur,
        Nec rex nec sapiens, / Salomon tamen vocatur.
        Pediculus cum sex / pedibus me mordet vbique;
14   Si possum capere / tokl tobl debet ipsem habere.

Lines 1-6 here attack friars generally, while lines 7-10 verberate the Carmelite Friars of Ely particularly. Wright made the interesting point that in his day, "two lines . . . are still popular among schoolboys in the following modified form: *Tres fratres coeli navigabant roundabout Ely; Omnes drownderunt qui swimaway non potuerunt*," and he further remarked that "the expressions concealed by the cypher . . . are rather gross, and do not speak much for the morals of the Carmelites of Ely."[2] This remark set me to examining the cipher, of course, and I succeeded in decoding it. It merely involves substitution of the next letter in the alphabet, so that if the encipherer began with an *a*, he would write *b*, if with a *b*, he wrote *c*, and so on.[3] Thus, in line 8, *gxddbov xxkxx3t pg ifmk* is written for *fuccant uuiuis of Heli*, with *fuccant* formed on the same lines as *drencher-unt* in the next line (9). The friars of Ely, according to the poem, will never get to heaven, because they are *fuccant* the wives of Ely. To this elegant criticism the rhymer ads that they will all drown because they have no *steersman*—no doubt a double entendre—and further, that friars with knives are going around and swiving men's wives, this being of course the same assertion made by most critics of the ubiquitous medieval friars, as for instance in Chaucer's General Prologue to the *Canterbury Tales*, where he describes the Friar as having his hood *ay farsed ful of knyves / And pynnes, for to yeven faire wyves.*

We observe that our medieval scribe has enciphered not only *fuccant*, but also *suuiuit*. Obviously these words were synonymous at this time, and the modern version had not yet pushed out the older *swive* as yet.[4] But this brings us to the important question: Just when was the poem written, or at least when was it written into the manuscript?

Inspection of the script and hand shows that it could have been almost any time in the middle or later fifteenth century. Use of þ (thorn) and 3 (yogh) would seem to rule out a dating in later sixteenth century, but it is not possible to assign a precise date on palaeographic grounds alone, and I have not had time to look for historical references or other evidence that might pin down the date of transcription. Wright said the date was "of the fifteenth century," and this is Max Förster's opinion also (*Anglia* vol. 42, 1918, pp. 198, 207), though Förster specifies that the MS. is of the latter part of the century, i.e., ca. 1450–1500. And editors of the *Middle English Dictionary* have also assigned a date of ca. 1500 to the MS.; in my opinion, the date is palaeographically more likely to have been ca. 1450–75 than 1500. In any event, it is almost certainly as early as Dunbar's poem, and very probably earlier by some years.

But a final problem must be spoken to: Why did the scribe encipher those passages? One might simply think he was keeping these naughty words away from uninitiated eyes, and perhaps that is the case. But if so, then why did he also use the cipher in line 14 (the last one given above) for the words describing what he will do to the lice biting

431

him if he can catch them? Those words, as we see by deciphering *tokl tobl*, are just *snik snak*, and it is hard to see why the poet or scribe should have thought them obscene enough to put the figleaf of his cipher over them. Perhaps, of course, *snick-snack* was accompanied by an obscene gesture, of a sort not hard to imagine, and the audience would have rolled in the aisles at the thought of doing that to a body-louse.

Which brings us, surely, to the realization that the cipher is meant not to conceal as much as to reveal. Like a bikini, it is meant to draw attention rather than baffle it. *Snik-snak* put straightforwardly onto the page is not half so funny as *tokl-tobl* becomes, when one has the *Aha!* pleasure added to the *Yeah!* one: it is the slight stammer of the humorist before he gets the right word out, making the joke funnier. Now, I might be wrong: but the cipher is so *very* simple, and the whole point of a riddle is to have an answer, after all. So it is my opinion that the medieval scribe here was not really showing how shameful the words seemed to him but adding a little extra spice to the joke of using the words about friars. Instead of *obeying* a taboo, that is, the scribe was *exploiting* it: this is a case of what Allen Walker Read (in *Language* vol. 40 no. 2, April–June 1964, pp. 162–66) has called "a type of ostentatious taboo." In fact, what the scribe was doing is very like what we do when we print "f--k" while expecting that every reader will know that the word meant is—well, you-know-what! We have lately enriched our vocabularies in this area, too, with the word *bleep* (*bleeping*), which has replaced earlier *blank*, *blankety-blank*, not to mention *s.o.b.* and the like. Who knows? We may soon see, with returning censorship, ciphers replacing these acronyms and replacements.

NOTES

[1] I was able to inspect the manuscript (Harley 3362), and here acknowledge the kindness of the staff of the Students Room of the British Library in providing access as well as the marvelous services and facilities for study which make it such a pleasure to work there.

[2] *Reliquiae Antiquae* Vol. I, p. 91.

[3] A cipher very similar to this occurs in B.M. MS. Sloane 351, fol. 15, from which Wright prints it (*op. cit.* Vol. II, p. 15). Wright says this MS. also is "of the fifteenth century."

[4] The definitive history of the obscenity symbol, including its

etymology, is now being worked out by several scholars, notably Allen Walker Read. It may well be of Flemish origin. Certainly one would want to know the details of how it entered English and why it came to replace *swive*. It appears that the latter word was indeed perceived as a gross term, and its written appearances seem confined primarily to invective or comic contexts; the first *OED* citation for *swive* is for the gerund *swiving*, used in the "Song of Lewes" (written ca. 1265 A.D.) as a term of contempt: the poet says that Richard of Cornwall spent all his treasure on *swiving*, and clearly it was not just uxorious activity that the poet had in mind. Chaucer used *swive* only to describe adulterous or clandestine fornication, and one can see how a word in such a smelly role will easily give way to another more foreign and vigorous: it is much easier and funnier to swear in a foreign language, as Americans have found with the British *bloody*, for instance.

VAN GOGH, VAN GOGH, VAN GOCH

It seems rather rough
On Vincent Van Guff

When those in the know
Call him Vincent Van Go

For unless I'm way off
He was Vincent Van Gogh.

Joe Ecclesine
Rye, New York

Gloria in extremis . . . .

The County Council of Buckinghamshire, England, has struck a low blow against women's lib. The municipal parking garage has restrooms, side by side, marked "Gentlemen" and "Disabled," respectively. *Sic transit Gloria Steinem.*

The Seat of Our Affections

Clair Schulz
Clinton, Wisconsin

It is impossible to say when I first developed this fascination with bodies, but once implanted in my brain there was no ousting it. Some may call it an unnatural interest in an unpleasant subject and they may be right. But that won't stop me from recording the results of my impassioned study of anatomy.

Those who expect to find the confessions of a voyeur or a coroner here had best look elsewhere; my interest in the body pertains to the sentiments that go with it for it is the passions that attend the body that give it life. Even Frankenstein realized this. If he had found his creation devoid of emotion, he would have stamped *Reject* on his forehead and torn him limb from limb (being careful to tear along the perforations).

What began as a casual inquiry during my collegiate days has now become an avocation. It has sharpened all my senses, above all the sense of hearing. Most people are not even aware that I possess this sensitivity. As long as conversations stay away from bodies, I appear to be just another disinterested party. But let someone drag in a torso or limb and slap some emotion on it and I will digest every morsel.

Traditionally, people have assigned the emotions to three parts of the body: the stomach, the heart, and the head. The stomach is the source of gut reactions and it occasionally serves as a gateway to the heart. The heart, because of its association with the soul, has become a symbol of love and spirit in expressions such as "Peg o' my heart" and "She's got a lot of heart," variations of the latter being given so much mileage by comedians that one could attribute the death of burlesque to heart failure. And, when someone says, "She's got a good head on her shoulders" or "Let's put our heads together," he is obviously referring to the center of the intellect.

For years the three lived in harmony, each carrying out its separate duties and each being content in its own realm. Oh, occasionally there are some rumors of an uprising. A dish of ice cream might cause the stomach to go to a person's head or excitement carry the heart as far as the throat, but they soon fade away. They've always known their place.

But now a usurper has appeared. It was there all the time, but few paid any attention to it. Gradually, in degrees so small as to be imperceptible to most people, it has crept into the language and now rivals not only other parts of the body for dominance but also challenges all the words in certain individual's vocabularies for frequency of use.

How does it manifest itself? In many forms.

Perhaps it appears most frequently in situations of anger. My research has shown that very often during crises one person will request another to place some unidentifiable *it* in a specific location. Paradoxically, if this proves ineffectual, this same person who made the request will often ask the other person to kiss this portion of his own anatomy in a gesture of apparent goodwill.

Or it could be something just short of anger that causes its invocation. If a series of events brings about a feeling of irritation within a person, he is likely to say that any person or thing is causing him discomfort. At one time this arbitrarily placed affliction was said to take root in the neck. Lately, the sensors seem to have dropped about two feet.

It seems not only sensitive to varying levels of exasperation but to changes in temperature as well. Indeed, it can readily claim the title of the Body's Thermometer. Apparently, it reaches 32° faster than any other part of the body. The nose was formerly considered to be a reliable instrument, but I can't recall its accuracy being tested since a cold November day when a little girl I know looked up long enough from her hula hoop to tell her mother, "I'm freezing my nose off." The increased dependence upon the newer device may result in more people being accused of wasting time by standing around while checking the temperature with their fingers.

Not only has this part developed into the body's weather station; it also strives to become its classroom. At a time when learning was believed to originate in the brain it was not unusual to hear a parent say to a child, "If you don't mind me, I'm going to give you a good hit across the side of the head." Despite the pleading of educators against training by punishment, threats are still used to control conduct or to suggest correction. However, current usage indicates that certain traits can be taught without risking cranial lumps or welts on the backs of hands. The foot now serves a tutorial purpose once reserved for the hickory stick, although the sector of the body receiving the instruction has

435

not been altered. The word *good* remains in the incantation delivered by the teacher and it usually is followed by the word *swift*. Some football coaches have found films of the activity *too* swift, and so they have employed slow motion techniques to illustrate the importance of keeping the head down and follow-through to their field goal kickers.

This movement to take over the functions of the head seems to be gaining momentum. There was a time when people, in describing periods of emotional stress, would say that they were working or worrying their heads off. No more. This change of address for the sentiments has resulted in a substantial decrease in the number of mothers who ask their children how hard they have been playing.

Even the location of the sense of humor has been questioned. Just as people centuries ago were certain where the four humors of the body were to be found, modern man seemed confident that gibes and gambols resided within the chopfallen or chopful walls of the skull. A person who showed unrestrained amusement was said to be "laughing his head off." The popularity of this saying is being threatened by a similar expression, although it is doubtful that the newer form will achieve supremacy because smiles are seen only on faces.

Whether the head will retain its distinctive features or whether it will lose its leadership and become assimilated is a question posterity will answer. There is no doubt that it has lost ground. I find myself cringing involuntarily when I hear a forlorn gambler forgo the standard "I lost my head" for a more desperate statement of despair. And sometimes at night I conjure up surrealistic scenes involving guillotines as I consider how the course of French history would have been altered had this interchange of linguistic function been prevalent during the days of the Reign of Terror.

Despite these disturbing developments, I continue my self-appointed role as the body's watchdog. My research has taken me to "The Miller's Tale," and in the near future I may be able to conclusively relate Chaucer with this newest phenomenon. It will be published as soon as I can account for the lag of six centuries.

I listen, as before, but my friends say that lately I have replaced my indifferent expression with one bordering on bewilderment. I have the feeling that they are tossing their members into the conversation to see if the old eyes, ears, nose, and throat man will come alive. Perhaps they read my face correctly; maybe they are humoring me. All I know for certain is that the next time I see a man holding his wrist and asking the question "Heads or tails?" I will be able to sympathize with his confusion.

EPISTOLAE

I just read the first issue of VERBATIM on my husband's subscription. Generally, I enjoyed it. However, the lead article, "Hear Finish Before (Pause) You?", contains a serious error.

Cued Speech is not a sign language system as stated by the author. Cued Speech is the antithesis of sign language in that it is a means of providing a visible analog to *spoken* English. Because the hand is involved, many persons who have not read the very clearly written material by its inventor, Dr. Orin Cornett, a Vice President of Gallaudet University for the Deaf, naively assume it is a manual or sign language system.

M. Carolyn Jones, Ph.D.
New Orleans, Louisiana

I was very interested in two pieces in the current VERBATIM—the one on cockfighting and all its gifts to English, and your comments on Aristides' comments on *6,000 Words*.

As to the former, I am simply astounded. As to the latter, I have to say that I couldn't agree with you more completely. Why do supposedly intelligent people think that dictionaries should be school marms? I remember the flurry when *Webster's Third International* first came out—and Rex Stout's Nero Wolfe threw his copy into the fire! How unutterably silly. And yet it keeps on going.

In fact, I like the vitality of English vocabulary nowadays. Mind, I say vocabulary, not usage; but as to usage, in my memory of things (admittedly only half a century) it has never been very good, overall, and I think back to themes my father wrote in elementary school in 1900: even then, in a good school, the style was terribly stilted (although "correct"), and I think I prefer liveliness with error to correctness without life. You may disagree.

Charles Van Doren
Chicago, Illinois

The Growing Use and Abuse of *Literally*

Elaine F. Tankard and
James W. Tankard, Jr.
Austin, Texas

We have noticed a growing use of the word *literally* in the past year. Recently we heard a well-educated friend use the word three times in the course of an evening's conversation. *Literally* is also showing up more and more frequently in the mass media, unfortunately with a growing lack of precision. Theodore M. Bernstein writes in *The Careful Writer: A Modern Guide to English Usage* that "literally means true to the exact meaning of the words." Many people misuse the word to mean *figuratively* or *virtually*. Others just use it as an unnecessary superlative.

We have found examples in the following three categories of usage:

INACCURATE (AND OFTEN ABSURD):

> An official at the U.S. Government Printing Office wrote, " . . . we were literally swamped with your orders."
>
> A brochure advertising calendars stated, ". . . we know that you are literally flooded with calendars from which to choose . . ."
>
> A TV commercial for a teriyaki sauce spoke of "a flavor that literally sparkles."
>
> In the James Bond film *The Man with the Golden Gun*, one of the characters says the highest bidder for solar energy "will literally have the sun in his pocket."
>
> A noted Black author said in a speech, ". . . for generations the talents of Black people were literally poured down the drain."
>
> A psychologist reviewing for a journal wrote that a book was "literally mind expanding."
>
> Another psychologist reviewing a book for the same journal wrote that it presented a consensus that "literally scares the hell out of me."
>
> An editor for a different journal wrote the following ponderous sentence: "During the past few years, scientific interest in and attention to the nonverbal components of human behavior and the relationship of human beings to their physical environment have literally mushroomed."
>
> *The New York Times Book Review* contained this state-

438

ment: "Following literally in the projected footsteps of Harper & Row, . . . we headed out to California to see if the grass was any greener."

A minister told a city council his telephone "has literally rung off the hook" since a newspaper published a series about massage parlors.

ACCURATE BUT UNNECESSARY:

A psychologist reviewing for a journal wrote: "This is a most readable book. It is literally exciting."

A high-brow magazine wrote in a letter seeking subscribers: "After screening literally hundreds of mailing lists, we came up with a relative handful of names like yours . . ."

A labor leader said during a TV interview: "We've just literally got to reduce the work load."

CORRECT:

A news magazine wrote about Gary Gilmore: "The sentence of death was carried out, eighteen minutes late, only after an extraordinary round of desperation appeals — the last of which was turned down by the U.S. Supreme Court as the prisoner literally sat facing execution."

Sometimes a careful writer will use a word like *actually* where a weaker writer would use *literally*. The following is from a short story by Ann Beattie in *The New Yorker*: "It hurt her badly, made her actually dizzy with surprise and shame, and since then, no matter who the guests are, she never feels quite at ease on the weekends."

The fact that we found only one instance in the "correct" category makes us conclude that it is difficult to use *literally* accurately. We would argue that the word should be saved for those rare cases when something that is usually metaphorical or figurative is actually true.

EPISTOLAE

May I submit the title of an award received by a good friend from Manzano AF Base, N.M., in July 1968: *Defense Atomic Support Agency Suggestion Award Certificate*.

Lester Noyes
University of Colorado
Boulder, Colorado

Illicit Threesomes

Elaine Von Bruns
Middlebury, Vermont

Introduce a legal word couple to a third word and you may set into language a newly meaningful relationship.

Sometimes the single will cling to one partner of the couple, sometimes to the other. And sometimes, if he's built like one of the partners, only bigger, he'll break up the couple and claim the other partner for himself. In two of the cases mentioned below, the newcomer brought along friends, linked by hyphens.

Occasionally, the interplay will change the appearance and even the character of the partners. For better? For worse? You be the judge.

COUPLE	THREESOMES
ball and chain	*ball and chain*STORE 'shopping mart for sadomasochists'
comb and brush	*comb and brush*-OFF 'a new way of parting'
Thanksgiving turkey	*Thanksgiving turkey* TROT 'Pilgrim frolic'
tar and feather	*tar and feather*BED "You've made your bed, now lie in it," said the Patriot to the Tory.
draw and quarter	*draw and quarter*BACK 'occupations of an artistic athlete'
scotch on the rocks	HOP*scotch on the rocks* 'game for the inebriated'
running nose	*running nose* DIVE 'hangout for snifflers'
dinner pail	*dinner pale*FACE 'nervous guest'
threadbare	*threadbear*HUG 'lukewarm welcome'
stop and go	*stop and go*-GO 'traffic signals from a lissome policewoman'

black-and-blue	*black and blue*LAWS
	'the punishing edict of
	never on a Sunday'
milk and honey	*milk and honey*MOONERS
	'Prohibition-era
	newlyweds'
bow and arrow	*bow*TIE *and arrow*
	'Robin Hood goes formal'

. . . sometimes he brings along friends:

fish and chips	*fish and chips*-OFF-THE-OLD-
	BLOCK
	'back-home lunch'
bird in the hand	*bird in the hand*-ME-DOWN

. . . and sometimes he comes between them and claims a partner for himself:

cloak and dagger	*cloak and* DAGUERREOTYPE
	'old photo of Zorro'
barbershop pole	*barbershop* POLTERGEIST
	'spirit in the hair tonic'
bottleneck	*bottle*NECROPHILIA
	'unmentionable interaction
	with nonreturnables'
sock hop	CAS*sock hop*
	'fun for clergymen'
skin and bones	*skin and* BONSAI
	'Japanese strip show'
cash and carry	*cash and* CARRION
	'profits from graverobbing'

Do you know of any other swinging word couples-about-town?

EPISTOLAE

I enjoyed reading "Menu Barbarisms" [III, 2]. Here are two examples suggesting that the problems are international. On a recent trip to South America I found the following items on menus: *Aristu* 'Irish Stew'; *Pitipua* 'petits pois.'

Guy P. Pfeffermann
Chevy Chase, Maryland

441

To Understand America (and Americans) . . . .

John O. Herbold II
Lakewood, California

Story has it that in the early days of the 20th century a college professor exclaimed: "To understand America, you must first understand baseball." And he was probably right, for outside of the horse ("you can lead a horse to water . . .," "horse of a different color", "cart before the horse" etc.,) no other single concrete noun has contributed as many terms as has the "horsehide" sport.

Even Americans who have rarely seen a baseball game will find themselves sprinkling many of the following terms into their daily conversation:

1. He was born with two strikes against him.
2. He couldn't get to first-base with that girl.
3. He sure threw me a curve that time.
4. I'll take a rain-check on it.
5. He went to bat for me.
6. I liked him right off the bat.
7. He was way out in left-field on that one.
8. He's a foul ball.
9. I think you're way off base on that.
10. It was a smash hit.
11. Let's take a seventh-inning stretch.
12. I hope to touch all the bases on this report.
13. Could you pinch-hit for me?
14. He doesn't even know who's on first.
15. I just call 'em as I see 'em.
16. He's only a bush-leaguer.
17. Major League all the way.
18. We'll hit 'em where they ain't.
19. He was safe a mile.
20. He has a lot on the ball.
21. He really dropped the ball that time.
22. We'll rally in the ninth.
23. No game's ever over until the last man's out.

And is there any term in our language more synonymous with failure than "to strike out"?

Had President Nixon stayed in office a while longer, it's possible that football might have begun to approach baseball in the number of terms used (*game plan*, *kick-off*, etc.); but the Nixon *team* got its *signals crossed*, so now *it's a whole new ball game*.

Baseball, like other occupations, has its own particular terminology and nomenclature, understood only by the esoteric few and not by the everyday fans (*fan* from *fanatic*).

For instance, your grandfather would speak of Christy Mathewson's *fadeway* or Walter Johnson's *inshoot*. Three-fingered Brown threw an *outdrop*, and in those days you might knock an opposing pitcher *out of the box* (though rarely one of the aforementioned trio).

Your father spoke of Bob Feller *throwing heat*, while Tommy Bridges had a good *deuce*, *jug*, *hook*, or *Uncle Charlie*—all synonyms for the curve-ball. Jim Tobin threw a *butterfly* pitch because he *pulled the string on it*, thus making it come in slow.

Today the pitches are pretty much the same, but the terminology has altered some, largely because of the influx of Black players.

The fast ball becomes *the express*; the hard curve is a *slider*; and the off-speed pitch is simply referred to as *the change-up*.

And whether you call a high, hard one thrown at the batter's head a *purpose pitch*, a *knockdown pitch*, or a *bean ball*, the message remains the same: *Metala en su oreja* ('stick it in his ear!').

As mentioned, the Black players have brought in some colorful terms of their own. A pitcher who throws hard can *really bring it*. The catcher for some strange reason is often called a *back catcher*. A good hitter is described as being a *baaaaddd* hitter, and *nobody walks but the mailman*. A player who excels can *get it done*, and if he hits well, then *he can really stick it*.

One never knows what some Black players are going to do with verbs. Some omit them altogether: *You out*. While others use the word *be* in its pure form: *You be out, brother*.

Chicano baseballers love to talk in slang terms, often in Spanish. Hitting the ball well means that you got good *wood* on it. But they have no real word for *bat*, so they call it *lena* or 'wood.' One of their most derogatory terms—often directed toward umpires—is the word *guy* used in place of the name. "Hey, guy, wise up, you cabeza de melon" ('melon head'). If they really get upset, they'll call you *tonto*

443

('dumb') or *estupido* ('stupid'). When speaking English, the Latin ball players can likewise be most amusing: "Hit to me the ball." "His fast ball—he doesn't have any," and "he throws several quick."

I can remember losing one game to a Latin team when a homerun got lost in the bushes enabling the Mexican team to defeat us 11-9. After the game I exclaimed, loud enough for the victors to hear, "We'd have won the game had it not been for those dumb bushes."

A bit of Latin wisdom followed which I've never forgotten: "Well," replied the player who'd hit the homer, "the bushes—they are the same for everybody."

Everyone knows that the trite clichés of the Grantland Rice era have been largely eliminated. Today a bat is a bat, not a "mace," "club," "willow," or "stick." The plate is no longer a "dish," "pentagon," or "home." Umpires are umpires—not "arbiters" or "men in blue"—and we no longer are besieged with such terms as "hot corner," "keystone," "Texas Leaguer," "flyhawk," "maskman," and "grasscutter."

And baseballers still retain two other traditional traits: one, they abbreviate everything they can—DP, RBI, ribbie, "two," BP (batting practice), PFP (pitchers' fielding practice), K (strike out), etc. And two, they always use the historical present tense in retelling tales of the past: "I was waiting on the on-deck circle, and Williams is hitting. Well, Cleveland has Bobby Feller going today, and he's mad at Williams because Williams hit a homer off him the inning before, so while I'm standing there . . . ."

An interesting note is that most of America's teens and pre-teens are pretty basic in their language—a bat is simply a bat, a pitcher's a pitcher, and so on. Even the Japanese have borrowed most of the American terms with slight alterations. They play *dabulheddas*, and they have an outfield consisting of a *left-o*, *cent-o*, and *right-o*, plus a *thard-o*, *show-to*, *secand-o*, and *fast-o*.

But as mentioned, the American youngsters are not really sports idol worshipers the way their fathers and grandfathers were; and while sports may open many doors to them, they also open numerous mouths in a big yawn. We find this to be pretty much "par for the course." Oops! That's a golf term, and that's "one strike against it," all of which makes it a mixed metaphor or something.

The Sinister Side of the Language

J. Frank Schulman
Houston, Texas

Why does *left* get such a bad deal from language? In most languages *left* has unpleasant associations.

In English, *left* has associations of political radicalism. It also means 'abandoned.' *Left-handed* means 'unflattering, dubious, insincere.' *Right*, on the other hand, means 'correct, good, or proper.' The German words *links* ('left') and *rechts* ('right') have similar meanings.

In Latin, the word for *left* is *sinister*. Sinister connotes 'evil, cunning, scheming.' The word for *right* is *dexter*, from which derives our word *dexterous*, meaning 'skillful, clever, or artful.'

In French, *gauche* means, besides 'left,' 'awkward, tactless, clumsy, lacking in social grace.' *Droit*, 'right,' has the usual meanings of 'correct, good, and proper,' and also means 'law.' Even more to the point is that *gauche* means the same as *maladroit* ('bad right'). In German, *linkisch* means 'maladroit.' *Gouache* also refers to a school of painting in which paint was piled high on the canvas. It was considered ugly and in bad taste.

In Spanish, too, *izquierda* ('left') has the same unpleasant connotations, including political radicalism, and *derecho* ('right') means 'law,' as it does in French. The same is true of the Portuguese words *esquierda* and *derecho*.

In no language does the word for *right* have these unpleasant connotations. The languages seem to have conspired against the left-handed of the world. Everything from can openers to golf clubs is designed for the right-handed. The single exception seems to be the typewriter, the keyboard of which favors the left-handed. Perhaps Christopher Sholes, its inventor, was left-handed.

One suspects there is a sinister plot by the linguists. We can speculate about the reasons for this moral distinction between left and right. The political difference comes from the habit in France and Germany of Communists sitting on the speaker's left in Parliament, and Fascists sitting on the speaker's right. Another reason may be that left-handed people were considered peculiar, perhaps victims of some evil force. Until quite recently it was thought best to retrain left-handed people. They often became clumsy as a result. A doc-

445

toral dissertation concluded that serious psychological consequences follow from this retraining.*

Clearly, the word *left* has been dealt a left-handed blow. Is this right?

---

*Dra. Bettina Katzenstein, University of Hamburg, 1930.

EPISTOLAE

Norman R. Shapiro had a number of interesting things to say [III, 3], but for me his remarks about *bravo* were not among them. Shapiro writes, "When an Italian shouts *bravo*, for example, he isn't just voicing indiscriminate onomatopoeia; he is using a bona fide adjective. (Hence the feminine, *brava*, to a deserving diva.)" My problem with that is not only a bit of puzzlement over *bravo* as onomatopoeia, but also the fear that he is helping to perpetuate a most unfortunate practice.

Bravo comes in two forms. As an adjective, *bravo* is indeed inflected; male and female were they created. And as an adjective, *bravo -a*, means, according to Cassell's, "able, clever, skillful; capable; honest; plucky."

But this is not the whole story. *Bravo* also is entered in this fashion: "bravo! *inter*. Bravo! Fine!" This is immediately followed by "Da Bravo! Courage!" Obviously, in its incarnation as interjection, *bravo* is *not* inflected. The divine diva bows to the same *bravo* as does the towering tenor.

Among American dictionaries, *Random House* declares, under the entry, *bravo*: "*interj*. well done! good!" *Webster's Third* does have an entry for *brava*, which states: "Bravo—used interjectionally in applauding a woman." The OED Universal edition says: "Bravo" *int* and *sb*, 1761 [It. *bravo* superl *bravissimo* (also used).] Capital! Well done! Hence, as *sb*, a cheer."

To turn to the review of *The Phrase-Dropper's Handbook*, the commentator dropped one phrase all the way: It's *Revenons à nos moutons*. One hopes "Revenons à moutons" is not in the book, but rather is a typographical error.

Haven't we enough problems in our language?

Wesley First
New York, New York

The New Orthography

Ellen Perkins
San Diego, California

One of the heart-warming scenes of *How Green Was My Valley* has young Huw, driven by his schoolmaster's sneering at a mispronunciation, finally erupt: "I do not think it a shame to have read more words than I ever heard pronounced." An inspiriting moment for those who love language and learning. Consider it also a key to coping with the rapid progress of our loved language toward The English of the Future. Our high school students are pointing the way. For they do not think it a shame to use more words than they have ever seen written. All we need to do is loosen up a few prejudices and follow their lead.

The commonest principle in creative spelling is the phonetic one, of course. *Mestup*, since that's what the rules of spelling and punctuation are, has a certain logic, as do *froogley* ("These Japanese lived very froogley") and *next store* ("We lived next store to Joey"). G. B. Shaw himself could not have done much better than *skwormed*, *angches*, and *Pencil vanea*, all created, as are all the new spellings herein, by students. Or *perrigraff*. For that one we have to scrap our exhilarating mini-lecture on Greek roots, but it never did much for *phycology*, either. As our young writers would be quick to say, "*Ph*, *ps*, Greek, shmeek, you know what they mean." And if you are willing to discard mere pickiness, you know what *taken for granite* and *scuenting* mean, too. Or why not the grand flair of *nateral fenoninum*? One would swear, if I may quote, that's the way *it supostube*.

These wholesome simplifications may arise from a widespread opinion that the language is well enough supplied with fancy forms and spellings. However, disagreement is the stuff of progress; happily, someone out there prefers the gentility of *no doubtly*, the delicacy of *coughen*, and the pure flourish, I guess, of *laight*. There is a taste for the elegant in the old U.S. of A. *surprizing le enought*.

We come now to what can only be seen as phycological fenoninums. Not being one of those head doctors whose title I can no longer spell (conditioning, accidental or otherwise, being what it is), I can but lay these before you as they came before me. They are exact in every detail of diction and punctuation; I would not trifle with scholarly accuracy

447

in such a matter.

1. Although our societies are formed by man, he isn't able to flunksuate with it's pace.
2. Everything was fine until one day a man and a lay drove up in a van.
3. As a catholic priest one spends most of his time teaching, praying, giving sermons, and absorbing sins given out by daily confessors. (This was not the student whose paper included a paragraph on the rituals of *whorship*.)

And moving ever deeper into the psyche,

4. The West's women's doubles team brought the team back from a four-game deficate.

Perhaps properly trained researchers will get funding for a study of these. Surely they belong not to a teacher but to a *shitisatris* (sp?).

Well. To end on a positive—even exuberant—note, a whole glorious welling up of creativity exists that cannot really be classified, though by backing off enough one can see it as a kind of simplification—beating the universe to the ultimate entropy. For example, there is the man who had extra income aside from his job because "*he was a member of the notor republic*." Not a *horrobile* mistake, but art in language. And a *chairtable* is not a piece of furniture but an adjective meaning generous and kindly. A *chesser-drawers*, on the other hand, is furniture, as is a *chester doors*, but you would have known that all right, even if I *hadaded* told you. *Tenashoes* equals *tenershoes*; a world of possibilities opens up here. And a *stewdress* works on an airplane, after she *graduwayts* from training.

Maybe it's significant that these alternative spellings developed in Southern California, where free spirits flower like the gorgeous *bogangadilia*. Let's hear from the rest of the country. Four cheers for the future and *uter caoues*!

EPISTOLAE

An addition to John G. Caffrey's "Menu Barbarisms" [III, 3]: A restaurant near Joplin, Mo. serves "ho-made bread." As *ho* is used by prostitutes for 'whore,' I am puzzled whether this bread is made at the home of a *Mo-Ho*.

Reinhold Aman
Waukesha, Wisconsin

The Encompassing Circle

Arthur J. Morgan
New York, New York

It is one of those ironies which are not infrequent in language that two such disparate, not to say opposed, expressions as Ku Klux Klan and "kike" should share a common derivation. But let us trace them individually.

The vituperative and contemptuous appellation *kike*, started, as such epithets often do, in a fairly innocuous way. In the last century there were a great many Jewish peddlers and tinkers traveling the byroads and hinterlands of the country. Many of these men were illiterate, at least in English. When called upon to sign his name, being unable to do so, the Jewish peddler often had to "make his mark."

However, for religious reasons, he would not make a cross, but offered to draw a circle instead. The Yiddish for a circle was *keikel*, which in time was corrupted to *kike*, and as often happens with ethnic appellations, deteriorated into a slur when its origin was forgotten. (Cf. *gringo*, from "Green grow the lilacs, O," a song that was popular among the American soldiers during the troubles with Mexico. Many other examples could be given.)

Now, how about Ku Klux Klan? Eric Partridge attributes the first part, Kuklux, to a distortion of the Greek *kyklos*, 'circle.' The deliberate distortion, and the use of κ's and x's were intended to make the name more mysterious and frightening, but it merely meant 'Circle Clan' to start.

But that very word *kyklos* was the origin of the Yiddish *keikel*. Most Yiddish words come from German, but circle in German is *Zirkel* or *Kreis*; this word *keikel* goes back to the Jewish dialect Yevanic, analogous to Yiddish, except that the vocabulary was Greek, rather than German. Like Yiddish, the written language used Hebrew characters.

In fact, during the long years of the diaspora, the wandering Jews have had a dozen dialects, written in Hebrew letters, but with words derived from the language of their current (or previous) hosts. Thus a book which looks like Hebrew may actually be in Persian, Arabic, Berber, Greek, French or Provençal, Italian or Spanish. The latter, called Ladino, is still spoken and even written, today. It's a wide, wide circle.

Who Do You Believe?

For those readers who consider "incorrect" grammar indefensible, the first of the following letters provides an interesting (if indefensible) rationale: it is a good example of solecistic (as contrasted with syllogistic) reasoning. The second letter here reproduced expresses a rational approach to the problem, puristic attitudes notwithstanding.

Mrs. Dorrice R. Morrow
Swarthmore, PA   November 13, 1973
Dear Mrs. Morrow:

We are aware that your dislike for the interrogative "Who are we pleasing?" is sometimes shared by others. Some people insist that this sentence should read, "Whom are we pleasing?" But the use of the pronoun in an interrogative sentence, as here, needs to be distinguished from the pronoun in "For whom the bell tolls" or "to whom it may concern."

When "who" is used as an interrogative pronoun, it is unnatural English to use its objective form, even when it is the object of a verb or preposition. Noah Webster said that "Whom did you speak to?" is "hardly English at all" but . . . "is a corruption, and all the grammars that can be found will not extend the use of the phrase beyond the walls of a college."

When the word stands before a verb, as in "Who am I trying to please?" the nominative form is preferred. The form "whom" is required when the word follows a preposition ("To whom am I to send the letter?").

The invariable form "who" in interrogative constructions was found in older and early in modern literary English. Shakespeare used it. Speaking of this, the noted grammarian Curme says, "The use of the nominative *who* as object is never ambiguous since . . . 'who did they meet?' indicates that *who* . . . modifies the verb and cannot be the subject?"

Sincerely yours,
The Editors

Dear Mrs. Morrow: May 29, 1975
Thank you for calling to our attention the misuse of "who-whom" in the Monitor. Unfortunately, this seems to be a fairly common error in today's world. We do not condone it in any way and try to be alert against it. But we do not always succeed.

We try to uphold the highest standards of proper grammatical usage in the Monitor. Alert readers are of great help in motivating us to maintain our high standards and we appreciate your concern.

Sincerely,
Dewey F Ray
Chief of Copy Desk

The reference to George O. Curme draws one to his two books, *Parts of Speech and Accidence*, Heath, 1935, and *Syntax*, Heath, 1931: the latter contains the quotation cited by "The Editors" of *The Christian Science Monitor*. It is on page 101 in a section that concludes with the comment, "In general, however, the use of *who* for *whom* is receding in all functions in the literary language." Such usage is also called "careless language" by Curme.

A further comment appears in *Parts of Speech*: 'I don't know *who* (instead of *whom*) he plays with.'

The relative pronoun always has the case form required by the construction of the clause in which it stands . . . . In ['I will go with *whoever* I like,' *who* is the object of the preposition *with*. We should withstand the strong drift here toward the modern forms and use the more expressive older ones. [pp. 166-7]

As we have in general abandoned the use of the old inflectional endings in favor of modern means of expression, there is also here in colloquial speech a strong tendency to employ modern forms—. . . : '*Who* (instead of *whom*) did you meet?' '*Who* did you give it to?' . . . . In choice language the tendency is to withstand the very strong drift here toward the modern forms and use the more expressive older ones. [p. 171]

There is no mistaking how Curme expressed himself, and the quotation in The Editors' letter is an explanation of why *who* replaces *whom* in certain constructions: it certainly cannot be construed as having received the grammarian's approval.

[*Incidentally*, VERBATIM *is planning to publish a reprint of Curme's two books, one of the best and most complete reference grammars of contemporary English, rife with examples from literature. It would help greatly if readers could provide us with some indication of their possible interest in having such works in their libraries. Both books have been out of print since 1963.*—Editor]

Exceptions to the Rule

Gary S. Felton
Los Angeles, California

All of us have grown up learning countless rules or laws of nature and the universe. We learn these rules or laws well and find eventually that most of the time they hold up and operate as expected. Nevertheless, as with most things in life, people encounter inconsistency about rules or laws and the domains they refer to. Often there is some exception.

One way offered to deal with, allow for, or rationalize the exception is to state that there *are* some exceptions and then, where applicable, learn them, understand them, and accept them. Another approach is to continue to analyze exceptions and "fit" them into the rules. Some people are more earthy about such matters, however, and treat with levity the fact that life is not always consistent and existence is not always predictable.

One of the outgrowths of this latter approach is a number of pseudo-scientific statutes or laws. These statements incorporate known experience with generalized expectancies about existence and give us something to laugh about at ourselves and our universe. Such "laws," as they generally are referred to, usually are named after their discoverer. In giving us a fascinating and amusing look at ourselves, the laws relate to several domains of our day-to-day experience, particularly scientific research and the study of behavior, and are presented below for interested readers.

Laws

Agnes Allen's Law.[7] Almost anything is easier to get into than out of.

The Bougerre Factor[1] [pronounced "bugger"; same as *The Soothing Factor*]. Characterized as changing the equation to fit the universe (mathematically similar to *The Damping Factor*) and has the characteristic of dropping the subject under discussion to zero importance.

Bromiley's Maxim.[2] What's not worth doing is not worth doing well.

Diddle Coefficient.[1] Characterized as changing things so that universe and equation appear to fit without requiring a change in either (combination of *The Bougerre Factor* and *Finagle's Constant*).

Fetridge's Law.[6] Important things that are supposed to happen do not happen, especially when people are looking or, conversely, things that are supposed to not happen do happen, expecially when people are looking.

Finagle's Constant.[1] A multiplier of the zero-order term; may be characterized as changing the universe to fit the equation.

First Law of Experiment.[1] In any field of scientific endeavor, anything that can go wrong will go wrong.

Fourth Law of Experiment.[1] If in any problem you find yourself doing an immense amount of work, the answer can be obtained by simple inspection.

Gumperson's Law.[6] The vacant parking spaces are always on the other side of the street; you can throw a stubbed-out cigarette from a car window and start a raging forest fire, whereas it will take an hour and a half to get a blaze going in a fireplace loaded with dry wood and sloshed with kerosene; grass seed planted in rich soil, fertilized and kept moist, will not grow, although a few seeds may blow onto the blacktop driveway, settle into a crack, and there take root and flourish.

Murphy's Law.[3,7] If anything can possibly go wrong with a design, test, or experiment, it will.

Nichols' First Law.[7] Success occurs when preparation meets opportunity.

Nichols' Fourth Law.[7] Avoid an action with any unacceptable outcome.

Parkinson's Law.[5] The idea that work expands to fill the time allotted to it, as by a worker's slowing his pace or embellishing a task so that he does not finish it ahead of schedule.

The Peter Principle.[4] In a hierachy, every employee tends to rise to his level of incompetence.

Rule of the Way Out.[1] Always leave room, when writing a report, to add an explanation if it does not work.

Second Law of Experiment.[1] It is usually impractical to worry beforehand about interference; if you have none, someone will supply some for you.

Second Law of Experimental Psychology.[2] Training takes time, whether or not anything is learned.

Smith's Law.[7] One ought to finish what one starts.

453

Colonel Stapp's Ironical Paradox.[7] The universal aptitude for ineptitude makes any human accomplishment an incredible miracle.

Third Law of Experiment.[1] In any collection of data, the figures that are obviously correct, beyond all need of checking, contain the errors.

Third Law of Experimental Psychology.[2] Any well-trained experimental animal, in a controlled environment and subject to controlled stimulation, will do as he damned well pleases.

Zahner's Law.[7] If you play with anything long enough, it will break.

Some of these laws also have corollaries. For a detailed look at them please check the references. I am eager to hear from any readers who know more of these laws inasmuch as *any compilation of exceptions to the rule will always be incomplete (Felton's Law).*

[1] Aurelian, L. Science conquers all. *Intellectual Digest*, 4:47 (Mar.) 1974.

[2] Hebb, D.O. What psychology is about. *American Psychologist*, 29: 71-79 (Feb.) 1974.

[3] Murphy's Law and its corollaries. Unpublished anonymous manuscript available through the author.

[4] Peter, L.J. and Hull, R. *The Peter Principle*. New York: William Morrow & Company, Inc., 1969.

[5] Parkinson, C. Northcote. *Parkinson's Law and Other Studies in Administration*. Boston: Houghton Mifflin Co., Sentry Edition, 1957.

[6] Smith, H.A. *A Short History of Fingers (and Other State Papers)*. Boston: Little, Brown and Company, 1963.

[7] Smith, J. The lawful truth. *Los Angeles Times*, Part 4, p. 1 (Jan. 13) 1977.

More -*ine* Adjectives

Jay Dillon
Gladstone, New Jersey

In her piece, "Animal-Like [*sic*] Adjectives" [III, 3], Miss L. T. Jewell not only presents a corpus of some thirty-five "animaline" adjectives, but cites also several amusing examples of their journalistic use with reference to human behavior, features, and affairs. While I am unable quite so readily to contribute to her stock of amusing usage, I have managed in a few hours' time to more than quadruple her corpus.

Forty-two of my new-found animaline adjectives refer to birds:

alaudine skylark W*
alcine auk W
alcidine auk, puffin, etc. W
alectoridine crane, rail, etc. W
anatine duck 1862-1893 OOsW
avine bird 1881 OW
buteonine buzzard 1865-1874 OW
charadrine plover W
ciconi(i)ne stork 1874-1893 OsW

columbine dove c1386-1835 OW
corvine crow 1656-1886 OW
cuculine cuckoo OW
cygnine swan W
dacelonine kingfisher W
didine dodo 1885 OW
falconine falcon OW
fringilline finch 1874-1893 OW
fulicine coot W
fuliguline eider, etc. 1862-1893 OsW

---

*In this, and other lists below, the individual forms are followed by the common names of the species, genera, etc., to which they refer, the dates of the earliest and latest citations at hand, and sigla reporting each form's presence in one or more sources. The absence of a particular siglum after a form shall signal that form's absence from the source referred to by that siglum. The sources are the *OED* (O), its supplements (Os) and the second edition of *Webster's New International Dictionary* (W).

galline domestic fowl
1868-1895 OW

garruline jay, magpie
W

hirundine swallow
1831 OW

ibidine ibis 1875
OW

laridine gull, etc. 1877
OW

larine gull OW

meleagrine turkey W

milvine kite 1727-1842
OW

nestorine kea, kaka W

phasianine pheasant
1868 OW

picine woodpecker
1890 OW

psittacine parrot 1888-
1895 OW

ralline rail 1885-1892
OW

sittine nuthatch 1829
OW

strigine owl W

sturnine swallow 1809
OW

tetraonine grouse,
ptarmigan, etc.
1868-1885 OW

tringine sandpiper OW

trochilidine humming-
bird 1885 OW

trochiline humming-
bird W

turdine thrush 1890
OW

volucrine bird 1881
OW

vulturine vulture 1647-
1886 OW

Fully fifty-four of my discoveries have to do with land
animals:

alcine elk, moose W

antelopine antelope W

aspine asp 1644 O

bisontine bison 1885-
1887 OsW

bubaline hartebeest
1827-1907 OsW

caballine horse 1430-
1878 OW

cameline camel 1865
OW

capreoline roe 1835
OW

cricetine hamster W

crocodiline crocodile
(1730-6)-1755 OW

crotaline rattlesnake
1865-1882 OW

dasyurine dasyure
(1839-47) OW

didelphine opossum
1847 OW

gazelline gazelle OW

giraffine giraffe 1901
OsW

hippopotamine hippo-
potamus 1883 OW

hippotigrine zebra W

hirudine leech W

hominine man 1883-
1959 OOsW

hyenine hyaena (1884-
5) OW

hylobatine gibbon OW

hystricine porcupine
1883 OW

leporine hare 1656-
  1877 OW
lumbricine earthworm
  1890 OW
lyncine lynx W
macropine kangaroo
  1888-1891 O
macropodine kangaroo,
  wallaby, etc. W
megacerine (extinct)
  Irish elk W
megacerotine (extinct)
  Irish elk 1884 OW
megatherine (extinct)
  American sloth W
mephitine skunk W
moschine musk deer
  OW
musteline weasel, mink
  1656-1891 OW
noctilionine bat 1844
  O
ovibovine musk ox OW
pantherine panther
  1656-1890 OW
pardine leopard (1859-
  63) OW
procyonine raccoon,
  kinkajou, etc. 1883
  OW
pteropine bat 1844 O

rangiferine caribou,
  reindeer, etc. OW
rhinocerine rhinoceros
  1879 OW
rucervine Indian
  swamp deer, etc.
  1881-1891 OW
rupicaprine chamois
  1827-1891 OW
sabelline sable 1888-
  1891 O
salamandrine salaman-
  der 1712-1888 OW
sciurine squirrel 1842-
  1883 OW
soricine shrew 1781-
  c1878 OW
talpine mole 1860 OW
tapirine tapir
  1891 OW
tigrine tiger 1656-1908
  OW
tolypeutine armadillo
  OW
vaccine cow 1799-
  1881 OW
vituline calf 1656-1870
  OW
viverrine civet 1800-
  1885 OW
zebrine zebra OW

Insects account for six more such terms:

acarine mite 1828 OW
anopheline mosquito
  1920-1964 Os
bombycine silkworm
  W
culicine mosquito
  1921-1964 OsW

formicine ant 1885
  OW
vespine wasp 1843-
  1884 OW

Marine beasties supply ten animalines:

cyprine carp 1828 O
delphine dolphin 1828
  OW
delphinine dolphin O
homarine lobster 1880
  OW
manatine manatee OW
megapterine hump-
  back whale W

octopine octopus 1914
  OsW
ostracine oyster 1890
  OW
phocaenine porpoise
  1890 OW
phocine seal 1846 OW

Finally, beasts of the mind occupy the last three places in my extended corpus:

basilicine basilisk 1855
  OW
sphingine sphinx 1961
  OW

sphinxine sphinx 1845
  OW

I cannot pretend that the above lists are complete, or even nearly so; the relative ease with which they were compiled suggests that there are at least one or two hundred more such terms lurking about, waiting to be unearthed by someone with more time and interest than I can devote.

Miss Jewell's identification of *-ine* as "Middle English, [meaning] 'pertaining to'" mystifies me. For it seems to me perfectly obvious, and is readily confirmed, that English adjectival *-ine* simply represents Latin *-inus*, and perhaps occasionally French *-in*. Moreover, the suffix appears not to have been productive in English before Elizabethan times. Thus, *-ine* is not Middle English at all, although it is collaterally related to Middle English *-en* 'made of—, (*brasen, golden, lether(e)n, wollen*), by way of Indo-European **-ino-*, Common Germanic **-ina-*, and Old English *-en* (*braesen, gylden, leðren, wyllen*).

Finally, it must be remembered that there is no consistent morphological difference whatever between the animaline adjectives and such other adjectives as *feminine, genuine, marine,* and *sanguine*. The distinction is purely a semantic one, and it is not always easy to demarcate the animaline from the other adjectives in *-ine*; does *hominine* belong in the above list of land animals? If Miss Jewell includes both *caprine* and *hircine*, ought we to add, then, *masculine* and *feminine*? Ought adjectives in *-ine* for fabulous beasts to be included? What of *didine, megacerine,* and other adjectives for animals prehistoric, extinct, or both? Ought I to have included *sylphine* and *nymphine*? Miss Jewell's *animal-like* and my *animaline* have thus far meant whatever she and I have wanted them to mean; should these words ever be used again, they will mean whatever they are intended to mean, or are taken to mean.

♈♈♈♈♈

EPISTOLAE

The reason that I don't subscribe to *The American Scholar* is precisely what you say. I haven't returned my Phi Beta Kappa key, but I have been infuriated by some of the articles, which I stingily glance over in the local library. I doubt, however, that your "Permissions" will go anywhere in face of the present paranoia in the public's public.

Other less important comments: Off and on, mostly off, I have made comments about my own name in ANS Bulletins. Schulz should not be so concerned. He should feel elated. My mail, as you can suspect, comes much the same way: Ms., Mrs., Mr., and Miss, and sometimes just zero. It gets me on all kinds of mailing lists, all of which I thoroughly (no counter word) enjoy. I have been involved in Women's Lib groups—by mail—(no pun), gay groups, and probably others because of the name. One book on names gives the full etymology of my name. The editor then acknowledges that I sent him the information, meanwhile thanking graciously Miss Kelsie B. Harder, Executive Secretary of the American Name Society. I had neglected to let him know. I got a page and a half in the introduction. Another good story corresponds with Schulz's, although with a different twist. When I was a student at Vanderbilt, a professor called the roll, Miss Harder. I replied, "Mrs. Harder," for I was married at the time. He never called my name again, just skipped it when he called the daily roll. Furthermore, he gave me an "A." James Dickey was in that class. More on Dickey some other time!

Kelsie Harder
The State University College at Potsdam

Notes from the Compound World

Caryl Johnston
Boston, Massachusetts

According to the famed mytho-grammarian Maxim Mütter, compounds (*snow-white*, *rose-red*, *upsy-daisy*, *shaggy-dog*, etc.) are the harbingers of a new epoch of consciousness. In contrast to the modern uncompoundish or analytical tendency, they herald a new power or faculty which Mütter termed "magistic." (The verb, *to magist*, means 'to conceive, or to engage in the labor of conceiving, the gist of something in an image.') Linguistic philosophers, who are the kind of people who like to separate their words into distinct and clearly-defined operable units (as, for example, in the assertion that there are two apples in this cart, and three oranges in that cart) simply balk at the $2 + 2 = 5$ mentality of most compounds. (Take, for example, the notorious query: "What is the meaning of *applecart* in the statement: 'Don't upset the applecart'?") According to Mütter, it (the noncompoundite intellect) "is unable to split in one lightning-stroke (*blitzkrieg*) the complex welter (*plexwelt*) of ideas, associations, and images which compounds, denoting permanent or transient actions, qualities, or states, represent." The mind is thus hurled, willy-nilly, into the very jaws of duality, and forced to entertain simultaneously two dissimilarly-compatible concepts, which, however, still fall far short of the intended meaning. It is precisely in this quality of falling-farshortedness that compounds are so peculiarly noted, and for which Mütter reserved only words of highest praise.

Some of Mütter's conclusions have been slightly modified over the past century, due to the discovery of compounds involving trinitarian, quadripartite, cinquefoil, or even sextuplet conceptions. Dr. Algol Blauhaus, a student of magnitudes, has claimed to discern infinite digression in the series of conceptions, and deals only with magistian infinity-factors, a branch of the science which is still, so to speak, in its infancy. In any case, despite the constant unearthing of new data, the basic compost made by Mütter has sprouted what in this century has come to be known as the Society for the Preservation of Ancient Compounds. The name can be somewhat misleading, as Society members seek not only to preserve ancient compounds, but also avidly promote the science of magistics. They also openly encourage the assimilation of infinite digressions.

This avowed and open activity on the part of SPAC members is watched with panic on both sides of the Atlantic by language technicians and computer specialists, people who are somewhat derisively referred to by Society members as *compeeps*. (Panic: *ealu-scerwen*, 'terror as at the loss of ale.') It has been pointed out by members of the pro-compound party that a person who panics at the proliferation of compounds is probably a *nincompoop* 'non compos mentis' if not *niçakeçaçmaçrunakhas*, 'he who has short hair, nails, and beard.' The compeeps, in turn, call the compounders *kunophron*, 'having the soul of a dog,' and *boukephalos*, 'with the forehead of an ox' (*Front-de-Boeuf*).

Debates on both sides of the compound fence are aired over most stations, and compound-slung epithets frequently jam the ears of the listening public. From Hoboken ('smoke pipe') to Derby ('village of wild beasts'), from Punjab ('five rivers') to Algonquin ('those on the other side of the river'), compound-keepers have been spotted, trapping and talon-tagging possible topics before mating them. Often demonstrations on behalf of compounds are held, as the one which we recently attended in Massachusetts, 'blue hills.' (Incidentally, the five brothers Padavas were there, 'having their mother for sixth (companion)'—*matri-śastha*.) Professor Leichen-Bleich ('pale as a corpse') spoke for the computer people, calling the compounders *chairekakoi*, 'those who rejoice in evil,' and *ethelorhetoroi*, 'pretending to be orators.' He also denounced the whole compounded controversy as being nothing more than an insipid quibble over *piqsirpoq* and *qininqsug*, 'drifting snow' and 'snowdrift.' The noted Boston Brahmaness *Nihçvasa-parama*, 'sighing a great deal,' or 'regarding sighs as the supreme thing,' countered appropriately for the Archaic Society by discoursing upon the dekeeping-childlightsomeness which certain compounds have, the *ambologera*, 'who puts off old age.' She also spoke feelingly for the kind of compound which has the *dakethumos*, 'that bites into the heart.' Professor Leichen-Bleich, attempting to pun upon Ms. Nihçvasa-parama's multi-sibilance, reminded her of the Spartan woman 'who shows her thighs' (*phainomeris*); and, as for biting into the heart, he'd just as soon be 'wounded by a thorn' (*akanthoplex*). But Herman Stockfest ('firm as a stump'), snorting visibly, called the spokesman for the compeeps an old fly-flapper (*proboscis*) and a shuffle-foot who spoke nothing but fatback, a composite which seems to have carried the day as no one could come up with an immediate Greek, Latin, or Sanskrit equivalent.

Compounders and polysemiasts are urged to send samples of their work to the Archaic Society, which is always glad to supply interested members of the public with compounds for new or old diseases, states, conditions, or habits of mind. Cremnophobics, for example, afraid of falling from cliffs, should be happy to know they no longer need to be classed with ordinary acrophobics. Those with an excessive fear of holy places should jot down *hagiophobia*, and at long last 'fear of Friday the 13th' can take its place in our growing family of componderables as the insidious triskaidekaphobia. And finally, those of you who, like the compeeps, cringe at compounds, can always take comfort that *floccinaucinihilipilification* is just the word you've been waiting for.

EPISTOLAE

I can contribute two additional Menu Barbarisms to those listed by Dr. McCaffrey in the December 1976 issue. Both were perpetrated by restaurants in the Washington, D.C., area: *Tornado Rossini*; *Steak Joan of Arc*.

J. F. O'Connor
Silver Spring, Maryland

Re: " 'Ouch!' he said in Japanese" [III, 1]. I dunno about you academic types at all. The only time I might use "ouch" would be in reaction to a minor irritation, such as a flu shot. I certainly do not consider the word to convey "vocalized pain itself . . . ." Were I to hit my finger or thumb with a hammer while trying to drive a nail into wood, I would use any of a number of expletives such as s—, f*** or even AAAAAHHooouuuwww! But I'm damned if I'd ever consider "ouch."

C. A. Peddle
San Francisco, California

Self-referring Words

Alexander J. Pollock
Northbrook, Illinois

Self-referring sentences, notably the paradoxical "This sentence is false," are sufficiently familiar. But the notion of self-referring *words* was new, at least for me, when it occurred to me the other day while I was waiting for an elevator. Self-referring words denote or describe themselves—for example, the word "word" is itself a word, and the word "useful" is itself useful.

I was already intrigued by these words by the time we were riding up on the elevator. Other readers of VERBATIM may wish to participate in answering three questions which self-referring words raise:

1. How many of them are there?
2. Can we formulate general principles about them?
3. How widely are the categories "self-referring" and "nonself-referring" applicable?

Having posed the questions, any logophile of spirit must attempt answers.

It is obvious that the vast majority of words are not self-referring. My current list follows:

1. Nouns

THE WORD:	IS ITSELF A:
a. *word*	word
b. *term*	term
c. *noun*	noun
d. *substantive*	substantive
e. *symbol*	symbol
f. *sign*	sign

2. Adjectives

THE WORD:	IS ITSELF:
a. *useful*	useful
b. *English*	English
c. *français* (etc.)	français (etc.)
d. *acceptable*	acceptable
e. *unobjectionable*	unobjectionable
f. *intelligible*	intelligible
g. *meaningful*	meaningful
h. *understandable*	understandable
i. *thinkable*	thinkable

j. *sesquipedalian*	sesquipedalian
k. *ordinary*	ordinary
l. *analyzable*	analyzable
m. *inflected*	inflected
n. *polysyllabic*	polysyllabic
o. *definable*	definable
p. *expressible*	expressible
q. *printable*	printable
r. *writable*	writable
s. *pronounceable*	pronounceable
t. *speakable*	speakable
u. *utterable*	utterable
v. *learnable*	learnable
w. *teachable*	teachable

I have so far three principles:

1. Only nouns and adjectives can be self-referring. This is because words themselves are objects in the cultural world; thus they can only be referred to by names or descriptions of objects, i.e., by nouns or adjectives.

2. Self-referring nouns are always grammatical or linguistic terms applicable to nouns. This appears to be the only way for a noun to name itself.

3. Self-referring adjectives have a wider range of meaning than self-referring nouns, because they can express many aspects of words (than which nothing has more aspects). The self-referring adjectives listed above bring out, respectively, that words are:

      a. practical

      b-c. in some language or other (This class of self-referring adjectives is represented in each language I am familiar with by one word—namely the adjective which describes words, including itself, as being in that language. As an aside, I wonder if, of the few thousand languages there are, any is so unselfconscious as not to have a word for itself, as one language among many?)

      d-e. socio-cultural

      f-i. cognitive

      j-k. stylistic

      l-n. structured

       o. semantic

      p-u. variously expressible

      v-w. pedagogical

My question here is whether, in principle, every noun

and adjective can be unambiguously classed as either self-referring or nonself-referring.

It is clear that there might be disagreements about the classification of given words, for reasons such as:

1. Different senses of the same word—for example, *sign* in the sense of 'an indication of meaning' is self-referring; in the sense of 'an inscribed board used for advertising' it is not.

2. Differences in taste or opinion—some people might think *interesting* interesting and *euphonious* euphonious; other people might not.

3. Differences in theory—some people might speculate that words in some sense exist or are things, thus making *existing* and *thing* self-referring; others' speculations might reach opposite conclusions.

Such disagreements are not objections *in principle*, however. In principle, we can sort out the senses of words, and settle or at least understand and handle differences of opinion, taste and theory. But is there a word which cannot in principle be assigned to one of our two categories?

It seems to me there is one: the word *nonself-referring*. If *nonself-referring* is nonself-referring, it obviously describes itself and thus must be self-referring. If, on the other hand, *nonself-referring* is self-referring, then it must describe itself and be nonself-referring. So the self-referring word can lead us to paradox equally as well as the self-referring sentence.

Doubtless, as journal articles say, further research of this intriguing subject is needed. And the inviting field of the self-referring *phrase* lies all untrodden before us.

EPISTOLAE

I was delighted to read *Hear Finish Before (Pause) You?*, since one rarely comes across articles on sign language that deal with Ameslan rather than Signed English. (In fact, one all too rarely comes across articles on sign language at all.) Ms. Brown, rightly stressing the fact that Ameslan has a grammar of its own, uses some of the most salient differences between its syntax and English syntax to illustrate this fact: "it lacks articles, and plurals and verb tenses are supplied either through context or by the addition of the word 'finish'."

Readers might be interested to know that Ameslan happens to show many remarkable similarities to Chinese in its syntax: e.g., that identical quotation applies to Chinese! I have all too often heard the naive claim that neither Ameslan nor Chinese "has a grammar." In fact, both have quite intricate grammars; what they don't have is word-endings, which the Latin-minded often think of as the only kind of grammar. I wish, however, that Ms. Brown hadn't devoted quite so much attention to idiomatic expressions (real or apparent), since idioms tend to obscure the grammar of a language rather than to illuminate it.

I have two other minor criticisms of Ms. Brown's article. First, her folk-etymologies of the signs for male and female ("long ago someone must have decided men have minds while women have mouths") are not borne out by researchers in the field. The standard etymologies are reflected in Lottie Riekehof's excellent lexicon, *Talk to the Deaf*, and in Harry Hoemann's thorough and thoughtful text, *The American Sign Language*: according to Hoemann, "the male gender marker was based on the custom of tipping a hat, and the region of the forehead serves as the gender marker for male kinship signs. The female gender marker was derived from the bonnet strings tied under the chin." A different etymology occurs in William C. Stokoe's pioneering *Dictionary of American Sign Language*. Stokoe, the recognized authority on the linguistics of Ameslan, writes of the sign for "female": "Epée himself states that it was selected because of the hanging curls prominent in the coiffures of the day. Curiously enough there is a traditional ASL etymology too which makes the sign an indication of the ladies' bonnet strings." [Epée, an eighteenth-century French abbé, is the father of the modern American and French sign languages.]

Finally, Ms. Brown leaves the reader with the unfortunately inaccurate impression that sign-language classes and textbooks all teach Ameslan. Would that that were so, but in fact a great many of them teach Signed English. The signs are the same, but the grammar of Signed English is English grammar, often complete with English suffixes and prefixes. There's nothing wrong with Signed English if that is what you really want to study, but you should know just what you're getting before you enroll in a class or buy a textbook. If you want Ameslan, be sure you're really being given Ameslan.

My criticisms, however, are definitely outweighed by the positive aspects of the article. (In fact, they are even outweighed by the mere fact that an article appeared on Ameslan in the first place.) Perhaps the best thing about Ms. Brown's article is the simple fact that she makes it clear that

Ameslan is indeed a *language*, not just a lexicon of signs.

I was not so delighted to read your own "Obiter Dicta," in which you display a surprising ignorance (or willful disregard?) of the meaning of the term "affirmative action." You say that "what is probably intended is the sense of *assertive* action; in other words, 'We don't shilly-shally when asked for a decision on an application.'" But this is *not* what is intended at all! It isn't even close: the term really means that the employer will *affirmatively* (= "assertively," as you put it) seek out women and members of minority groups. Not only will he give equal opportunity to those who show up applying for a job, but he will also assertively try to get applications from types of people who do not usually apply. The term "affirmative action" arose fairly recently in response to those companies that claimed that the lack of women, handicapped persons, blacks, etc., in high positions was due to the fact that very few even applied for those positions. "Affirmative action" companies are now accepting an obligation to do something about this situation, to do something *affirmative* rather than the simple *negative* action of *not* discriminating against qualified minority applicants.

The quality of VERBATIM is remarkably consistently high, an occasional *lapsus* like the squib on "affirmative action" notwithstanding. I look forward to each issue. Keep them coming, and how about some more articles on sign language and some articles on animal communication, child language, and other psycholinguistic topics?

Laurence J. Davidson
Cambridge, Massachusetts

Where have you been? *Affirmative action* is a phrase that has been around for some time. It means, "We not only believe in equal opportunity; we act to affirm that belief by seeking out and giving preference to people from groups that have suffered from lack of equal opportunity."

Don't knock it.

Margherita S. Smith
Annandale, Virginia

"Affirmative action" is required of companies which hold Government contracts, or subcontracts.

It is Government English for the requirement that the

company not sit back waiting for members of ethnic minor-
ities, handicapped persons or women to apply for jobs, but
actively engage in recruiting such prospective employees.

Incidentally, this is sometimes described as "seeking
employees from minority groups," or even "seeking minor-
ities," despite the fact that, as any census will show, women
constitute a majority.

To continue with the fairer (though occasionally more
unfair) sex, Mr. Norman R. Shapiro parenthesizes, "Hence
the feminine, *brava*, to a deserving diva."

Wrong.

To a deserving diva, for a superlative performance, I
might shout, "*Bravo!*" This is an exclamation and is uninflected.
The boys in the balcony, whether amateur fans or professional
claque, who shout "Brava!" may be doing the lady an in-
justice, since it refers to the diva, not her performance, and
merely makes a statement that she is good, honest, or possibly
even brave. (To be up on that stage?)

Arthur J. Morgan
New York, New York

*As readers may be able to tell, quite a few people have
written to comment on the brief article about* affirmative
action. *It is important that the record be set straight;
equally important is the point that the words* affirmative +
action, *in juxtaposition, mean only what readers (and the
government and employers) say they mean by virtue of conventionalized jargon. Unfortunately, the convention had
not yet reached VERBATIM. The other phrase often
appearing in want ads,* "We are an equal-opportunity
employer," *seems to have no stigma and to state a position
more clearly. Any further comment would be social and not
linguistic.*

—*Editor*

Mail Lib—Rejoinder

Claire K. Schultz
Line Lexington, Pennsylvania

Because of the similarity of names, a friend sent me a
copy of Clair Schulz's "Mail Lib" [III, 4].

I can relate easily to his feelings because, generally, all of the same things have happened to me in reverse. Confusion on the part of others about one's sex is particularly difficult during the formative years, when self-identification is yet to be achieved. However, the effects of bisexual names can affect even one's descendants. I remember my children's disappointment when I received a letter from President Truman, which they wanted to show off at school, but no one would believe that Mr. Clair Schultz was their mother!

My purpose in responding is to focus on another aspect of mail lib—that taken with one's address. Fortunately, these liberties are corrected to some extent if one lives in a rural situation.

The addresses below, reproduced from envelopes, show how the simple address in the byline above is misunderstood, misspelled and adorned, and how the mail gets delivered in spite of a myriad of variations. There are many more examples than can be printed here—I have enclosed only some of them, to demonstrate the exercise of communication, on a day-to-day basis.

Prof. C.K. Schultz
Line Lexington
PHILADELPHIA
USA

Mr. and Mrs. Schultz
Metropolitan Museum
 of Art
Line Lexington,
Pennsylvania

Mrs. SCHULTZ
Milltown Pike
Line Lexington,
Pennsylvania (U.S.A.)

Mrs. Claire K. Schultz
Little Twon Line
Lexington, Pennsylvania

Miss Claire Schultz
Libre (?)
Lexington, Pennsylvania

Mr. Schultz
Hilltown Pike
Lima - Lexington, Pa.

Mrs. SCHUTZENBER-
 GER C.K.
SCHULTZ
Hilltown Piks
LINE LEXINGTON
(Pennsylvania) U.S.A.

Mrs. C.K. Schultz
Line Pa 18932

Mr. Claire K. Schultz
Line St
Lexington, Pa

Mrs. Clair Schutz
Line Washington,
Pennsylvania, 18932

Mr. C. Schultz
Lyon Lexington,
Pennsylvania

Mr. Claire K. Schultz
Line Lexington Pa.
 Biology
York Co. Pennsylvania

"Ormonyms"

Ormly Gumfudgin
La Crescenta, California

Being a columnist of little note nor long remembrance, I've used my column as a vehicle to play with semantic oddities and explore the possibilities of various word combinations; mostly in a semi-humorous vein. What I'm saying is that nobody has complained—so far, anyway.

Among the first items I developed was the "profundrum," a word I created to encompass various statements I've developed (and collected) to make the reader think a little more than usual. A few random examples are:

> *Happiness is no laughing matter.*
> *Anything worth doing is worth doing.*
> *Why not take your mother-in-law out to the next swap*
>   *meet and see what you can get for her?*
> *He who laughs, lasts.*
> *The darker the light, the darker the dark.*
> *People never go there anymore; it's too crowded.*

In the meantime, I've graduated to what I term "ormonyms" because I didn't know what they were. I sent some to Mr. Urdang who claims they are "junctures" but he hasn't convinced me on this as yet. However, I have to give his comments serious consideration because he really knows more about this semantic business than I do.

The main purpose of this article is to get some more comments concerning this semantic exercise from our learned brethren. My main rule is that they read differently but sound the same. It would be most interesting to see if anyone else is creating/saving such semantic oddities—and what they may have come up with.

Here are some examples I've created—with a few which have been contributed by my readers:

> *The stuffy nose can lead to problems.*
> *The stuff he knows can lead to problems.*
>
> *Where is the spice center?*
> *Where is the spy center?*
>
> *Are you aware of the words you have just uttered?*
> *Are you aware of the words you have just stuttered?*
>
> *That's the biggest hurdle I've ever seen!*
> *That's the biggest turtle I've ever seen!*
>
> *I'm taking a nice cold shower.*
> *I'm taking an ice cold shower.*

He would kill Hamlet for that reason.
He would kill Hamlet for that treason.

You'd be surprised to see a mint spy in your bank.
You'd be surprised to see a mince pie in your bank.

Some others I've seen . . .
Some mothers I've seen . . .

Here are a couple of examples which do not qualify:

Reading in the library is sometimes allowed.
Reading in the library is sometimes aloud.

A politician's fate often hangs in a delegate balance.
A politician's fate often hangs in a delicate balance.

My reason they don't qualify is because they are too easy. It's using two words that sound the same or similar.

Mr. Urdang sent me an example of junctures which was the sound of "white shoes" and "why choose." I tried to put these into a duplicate sentence to qualify them for an ormonym. I haven't made a rule about punctuation as yet so I tried to make a sentence out of them. A bit awkward, but here's how it worked out:

White shoes; the trademark of Pat Boone.
Why choose the trademark of Pat Boone?

Maybe what I'm doing is taking junctures and making a sentence with them and that's what an ormonym really is. Anyway, it's fun and maybe it serves to crack a smile here and there; if so, it's worth it.

I'd appreciate any input; pro, con or whatever is in between. And maybe we need a word for that—or is there one already?

♥♥♥♥♥

EPISTOLAE

In my article, "That Dirty Bird," I have mentioned my discovery that shitepoke first appeared in print in the 1775 *First Book of the American Chronicles of the Times*, antedating the *OED*'s single citation of ca. 1850. In subsequent research, it turns out that my "discovery" was itself antedated by Mitford M. Mathews in his *Dictionary of Americanisms*. Mathews cites *The First Book of the American Chronicles of the Times* as the first printed appearance of the term *shitepoke*.

My "discovery," then, is due to nothing but incomplete scholarship!

I'm sure other readers of VERBATIM have already discovered this error, so let me apologize for my faulty and misleading reference.

Steve Hicks
Lawrence, Kansas

✉

In his article, "That Dirty Bird," on the onomastic migrations of the shitepoke [III, 3], Steven R. Hicks makes passing reference to the intriguing word *shyster*, an American colloquialism dating from at least as early as 1846 (see Mitford Mathews, *Americanisms*, 1966). Like Mr. Hicks, I have always taken for granted that it derives from the German *Scheiss*, 'shit,' (despite other esoteric possibilities put forth by Mencken). Not, however, via *Scheisser*, as he assumes along with Partridge and others, but rather from an oral form *scheiss*-ster, by analogy with so many nouns in which the venerable suffix *-ster* originally implied contempt. (Needless to say, it no longer always does so: witness *youngster*, *roadster*, *songster*, and scores of others.) Partridge supposes a transmission from German through Yiddish. This is, I think, a debatable suggestion, since the usual Yiddish word for the substance in question is *drek*, not *scheiss* (which, if used at all, would very likely have undergone a standard vocalic shift—moved its vowels, so to speak—and been pronounced "shayss," hence an unlikely forebear of *shyster*).

But scatymological considerations aside, readers may be interested in another proposed derivation, found in Farmer and Henley's *Slang and Its Analogues* (1890-1904). This invaluable volume, reprinted by the Arno Press in 1970, offers the following citation:

1871. DE VERE, *Americanisms*, . . . This is the SHYSTER . . . Ill-reputed men [who] offer their services to the new-comer, compel him to pay a fee in advance, and then—do nothing. On the contrary, they fight SHY of him, and hence they have obtained their name.

However logical this early etymology, partisans of *Scheiss* will probably not be budged.

At the other end of the alimentary canal, John G. Caffrey, in the same issue, calls attention to the phenomenon of what he terms the "dropped d" in names of foods and dishes (*chop sirloin*, et al.). Many common examples might be added to his list. Foremost among them, *ice coffee*, *ice tea*, and especially *ice cream*. The *OED Supplement* documents this last apocopated form in a passage from 1744, decades before Dolley Madison introduced the White House to her dessert. The original, *iced cream*, is attested as early as 1688. Coincidentally, cream also provides a recent example of what can be dubbed an "added d." Some dairy food companies have lately taken to calling their product *soured cream*, apparently in an effort to destigmatize it somehow by giving the impression that it has been "soured" intentionally and that it hasn't just turned "sour" through age or neglect.

Norman R. Shapiro
Wesleyan University
Middletown, Connecticut

Mr. Pete Chappars was apparently misinformed about the special meaning of *to signify* amongst blacks [III, 3] by what must have been inarticulate informants.

This peculiar meaning of *to signify* (not confined solely to any one part of the country, I might add) is to make an oblique hint or remark, an indirect intimation or an insinuation. In short, innuendo.

From time to time popular music of all sorts filters down to some of us lovers of the classics. One such occurrence was the 1965 recording of Wilson Pickett's "Mustang Sally." If memory serves me right, here is a part of the lyric for Mr. Chappars' edification:

I bought you a brand new Mustang, a 1965.
Now you come around signifying, woman.
You don't want to let me ride.

Thomas Daniel
Warren, Ohio

Years ago a black man I knew well finally objected, one day, to my "signifying." I asked what that meant. I was told that this word described the subtle, yet pointed way in which I verbally probed to uncover whether he had done a particular thing or had been in a particular place. In plain English, had he been with another woman. It also described the case in which I let it be known very indirectly, by what I said, that there was a piece of information I had that he might have preferred I hadn't.

My probing had not been direct, as was the discussion

473

you described going on in the parking lot. I understood that directness was definitely not a quality of signifying! Rather, it is that idle, spoken-yet-unspoken, semi-hidden *signaling* that is thought to be especially well cultivated by women. It avoids direct confrontation.

Incidentally, it is not unusual for blacks to protect important parts of their language from knowledge by the whites, so you may have been deliberately misled. Too bad, because black language has a rich history. But after all, it is a way to remain on guard and retain privacy in a still hostile environment.

Vera C. V. Karger
Stamford, Connecticut

VERBATIM

THE LANGUAGE QUARTERLY

Vol. IV, No. 2   September 1977

EDITOR: LAURENCE URDANG

We Shall Know Them By Their Roots

Clair Schulz
Clinton, Wisconsin

Of all the aspects related to the institution known as rock music, one of the most intriguing is the names groups choose for themselves. Whether the names are ordinary or outlandish, they sometimes become so much a part of our culture that, for instance, a casual reference to the *Four Seasons* or *Dawn* is just as likely to remind people of tunes as of time. True, most groups vanish after a short period of popularity, but many of their names remain suspended in the same web of nostalgia that holds glutinously to memories of first dates and aborted dreams. The parade of names that follows is for those who want to hear their favorites one more time.

Some groups began merely by counting heads. There

were *Four Tunes*, *Aces*, *Preps*, *Freshmen*, *Tops*, *Fellows*, and *Lads*. One-upmanship has been practiced by the *Fifth Dimension*, *Five Americans*, *Dave Clark Five*, and *We Five*, although they too were outscored by the *New Colony Six* and *Six Hits and a Miss*. Still others (the *Association*, *Group Image*, *Gallery*) banded together under corporate entries.

Music itself has been the inspiration for a number of groups. The *Band*, *New Vaudeville Band*, *Chords*, *Chordettes*, *Crescendos*, *Accents*, *Monotones*, *Cleftones*, *Sparkletones*, *Delfonics*, *Gerry and the Pacemakers*, *Merseybeats*, *Easy Beats*, *New Beats*, *Delta Rhythm Boys*, *Rhythm Heritage*, *Amazing Rhythm Aces*, and *Blue Notes* identified with musical terminology. The *Bells*, *Roxy Music*, and *Earth Opera* struck melodic notes, whereas the *Ding Dongs*, *Platters*, and *Music Explosion* selected less pretentious titles.

Ever since *Bill Haley and the Comets* blazed across the rock and roll heavens many troupes have considered themselves children of light. The *Chi-lites*, *Limelites*, *Lovelites*, *Fireballs*, *Firefall*, *Flares*, *Flames*, *Flaming Ember*, *Lamp of Childhood*, *Silhouettes*, *Reflections*, *Shadows of Night*, *Rays*, *Link Ray and his Ray Men*, *Clear Light*, and *Flash* represent direct and oblique references to light, countered by the extraterrestrial illumination provided by the *Moonglows*, *Sounds of Sunshine*, *K.C. and the Sunshine Band*, *Ars Nova*, *Morning Star*, *Starbuck*, and *Joey Dee and the Starliters*. Artificial energy emerges from the *Magic Lanterns*, *Edison Lighthouse*, *Electric Light Orchestra*, *Electric Flag*, *Electric Prunes*, and *Pacific Gas and Electric*.

Brilliance is also apparent in the colors rock artists select to represent them. The favorite hue appears often: *Blue Suede*, *Blues Image*, *Blue Oyster Cult*, *Blue Bells*, *Blue Cheer*, *Blues Project*, *Blues Magoos*, *Moody Blues*, and *Schocking Blue*. Other colorful performers include *Redeye*, *Redbone*, *Pink Floyd*, *Frijid Pink*, *Rose-colored Glass*, *Savoy Brown*, *Soft White Underbelly*, *Average White Band*, *Deep Purple*, *New Riders of the Purple Sage*, *Silver Convention*, *Quicksilver Messenger Service*, *Argent*, the *Inkspots*, and *Yellow Pages*.

Love and domestic life are not only the themes of most popular songs; they have also served as afflatus for singers seeking an image. Affection has been expressed by *Love*, *Love Affair*, *Love Unlimited*, *Ruby and the Romantics*, *Heart*, and *Kiss*. There have been a number of siblings such as the *Osmonds* and *Jacksons* who have recorded under surnames, but groups that lack common bloodlines have also invoked familial ties. Relatively speaking and singing were the *Brotherhood*, *Flying Burrito Brothers*, *Righteous*

Brothers, Big Brother and the Holding Company, Mamas and the Papas, Every Mother's Son, Mothers of Invention, Family, and *M(other) F(ather) S(ister) B(rother).*

Young people have been unjustly accused of having no sense of time or place. The calendar and clock have been duly noted by the *Tymes, T.I.M.E., Moments, Midnighters, Dusk, 8th Day, Wednesday, Ten Years After,* and *Ides of March.* The *Belmonts* that backed Dion DiMuci in the fifties derived their name from a street in the Bronx, and since that time the nation's largest city has spawned *New York City, Brooklyn Bridge,* the *Lower East Side, Manhattan Transfer,* and the *Manhattans.* The tradition of paying homage to home territory has been carried on by *Chicago, Boston, White Plains, Orleans, Bay City Rollers, Nazareth, Detroit Emeralds, Black Oak Arkansas, Kansas, Ohio Players, Herb Alpert and the Tijuana Brass,* and *Sergio Mendes and Brazil '66.* (The last group truly changed with the times; they are now known as *Sergio Mendes and Brazil '77*). Additional lessons in geography are provided by *Jay and the Americans, America, American Breed, Ronnie and the Daytonas, B.J. Kramer and the Dakotas, Cimarron, Left Banke, Ozark Mountain Daredevils, Linn County,* and *Stone Country.*

Transportation to these places may be achieved in a variety of ways. Among the groups that used automobiles for extensive mileage are the *Rivieras, Fiestas, Edsels, Impalas, El Dorados, Falcons, Fleetwoods, Fleetwood Mac, Thin Lizzy, Cadillacs, L.T.D., Booker T. and the M.G.'s, Flash Cadillac and the Continental Kids,* and *Mitch Ryder and the Detroit Wheels.* Other methods of travel have been obtained via *R.E.O. Speedwagon, Orient Express, Ohio Express, B.T. Express, Caboose, Sea Train, Grand Funk Railroad, Dixie Flyers, Led Zeppelin,* and *Jefferson Airplane* (later *Jefferson Starship*).

People mystified by the feral gyrations of modern dances will not be surprised to discover that many groups captured their names from wildlife. The *Animals, Tarriers, Chipmunks, Teddy Bears, Monkees, Critters, Herd, Turtles, Murmaids, Crickets,* and *Beatles,* as well as *Crazy Horse, Stone Pony, Howlin' Wolf, Sopwith Camel, T. Rex, Buffalo Springfield, Elephant's Memory, Kangaroo, Rhinoceros, Three Dog Night,* and *Country Joe and the Fish* borrowed from the animal kingdom. Flying above the earthbound beings are the *Byrds, Yardbirds, Larks, Jayhawks, Ravens, Flamingos, Pelicans, Orioles, Sandpipers, Eagles, Robins, Swallows, Wings,* and *Crow.* (The *Penguins* and *Iron Butterfly* performed well, but could not get off the ground.) The call

477

of nature has also been answered by the *Gladiolas, Clovers, Rose Garden, Earth Wind and Fire, Rare Earth, Mother Earth, Nitty Gritty Dirt Band, Seeds, Gladys Knight and the Pips, Grass Roots, Fever Tree, Hollies, Beach Boys, Ocean, Surfaris, Mad River, Credence Clearwater Revival, Zephyr, Hilltoppers*, and *Mountain*.

Parents frequently complain about the cost of feeding and clothing teenagers, and even when not lamenting their fate are reminded of it by the artists who record the albums they themselves often purchase for their sons and daughters. Fruits and vegetables are represented by the *Silver Apples, Crabby Appleton, Lemon Pipers, Moby Grape, Wild Cherry, Grapefruit, Raspberries, Strawberry Alarm Clock*, and *Ultimate Spinach*. The simple fare offered by *Hot Butter, Bread, Goldie and the Gingerbreads, Sugarloaf, Honeycombs, Peanut Butter Conspiracy*, and *Marmalade* whet appetites for the *T-Bones, Joy of Cooking, Main Ingredient, Hot Tuna*, and *Captain Beefheart and his Magic Band*. Liquid refreshment and sweets are readily available from the *Lovin' Spoonful, Tea Set, Creem, Hot Chocolate, Humble Pie, Vanilla Fudge*, the *Candymen*, and *1910 Fruitgum Company*. After such a rich diet, people might feel compelled to settle down in easy chairs and wrap themselves in the rhythms of the *Satins, Turbans, Weavers, Hollywood Argyles, Orlons, Velvet Underground*, and *Chiffons*.

Another parental concern, that listening to rock music brings impressionable minds under Satanic or necromantic influences, is only partially correct. Certainly names such as the *Zombies, Enchanters, Undertakers, Mindbenders, Temptations, Temptress, Grateful Dead, Styx, Spooky Tooth, Pickettywitch, Coven*, and *Black Sabbath* are not apt to instill *joie de vivre* in human breasts. But counteractive forces are presented by the *Shangri-Las, Soul Stirrers, Soul Survivers, Sweet Inspirations, New Hope, Seekers, Searchers, Meditations, Devotions, Nice, Miracles*, and *Angels*.

It should be freely admitted that there are negative elements of a mundane nature present as well. Ensembles like the *Who, Guess Who*, and *Question Mark and the Mysterians* arouse suspicion. The *Mugwumps, Charlatans, Casinos, Trashmen*, and *Young Rascals* are merely mischief makers compared with the *Churls, Corsairs, Intruders, Highwaymen, James Gang, Mob, Village Stompers, Stampeders, War, Bloodrock, Lost Generation, Stealers Wheel, Bad Company, Badfinger*, and *Scaffold*. Transients who formerly adhered to the *Drifters, Paupers, Coasters, Vagrants*, and *Rolling Stones* have more recently found a voice in the *Runaways*, an all-female band that exudes sensuality in a manner that might only be surpassed by the *Demimondes* or the *Trulls*. There also exists a multitude of groups whose names seem to belong on the tattooed arms of street gangs, foremost among them being the *Rockin' Rebels, Tornadoes, Hurricanes, Raiders, Kinks, Dominoes, Outsiders, Hombres, Ramrods, Ventures, Del Vikings, Gaylords, Olympics, Marcels, Spinners, Contours, Youngbloods, Doors,* and *Los Bravos*.

Those who foresee a slide into decadence need not despair, for each pejorative can be balanced with names reflecting breeding, royalty, and even snobbishness. Despite the egalitarian lyrics of many popular songs, groups like *King Curtis and the Kingpins*, the *Kingsmen, King Crimson, Queen, Royal Teens, Royal Guardsmen, Teen Queens, Amboy Dukes, Essex, Barons, Regents, Viscounts, Buckinghams, Imperials, Crests, Coronets,* and *Sam the Sham and the Pharaohs* exemplify the monarchy rather than the great unwashed. Less regal but still displaying elitist sentiments are the *Commodores, Cavaliers, Elegants, Beau Brummells, Champs, Supremes, Gentrys, Chairmen of the Board, Friends of Distinction, Presidents, Rocky Fellers, Magnificent Men, Great Society, Uniques, Originals, Stylistics, Fortunes, Classics IV, Influence, Eden's Children, Sapphires, Diamonds,* and *Pearls Before Swine*. To indicate gentility, groups have taken residence in the glamorous surroundings of *Procol Harum, Crystal Mansion, Wadsworth Mansion, Glass House,* and *Taj Mahal*. There is even status in the names adapted from magazines: the *Vogues, Playboys, Vanity Fare,* and *Harper's Bizarre*.

Perhaps one day an artist will translate the incongruity of the noble coexisting with the villainous into rock music's escutcheon: a white sport coat opposite a black leather jacket.

This is quite obviously not an inclusive list. There are scores of groups who, by selecting a unique identity, defy categorization. Where, for instance, would one place *Soft Machine, Bagatelle,* and *Status Quo*? *Status Quo* is not only a distinctive but also a highly ironical choice for singers and musicians who perform in the most transitory field of entertainment. But even in this rhythmic world of perpetual change there is one constant: all groups, regardless of size, sex, or temperament, can trace their origin to the greatest of recording artists, *Noah Webster and the Lexicographers*.

Scoring Jargon

David C. Ferris
Exeter University

Compare this:

> To everything there is a season, and a time to every purpose under the sun. A time to be born and a time to die, a time to plant and a time to pluck up that which is planted

With this:

> Over the past ten years the school has evolved a child-centred individual-learning situation with a degree of integrated day organisation and close co-operation between each year's mixed-ability classes. Basic-work morning programmes are carefully structured but allow for integration . . .

Both passages are true enough exemplars of their times, the former from the Authorised Version, the latter from a recent advertisement for a Junior School teacher. Contrasting the two suggests that the language has gained in the past 350 years something that it could well do without. Loosely, we can call it "jargon," but it would be unfair to leap on our high horses every time we read a passage that contains unpleasantly long words and which does not make much sense to us; if we hear that

> Reaction kinetics and gas absorption, as well as catalysis and granulation, are technical fields in which the Division is particularly interested

we can do little but admit that nowadays there is more to fertiliser than following a horse with a shovel.

So this attack is addressed only to the inflated verbal pomposity that we might call bullfrog jargon. The school advertisement quoted above is by no means the most repellent abuse of English available, but I used it because it does at least seem to have been intended seriously, unlike perhaps,

> The structured structure by reason of its symbolic efficacy ongoingly structures the structure.

Although you never meet anyone who writes it himself, jargon somehow continues to rampage over English like the tendrils of a creeping jungle. It would be easier to resist if we could pin down a little more precisely what it is, and maybe the enterprise has a certain grisly interest of its own; earlier resistance fighters have of course made their forays, but tended to add a salvo of personal preferences as to style, and besides did not have the dubious advantages of the New Linguistics.

One thing they agreed was that we must all stamp hard on polysyllabic verbalisations. Actually, however, it is too naive to assume simply that 'jargon' equals "long words" even though we can see why we feel the temptation, when the enemy called taxmen *inland revenue officials* or when mockery devises *artificial bipartite abdominal integument* as a replacement for *trousers*. Admittedly there is a link; *experimentation* instead of *experiment* is a well-known type of irritant, while *experiment* itself could often give way to *test*. This is not at all to say that the words in each pair always mean the same thing, only that they sometimes do and that in such cases life would be more comfortable if writers would use the shorter one. Yet even if we could cajole, bribe, or threaten out of use all words of more than two syllables, things would not be that much better. Some people shrink from using one word where ten will do and entangle themselves in Byzantine wiles to avoid our everyday monosyllables; so *now* disappears underneath *at this present moment in time*. Switching our scrutiny to the number of syllables in a sentence does not help much either; we can shorten the unexciting but straightforward

> to judge from what is happening now, things will go on getting worse

to

> current trends indicate a continued decline

which, however, now reeks of jargon. Length simply is not blameworthy in itself; other factors are lurking in the undergrowth.

One noticeable thing about jargon is its cargo of vogue words. For no very clear reason certain weeds or animals sometimes undergo a huge and rapid leap in numbers and threaten to upset the natural system where they live; in much the same way certain words start breeding like rabbits and make an increasing (or "ongoing"?) nuisance of themselves. Today we are plagued by "open-ended" "meaningful" "commitments" "escalating" in all too many "situations." Sometimes vogue words succeed in keeping the territory they have seized, for it is not frequency as such, but sudden increase in frequency that makes them objectionable. More often they have their heyday and then pass on out of the limelight; *orchestrate* and *organic* are examples that seem to be fading into the darkness already.

However, although we may look askance at vogue words they do not really seem to be longer than the common run, nor does their presence of itself turn a text into jargon. Another hare that invites pursuit is the idea that unusual recherché words are the linguistic villians. After all, *marmalade* and *mother* are not jargon but are common, while *mode* and *median* are jargon but are not common. On this view vogue words annoy us precisely because they forsake their proper rarity and make an indecent exhibition of themselves. Unfortunately, the hare turns out to be a wild goose; there are plenty of words that tend the other way. For most readers the average "rarity" of

the piebald mare trampled the yarrow underfoot

must be much higher than of

the identical theory offers a basis for development

but the latter is jargon, the former plain.

So consider *flibbertigibbet* and *tatterdemalion*. At a guess these words get used fairly sparingly and they are certainly not short. Yet there is something reassuring and solid about them that seems to make them proof against corruption; we could sum it up by saying that they are homely rather than official; they are the sort of words we may have met among friends or family, and not in textbooks nor in some official report. There are large overlaps between homely words and those of native English (those not known to have been borrowed from another language) and between official words and those derived from the classical languages, though the agreements are not complete.

Homeliness brings with it two traits, both of which a word must have to earn our highest esteem. One is simplicity. The classical origin of most official words explains why so many start with prefixes like *contra-* and *anti-* or end with suffixes such as *-istic* and *-ational*. It is a good rule of thumb that where you find many affixes you have a jargon-ridden writer, but the etymology does not matter in itself. What does matter is the amount of brainwork demanded of readers. Vague as it may be, a proper slice of meaning is linked to such affixes in many of their occurrences (contrast *archaic* and *archaistic*); and there is evidence that an effort is needed, even if a very slight and subconscious one, to glue together the meanings of affix and root so as to decide roughly what the whole should mean, an effort not required for words that are, in English, simple, like *strong* or *chrysanthemum*. These tiny hurdles keep tripping our brain as it follows its semantic path and this is where length comes in. Naturally the more affixes are added to a root the longer the word becomes; but the trouble is caused not by length *sensu stricto* but by complexity.

The second point about homeliness is illuminated by words like *ocelot* which we might well first come across in a textbook; certainly, ocelots were not plentiful around my mother's knee. Yet it would seem odd to describe the name of an animal as jargon. Trying to explain this forces us to admit a cleavage in English between words that are in some way tangible or "real," and those that are abstract. We might agree in practice about the allocation of many items, but it is impossible to give an exact rule about where to draw the line, and what is more it will by no means coincide with what science would tell us; for instance, unicorns must be real whereas semanticists, regrettably, might be abstract.

We are now nearly able to devise an index to assay the linguistic virtue of English words, but fair play imposes one caveat. A word like *international* is abstract, borrowed from Latin with both prefix and suffix, and very often met "officially"; its appearances in advertisements even smack of the vogue word. However, we cannot throw many stones at it, simply because there is often no easy brief alternative (think of *international opera-singer*). Many words look suspiciously like jargon but escape with unsullied character because there is just nothing else that will do so well in the same place. That said, here is the index, built on the above remarks; naturally, we assume some give and take in the workings.

(1.) If the root of the word is "native" English; or (should it be borrowed) if the whole word cannot easily be replaced by another that does have a native root,
   SCORE 1.

For other roots,
   SCORE 2.

(2.) For every affix except *-ing*, *-ed*, *-en* and *-s*,
   ADD 1.

(3.) If the root is a bound morpheme (that is, if it

483

cannot stand as a word in its own right, like *-ceive*),
ADD 1.

(4.) If the word as a whole has an "abstract" meaning,
ADD 1.

(5.) If the word is a vogue word,
ADD 2.

Actually, it is far too optimistic to believe that this index could help in rooting out jargon; I merely offer it to readers so that they may amuse themselves in a melancholy way, gauging the monstrous growth of the weeds closing around the language.

The natural next move is to work out an index for texts. This means sniping at the Hydra of structural jargon; for even if they use only low-scoring words, writers can still make things awkward to understand or at least less attractive by using them in complex structures with plenty of subordinate clauses and dependent phrases. It is here that the legendary compilers of government regulations show their true mettle. Sadly, it is out of the question to work out a thoroughgoing system, if only because far too little is yet understood about the freedom with which our language lets us play around with the shape of sentences. But we can cook together a few ideas of our own and other writers, to give something like this:

(1.) Add together the jargon scores for all the verbs, adverbs, adjectives, and nouns other than names.

(2.) For every passive verb,
ADD 1.

(3.) For every double negative (as famously guyed in Orwell's *a not unblack dog was chasing a not unsmall rabbit across a not ungreen field*),
ADD 2.

(4.) For every subordinating conjunction,
ADD 2.

(5.) Divide the result by the total number of words in the text.

One important ingredient is missing, namely some means of measuring how complex the ideas are that the writer is trying to convey; any hack could score well describing the adventures of Tom and Jerry, but a laureate could, and indeed should, score rather high in expounding Kant's philosophy. This may be why editorials in the more picturesque newspapers score lower than *The London Times*. For that matter, something similar applies to the word index; ideally, we should mark different degrees of vacuity on a scale leading towards total meaninglessness, and adjust our sense of outrage accordingly. Yet, it is extremely difficult to pry into the inner anatomy of words to see how far the essence of meaning is diluted, nor is there much hope of getting wide agreement between, for instance, political theorists and theologians. At present, the best available remedy seems to be marking words as abstract or tangible.

One last observation is that here as often elsewhere both extremes are suspect. A very low score betrays a failing in that such writing would be more like babytalk than good English. On the other hand, the indices presuppose that high scores are a greater threat—signs of floundering intellect, or even mental bankruptcy; that is why I am interested, and sorry, to find after marking a range of texts that the highest scores of all were fairly consistently those of works on theoretical Linguistics.

EPISTOLAE

Nine words with *oto*? What a hornet's nest that will stir up! The photographers will be annoyed, and all the otologists. (There are at least a dozen eartickling relatives of that one.) The gardeners will throw a croton or a cotoneaster or a sotol; you'll be told to jump in the Potomac without a rotor. No one will kotow to you, or serenade you on a koto; rather, you'll be threatened with celotomy or colotomy, equally uncomfortable, or with banishment to Cotonou or Cotopani. (There's one of those in Colorado as well as in Ecuador.) Notoungulates and lotophage will vie with potoos and potoroos to bring you notoriety—and that's not one patch of what you'll hear from readers who have access to a big Webster or Oxford!

John Sinor in the San Diego Evening Tribune had his readers on their *otos*, trying to find the four English words that end in *gry*.

Try *that*, Richard Manchester.

But I am going to buy your book because—lucky me—I have three grandsons who love words.

Barbara Marsh
San Diego, California

485

BIBLIOGRAPHIA

LOUISIANA PLACES: A Collection of Columns from the Baton Rouge Sunday Advocate 1960 - 1974, by Clare D'Artois Leeper, Legacy Publishing Company, 1976, 264 pp. $19.95

On February 7, 1960, under the heading of "Louisiana Places: Those Strange Sounding Names," the Baton Rouge *Sunday Advocate* published a brief account of *Natchitoches*, the name of "the oldest town in Louisiana," deriving it from "paw-paw eaters," the name of a Caddoan tribe. This short discussion turned out to be the starting point and set the tone for a regular column on Louisiana place names (mostly names of towns and post offices) which Mrs. Leeper has conducted ever since. The fruits of the first fourteen years of her labors, about 770 items in all, have now been gathered and published in book form. The collection, while preserving the original wording of the first printing in all instances, presents the names discussed in alphabetical order. Although making them more easily accessible, this arrangement also exposes some of the major weaknesses inherent in the "permanent" reprinting of what once were intended to be "occasional" pieces, i.e., the conversion of a weekly newspaper column into a book without the required thorough revision.

The most noticeable of these shortcomings is undoubtedly the presence of a number of verbatim duplications (as under *Arizona*, *Bordelonville*, *Bunkie*, *Converse*, *Dry Creek*, and several others), which makes sense in a series of articles written over many years—at least partly in response to readers' enquiries—but tends to annoy the reader. As the author of a similar column in a monthly magazine, this reviewer is very much aware of the strong temptation to convert such contributions into a book, especially when encouraged by appreciative readers, but only under exceptional circumstances can such a conversion be carried out successfully and should therefore usually be avoided; it should never be attempted without the provision of an overview through a summarizing Introduction or Conclusion.

Having expressed an understandable dissatisfaction with the inappropriate process which created this volume, one is pleased to discover that the original subtitle, dropped in May 1965, does not imply the kind of exclusive hunt for the quaint and the curious which is so often the pursuit of the local onomastician. Naturally, several place names whose major attraction lies either in their intriguing surface meaning (*Aimwell*, *Bayou Bonne Idee*, *Converse*, *Forlorn Hope*, *Fort Necessity*, *Gin Lake*, *Lick the Skillet*, *Luna*, *Spoon Full*, *Sunset*, for example) or in their exotic sound/spelling (*Anacoco*, *Atchafalaya*, *Choupitcatcha*, *Maringouin*, *Natchez*, for instance) are discussed, but their inclusion does not seem to stem from the notion that such names are more worthy of enquiry than those which apparently contain no such mystery (*Bailey's Dam*, *Baldwin's Store*, *Big Bend*, *Branch*, *Buchanan's Ferry*, *Center Point*, *Cotton Valley*, *Oak Ridge*, etc.). For the name scholar there is no such creature as a "pedestrian" or "uninteresting" name, and Mrs. Leeper is clearly well aware of the full scope and potentialities of onomastic research.

Naturally, the geographical location and documented history of Louisiana predict a sizable native American and French admixture to the state's place-nomenclature, but while there does not appear to be any particular toponymic marker with regard to the former, a generic like *bayou* serves its purposes well as an indicator of the settlement area of the Louisiana French, as was demonstrated by Robert C. West over twenty years ago. The volume under review lists twenty-eight names in which this term, borrowed by the French incomers from the Choctaw *bayuk*, occurs as the first element; close scrutiny of the specifics of these names (*Chene Fleur*, *Adois*, *Alabama*, *Barbue*, *Beaucoup*, *Bonne Idee*, *Bushley*, *Castine*, *Chene*, *Chicot*, etc.) would be in itself a rewarding undertaking, opening up a fascinating range of cultural influences and naming practices, from the straight-forward to the bizarre.

As is to be expected, however, a study of Louisiana place names is not so much an exercise in linguistics as an investigation of local and regional history, and the better one knows the people behind the settlements, the first settlers, the first postmasters, the landowners, their wives and daughters, the easier is the task of unraveling the strands woven into some of the name stories; for if there is one chief factor which dominated the naming of Louisiana places, it is the recognizable American phenomenon of the shift from a personal name to a place name, as a gesture of grateful commemoration (*Addis*: after J.W. Addis, an official of the Texas & Pacific Railroad; *Akers*: after William W. Akers, the first postmaster; *Allen Parish*, after Henry W. Allen, Confederate governor of Louisiana; *Allen Settlement*:

after Mr. Allen, the first Justice of the Peace; *Amelia*, after Miss Amelia Dupuis, the deceased bride of the first postmaster; and several dozen more). It is in the exploration of this toponymic category, which forms such an astonishingly high proportion of the names on the Louisiana map, that Mrs. Leeper is at her best seeking out relevant information wherever it may be hidden. Thus the examination of a naming process frequently becomes the detective story of an eminently human event, and *story* and *history* merge again, regaining their former etymological unity.

Under these circumstances, who wants to attribute blame if the narrative impulse sometimes wins out over scholarly sobriety? Nevertheless, it would have been useful to have indicated in some way when a (migratory) place-name legend is recounted rather than a historical fact; otherwise, "West we go" as an answer to the question "Where do we go from here?" will become accepted more than locally as the true story behind the name *westwego*, and *Sunset* will continue to be thought of as having been named either by workers building the Southern Pacific Railroad, at the end of a heavy working day, or, alternatively, by inhabitants of Grand Coteau over whose community "the sun would have set," if the new railroad had not gone through it. Such folk-etymological reinterpretations hardly ever manage to retrace the original naming process, although their value to the student of folk narrative is, of course, undeniable.

Perhaps the special fascination, even virtue, of *Louisiana Places* lies in this very mixture of the sober and the sentimental, the rigorous and the romantic, the felicitous and the folksy. Just as they have done for the people of Baton Rouge since 1960, Mrs. Leeper's 770 place-names will now serve for those beyond the circulation area of the *Sunday Advocate*, as keys capable of unlocking some of the otherwise closed doors of Louisiana settlement history. On the whole, those who trust those keys will not be disappointed. They may, however, well join this reviewer in wishing that the author would soon provide us with a second book (beyond the supplements already promised), which, by abandoning the alphabetical arrangement, will give us that overall summary that the present volume lacks and which will treat the place names of Louisiana in the context of linguistic, social, cultural, and economic history. In the meantime, those of us involved in the Place Name Survey of the United States are grateful for another

488

important stone in this country's toponymic mosaic.

W.F.H. Nicolaisen
State University of New York at Binghamton

. . . *As we were going to press, we received word that the two supplements to* Louisiana Places, *one for 1975 and one for 1976, are now available. $2.50 each, paperback.*

—*Editor*

⌒

INDIANA PLACE NAMES, by Ronald L. Baker and Marvin Carmony, Indiana University Press, 1975. xxii + 196 pp. $7.95.

In the 1960s, the American Name Society established a commission to undertake a Place-Name Survey of the United States. The massive project is now well under way and is estimated to take 25 years to complete. It will result in a multi-volumed dictionary roughly comparable to the 50 or so volumes of the English Place-Name Society's *Survey of English Place Names*, published over the last half-century by Cambridge University Press. The dictionary will include definitive information on the historical, linguistic, geographic, and folkloristic aspects of the names and of the naming process of such artificial and natural features as cities, counties, streams, and the like. Meanwhile, approximately half of the states have place-name dictionaries of some sort and of varying degrees of completeness and accuracy. *Indiana Place Names* grew out of materials gathered for the national Survey and could well serve as the model for other studies which will doubtless appear over the next several years while we await the publication of the projected national study.

Indiana Place Names consists mainly of a 16-page Introduction and a 186-page glossary. The book offers information for the general reader about 2,271 villages, towns, cities, counties, streams, and lakes in the state, with emphasis on settlement names. It is quite selective in its coverage and is by no means a gazetteer, as the editors point out. Individual entries vary in length from a couple of lines to nearly a page and include information on spelling, pronunciation (including stress pattern), alternate names, type of

489

name (e.g., village, county), location, origin, and legends. The average entry has perhaps 6-8 lines.

In the Introduction, Professors Baker and Carmony classify the place-names into the following categories: names of persons, names from other place-names, locational names (*East Fork Tanners Creek, Half Way Creek*), descriptive names (*LaPorte, Plum Tree, Badger Grove*), inspirational names (*Harmony, Waverly, Troy*), humorous names (*Santa Claus*), Indian and Pseudo-Indian names, names from other languages, incident names (*Cyclone, Treaty Creek*), names from folk etymology, coined names, mistake names, and names from legends and anecdotes. The editors are thus able to account for an impressive variety of memorable names, including *Antiville, Beanblossom, Correct, Daylight, Jacks Defeat Creek, Needmore, Popcorn,* and *Pumpkin Center.*

Among the most interesting names are those derived from folk etymology and those that are mistake names. How much more American-sounding can a name be than *Gnaw Bone,* especially when we learn that it is a corruption of the French name *Narbonne?* Similarly, *Mary Delarme Creek* is a version of *Marais de l'Orme,* 'Elm Swamp.' *Correct, Siberia,* and *Taswell* should have been, respectively, *Comet, Sabaria,* and *Laswell.*

Some 31 of the names covered are derived from legends, and for many other names legends have been included. As the authors point out in the Introduction, the legends often suggest the prejudices and humor of the people telling them, and whether the legends accurately account for the names or not, they indicate what the names mean to the people who use them. It is fun to know that local legend attributes the name Eugene to a drunk who, having lost his wife, tried to call her ("Oh, Jane!"), but could only manage to say "Eu, Jene."

The authors not only analyze and classify the names treated in the book, but also discuss the pronunciations of these names, pointing out characteristics of Indiana speech as they occur in the names treated and noting other phonological reasons for the pronunciations recorded. Thus, the pronunciation of *Morristown* as if it were spelled "Morsetown," the loss of the final -*t* in *East Liberty*, the pronunciation of *Bainbridge* as "Brainbridge," and of *Putnamville* as "Putmanville" are explained in light of the authors' sound knowledge of the phonological development of language in general and of American English in particular. The discussion can generally be understood quite readily by the non-linguist, and such terms as metathesis, substitution, and assimilation are worked unobtrusively into the explanations.

The book has flaws, but they are relatively minor. For instance, the definition of a place-name given in the first sentence of the book needs explanation. The authors mention no other studies of Indiana place-names in their Introduction, they do not allude anywhere to the fact that an important national journal is published in the field (*Names: Journal of the American Name Society*), nor do they mention what is perhaps the most popular book on names, George Stewart's *Names on the Land*. And they offer no explanation of the purpose or scope of the national Place-Name Survey. The general reader, to whom this book is addressed, needs to know about these things.

It would help the general reader, too, if the relationship between the pronunciation of Indiana place-names and the dialects of Indiana were made clearer. To this end, more of the distinctive features of Indiana dialects need to be emphasized. More information on the method used to select the names studied and on the method used to select the works included in the Bibliography would be useful. Are the works in the Bibliography works consulted, works of general interest, or what? In any case, the publisher should be mentioned for each work listed. More explanation of why and how the particular pronunciation informants were chosen is also needed.

As excellent as the pronunciation section is, some matters are handled superficially. It is not enough, for example, to account for *Floyds Knobs* becoming *Floyd Knobs* by saying that this sound change occurs "because the combination is hard to pronounce." Why not say that since the *-s* in *Knobs* is anticipated, the speaker drops the *s* in *Floyds*? In addition, the pronunciation key is inadequate, and the printer, apparently, has introduced into it several errors. Finally, although the book has a beautiful map in an envelope inside the back cover, the reader is completely frustrated when he discovers that the coordinates of the map in the glossary do not refer to this map at all, but to a highway map which is not included in the book!

A measure of the book's success is that it whets the appetite for more than its format can accommodate. For example, it would be interesting to know much more about the origins of the names treated and about the nature and role of topographical terms in the naming process. The discussion of dialects would be even more valuable if some note were taken of social dialect differences. Someone needs to compare the pronunciations documented here with pronunciations found in dictionaries, and an analysis of syllable divisions might tell us more about the nature of English words and their formation. Meanwhile, onomasticians everywhere may well be grateful to Professors Baker and Carmony for a careful and useful study which will help the general reader understand the value and fun of a discipline which is perhaps just now coming into its own in the United States after a quarter-century of serious study by hundreds of scholars and laymen alike.

W. Bruce Finnie
University of Delaware

EPISTOLAE

Since most of your readers appear to be supersleuths, I await the charge that there is no chapter on Howard Cosell in *A Civil Tongue*. I had written "Criticism in the chapter *of* Howard Cosell, etc." and it came out "Criticism in the chapter *on* Howard Cosell, etc."

One or two of the items in III, 3 brought back to mind a book manuscript I once failed to sell. It was titled "Psychiatric Cook Book." I list a few of the recipes:

Plum Loco Pudding
Stuffed U.N. Conches
Inn Bread
Kooky San Jacque
Lemon Derange Pie
Apple Jitters
Fruit Conflict
World's Fear Special
Poultry, Geist
Milk of Amnesia
Traumatic Ketchup
Powdread Milk
Addle, Pate
Raw Shacktoast
Sib Ling Chow Mein
Dream of Celery Soup
Shocked Liver
Shuddered Wheat
Oafmeal Cookies

Freud Oysters
Inferiority Cornflakes
Accident Prune Pie
Schizo Farina
Filet of Timid Sole
Depressed Duck
Moronated Herring
Group Therapea Soup
Egg Foo Jung
Oddballed Eggs
Menthol Blocks
Confused Manna
Lobster Claws, Trophobia
Withdrawn Butter Cookies
I Qcumber Salad
Padded Celery Soup
Senilla Tea
Mixed Nut Cake
Oedipus Compote

M. Panzer
New York, New York

Twenty-six Sticks

Alden Stahr
Columbia, New Jersey

Oscar Ogg, in his *The 26 Letters* (Thomas Y. Crowell 1961), maintained that the Phoenicians invented our alphabet. But I hold that they didn't need to "invent" it — all they had to do was go out among the Cedars of Lebanon and pick up an alphabet very handily with the aid of a bronze dagger.

I made this startling etymological discovery when my young son Stanley was having difficulty learning the alphabet. I took him out in the woods, and with the aid of a penknife and a high degree of pertinacity we played a game of finding the building twigs of communication.

It's possible, of course, to start with *A* and find the letters in alphabetical order (what else?). But the rewards come sooner if we take any letters that come along and gather them helter-skelter until we have the whole twenty-six. Trees and bushes out in the open are too regular in their growth to have any but *I-V-Y* letters. If you want the odd, difficult letters, go where the undergrowth is thick and branches must twist and sometimes bend backwards as their leaves reach for sunlight. Certain trees have growing patterns that make them good sources of special letters. For example, the branches of wild cherry and gum often grow at right angles to each other to yield such letters as *L*, *T*, *E*, and *F*. Grapevines, wisteria, poison ivy (!) or other climbers are good sources of curvy letters such as *C*, *G*, *J*, *O*, *P*, and *Q*. Here is where Stan and I found the individual letters:

A - prickly pear

B - wisteria

C - wisteria

D - apple tree

E - wild cherry

F - wild cherry

G - prickly pear

H - spice bush

I - any bush (even ivy!)

J - wisteria

K - gooseberry bush

L - oak tree

M - hemlock tree

N - mulberry

O - Virginia creeper

P - wisteria

Q - wisteria

R - apple tree

S - wisteria

T - gum

U - wisteria

V - maple

W - mulberry

X - black birch

Y - spice bush (or any tree)

Z - prickly pear

493

BIBLIOGRAPHIA

SEXISM AND LANGUAGE, by Alleen Pace Nilsen, Haig Bosmajian, H. Lee Gershuny, and Julia P. Stanley, National Council of Teachers of English, 1977, 203 pp., paper, $5.95.

RESPONSES TO SEXISM, Ouida Clapp, ed., National Council of Teachers of English, 1977, 150 pp., paper, $4.50.

In the course of developing *Sexism and Language*, the authors sent a questionnaire designed to "survey people's attitudes on the issue of sexism and American English" to 200 randomly selected editors and members of academic organizations concerned with English. Within this elite group an obvious struggle is going on between those sensitive to the broad currents of linguistic change already at work and those blindly committed to the status quo. Representative of the latter was the following response: "Our editorial policy . . . is more concerned with clarity and a certain purity . . . than it is with the rather laughable and probably hopeless attempts (and meaningless ones, at that) to rid English of all sex-determined language."

The two books dealing with sexist language recently published by the country's largest professional organization of English teachers will probably not enlighten so confused and self-righteous a "thinker," but for those more alert and open-minded, they provide solid, well-documented evidence of the damaging influence on both sexes of some of our most cherished linguistic habits.

Responses to Sexism, the current manual in the NCTE's Classroom Practices series, contains 26 teaching units designed to help students recognize sexism in its many subtle forms and to develop flexible attitudes toward human individuality. Five of the units focus specifically on language and form a useful supplement to the longer volume.

Sexism and Language is an ambitious effort to analyze obstacles to sexual equality both in the vocabulary and grammar of standard English and in its use in several disparate subject areas—law, literature, marriage, dictionaries, and children's books and teaching materials. Inevitably the result is uneven. Like many publications put together from papers related to each other only by their authors' common concern, the book lacks a sense of progression. Further, the distinction between language itself and how it is used is often blurred: much of the analysis deals with the stereotypical images of females and males perpetuated through written materials rather than with words themselves or the exclusionary gram-

494

matical "rules" imposed on children by generations of well-meaning teachers.

Despite these weaknesses, each of the eight essays in the book contains valuable insights. Stanley's "Gender Marking in American English: Usage and Reference" demolishes any lingering belief that masculine-gender "generic" forms are sexually inclusive. Arguing that the "generic" encourages writers and speakers of English to perceive the male sex as the social standard (p. 62), Stanley uses extensive quotes from contemporary writers, both male and female, to demonstrate her case.

Nilsen's description of her work with young children, in which she tested their responses to William Labov's Type I (naturally developed) and Type II (formally taught) rules of grammar, supports Stanley's conclusions (p. 178). In other essays Nilsen discusses the definition of sex-roles conveyed through both slang and standard English. Her introductory article, which traces the media's handling (from 1970 to 1976) of linguistic sexism as a social issue, will serve as a useful chronology for future students of the subject.

Bosmajian's "Sexism in the Language of Legislatures and Courts" provides historical perspective on the way "women have been defined, labeled, and stereotyped as (1) mother and wife, (2) infantile and incompetent, (3) seductive and immoral, and (4) nonpersons and nonentities" (p. 77).

Gershuny explores the pervasive consequences of prejudiced Biblical translations: for example, the failure to render the Hebrew *'adham* (translated Adam) as the equivalent of "human being" in Genesis 2. Her discussion of subliminal sexism in dictionary definitions includes the best analysis in the volume of the harm done males (as well as females) by linguistic stereotyping (pp. 147ff).

The Valuable "Guidelines for Nonsexist Use of Language in NCTE Publications," which the Council published in 1976 is included as an appendix.

As long as teachers, writers, and editors ignore the androcentric bias of standard English, its maiming—and obscurantist—effects will continue. As these books demonstrate, however, pressures for change are widespread and sometimes come from unexpected sources. One reply to the questionnaire the authors of *Sexism and Language* sent out came from an editor who wished to remain anonymous: "We have made few, if any, changes," he wrote, "and do not plan to do so." Tucked in the same envelope was a second, unofficial response: "This is a note from _____'s secretary," it said.

"His answer and the deletion of his name speak for themselves. I'm working on him."

Casey Miller and Kate Swift
East Haddam, Connecticut

📖

WESTCOUNTRY WORDS AND WAYS, by K. C. Phillipps, David & Charles, North Pomfret, Vermont, 1976. 144 pp. $10.95

As long ago as 1905 the great British dialectologist Joseph Wright observed: "There can be no doubt that pure dialect speech is rapidly disappearing even in country districts, owing to the spread of education, and to modern facilities for intercommunication." The gloomy foreboding implicit in this remark has been largely borne out by subsequent events: the spread of literacy and education, and the snobbery that too often accompanies them; the improvements in transportation and travel, which have brought a shakeup of a hitherto stable population; the calamitous influence of two world wars; the coming of radio and television—all have had a hand in the standardization of speech and the decline of colorful localized variations in it.

Having said all that, it comes as a surprise perhaps to think that English dialects are still "alive and well" in many parts of the U.K. The nation-wide Survey of English Dialects (SED), organized by Leeds University, was not launched until 1947, yet it found a wealth of material to record during the 1950s and 1960s.

Dialect is one of the most enduringly popular and approachable areas of linguistics. It often evokes nostalgic reflections on the past, and the humor and practical "horse sense" it often embodies seem to epitomize solid stable values in an all-too-changing world. Although for modern linguists, dialectology is still somewhat rooted in the era of comparative philology, many people with an interest in local words and their origins do their share to preserve both the study and practice of dialect speech. Local dialect societies flourish throughout the British Isles.

The wish to preserve, to "gather up the fragments that remain, that nothing be lost" is a vital element in K. C. Phillipps's *Westcountry Words and Ways*. It is a thoroughly enjoyable book, aimed both at the enthusiastic "word-buff" and at the person who is interested in a bygone way of life.

Dealing specifically with the dialect and customs of Cornwall and West Devon, the book presents us with an abundance of absorbing data all put together in a highly readable, often humorous way. In a 19-page discursive introduction, Mr. Phillipps, lecturer in English at Leicester University, briefly chronicles the history of dialect research and points up some interesting aspects of Westcountry speech: how it makes use of humorous similes like "You'm like a cow handling a musket," or turns coarseness into a virtue, as in "The devil shits luck for some, but when he comes to we, he's hardbound [constipated]." Mr. Phillipps mentions how scientific modern dialectology is; he deplores the lack of interest in the International Phonetic Alphabet exhibited by dialect enthusiasts and general readers alike— but he shrewdly avoids using phonetics himself in this book.

The main part of the work, also discursive, although arranged alphabetically under keywords, is really a detailed expansion of some elements of the introduction. The keywords act merely as points of departure for entertaining, often anecdotal articles on Westcountry life and language. The arrangement suits the browser rather than the reader looking for something specific, and despite the presence of an index the linguist wishing to know about the Celtic element in Cornish English, for example, will have to realize in advance that much of what Mr. Phillipps has to say on the subject is contained under the keyword PADGY-POW.

This unsatisfactory arrangement is regrettably not the only drawback of the book; there is also one that arises from Mr. Phillipps's desire to prevent interruptions in his text. Thus the rather unusual method is employed of referring to an endnote by using a key phrase rather than a number. It was rather disconcerting to find that without realizing it I had read a passage on which there was a note, even though the author explains his system in the preface.

Yet these points are rather pedantic quibbles. This is not a reference work and my judgment of it is based on its entertainment value, which is very high. *Westcountry Words and Ways* is a thoroughly well-researched book. The author has gone to local magazines, learned journals, works of literature, and old dialect glossaries and dictionaries, and has also drawn on his own experience as a Westcountry dialect speaker.

True, the book is very often parochial in character, and we have the inevitable lamentation for the loss of things past and detestation of things present (especially motorways and city-dwellers). But in case you think that Westcountry dialect is like a wine that doesn't travel, just dip into this book and see if you can resist the humor of remarks like "If that hedge wudn' there he'd a gone right through 'un," or a sign on a beach saying "Do not sit in deck-chairs with wet bathers."

William Gould
Aylesbury, Buckinghamshire, England

□

CLASSIFICATION AND INDEX OF THE WORLD'S LANGUAGES, by C.F. AND F.M. Voegelin, Elsevier, New York, Oxford, Amsterdam, 1977, ix + 658 pp. $39.50

This is a nonobjective review. It has to be. Faced with an index of thousands of names of languages and dialects, only a minute fraction of which are familiar to him, the poor reviewer pursues his feeble ken to an *O altitudo!* and marvels at the courage that undertakes such an impossible task. That the task, though mainly shouldered by the Atlantic (= 'Atlaslike') team of the Voegelins, was shared to a certain extent is inevitable. Over forty distinguished consultants assisted, plus a number of graduate students. Was there enough help? Perhaps not. Perhaps there never can be.

The book is based in part on previous work. In twenty separate numbers of *Anthropological Linguistics* (1964–66), the authors gave us *Languages of the World*. Now, with an NDEA contract and the help of the consultants referred to, they have provided a complete revision according to a model provided by Charles F. Hockett ([ix]).

Let me say that the book is superior to others of the sort known to me—which does not imply lavish praise. The nit-picking that follows will be directed at nits that should not have been found in such a volume. The introduction makes a debatable remark in the first sentence: "one century [has elapsed] since the recognition that all the languages of the world could yield proto languages." This certainly needs qualifying (with "theoretically" or the like?), for what are we to do with Burushaski and all the other languages with no known relatives?

In approaching such a dazzling work, a reader soon turns to his own pet fields of interest or fortuitous areas of useless knowledge. Thus I turned first of all to Celtic, hardly an out-of-the-way realm compared to Chorotega or

Upper Cowlitz, granted, but possibly less familiar than French or German to some readers of *Verbatim*. Here I was self-righteously appalled. I found the traditional divisions of *p*-Celtic and *q*-Celtic, but with no explanation of the terms and with no reference to embarrassing contradictions in Gaulish or to recent illumination emanating from discoveries in Spain. I realize that limitations of space are crucial. But space could have been saved in giving the number of monoglot speakers of Welsh in four digits, instead of a fictional six. And the name of the Breton town Vannes takes slightly less ink than the incorrect *Vannetais* (= the dialect, not the town). To say that Breton is "probably an off-shoot" of Cornish saves space, to be sure, by avoiding many problems. The statement on Patagonian Welsh is most ambiguous: "spoken in Chubut Territory, Patagonia in South America in 1891" (p. 103); it is still spoken there! In listing the counties in which Welsh dialects (North and South—an intolerable oversimplification for anyone even slightly acquainted with Welsh dialectology) are spoken, the book provides an unpardonably incomplete statement. Manx, called "extinct in this century"—possibly a true statement—was presumably still alive and doing poorly when the book was written, for the last native speaker (born in the 1870s) lived on with Celtic stubbornness until 1974. There are still speakers, however, who learned it as a second language.

Let us look at Germanic, the group to which English belongs. A rather old-fashioned division is chosen (East, North, and West Germanic), although we are made aware of alternative theories (p. 139). But what evil genius led the authors to divide Scandinavian into Continental and Insular Scandinavian? A great many speakers of what are called "Continental" Scandinavian languages live on islands. We might well ask why English is not called "Insular West Germanic"! There is, however, greater fault in historical distortion. The Faroese would be justifiably incensed to learn (p. 141) that their islands are "Dutch-administered"! They never have been, and even the Danish control is slackening more and more in a surge of Faroese nationalism. The figures on speakers of Faroese (and Icelandic, too) are too low, as contrasted with those of Celtic speakers, which are, for the most part, too high. Perhaps the relative exuberance or mendacity of trusted consultants is to blame.

Including English-based Creoles as members of West Germanic, while no doubt intriguing to anthropologists, lends considerable distortion to the classification, especially when the numbering system implies that English (No. 5 in the Germanic group) is more or less equivalent to Gulla (No. 7), or that German and Dutch together ("Netherlandic-German") have somehow the same statistical weight as, e.g., Beach-la-mar (No. 16, p. 144), with its 50,000 speakers!

Another hobby of the reveiwer's is Armenian. In this book we find a traditional classification which, while not damnably wrong, was nevertheless shown by the outstanding Armenian linguist Hrachia Acharian/Ajarian as early as 1909 to have certain shortcomings. In his dissertation at the University of Paris, one of the few works by him not written in Armenian, but in French—and therefore accessible to the West, including Indiana—he gave syntactical and morphological proof of a much better tripartite division. Meillet's notion that Armenian was most closely related to Greek is based on eclectic features and, despite endorsement by Eric Hamp, for whose linguistic acumen this reviewer has boundless respect, is probably not well-founded; it is, nevertheless, accepted in this volume.

Living in Yonkers, N.Y., I am interested in a group of neighbors who call themselves "Assyrians." In fact, the two centers of Assyrian activity in the United States are Yonkers, N.Y., and Flint, Michigan (the latter also has Druses, to make the picture more intriguing). At the Assyrian National Headquarters in Yonkers one hears, from the lips of people so gentle that they can hardly ever have come down like a wolf on the fold, that they speak the "language of Jesus Christ" (unaltered). How does a book like the present one give an average citizen information on such matters? Not at all. Assyrian is discussed only in its usual connotation, as a "dialect" of ancient Assyro-Babylonian. Even if one looks up Aramaic, bearing in mind the spoken language of Palestine at the time of Christ, there is still not much help. Somewhere under "Modern Aramaic" this so-called Assyrian language should be included, but it is far from clear, in the present classification, where it belongs. (Incidentally, here, as well as in other places in the book, the use of such a paltry device as the semi-colon baffles the poor reader. Such an admission of one's own inadequacy ought to be eschewed, but it is difficult for me to tell whether a given semi-colon is a wall excluding extraneous elements, or a gate granting access, or a permeable membrane allowing osmosis. A look at p. 303 makes me vote for East Aramaic; but I could be wrong, and my neighbors, if dependent on works like this, will continue to confuse themselves with Christ and possibly Nebuchadnezzar as well.)

If these areas about which I know a thing or two (hardly three) evince so many defects, how can I have any great confidence in the accuracy of those sections (most of them!) where I know nothing? Logicians tell me that this is faulty reasoning. I do not believe them.

There is a bibliography, called "References" (359-383). Now, despite the worldwide scope of the material covered, well over two-thirds of the books listed (articles, too) are in English. Moreover, in those titles in foreign languages, there are incredibly glaring errors—in German, French, Russian, etc. Can you believe that there was an *Akademie der Widdenschaften* in Vienna? There are many signs of haste in this portion of the book. Perhaps the printer should not be paid.

I wonder how many people can afford the price of the volume? I cannot. I am also not convinced that such a work is really possible. We may need an encyclopedia instead. We also need maps. The ancient Meillet-Cohen had them, and I still consult them with some profit, although not for all parts of the globe. We probably also need tapes and films and many other things.

Come to think of it, there probably hasn't been a completely satisfactory and satisfying work on language since Panini, and even that great grammarian is said to have had his faults. There is, however, one great merit (in addition to many others, despite my strictures) and that is: its overwhelming list of languages should give pause to those friends (now, perhaps, ex-friends) of mine who mouth sweeping utterances about "all languages."

Robert A. Fowkes
New York University

📖

EPONYMS DICTIONARY INDEX: A Reference Guide to Persons, Both Real and Imaginary, and the Terms Derived from Their Names, Ed. by James A. Ruffner, Gale Research Co., 1977, xxviii + 730 pp. $45.00 [Available only directly from the publisher.]

For those readers not in the mood to reach for the dictionary, an *eponym* is defined by the *Random House Dictionary (Unabr.)* as 'a person, real or imaginary, from whom something, as a tribe, nation, or place, takes or is said to take its name: *Brut, the supposed grandson of Aeneas, is the eponym of the Britons.'*

Among all of the medical, anatomical, biological, and other names (e.g., *Shick test; Voight's lines; Swainson's hawk, thrush, cliff swallow, warbler,* and *warbling vireo; Swammerdam's vesicle; Unwin's extensometer,* etc.) are nestled *Peter Principle, Munchausen's syndrome,* and *Murphy's law* (attributed to 'Murphy Edsel?'). Browsing around, one finds such gems as *Queen Elizabeth's pocket-pistol, Knipperdollings,* and *Yongjong era.* Moving in the other direction (to the eponyms themselves), we can be dismayed that *Brillat-Savarin,* besides meaning 'gastronome,' has provided the name only for *Savarin,* which is a kind of egg bread (and of course, a brand name for a coffee), while *Pierre Paul Broca* gave his name to about ten anatomical spaces, angles, and other details. *William Carey Brinkerhoff,* although only *B.'s speculum* appears to have been named after him, ought at least to have a longevity potion named in his honor: he appears to be alive though born in 1861. [For the less fleet of fingers, that's 116 years.]

Extremely useful as reference, especially for etymologists, this book lists 20,000 terms and their 13,000 eponyms. Moreover, each is documented by reference to one or more of the 500 biographical sources neatly listed in a bibliography at the front. *Silhouette, Ferris wheel, poinsettia, boycott, nicotine*—they are all there.

Inevitably, as the editor suggests in his Preface, some items have been missed, but the only omission we noted was of *Urdang's Law,* "If you want a book badly enough you will buy it regardless of the cost."

EPISTOLAE

Below is the answer to a query regarding a word in *Mariah Magazine* (Fall) found on page 58.

> Thanks for your inquiry. A *hornsmith* is a person who crafts or carves items out of horns or bones (or synthetic substitutes such as plastic nowadays). Items might range from a belt buckle to a knife butt. *Hornsmith* may be part of western Rocky Mountain vernacular.

George O. Morrison
Monrovia, California

CHEERS & JEERS

The menu of the Sunningdale Country Club, Scarsdale, N.Y., offers: *crisp Long Island duckling, "Montmerancy,"; soft shell crabs, sauteed almondine; tournadoes of beef, "Forestiere"* [guaranteed to give you wind?]; *and mocca layer cake,* and *All entries* [are] *served with soup, salad, fresh vegetable, potato & coffee.* What we want to know is whether serving potato with the coffee is a rebellious reflex against the (California-inspired) practice of serving a salad with the appetizer? [Richard M. Lederer]

Sign on a restaurant in Richmond, Virginia: *veal parma john.* [Mrs. Howard Williamson]

Comments about self-referring words in VERBATIM [IV, 1] have evoked some interesting correspondence from several readers. Now a letter from Geertrui H. Garbolevsky on quite another subject sparks the invention of the self-canceling phrase. She provides the following, from "one of the better known universities in the Tidewater, Virginia, area": *This card entitles this student to attend your class. Students who report without this permit should be sent to the Registration Center to determine their registration status.* [How does the instructor know what to do about students who have no card?] Another gem, from the railroad station in Amsterdam: *We give no information.* And a long-time favorite of ours, to be found on every Band-Aid and other sterile gauze pad package made by Johnson & Johnson: *Sterility not guaranteed if package is opened.*

Two candidates for the *Word Most Often Misspelt: minuscule* (usually "miniscule"); *millennium, millennia* (usually "millenium, millenia"). On the basis of actual count, the latter misspelling is actually preferred by *The New York Times,* which, significantly enough, considers itself "the Keeper of the Anals" (or is that Annals?).

This season's candidate for the word most often misused: *bemused.* It means 'confused, befuddled; lost in thought, preoccupied'; it is more often misused to mean 'amused,' usually by journalists.

Words of Size and Shape

I am fond of words. I like the pulsing, throbbing ones that send a sentence bounding: *plummet, succubus, plunge*, or the angular ones that tear their way through—*shock, stark, acrylic, act*. Although not enthusiastic about the thin words that set the teeth on edge—*needle, skewer, shrew*— nor the chameleons that change their color to hide their meaning: *appears, figuratively, alleged*, I truly admire the big, full-blooded ones that stand like a bulwark, making the verbs work like hell to overcome them: *dungeon, mawk, holocaust, turgid, gothic*. There are light words that float their message—*pastoral, serene, languid*, and there are the cossacks that thunder through the mind: *savage, murder, cauldron*. I like the crisp words, too, those that make thoughts dance: *crystal, dazzle, crackle*. Still, I am aware of the tyranny of pure definition as it strips some words of their inherent, almost restful euphony—*gangrene, influenza*. Some there are that have a way of grouping themselves into an invitation to join them in a journey—*down across the ways*, or summon me to view an exciting panorama of space and time: *dawning of an age, a field of stars*, or that give me a trip along land- scapes of nostalgia: *twilight of an era, corridors of time*. Yes, sir. I like words. Each is a nucleus upon which misty thoughts— concepts—can condense to become vivid with life and color. And I am most fortunate for I have thirty-five thousand of them immediately at hand, and quick access to a quarter million more. Yes, indeed. I like words.

John P. Kidner
Alexandria, Virginia

EPISTOLAE

As you probably already know, the commonly used "four letter words" of 1977 were rarely, if ever, printed in the early days of our country. As a matter of fact, when spoken, it was only in private conversation—and then in a lowered voice.

This is leading up to the article, "That Dirty Bird," which appeared on the front page of Volume III No. 3 of your publication.

My boyhood home was in Minnesota (where herons and their habitats are numerous). My uncle who was born in Iowa well before 1850 told me (who was born in 1903) that the popular name of "That Dirty Bird" was derived from its habit of evacuation when disturbed and taking flight. According to my informant, the bird was called *shit-puke*, an easily acceptable explanation considering both the fact that the birds were numerous and immediately flew away from the disturber so that it was difficult to tell whether the bird was regurgitating or was evacuating its bowels. Hence the double "shite-poke" name.

There is little or no need to consult erudite dictionaries. "Ask the man who has seen scores of the Dirty Birds." Incidentally, the effluviae are white or brownish white and in many places stain the bulrushes where the heron makes its home.

George R. Downs
Denver, Colorado

⊠

I would add the German word *Kafer* to the list in Mr. E. E. Rehmus' penultimate paragraph of "La Cucuracha" [III, 3].

John P. Jehu
Albany, New York

⊠

A woman in our town is well-read and well-traveled and holds at least two academic degrees. Yet she speaks of the Hillamanian Mountains in Tibet, Simonese cats in Thailand, and Flamingo dancers in Spain.

"You mean Flamenco," someone murmurs, and she replies, "Yes, that's what I said: Flamingo!" After a week in Taxco, where the Mexicans corrected her daily, she still called the town Tacos.

What causes this aberration? Where is the malfunction?

Needless to say, her friends are enchanted. She serves steak with Bordello sauce. Her young nephew watches a TV show called Sesame Seed. Her dining room set was designed by Drunken Phyfe.

L. E. Braun
Detroit, Michigan

⊠

"I" before "e"
Except after "c,"
Or when sounded as "ay"
As in "neighbor" or "weigh," EXCEPT IN

Neither could either weird, surfeited, counterfeit sheik raise a stein, seize the height by stealth or sleight, or summon the leisure to make an obeisance by the seismograph on the weir.

Sheik and *obeisance* were of course once exceptions like *neighbor* and *weigh*, but no longer, at least in the U.S.

Harry L. Arnold, Jr., M.D.
Honolulu, Hawaii

H. N. Meng [III, 1] asks if *spit*, as in *spit and image*, might not be a truncated form of *spirit*. N. Shapiro suggests [III, 3] that we are dealing with "honest-to-goodness spit" (with which opinion I fully concur) and quotes a 15th century French phrase to substantiate his opinion: *son père tout craché.* Proverbial expressions have a way of bouncing back and forth across territorial boundaries and surely one of the most exciting, though frustrating, studies must be the search for the original version of any given proverb. Later reflections of this French phrase may be seen in Mateo Aleman's *Guzman de Alfarache* (Pt. I, 1599) where we find the phrase "*le decia que era un estornudo suyo y que tanta similitud no se hallaba en dos huevos,*" (Clasicos Castellanos, I, 93). James Mabbe, the English cleric who translated *Guzman* into English as *The Rogue* (1622), renders this line in his usual verbose fashion as "my mother would tell him, that I was like him, as if I had been spit out of his mouth; and that two Egges were not liker one another, than I was like him" (Tudor edition, I, 84), where the Spanish *estornudo* (sneeze) is rendered by *spit* (both, after all, being forms of forceful ejection). In Italian we also have the phrase, *e suo padre nato sputato.* M. P. Tilley, in his grand *A Dictionary of the Proverbs in England in the Sixteenth and Seventeenth Centuries* (1950) lists: *As like him as if he had been spit out of his Mouth* (M 1246) and dates the first example of its use as 1598.

It seems to me that the documented use of *spit* in such a context makes the expression *spit and image* a "corrected" form of an earlier participial use of *spit*, as in *spitten image*. Given this construction, the derivative *spit 'n image* (which puzzled Meng) becomes understandable and perfectly suits the meaning of the phrase as in: *he's the spit 'n image of his father*.

Ruth Brown, in her article on sign language, VERBATIM, III, 3, *Hear Finish Before (Pause) You?*, points out that nouns indicating the human male are signed above the nose while those belonging to the female are signed below the nose. She then, jocosely I hope, states that "long ago someone must have decided men have minds while women have mouths." The more charitable and traditional explanation associates the gender with the head piece. The sign for man is much like the gesture of catching hold of the brim of a hat (remember those curious items of dress?). The sign for woman, the thumb tracing a line roughly from the inferior tip of the auricle down to the chin, represents the string or ribbon from the woman's bonnet which was fastened beneath the wearer's chin.

E. J. Moncada
Gallaudet College
Washington, D.C.

It is well known that Milwaukee's largest ancestral group is German. Imagine the plight of a doctor's secretary who has to spell and pronounce names like these all day, every day:

Greiveldinger	*Promenschenkel*
Griepentrog	*Reifschlager*
Habersetzer	*Schwabenlender*
Klotzbuecher	*Seidenstricker*
Krautkramer	*Wesselschmidt*
Kronschnabel	*Schachtschneider*
Pflughoeft	

M. DeChant
Thiensville, Wisconsin

In a recent issue of VERBATIM [III, 2], "an (unspecified) number of years ago" was used. In my own writing I solve such a problem quite simply to my satisfaction by putting it: "A (n unspecified) number of years ago."

One further thought: Why is it that during Lent some bakeries produce "hot × buns" instead of "hot + buns"?

Donald Weeks
London, England

The Japanese word for insect is properly *konchu*, a more common word for insect or bug is *muchi*; the proper name for cockroach in Japanese is *aburamuchi*, literally 'oil-bug.' In III, 2 my letter concerning "The Enigmatic Eggplant" has the following error which is probably due to a misreading of my script: "Italian farmers who just cultivated" should read "Italian farmers who first cultivated."

M.R. Paskow
Sonoma, California

$\boxtimes$

In VERBATIM [III, 4], proofreader Barbara Marsh wondered why *chili* was so often spelled *chile*. It would probably be more in order to wonder why the Spanish word *chile* appears so often as *chili*. I don't know but I would guess that it is a result of an Anglo mispronunciation of the last syllable of *chile*. Yes, the name of the pepper is identical to the name of the country, and the vowels rhyme with *we-they*.

Donald E. Schmiedel
Las Vegas, Nevada

$\boxtimes$

The managing editor of the *Old Farmer's Almanac* suggested writing to you for help on a reference question I sent to them. We are trying to find the origin of the phrase, *old man winter*. It is such a common saying but I can't seem to get a handle on how it started.

Any suggestions you have will be greatly appreciated.

Carol Coon
San Francisco, California

. . . Readers may send their speculations, suggestions, etc., directly to Ms. Coon/Reference Librarian/Bay Area Reference Center/San Francisco Public Library/Civic Center/San Francisco, CA 94102. Editor

$\boxtimes$

Our "American-English" is fast becoming the international language that will eventually become the means for all the peoples of the world with which to exchange knowledge and ideas and to strive toward mutual understanding.

Unfortunately, our language in its present state is far from an ideal system of symbols, growing as it has from an array of northern European and Romance languages with a sprinkling of American Indian, Yiddish, and a few dozen other languages.

While this mixture has tended to develop an extensive lexicon, it has complicated it to a degree that endangers its usefulness. Therefore, steps must be taken now to purify and distill our language so that it can be used accurately and be taught to our children and to people of other countries quickly and easily.

Efforts such as yours are at work toward making our language a more accurate and useful tool for communication and should earn widespread interest and support.

Charles Bremer
Lincoln City, Oregon

The February 1977 issue was a delight. Walter C. Kidney, in "The Seating of Zotz" [III, 4], pointed out that reading widely leads to an extensive but not always *useful* vocabulary. (Emphasis added.) Au contraire.

Ten years ago I had a lunch interview with a writer/prospective employer. He said he'd always liked the word *borborygmus* and looked at me expectantly. "Oh yes," I replied brightly, "Greek for 'tummy-rumblings.' " The job was mine.

I had only learned the word two weeks previously from an amusing column in *The Saturday Review of Literature*.

Looking back, I bet the writer had learned the word from the same source. If you read this, Mark, I'll hear your chuckle.

Joanna B. Paxson
Washington, D.C.

A cartoon in VERBATIM [III, 4] revolves around the expression *to bend over backwards*. I am led to share with you an excerpt from a letter I received recently from Robert I. Colin, of Gloucester, Massachusetts.

When, before retirement, I worked at ITT in Nutley, N.J., I often had two-way correspondence with a gentleman working at an ITT subsidiary in Stuttgart, Germany. Our letters (and conversations at personal meetings) were often polyglot, since we both were handy in each other's languages.

In one of my letters to Stuttgart, I used the

phrase *bend* (or *lean*) *over backwards*. In reply, my
colleague wrote that he followed well all of my
letter, but "what is this thing about bending over
backwards?"

To explain it, I composed several instances where
that phrase would apply. Also I cited the (cumbersome)
German word, *überkompensieren* 'to over-compensate.'

Stuttgart was still puzzled. Some months later he
came to Nutley on a personal visit. In my office was
another ITT employee, a Frenchman. I knew that
Stuttgart, like many educated Germans, was proficient in
French, so I asked Etienne if he could explain what *bend
over backwards* would be in French.

Etienne paused a minute, and replied, "No. A
Frenchman would never bend over backwards."

Since then I've put the question to professors of
German, French, Italian, Spanish, and what have you.
All were stumped. There the matter rests. I conclude that
ethnic differences make certain notions impossible to
translate into other languages.

I gather from the Supplement to the *Oxford English
Dictionary* that *bend over backwards* originated in this
country and is seldom used in England. The earliest citation
in the *OED* is for 1926.

Some of your readers might be able to cite a similar
idiom from another language.

> Willard Espy
> *New York, New York*

I wonder if any other of your readers note a certain
deficiency in our English language. That is the proper word
or expression which means thinking of the clever answer or
the witty retort after the event has happened.

Germans say *Treppenwörter* literally 'step-words' while
the French say *les paroles d'escalier* or 'words of the
staircase.' Both of these expressions mean that you've
thought of the clever response while going down the stairs
AFTER you've left the party.

Of course, no one uses steps anymore. We use elevators
but "elevator words" seems too uplifting. If we used the
English term, we could call them "liftwords" which does
have a lilt to it, but nobody would know what you meant.

May I suggest that we use "wishwords" for these afterwards afterwords in the sense that "I wish I'd said that."

Do your readers have any other suggestions?

Martin Harris Slobodkin
Cambridge, Massachusetts

If the *milli-helen* of W. K. Viertel [III, 4] is accepted by the American National Metric Council, they will probably insist that it be written *millihelen,* i.e., without the hyphen. Also the official symbol would be *mH*.

Before it is adopted that body may insist that history be ignored and the definition be that a *helen* is the 'amount of female beauty required to launch one ship.' After all, *centigrade* has been changed to *Celsius* (not lower case), and for frequency the unit is a *hertz* (lower case) rather than *cycle*.

Since it is planned to eventually substitute 3.6 megajoule (symbol *MJ*) for a *kilowatt-hour*, the redefinition of *millihelen* to *helen* could be done at the same time.

F. W. Schaub
Decatur, Illinois

Ethel Grodzins Romm says silly hyphenation by computers [III, 4] is no joke for marginal readers. I would carry that further: it is a serious roadblock for young readers.

In Westchester County, N.Y., one of the nation's richest and best-educated areas, eight Gannett newspapers are promoting a Newspaper in Education program. This plan, it tells teachers, "reinforces the things you teach." So look at some end-of-line splits from these newspapers:

boo-kends	*houseb-roken*	*so-mething*
bul-lhorn	*looses-trife*	*someth-ing*
brea-kaway	*mor-gue*	*stil-lborn*
chee-seburger	*pru-ned*	*spo-kesman*
di-mestore	*ris-ked*	*storef-ront*
dinin-groom	*shel-lfire*	*surpri-se*
gues-swork	*shellf-ish*	*tee-naged*

These may evoke little more than ridicule from a discerning reader. I am concerned that some examples may lead to sloppy writing and mispronunciation.

Reasonably acceptable pronunciation is one key to peer respect. English is full of oral traps. The hazards compound when newspapers omit diacritics from foreign words as most of them do. *Habitué* without its accent easily becomes "ha-bi-too" for a 14-year-old who lacks French and hasn't heard the word.

Once the Linotype operator and the proofreader took pride in their work; few absurd divisions of words got by. Even when type is set electronically, means exist to provide logical divisions, even though it may take an extra pair of eyes. This is a hard pill to swallow for companies already saving millions through automation.

Ben Bassett
Larchmont, New York

"Aunt Minnie's Chicken Talk" [III, 4] finally answered my question of long standing, why Britons say "keep your pecker up" when they mean the chin.

Other pseudo-X-rated expressions we heard during our four-year stay in Scotland were: "Give me a wee tinkle," "Knock me up sometime," and, as my 16-year-old Scottish secretary announced one morning upon arrival at the office, "I didn't get my piece this morning."

The last one caused upraised eyebrows until she explained that a *piece* is a 'brown-bag lunch.' *Knocking up* means 'knock on someone's door,' and the *wee tinkle* has nothing to do with the water closet. Rather, it suggests the use of the telephone.

H. G. Frommer
Mequon, Wisconsin

Why does Barbara Walsh [III, 4] prefer *chili* to *chile*? When she finds *chile* on a menu, it is almost certain to be part of the phrase *chile con carne*, perfectly good Mexican for a dish which presumably originated in that part of the country which became Arizona, New Mexico and Texas. Why Americanize part of its name? Would she prefer 'kid al horno' to *cabrito al horno*, or 'turkey mole' to *mole de guajolote*?

Incidentally, Francisco J. Santamaría, in his monumental *Diccionario de Mejicanismos*, defines *chile con carne* as 'a detestable dish which, with the false designation of

512

Mexican, is sold in the U.S. from Texas to New York.' He must have eaten some of the canned stuff.

W.S. Tower, Jr.
Essex, Connecticut

⋈

Re your review of *Words and Women* in the September issue of VERBATIM: I quote, ". . . the unassailable fact is that all sages have always been male and we would defy . . . anyone . . . to unearth evidence . . . that the word has ever been used to refer to a female."

I cite the following passage from the first page of David Niven's *Bring On The Empty Horses:*

When Gertrude Stein returned to New York after a short sojourn in Hollywood, somebody asked her, "What is it like—out there?"

To which, with little delay and the minimum of careful thought, the sage replied, "There is no 'there'—there."

Joyce A. McConeghey
San Francisco, California

⋈

Perhaps the Austin Awareness League would find useful the avowed statement of Deacon Ephraim Stebbins of long ago, quoted in Burgess Johnson's *The Lost Art of Profanity*, Bobbs-Merrill, 1948. Said Deacon Stebbins, "Unabridged dictionaries are dangerous books. In their pages men's evilest thoughts find means of expression. Terms denoting all that is blasphemous, foul or obscene are printed there for men, women, and children to read and ponder. Such books should have their covers padlocked and be chained to reading desks, in the custody of responsible librarians, preferably church members in good standing. Permission to open such books should be granted only after careful inquiry as to which word a reader plans to look up and how he plans to use it."

I derived my appreciation of the language very early from my father who was a merciless critic. My mother was a church organist, and the current minister telephoned our home once and asked my father, "Is your wife convenient?" My father replied, "A strange question, and for what purpose I cannot imagine, but yes, I believe I would say that she is quite convenient," and hung up. My mother cried, the minister called again, and all turned out well after my parents were finally speaking.

Marianne B. Garland
Wellington, Kansas

513

Anglo-American Crossword Puzzle
No. 1
by Jack Luzzatto

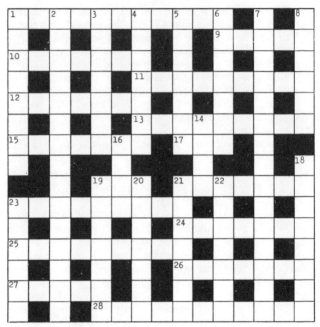

ACROSS

1 Secular pact has sensational effect. (11)

9 Suit that wears like iron. (5)

10 It's mean to be made to declare how old one is. (7)

11 Blushing about confused entree when back in the room again. (9)

12 D.C. current. (7)

13 Charms with stage appearances. (9)

15 Trained to be shot. (7)

17 Howl for back pay. (3)

19 De mortuis nil nisi bonum, burying a party man. (3)

21 Caliper shows it's a good copy. (7)

23 Detail cue to avoid misunderstanding. (9)

24 Goon caught in broken part of the defense wall. (7)

25 Sitter, at eve, takes the table linen. (9)

26 Bad rut in crooked back road puts the car out of drive. (7)

27 Clean non-nuclear missile. (5)

28 Comes back for more exorcising? (11)

DOWN

1 Step made in wild panic. (8)

2 Charge of the light brigade. (8, 7)

3 Confine mater in LM to the moon? (7)

4 Forced to comply by the small company creed. (7)

5 What old Boston fought for—bitterly, without tea! (7)

6 Coming back as something of a sailor, in a hopeless situation. (7)

7 See Ira inspire a man here? Ask his brother George. (8, 2, 5)

8 Dupers of their own sexuality? (6)

14 Gear (like jeans, perhaps) that becomes a popular fancy. (4)

16 Old governor seen coming back to the Orient. (4)

18 So constant a lust for liquor requires a locked cabinet. (8)

19 Understanding person at the drive-in. (7)

20 Femme fatale turns up as part masculine. (7)

21 Is sorry about the poor present. (7)

22 Something detected by smell. (7)

23 What artists take when leases are broken. (6)

EPISTOLAE

Reinhold Aman's letter in VERBATIM [III, 3] refers to Professor Fowkes's quest for a palindromic English city name. Is that on the level? (*Level*, by the way, is a Maryland town northeast of Baltimore.)

Carolyn Farkas
Cecil Community College
North East, Maryland

ANSWER to Anglo-American Crossword Puzzle (No. 1)

ACROSS

1. SPECTACULAR
9. ARMOR
10. AVER-AGE
11. RE-entere-D
12. POTOMAC
13. ENTRANCES
15. DRILLED
17. YAP
19. De M(ortuis)
21. REPLICA
23. ELUCIDATE
24. PAR-ape-T
25. SERVIETTE
26. NE-utr-AL
27. LANCE
28. REPOSSESSES

DOWN

1. ST-am-PE-de
2. ELECTRIC CURRENT
3. tram-M-e-L
4. CO-ERCED
5. LIBERTY (bitterly minus T)
6. RAT-TRAP
7. AMERICAN IN PARIS
8. PRUDES
14. RAGE
16. EYED (dey-E)
18. -TANT-A-LUS(t)
19. DIV-in-ER
20. MAN-TRAP
21. REPENTS
22. PER-FUME
23. EASELS

VERBATIM®

THE LANGUAGE QUARTERLY

Vol. IV, No. 3   December 1977

EDITOR: LAURENCE URDANG

We Do Not Talk Only With Our Mouths

Walburga von Raffler-Engel
Vanderbilt University

I N THE PAST, linguists have analyzed language as if words were the only means for conveying a message. They have ignored the fact that human communication is a combination of words and gestures.

When an Englishman shakes his head he indicates *no* as much as when he says so. To a Greek this same head movement means *yes*. To say *no*, he nods.

Cultures vary greatly in the meaning of gestures. I know of one American girl who waved goodbye with the palm of her hand open towards the Italian male whose attention she did not appreciate. Little did she know that in Italy one waves goodbye with the back of the hand and that showing the palm of the hand means 'come closer.'

Why have linguists taken so long to incorporate gestures into the analysis of language? Even those anthropological linguists who actually looked at their *informants* did not analyze body movements. Most of the time, they made note of them to serve as a prop for the time they would get down to the real business of analyzing the verbal transcript. In addition, the bulk of their transcripts came from monologs. Linguists seemed to ignore the fact that most of natural language occurs in dialog, within a conversational setting.

Stranger yet, the psycholinguists working with infants by and large ignored the obvious: eye contact and touch between mother and child, not to mention the infant's pointing at objects.

What all these linguists did was to transcribe what they heard and then work on their transcripts as if they were the real thing. What they did not realize is that spoken and written language are different media of communication. When we read in a piece of literature that a professor asked a student, arriving for a conference, why he had come, all the while keeping an eye on his watch, we realize that this professor did not encourage the student to speak. When we look at the linguist's transcript of such a speech act, we find no mention of the professor's gazing at his watch. An incomplete transcript makes a fully accurate interpretation impossible. The nonverbal component of human communication is as vital to the message as the verbal component. Anthropologists have recently become aware of how much information on nonverbal behavior is provided by the written records of the past. A new branch of anthropology, called *literary anthropology*, has developed with the task of extricating the forms of the nonverbal behavior of ancient civilizations from their writings, to be added to what otherwise may be deduced from visible records on tombs and other pictorial representations.

Psychiatrists, of course, have always incorporated the movement of the body in the analysis of human interaction. Belatedly, linguists too have come to recognize that people gesticulate while they talk. In 1941, David Efron published a remarkable book comparing the nonverbal behavior of assimilated and nonassimilated immigrants in New York City, showing how culture had influenced their body movements. Nobody noticed. In 1972, Efron's book was reprinted with a new title, and *Gesture, Race, and Culture* sold very successfully. In 1952, Ray Birdwhistell wrote his *Introduction to Kinesics* relating gestural behavior to spoken language. The term *kinesics* caught on among the linguists of the time, but in the 1960s, the *kineme* went the way of the phoneme. Now kinesics is definitely in again. A series of books on body language began to appear in the early 1970s, and this subject is now covered by ever longer chapters in new textbooks. Every meeting of linguists, psychologists, or anthropologists—and recently, also sociologists—has its section on nonverbal behavior.

The area is still new and the terminology is still in flux. What I propose is a tri-partite division: (1) *Body language* for bodily movements in general as they express the mood of the individual, nervously walking back and forth, fidgeting with his hands, or crossing his legs for a more comfortable sitting position; (2) *Kinesics* for message-related body movements which can substitute for a verbal expression or accompany a verbalization, reinforcing it, e.g., a German speaker can simply touch his forehead with his index finger or while doing so may say that such and such a person is a bit nutty; Mediterranean people have a rich repertoire of kinesic gestures; Anglo-Saxons are supposed to "keep their hands still"; and in one African language, numbers are always indicated by the fingers; (3) *Social movements*, probably the most important category of the three, comprises those movements of the body that are obligatory within social interaction. These are movements which children may be explicitly taught, while kinesic motions are generally acquired with verbal language. Greeting formulas, for example, enter into this category. In Europe, upper-class youngsters learn how to kiss a lady's hand without their lips actually touching the skin. Black Americans have developed the highly stylized art of the *soul handshake*. This ritual may take up to fifteen minutes and is seldom if ever practiced in inter-racial encounters. The hand may touch any part of the forearm—and even the elbow—giving a warm sensation of companionship. Among orthodox Jews, members of the same sex may hug each other, but men do not shake hands with women. The Japanese, who find the custom of hand shaking distasteful and unclean, greet each other with a deep bow. Persons of equal status get up at the same time—not an easy feat to accomplish because the two parties must ogle each other unobtrusively in order to synchronize their movements. When there is a disparity in status, it is very important that the person of lower status be the last one to get up. If a subordinate were to get up before his superior, the subordinate would feel highly embarrassed: it would be tantamount to his having insulted his superior.

It is in the realm of social movements that the generation gap is most apparent. Some young Japanese refuse to bow to their fathers, some young Europeans balk at handkissing altogether, and some young women feel that they are not truly liberated if they allow a man to hold the door open for them.

Research in kinesics is not easy. It requires a great deal of patience and technical know-how, first to videotape or film the subjects and then to analyze their behavior. One can start from the meaning and compare all the body motions that go on when an identical meaning is expressed verbally by any of the interactors, or one can concentrate on body parts and transpose on the editing tape all shoulder shrugs, foot tappings, and so on. Eventually, one is still confronted with the task of checking each of these separate body movements within all other movements that go on at the same time, thus forming a gesture cluster. Applauding with a sarcastic grin on one's face is not the same thing as applauding with a cheer.

Beyond the gestural behavior of people in conversation with each other, one can also research how people perceive and eventually reproduce the kinesic behavior of a third party, e.g., when talking about somebody who usually sits in a very formal manner, people themselves often straighten their posture. Making an analogy with *metalanguage*, I call this behavior *metakinesics*.

The relationship between the original kinesic movement of the model and the metakinesic movement of the reproducer is not one of absolute identity but rather one of sameness of proportion. The speaker who reproduces a kinesic model does so within his own body size, the speed of the ongoing conversation, and the limits of the space available between him and his conversation partner. His reproduction may be faster or slower and larger or smaller than the model, but it tends to maintain the same proportional relationship which obtains in the original for duration, range, and direction of movement.

Sex identification is very apparent in metakinesics; people copy movements most readily from those of the same sex. In addition to a natural inclination toward sex identification, in metakinesics one can observe strong sex taboos. These taboos seem much more pronounced in men than in women.

Men are more likely to copy men's behavior; they rarely copy a woman's body movements in exactly the same way she has made them. A strong taboo seems to intervene, and the movements are copied only approximately or incompletely. One female subject, mentioning a woman wearing a big earring, brought her hand to her ear in exactly the same fashion the woman talked about was in the habit of doing, while the male subject only touched his ear rather than his earlobe, and his hand remained there for a briefer period. Another male subject described a girl "gently playing with her hair." He cupped his hand in the fashion that the girl had done when stroking her hair, but he never actually touched his hair. On the videotape one sees the hand going up toward the hair and then, almost suddenly, arresting itself and performing the stroking motion in mid-air. The same male subject copied the eating motion of a woman by bringing his hand up, but again he arrested it just short of touching his mouth.

The process of metakinesics is basically psychological. The individual reproduces someone else's body movement within his own physical capabilities and social constraints, a process that is largely noninteractional.

The kinesic movements that go on during a conversational exchange are of a different nature. There is a constant interaction by which one conversation partner influences the other and vice-versa. The reciprocal influence is strikingly apparent in the body postures of interactors, which tend to synchronize. Sometimes they cross their legs, put their hands on their laps, scratch their heads, and so forth in what has been termed *interactional synchrony*. At times, one person who has not performed such an act in concert will "stick out like a sore thumb." In most interactions, in couples as well as in groups, there is a leader. This dominant partner establishes the tone of the conversation, which may be formal or relaxed, and the other participants then adjust their postures accordingly.

When an adult interacts with a child, he tries to accommodate his nonverbal behavior to the age of the child. The adult sits close to a small child, touches the child when he feels that the little one's attention is wandering, and makes use of extended movements of the hand and the arm to illustrate what he says.

In nonverbal behavior, as in all forms of human behavior, there are elements that are innate and common to all men, and there are specific forms which are culturally conditioned. Children are socialized into their cultures from the moment of birth. In North America, newborn babies are usually separated from their mothers and are bottle fed by a professional nurse at regular intervals. In other cultures, babies enjoy a playful body touch and rhythmic rocking by their mothers, who also sing to them.

As children grow up, they adjust to the kinesic behavior of their communities. Eventually, they establish a pattern of expectancy for gestural behavior similar to the expectancy which makes one's mother tongue understandable and other languages foreign. When, in the Vanderbilt Linguistics Program, this expectancy was tested by showing a videotape of a conversational interaction involving a certain amount of

521

gesticulation, persons from low kinesic cultures hardly noticed any details of the ongoing gesticulations, while persons from high kinesic cultures—such as South Americans—recalled most of the movements. It is no surprise to find that bicultural individuals have more than one kinesic code just as bilinguals possess mastery of more than one language.

In truth, we do not talk only with our mouths.

Explication de cricket

Mr. Herbold's list of baseball metaphors in VERBATIM [IV, 1] tempts me to submit an analogous list of cricket terms which have similarly been taken into the general language by the British. From my British-American dictionary (No. 21 on the VERBATIM Book Club list) I have culled some examples, to which I must append some interpretation and explanation, since very few Americans have the remotest notion about cricket and its mystique, and analogies to baseball are treacherously misleading. But let's try.

1. To *carry* or *carry out* or *bring out one's bat* is to 'stay with it,' 'outlast the rest'—the exact nuance depending upon the context. This expression applies to the batsman (batter) who is not put out during the match while his teammates fall by the wayside, and therefore leaves the pitch ('field') only at the end of his side's innings (yes, it has an -*s* in the singular: an innings is 'the period of play during which a side is *in* [or *up*]') carrying his bat with him, instead of leaving it for the next batsman, as used to be done in former times before everybody could afford his own bat. His ten teammates are all out; thus he has 'stayed with it' and 'outlasted' them.

2. To do something *off one's own bat* is to do it 'on one's own.'

3. To *get a duck* or *be out for a duck* is to 'fall flat on one's face,' to 'fizzle.' *Duck*, in this idiom is short for *duck's egg*, a British variant of *goose egg*, meaning 'zero' (or *nil*, as the British prefer to express it in scoring). Thus, a batsman who is out without scoring a single run is said to *get* or *be out for a duck*.

4. If one gets a duck in both innings (in first class, or major league, cricket, each side has two innings) one *bags a brace*. The term is used to describe a 'double fizzle,' as it were. You fall on your face, get up, and do it again.

5. A batsman who makes his first run is said to have

broken his duck. Hence to *break one's duck* is to have 'broken the ice,' 'made a start' and to 'be on one's way.'

6. To *have a good innings* is to 'have a good long life.' *Innings* is used metaphorically, like *inning* in America, to mean a 'turn,' an opportunity to accomplish an objective. *Innings* applies especially to a political party's period of dominance, or the term of a jobholder generally. But in context, a *good innings* means a 'life that is satisfying in both length and accomplishment.'

7. To *hit* (or *knock*) *someone for six* is to 'knock him for a loop,' 'knock the daylights out him.' In cricket, a ball hit beyond the boundary (roughly equivalent to *into the stands*) scores six runs, and a *six* is analogous to a 'homer.'

8. A *maiden over* is a bowler's achievement. He bowls (pitches) six balls, and that constitutes an *over*. If he can do this without allowing any runs, this is called a *maiden over* (a curious reference to virginity). Metaphorically, then, a *maiden over* is a 'successful ordeal,' one through which the protagonist has emerged unscathed.

9. To *queer the pitch* is to 'queer the act,' 'spoil someone's chances,' 'gum up the works,' 'throw a monkey wrench into the machinery' (or, as the British say, *a spanner into the works*).

10. To *be on a good wicket* is, like *being on a good pitch*, to 'be in a good spot.' To *be on a good wicket* with someone is to 'be in favor' with him. To *be* (or *bat*) *on a sticky wicket* is to be in a bad situation. *Wicket* has come to mean 'situation' generally. Thus, the newspapers spoke of the "American wicket in Vietnam."

11. To *up* or *draw stumps* is to 'pull up stakes,' 'clear out.' The stumps are the three upright sticks which form part of a wicket (here *wicket* means something else again) which the bowler tries to break each time he bowls, and any fielder with the ball in his hand can aim at as well while the batsman is running, in order to score an out. When the match is over, the stumps are pulled out of the ground and everybody goes home.

12. *At close of play* means (referring to anything) 'at the end of the day.'

13. *To play a straight bat* (considered correct form) is to 'play fair'—the very essence of cricket. Which leads to . . .

14. *It isn't cricket*, a sentence and a sentiment with which I'm sure we are all familiar.

Much of the above may be confusing, but space does not permit a dissertation on cricket—a game, a way of life, a religion. Suffice it to say that in Britain as well as in America, the national sport has been a fecund source of colloquialisms found in the everyday language of those who may never have attended a match.

Norman W. Schur
Weston, Connecticut

EPISTOLAE

There is an almost universal misunderstanding of the use of the ministerial adjective, the title "Reverend." All my life I have tried without success to correct editors, newscasters, parishioners, and the general public in the proper address of the clergy.

The easiest way to remember the rule is to equate the word *Reverend* with its counterpart, the formal use of *Honorable*. No one would address a judge as "Honorable" Jones, yet "Reverend" Jones is common practice.

The only time *Reverend* is used without an article before it is in a public address or in a letter addressed to the *Reverend Clergy* or *Reverend Fathers*, although now perhaps the adjective could precede *Ladies* or *Sisters* in some communions.

Always, in every other case, the correct form is *The Reverend Mister* or briefly *The Rev. Mr.* (or *Dr.* or *Mrs.*, *Miss*, or *Ms.*) Jones.

Years ago, I wrote a bit of doggerel which states the case. It reads, in part:

> The use of the "Rev." when you speak to your preacher
> Is as tricky a thing as I ever will teach yer;
> For he's not "Rev. Jones" though a seminary grad,
> He is "Mr." Jones and that's all my lad.

(The Reverend) Frederick W. Cropp
Santa Barbara, California

Winking Words

Philip Michael Cohen
Aliquippa, Pennsylvania

Twenty years ago, a group of Cambridge students decided to establish a sport where they could excel, the traditional ones being tiresomely full of experts. When they chose tiddlywinks and began standardising rules and equipment, they surely had no idea that it would become nationally prominent (with the aid of the Goon Show players and Prince Charles) and even take root across the Atlantic. There is now a small but enthusiastic community of U.S. winkers, concentrated at Eastern colleges but with colonies elsewhere.

This form of tiddlywinks offers great scope for strategy as well as physical skill, but even the most serious winkers retain a lighthearted attitude toward the game. This is particularly clear in the vocabulary. The two basic actions of the game are called *squidging* (shooting a wink with a special oversized wink, or *squidger*) and *squopping* (covering a wink with another, thereby paralyzing it).

While HYTHNLBTWOC was beating Zoo at the 1974 North American Championships, I was collecting vocabulary. The list which follows does not seem to have changed much since.

birthday or **Christmas present**   an unexpected stroke of good fortune, such as a bad shot by an opponent.

bomb   a long-distance shot used to break up a pile of winks. Also *v.i.* and *v.t.*

boondock   to shoot (a wink) far from the scene of action or off the mat. Incidentally, winkers who graduate & move away from the centers of activity are said to be 'boondocked.'

Bristol   an effective gromp (*q.v.*), developed at Bristol U., in which the squidger is held perpendicular to the pile and parallel to the line of flight.

butt   to knock (a wink) on or off a pile by shooting another wink at it on a low trajectory. Also **kick**.

click off   to remove a wink from another with a shot that ends by just touching (clicking against) the wink below, not moving it.

constipated   said of a position in which one has winks but, because they are squopping other winks, they are tied down and useless. (Free = unsquopped.)

dance   (of a wink) to wobble around on another wink, the rim of the pot, or the mat.

drunken wink   a wink that behaves unpredictably or bizarrely.

eat   to squop; especially, to squop thoroughly, completely covering the lower wink. Also, sometimes, **chomp.**

Goode shot   a shot used when one has a wink touching, but not on an unwanted pile. The wink is pressed hard into the mat and, when released, goes through the pile, thoroughly scattering it.

gromp   to move a pile as a whole onto another wink or pile. Also *v.i.* and *n.* Also **trundle**— an Ottawaism.

lunch   to pot an opponent's wink to gain strategic advantage; to trounce, especially in **get lunched.**

nurdle   to shoot (a wink) too close to the pot to be pottable or otherwise useful. Obsolete in England, where it originated in the early 60s.

perversion   any winks variation, such as Winks Tennis.

Petrie piddle   desquopping a wink by squeezing it out from underneath a pile.

piddle   to make microscopic adjustments in a pile, usually to walk it off a friendly wink.

shot   an exclamation of commendation for a good shot. *Antonym*: **Unlucky.** A Briticism, with some currency in America.

sub or **submarine**   *v.t.* or *v.i.* To shoot a wink (usually one's own) under another. In England called an **autosquop** or **ULU.** (The latter, pronounced YOO-loo, is said to refer to an unfortunate habit of the University of London Union team.)

EPISTOLAE

Here is a genuine entry from the Santa Cruz, California, telephone directory:

FÜTZI NUTZLE

Several years ago the Los Angeles Rams football team had a player named Vivyen Leigh; I am not sure if he is still active. An All-American college player of several years ago at Iowa University was named Wonder Monds.

William J. Cleere
Sunnyvale, California

The "Uphill Mississippi" Phenomenon and Openness to Unfamiliar Ideas

Robert L. Birch
Washington, D.C.

The statement that the Mississippi river "runs uphill" will usually cause a quizzical eyebrow to suggest further enlightenment. When it is pointed out that the distance from the center of the earth to sea level is greater at New Orleans than at the latitude of Minnesota, since the spin of the earth accumulates water around the equator, the responses begin to diverge.

One common reaction is the statement that since the Mississippi runs downhill "relative to sealevel" we should not say that it "runs uphill." Other reactions range from observing that, by this reasoning, Mount Chimborazo, in the Andes, is taller than Mount Everest, since it pokes out further into space, to the question as to whether it would take more energy to pull a freight train "uphill" from Chicago to New Orleans or "downhill" from New Orleans to Chicago.

Aside from its use as a psychological litmus paper, the question of the proper terminology to use in discussing the "uphill Mississippi" phenomenon can bring a number of magnitudes of the shape of the earth into perspective. Before thinking about the hydrostatics of this problem I would not have been able to guess whether the difference between the equatorial and the polar diameter of the earth were fifty feet or fifty miles. When a friend brought it to my attention that the difference is about thirteen or fourteen miles, I began to imagine waterskiing up the side of a thirteen-mile-high mountain of water as I traveled from the polar regions to the equator.

The next question that began to tease my layman's instinct for paradox was the question of what effect the slowing or speeding up of the earth's spin would have on the distribution of ocean waters and on the shape of the solid part of the earth.

After some frustrating library search and discussion with specialists, I found myself more than ever intrigued by the apparent indifference of the academic world to a phenomenon of such interest to me as a nonspecialist. If the students in colleges and universities are not given paradoxes to play with, they are quite likely to become dulled into the assumption that science consists of a number of dried and categorized bits of information, with no function for the sense of whimsy and the play of the imagination.

The current phase of my inquiry has to do with the mathematical handles that would be needed to correlate earth rotation rate with the sea levels suggested by raised beaches and similar phenomena.

OBITER DICTA

Ad Litteram

One reason so few Americans write letters is that we don't know how either to begin or to end them. We were taught, of course. Older Americans learned in school to begin a letter with something called the salutation, and to end it with something else called the complimentary close, both of these finely graduated in degrees of servility. (And why not? They were copied from eighteenth-century England. In that caste-conscious time and place, there was a proper amount of servility to squeeze out for every recipient. One might sign one letter with a groveling "I have the honour to be, my lord, your lordship's most humble and most dutiful servant" and the next with a curt "Yours ever.") Younger Americans, without ever having heard of salutations and complimentary closes, have picked up the surviving simplified forms of both, and feel awkward if they don't use them.

But they also feel awkward if they do. Our age values sincerity. It is obviously insincere to sign every letter "sincerely." Or to begin every one, even to people you despise, with the word *dear*. Dear enemy. Dear finance company which is about to repossess my car. Dear divorced husband.

Our age also values warmth. Warmth involves personal recognition—a warm smile is one that takes account of the person smiled at. But ritualized beginnings and endings by their essence deny recognition. Not only is the IRS official who writes to question your deductions not "yours truly" (if anything, you are his), but the stock phrase looks past you as if you weren't there.

Letters written to companies are especially difficult. Sex

as well as politeness is a problem. Say you're writing to Texas Instruments because you're not happy with your digital watch. Old style, you would begin the letter either "Dear Sirs" or "Gentlemen." But new style?

There is no new style. I have one friend who has started writing "Gentlepersons"—but this is conscious mockery, and not at all likely to catch on. "Sirs/Madams" would be suitable only for correspondence with the proprietors of a coed whorehouse. If elided to Smadams, it's ugly in a smeary, smudgy way. (Most words beginning with *sm*- are.)

What that seems to leave is "Hi, there," which may be all right if you're a cheerleader, and "Howdy," which works in spoken discourse only, even in Texas itself.

Letters that companies write to individuals aren't easy, either. No one knows how to sign them. "Yours truly" is fading fast, except in IRS offices. Regards are still popular, but threatened, because no one is really sure what a regard is. All agree that you must send several, and they must either be your best ones or warm ones, but that doesn't help much. Result: Many business men have begun to sign their letters "cordially." It's warm, all right: *cor, cordis* 'heart.' But then what happens to sincerity, if you claim to be writing from the heart to all the people on a mailing list you have just bought?

I have no solution to offer, except maybe to turn to extreme simplicity, simplicity as great as the "hello" and "goodbye" that make telephoning so easy. A couple of thousand years ago, an Egyptian cabinet minister sent a letter of official commendation to one of his senior colleagues. Here is' the complete letter. "Apollonius to Zeno, greeting. You did well to send the chickpeas to Memphis. Farewell." No problems of false cordiality, no insincere sincerity, no struggle over intimacy-level. We could do worse.

Noel Perrin
Dartmouth College

The first task of the student abroad is to find a suitable room. This I did and was signing a lease in Munich, where I had gone to live as a Fulbright Scholar. The question of *Kaution*, 'a deposit,' came up. I inquired politely whether it would be returned when I moved out. But I erroneously used *mich ausziehe* rather than *ausziehe*, so saying, "If I take off my clothes, do I get my money back?" The prurient landlord leered while his good wife explained.

While helping a roommate transfer belongings to a new apartment, a friend's overladen microbus was stopped along the highway. "What do you think you are doing?" the policeman demanded. "Why I'm helping this guy move," was the American's hasty reply. Or so he thought. He confused *sich umziehen* with *umziehen* so that the German heard "I'm helping this guy undress and change." Herr Offizer proved less sympathetic than my landlady. A traffic ticket was drawn up, but at least it cited no charge of indecent exposure.

Mich is accusative. But neither is the dative reflexive safe. I walked into a party one snowy evening, and at once my host asked if he might take my coat. "No thanks, I'm cold," I said when I should have phrased it, "It is cold to me." Conversation stopped. I had just announced that I was sexually frigid. Things went from bad to worse. As I began to warm up by the fire, I mentioned that now I was warm. Only this time, neglect of the reflexive rendered it, "I am homosexual." Thank goodness the company caught on before I blurted out, *Ich bin nun heiss*, meaning "I'm really turned on now, fellas."

Another trick the Germans play with their language is the preposition ploy. They simply Scotch-tape a preposition like a prefix onto a verb, and presto, they have a viable new word which likely has little to do with its parent. Idiom governs connotation of the compound. The non-native speaker must beware. I once informed house guests that they were welcome to stay with me, since I had often *umgebracht* friends at my place before. I should have said *untergebracht*. Terrified, they retreated to a nearby inn. 'To have (someone) spend the night' is *unterbringen*, whereas *umbringen* means 'to murder' them.

Somehow I made it unscathed through one year at the Universität in München. I certainly learned one thing: The profs don't teach you all you need to know in a seminar listed Deutsch Semester 3.

Nancy Barron
Santa Barbara, California

BIBLIOGRAPHIA

A GLOSSARY OF FAULKNER'S SOUTH, by Calvin S. Brown, Yale, 1976, iv + 241 pp. $12.50.

This is a useful, nontechnical glossary of Faulkner's words and phrases written mainly ". . . for any reader who did not share with him the time and place called Yoknapatawpha—

that richly regional Southern culture of the period between the two world wars." As the jacket summary implies, all readers will learn something from this book because the language and culture of those decades (1919–39) have undergone enormous change, and Yoknapatawphans who preserve the old regional and social dialects as well as the forms and values of those rural Southern folk institutions have little interest today in the literary accomplishments of their late, eccentric neighbor.

Calvin S. Brown is a rare exception among natives of Oxford, Mississippi. Now a distinguished professor of comparative literature at the University of Georgia, he writes this book with splendid credentials: he knows Lafayette County, Oxford, Faulkner, and Faulkner's writings extremely well. Although there is no substitute for native competence in the study of language and culture, he could have written an even better book had he attended more closely to the resources of cultural anthropology (and geography) in the delineation of his field and of descriptive linguistics (and dialectology) in the analysis and exposition of his materials. These limitations are reflected in the sometimes uneven and always nontechnical content of the glossary.

The text includes an introduction, a set of abbreviations, the glossary, and an appendix. The glossary elaborates words and phrases from those 22 novels and 27 stories that are set in *or* relate directly to the South. Including one-word transliterations of dialect spellings and cross references, the glossary has approximately 3,000 entries, about half of which are genuinely interesting. More than a few are so common that it is difficult to imagine what kind of speaker of American English is unfamiliar with *bird dog, corn bread, dandelion, lawn mower, prissy, rabbit's foot, razor strop, suspenders, skillet, trolley,* and *waterbug.* And could any user of the glossary have managed to get through *The Adventures of Huckleberry Finn* without understanding the large number of words that appear in that novel and the present word list? Even the most casual student of American literature should have no trouble with *a-holt, ast, ax* ('ask, asked'), *bar'l, beatin'es' b'ilin, bofe, caint, cheer* ('chair'), *clumb, coffin, cottonwood, crope, deef, doan, doggery, done* (aux.), *fur* ('far'), *galluses, gwinter, jimson weed, kaze* ('because'), *Mars, mourner's bench, nemmine, ourn, passel, p'int, plum, resk, ruther, Spanish moss, straw tick, 'sturb, tote, tother, tow-head* ('sand bar with cottonwoods'), *trash* ('base people'), *truck* ('junk'), *vittles, water moccasin, yonder,* and *yuther,* among the more obvious repetitions.

Against those dubious entries, however, stands a substantial body of information. Even with the elaborate discussions of flora and fauna, place names, and historical figure that seem extraneous here and even without authentic local pronunciations that could have been supplied in broad phonetic notation, Brown's vocabulary of artifacts and social interaction makes the book a valuable reference work. Descriptions of the forms and functions of the *bluegum, eating and drinking, froe, hame strings, lap-link, logger-head, maul, pot still, renter, ridge pole, sharecropper, Silver Shirts, third and fourth, vote-rousing picnics,* and *wagon stake* will not be found elsewhere in a modest handbook. Here is an example of authoritative work:

> *logger-head (C[ollected Short] S[tories of William Faulkner]: B[arn] B[urning]* 16): a double-ended, U-shaped hook used (one on each side) to fasten the TRACES to the HAMES. The hames have a series of holes (illogically called a ratchet), and the logger-head's two hook-ends are fitted into two of these. The choice of holes permits variation of the line of draft and hence the depth of plowing. (This term seems to be unknown to lexicographers.)

Equally impressive in thoroughness, and perhaps more useful in understanding Faulkner's South, are entries concerning race relationships:

> *bluegum (S[ound] (&)[and the] F[ury]* 84, 85; *CS: [A] Just[ice]* 343, 344): a Negro whose gums are blue rather than pink. In folklore he is viewed with that mixture of reverence and fear which constitutes awe. He has many strange properties, such as a fatal bite, and he is a particularly adept and powerful conjuror. I know of no exact parallel to Versh's story, but it is the general sort of tale frequently told about bluegums.

> *eating and drinking*: racial etiquette. Whites and Negroes were not expected to eat and drink together *socially*. The strength of the conviction depended entirely on the nature of the occasion; it did not hold at all for a casual snack on a job or on a hunt. (In the 1960s during the racially tense time when the Jackson, Miss., airport was under heavy police guard because of the invasions of "freedom fighters," I saw one of the white police guards and a black employee of the airport sitting side by side on a bench drinking Coca-Colas and chatting. This would have astonished outsiders, but was not even a matter for notice to anyone who understood the conventions.) As the number of persons involved or the formality of the

occasion increases, the taboo comes into effect. Minnie and Miss Reba would drink together if they wanted to, but in a larger group Minnie carried her glass back to the kitchen because "she declined to drink with this many white people at once" (*[The] Reiv[ers]* 113). When a group of whites had breakfast at the sheriff's, "they left Aleck Sander[black (*sic*)] with his breakfast at the sheriff's, and carried theirs into the dining room" (*[Intruder in the] Dust* 114). Similarly, Bayard Sartoris has to insist that the Negro family eat Christmas dinner with him instead of waiting until he has finished (*Sart[oris]* 347), just as Ned sets aside the drink which Colonel Linscombe pours for him in the company of a group of whites in the colonel's office, and will not drink it until told to do so (*Reiv.* 285).

And, despite the curious phonological description, no one should object to the following explanation when balanced against its instructive value to novice observers of Southern language and culture:

> *nigra* (*[The] Town* 84): Negro. This spelling represents the normal pronunciation of many Southerners who do not say *nigger*. (The *knee-grow* pronunciation, with both syllables stressed, is not indigenous to most Southern speech.) Faulkner's mountaineers use *nigra* where a north Mississippian of the same class would use *nigger* (*CS: M[ountain] V[ictory]* 751, 756, 758.)

The Class system within the white caste is closely related to sensitive problems of racial relationships that are critical to real comprehension of social interaction in the complicated microcosm of Yoknapatawpha. This glossary provides excellent sets of distinctions among renters, sharecroppers, and poor whites, and, although journalists and sociologists (from Cash and Dollard to Weller and McGill) have said much the same thing, Brown's coverage is much more concise and everywhere relevent to Faulkner's South:

> *shares, farming on* (*Sart.* 277; *S&F* 298; *Abs[alom, Absalom!]* 209; *[The] Ham[let]* 238): any of various forms of farm tenancy in which the tenant pays his rent in the form of an agreed upon share of his crop. Such arrangements often, but not always, include credit at the farm store or commissary. The share of the crop given to the owner depends on the nature of the tenancy, the ownership of tools and animals used, and the particular crop involved (see THIRD AND FOURTH). Faulkner refers to the three basic classes in his referenct to "the Negro tenant-

or-share-or furnished-hand" (R[equiem] f[or] a N[un] 245). The tenant simply rents the land for cash and keeps whatever he produces. The "share-hand" provides his own equipment and pays one third of his corn and one fourth of his cotton as rent. A "furnish-hand" (more often called a sharecropper) is dependent on the owner for equipment, seed, food—everything—and pays one half his crop. This payment includes the use of equipment, but food is simply charged at the commissary, to be paid when the crop is sold.

And many more interesting and useful entries are catalogued in Brown's guide to Yoknapatawpha: a respectable set of moonshine terms, e.g., *blind-tiger, bustskull, kettle, pot still, run,* and *white mule*) and fine glosses of *coon, deer, fox,* and *'possum hunting;* of *bears, barns,* and *boll weevils;* of *easy riders* and *Uncle Bud:*

Uncle Bud moved across the water
To keep the boys from screwing his daughter,
    Uncle Bud.
Corn in the crib what ain't been shucked
And a gal in the house what ain't been fucked,
    Uncle Bud.

One surely would have appreciated the remaining stanzas and the arrangement (guitar chords, at least) of this old favorite.

Had Brown consulted Odum and Vance, he might have improved the cultural geography of his book, e.g., the discussion of *delta* is incomplete (failing to integrate the five components, the basins of the Atchafalaya, Red, Ouachita, St. Francis, and Yazoo rivers, each of which is legitimately described as "a delta") and, like the ambiguous term *Black Belt* (apparently not part of Faulkner's lexicon), easily misunderstood (*Mississippi Delta*: all five components with reference to the river, but only the Yazoo with reference to the state). Cultural maps, such as those provided by Odum and Vance, would have been more useful than his reprinted essay from *PMLA* in identifying the subregions of the South: from Virginia to Texas there are at least 44 of these, and the heart of Faulkner's South—Lafayette County, Mississippi—is set squarely in the middle of the Interior Ridge of Tennessee and Mississippi, from the Buford Pusser's "Walking Tall" County in McNairy County in the north through Oxford to Philadelphia and the badlands to the south.

Had he made better use of the available materials of American linguistic geography, many entries could have been improved with respect to both accuracy and sociohistorical implications, e.g., several hundred of the entries in the word list have been systematically investigated in the Linguistic Atlas of the Gulf States project (based in Atlanta). Its findings might have improved some of Brown's entries. A *fice*, for example, is usually not just a 'small mongrel dog,' but a 'noisy and contentious, dyspepsic little dog,' usually spelled *feist* (probably from OE *fistan* 'to fart,' cf. Scot. *fist dog*, Eng., *feisty* and *fizz*). This is reinforced in Faulkner's "Shingles for the Lord," where the dog, one of the central points of interest in the story, is called "that trick overgrown fyce," with *trick* (a word omitted from Brown's list) surely meaning 'troublesome.' Indeed, many Southern folk speakers believe the *feist* (*fice/fyce*) is a breed apart, as distinctive as the Catahoula cur.

Although most of that information is available in any good dictionary, as is so much of this glossary, the historical dictionaries should have been used more carefully by the compiler. The definition of *juke joint*, 'a cheap restaurant or cabaret with music furnished by a jukebox,' is both misleading and interesting. It implies the place takes its name from the coin-operated phonographs, which had no currency according to the *Dictionary of Americanisms* before the end of World War II (but check the release date of Glenn Miller's "Jukebox, Saturday Night"). At any rate, *jook joint* is older (DA 1942), and *jookhouse* ('whorehouse'), according to L. D. Turner has African etymons (Wolof and Bambara) and was observed in Gullah in the 1930s. The matter is interesting because, if jukeboxes were played in juke joints during the days of the WPA (i.e., prior to WW II), Faulkner's reference in "Shingles for the Lord" is acceptable; if not, it is an anachronism.

Similarly, the glosses of *blind tiger, fatback, flying jenny, side meat,* and *sowbelly* are incomplete, but the definition and explanation of *greens* is perhaps the weakest. If outlanders are really to be taken into consideration, this will not likely be helpful: "any leaves that can be or have been boiled for eating. Greens, used alone, implies cooking. If the leaves are to be eaten raw, they are called *salad greens.*" Since virtually all flora *can* be boiled for eating, a reader might assume that Yoknapatawphans eat grass, if not the foliage of jasmine, spiraea, honeysuckle, and Cherokee roses. According to Brown's introduction, such interpretation is not at all far-fetched: he notes that the Shreve McCannons are unfamiliar with all of those plants and that a college student at Cornell, "A bright girl from Brooklyn," thought Lena Grove was contemplating dressed pelts when she said in *Light in August,* "I have come from Alabama: a fur piece. All the way from Alabama a-walking. A fur piece."

Brown also says in that same paragraph of the "Introduction": "One man's obvious is often another man's puzzle." Although a phonetician, lexicographer, or linguistic geographer could easily turn that line against the author of *A Glossary of Faulkner's South*, it would not be wise to do so. There are dozens, perhaps hundreds, of insights in this book that will improve every reader's understanding of both Faulkner and his South. The native speaker always knows the dialect better than the observer, and, when that native speaker is also a good literary scholar, his contributions to both lexicography and philology are certain to be useful. To have this book nearby when reading Faulkner is to have the steady company of a solid authority.

Lee Pederson
Emory University

New symbol, new word.

VERBATIM takes pride in introducing the *questpersand*, designed and defined by John Langdon, Wenonah, New Jersey.

It is pronounced "and?"

536

*KIL*ometer or ki*LOM*eter?

John R. Sinnema
Baldwin-Wallace College

Newspapers have recently announced that the Federal Highway Administration has drawn up plans to convert highway speed limit signs to the metric system next year. Signs will read, for example: Speed Limit 80 km.

While scientists are sure to welcome progress toward conversion, they may be at odds with each other over the pronunciation of the word *kilometer*. Linguists, in general, will tolerate either pronunciation given in American dictionaries: *KIL*ometer, accenting the first syllable; or ki*LOM*eter, stressing the second syllable. The *Oxford English Dictionary* and the *Oxford Universal Dictionary* give only *KIL*ometer, as did the 1927 edition of the 1901 *Webster's New International Dictionary*.

Many teachers seem to prefer ki*LOM*eter. Indeed, one teacher has been known to have militantly promoted it and attacked *KIL*ometer by displaying a poster showing someone vainly pounding a "meter" with a mallet while saying, "You can't kill a meter."

Be that as it may, at least as long ago as 1940, Willibald Weniger's *Fundamentals of College Physics* supported *KIL*ometer with this note (p. 14):

> The names of metric units are accented on the first syllable. Confusion sometimes arises in pronunciation of words ending in "meter." If such a word is the name of a unit, it is accented on the first syllable, but if it is the name of an instrument . . ., it is accented on the syllable ending in the "m" of "meter."

The stress on the second syllable, *-OM*eter, is known everywhere in the instruments *thermometer, barometer, odometer, speedometer, micrometer,* and in perhaps fifty others. The word *micrometer* now seems to be used only to refer to the instrument for measurement, the former usage *MI*crometer now being supplanted by the word *micron*. This gives a clue to the reason for the double pronunciation of *kilometer*. No instrument is or has been indicated by it, only the unit of measure. Thus no confusion can result, whichever accent is used.

More Than Meets the *-ine*

Sam Hinton
Lecturer in Folklore (and former Director of
the Aquarium-Museum)
University of California, San Diego

L YNNE TIESLAU-JEWELL [III,3] and Jay Dillon [IV,1] have discussed the use of the suffix *-ine* in converting an animal name to an adjective. They might like to know that this ending can have a special significance to zoologists, who might use it casually as a metaphor, but only under special circumstances in referring to the animals themselves. Thus an ornithologist might describe a colleague as having an aquiline nose, but would not use the word *aquiline* in reference to a bird of the eagle group.

The scientific name of an animal or plant consists of two words: the generic name and the specific name. These two together give us the name of a species—the only taxonomic category that actually exists in nature, usually defined as a group of actually or potentially interbreeding populations, reproductively isolated from other such groups. The larger hierarchical groups are artificial, set up by taxonomists for their own convenience and according to their own rules. The *genus* may be regarded as a group of *species* (although there are many monotypic genera, each with only one species, such as *Homo sapiens*; any group-name, or *taxon*, may be monotypic). The *family* is a group of genera, the *order* a group of families, the *class* a group of orders, the *phylum* a group of classes, and the *kingdom* a group of phyla. But this is by no means enough taxa, and it is often necessary to intercalate such terms as *subspecies, superspecies, subgenus, supergenus, subfamily, superfamily, suborder*, and so on, and some groups—such as the opisthobranch snails—have so many classificatory characteristics that specialists have used a number of less conventional taxa, including *tribe, group, infra-family, division*, and *subdivision*.

According to the rules agreed upon by the International Congress of Zoology, whose hundred-year-old *International Code of Zoological Nomenclature* is, although often revised, one of the oldest effective instruments of international agreement, two of these taxa are required to have standardized endings. All names of families must end in *-idae*, which is added to the stem of the included genus that is regarded as most typical of that family; and when subfamilies are set up, their names are formed in the same way, but with the ending -*inae*. (The family suffix is from the Greek *eidos*, 'a resemblance,' while -*inae* was invented for the purpose.)

Family and subfamily names are properly plural, and cannot be applied to individual specimens without additional words. It isn't good form to say "That fish is a Sparidae"; if you want to use the whole family name, it has to be in a construction like "Look! A member of the Sparidae!" This is awkward in informal conversation, and a custom—not sanctioned by the Code—has arisen, allowing you to drop the final -*ae*. So, as an English-speaking ichthyologist, you can say, quite correctly, "I think you've got a Sparid there." (A French colleague would reply "Oui, c'est une Sparide.") This would indicate that you knew the family to which the specimen belonged but were not certain of the smaller categories. You would not say "It's a Sparine" unless you were sure of the subfamily, and willing to exclude other Sparid subfamilies such as the Pagellinae and Boopsinae.

One word listed by Ms. Tieslau-Jewell is *accipitrine*, meaning 'hawklike.' This is fine when you want to endow a non-hawk with hawkish characteristics, but would not be used by one ornithologist to another in a conversation about birds. He or she might say *accipitrid* to indicate membership in the family Accipitridae, but *accipitrine* in this context would refer only to one of the accipitrid subfamilies—the Accipitrinae (the "true" hawks and eagles). This would considerably narrow the subject of discussion, excluding such subfamilies as the Circaetinae (serpent eagles), Circinae (harrier hawks), Milvinae ("true" kites and fish eagles), Elaninae (white-tailed kites), Perninae (honey-buzzards), Aegypiinae (Old-World vultures; New-World vultures, by the way, are in another family, Cathartidae), Machaerhamphinae (the African bat hawk), and Pandioninae (the osprey). (Not all taxonomists agree with all of this; for instance, the osprey is often placed in a monotypic family.)

This process of forming a vernacular word by modifying, in a traditional manner, a technical word, exemplifies an oral folk process among people to whom literacy is supremely important. There are no formal rules about it, and it's not usually taught in taxonomy classes; it's just a custom. And it is a more complicated custom, requiring more memorization, among botanists. They (like the bacteriologists) have their own Code of nomenclature. The botanical Code says that all plant family names must end in -*aceae*, except for eight very important families whose names were well established back in the chaotic B.C. (before the Code) years. Plant subfamilies end in *-oideae*, while the suffix *-inae* is used only to designate a subtribe—a taxon between tribe and supergenus, rarely used except in technical literature. As a result, the vernacular names of the family-groups are not as standardized as those of the zoologists, and you simply have to remember the customary way of informalizing each of them. To indicate membership in the Cruciferae, you say "a crucifer." A member of the Euphorbiaceae is called "a euphorb," with the accent on the first syllable, or more familiarly "a spurge." "A composite" belongs to the Compositae, a great family with 20,000 species. "A legume" is a member of the Leguminosae, while a specimen from the Scrophulariaceae would be termed "a figwort." This last is one of the well-established English names used at the family level; others are "the grasses" for the family Graminae, and "the evening-primroses" for the Onagraceae.

I'm not sure what customs are followed by the bacteriologists; they seem rarely to speak in the vernacular.

BIBLIOGRAPHIA

A DICTIONARY OF ONOMATOPOEIC SOUNDS IN ENGLISH AND SPANISH, INCLUDING THOSE OF ANIMAL, MAN, NATURE, MACHINERY AND MUSICAL INSTRUMENTS, TOGETHER WITH SOME THAT ARE NOT IMITATIVE OR ECHOIC, by Donald R. Kloe, Blaine Ethridge—Books, 1977, xi + 153 pp. $22.50.

In even the most superficial way, the knowledge that French dogs say *gnaf! gnaf!*, Japanese dogs say *han! han!* and English dogs say *bow! wow!* demonstrates that speakers of different languages hear the same sounds but reproduce them differently. English speakers say. *dog,* French *chien,* and Spanish *perro,* none of which is related, etymologically, to the other, even in the grand scheme of the Indo-European family of languages, to which all three belong. But, surely, one would expect onomatopoeic words to be similar.

The short story is that, in English and Spanish at least, they sometimes are similar and sometimes not. This dictionary examines the similarities and the differences; it is a fascinating piece of work, usefully arranged. Most important, it treats in a formalized way a segment of language rarely examined very seriously or systematically, yet, for all that, nonetheless revealing. At bottom, it says "Pooh! Pooh!" to the "Bow! Wow!" theory of language origin.

Just as surprising, in some ways, that certain sounds that we take for granted as onomatopoeic have very similar counterparts in Spanish is the revelation that many others about which we might have the same feeling, have quite different reflexes in Spanish. The author, a Professor at North Carolina State University, marks some entries "Word which is truly onomatopoeic" and others "Word with doubtful onomatopoeic characteristics." Since he has provided no detailed explanation of his techniques, we are left to wonder how he arrived at such decisions. For example, Kloe marks *coo* (as in *bill and coo*) as "truly onomatopoeic," which may be difficult to find fault with. However, *bill and coo* is similarly marked, and, while that may be correct, the image of a bird's wandering about uttering "bill and coo" strikes one as strange. The Spanish onomatopoeic counterpart is *zurear*, yielding *zurrrr, zurrrr* which, if one bears in mind the way Spanish *r* is pronounced, reproduces the sound of a dove more faithfully than *coo*.

Some of the close correspondences are interesting: [English/Spanish] *cock-a-doodle-doo/quiquiriquiar* (reminiscent of German *kikeriki*, Italian *chichirichi*, and French *coquerico*); *cuckoo/cucu*; *grr-grr/rr-rr*; *gobble-gobble/gluglu-gluglu*; and *hoopoe, hoopoo/hoopoe*.

This book, as the title promises, doesn't confine itself to animal sounds: under sounds of man we find *achoo/achu, boohoo/buhu*, and *gargle/gargarizar* among an assortment of biological noises that are best left to Alka-Seltzer commercials. There are some items missing: surely, if *susurrar* is onomatopoeic Spanish for *rustle*, the English equivalents, *susurration, susurrant, susurrous*, and *susurrus* should be shown.

Notwithstanding other, possible omissions—this review was not conceived as a fault-finding apparatus—the book is extremely useful and interesting. Its organization provides a two-column format, with each section (animals, man, etc.) divided in two: the first gives English as the source and Spanish as the target, the second, vice versa. There are bilingual glossaries, a complete index, and what looks like a pretty thin bibliography. The type is large enough for readers with a seeing disability; in case the number of pages is off-putting, it should be mentioned that the page size is 8-1/2"x11", but why it is is unclear.

When will compilers of dictionaries, glossaries, and other

reference books stop setting headwords for entries all in capital letters? They are hard to read and impossible to spell (since one cannot distinguish between words spelled with small or with capital letters).

JEWISH AND HEBREW ONOMASTICS, A Bibliography, by Robert Singerman, Garland Publishing, Inc., 1977, xii + 132 pp. $17.50.

This is *not* a book that gives the origins of Jewish and Hebrew names, but it does provide comprehensive information about sources where those origins and histories can be found. Following the bibliographer's succinct Introduction is a list of 1195 books, periodicals, and articles, arranged under such topical headings as "Biblical Names: Reference and Dictionaries," "Ancient Near East," "Greco-Roman Period," and moving on through geographic categories to "Individual Jewish Names." An interesting and useful Appendix provides an alphabetical index of some 3,000 Jewish surnames treated by Norbert Pearlroth in his column, "Your Name," which appeared weekly in the *Jewish Post and Opinion* between September 1945 and September 1976. That is followed by a brief index of "Individual Names," by which I suppose Singerman means given names, though my experience with people with the given names of Oppenheimer and Zakarbaal has been, to say the most, small.

The titles alone of works published during the Nazi regime are historically revealing: "Law Regarding Jewish Given Names (Second Decree for the Execution of the Law of August 17, 1938)," "Änderungen jüdischer Namen" ["Jewish Name Changes"] 1939; some later works bearing on the period are "The Nazi Name Decrees of the Nineteen Thirties," and "Jewish Emancipation Under Attack." In some cases, of course, there are only some sections of the sources that deal with onomastics, and these are noted.

At the price, this is not a book that any but the most ardent onomastician is likely to rush to buy, but even the more limited libraries should own a copy, for the work has been prepared with great care and obvious devotion. It is a pity that the publisher did not see fit to spend the small amount required to set the book in type rather than in that awful IBM typewriter face. However, it's the information that counts.

A DICTIONARY OF CATCH PHRASES, by Eric Partridge, Stein and Day, 1977, xv + 278 pp. $17.95.

At the outset, Partridge confesses that he does not know what a catch phrase (or c.p., an abbreviation he uses throughout) is. No matter: vagueness affords him the opportunity to include and omit material willy-nilly.

This may be a book of some interest and usefulness to British speakers of English, because the entries are predominantly British, but of somewhat less enchantment for Americans, because many expressions are not included and because those American c.p.'s that are treated are of questionable idiomaticity and fact. I fear that some of the informants on whom Partridge relied for American c.p.'s just don't know their stuff.

For example, **after you, my dear Alphonse—no, after you, Gaston** is given as Canadian in origin (1959). I heard the c.p. in America in the 1930s and am under the distinct impression that it was borrowed from an older vaudeville routine satirizing French over-politeness. In a quotation from a letter from Dr. Joseph T. Shipley under **remember Pearl Harbor**: "after the airplane strike of 6 December 1941 . . . ." Dr. Shipley, as far as I know, is an American: an "airplane strike" would, in American English, be usually taken to mean that the planes are either not being manufactured or not flying—not the same as an *air strike*. Similarly, the "day that will live in infamy" was Sunday, December 7, 1941—regardless of the side of the dateline you were on—a fact that used to be known to every schoolboy. Curiously, we find, "**Built like a brick shit-house**, mostly preceded by he's. A low Canadian phrase, meaning 'he's a very well-made fellow: C20." Balderdash! It is an American c.p. and almost *never* applied to a man. Besides, it is often followed, after a pause, by ". . . **and not a brick out of place!**" Another: "**all the traffic will bear**, often preceded by that's. Literally, it relates to fares and freights; only figuratively it is a c.p., meaning that the situation, whether financial or other, precludes anything more . . .. It is—Dr Douglas Leechman ['an authority on Canadiana'] tells me—said to derive from a US magnate's cynicism." Poppycock! First, what does "said to derive" mean? Second, *traffic* means 'trade, custom,' and the c.p. means 'charge as much as possible.' I have my doubts that it was ever used in what Partridge considers its "literal" sense.

Although I am familiar with the Thurber cartoon and have traveled for years in a crowd familiar with *The New Yorker*, I have never heard anyone say "All right—you did hear a seal bark." As far as I know, my hearing is unimpaired with regard to c.p.'s *and* the bark of the seal. Again, Partridge's American informants have either slipped badly or took delight in sneaking him some home-grown family expressions that the rest of us don't know. Where is "Sure as God made little apples"? "Nobody here but us chickens"? "No skin off my teeth?" ". . . or bust"?

The general presentation of the book could have been improved considerably by labeling Briticisms as well as Americanisms.

Partridge's comments are folksy and frequently as long-winded as they are inaccurate. **Pop goes the weasel**, which we (and Arthur Fiedler) have had up to here in America, is described as "Very English." **Polly put the kettle on and we'll all have tea** is described as "increasingly obsolescent" since WW2, yet I have often heard English people refer to it jocularly when they offer to put the kettle on to boil: "I'll be Polly."

All in all, the *Dictionary of Catch Phrases*, which resembles in spirit, if not in fact, Partridge's *Dictionary of Clichés*, might have seemed a good idea when conceived, and Partridge undoubtedly had a good time compiling it and writing the comments, but the result is uneven and, in places, downright inaccurate. It is also somewhat old-fashioned, to wit Dr. Joseph T. Shipley's comment of 17 February 1974 that **that's how** (or **the way**) **the cookie crumbles** ". . . is a rather frequent expression in [New York]." Perhaps it is among septuagenarians. On the other hand, some informants suffer either from a short memory or a long imagination. **Where was Moses when the lights went out?** is from an early 20c. riddle [the same vintage as "What's black and white and re(a)d all over?"], the answer to which is "In the dark" or, more elaborately "Down in the cellar in the dark."

POPLOLLIES AND BELLIBONES, A Celebration of Lost Words, by Susan Kelz Sperling, Clarkson N. Potter, 1977, 128 pp. $7.95 A VERBATIM Book Club Selection.

> For *dretching* the curly *crineted* child with a *fearbabe*, the *killbuck* was sent to a *kidcote* without an *eyethurl*.*

Someone has been having fun with the language, and good fun it is, too. A few hours spent with the *Oxford English Dictionary* alone could produce enough archaic and obsolete English words to satisfy any paleomorphophiliac, but Sperling, unwilling to leave it at that, has ransacked the nether reaches of Skeat's, Brewer's, Wright's and others' works to compile a glossary of 300-odd words that have, for some unaccountable reason, fallen into disuse in the language. And odd, indeed, many of them are. Not content with a glossary, the author has woven these relics into a collection of turngiddy tales (in which Teneris the Knight is prominently featured), snirtling telephone conversations with a Miss Fleak ['an insignificant person'], hoful synonym studies, and iqueme poems that cannot fail to confound and amuse. I utter a short prayer that crossword-puzzle compilers never learn of these words—I am having enough trouble as it is.

Not all of the words are as obscure [at least to me—but then I acknowledge an unfair advantage] as they might seem (or, perhaps, ought to be). For instance, I may be one of the few, but there are some people about who know what a *zarf* is and what *widdershins*, *welkin*, *tipsycake* [served at The Bell Inn, Aston Clinton, Bucks.—note for British readers], *spitchcock*, *prick-song*, *purfle*, *poop-noddy*, *misgloze*, and a few others mean. Whether you do or not, your adlubescence at this romp through should be undiminished, and that's no fadoodle.

> *Gloze: For *tormenting* the curly-*haired* child with a *something to frighten a baby intentionally*, the *fierce-looking fellow* was sent to a *prison* without a *window*.

EPISTOLAE

A.J. Pollock's discovery of the self-referring word [IV, 1] should probably be shared with the Apostle Paul. Writing to Philemon, Paul finds Pollock's very example useful in verses 10 and 11 when he writes:

> I appeal to you for my child Onesimus [meaning 'useful']. Formerly he ['Useful'] was useless to you but now he is indeed useful to you and me.

Paul uses *useful* not only as a self-referring word, but a paradoxical one as well. Of course, Paul was also familiar with the paradoxical sentence, quoting to Titus the classical paradox by the Cretan poet, Epimenides: "All Cretans are liars . . ." (Titus I:12).

In fact, I believe Paul would have enjoyed your publication and its Epistolae as much as we have enjoyed our very first issue.

Robert C. Connell
Portola Valley, California

In Verbatim [IV, 1], Alexander J. Pollock described his discovery of self-referring words. I am sure he will not be surprised to hear that he is one of a goodly company. Not only did I do so independently some years back, but I was not the first. It is probably re-discovered several times a year, as it is too simple and charming an idea to miss.

At first I called them *autonyms*, *paranyms*, and *heteronyms*, but as a quick consultation with the *Shorter Oxford* demonstrated that the originality of my terms was no greater than that of my discovery, I called them *autoscrips*, *parascrips*, and *heteroscrips*.

The *autoscrip* is what Mr. Pollock called a self-referring term, e.g., 'word.' *Parascrips* are self-referring in that they describe opposing concepts: e.g., *verb* describes 'verbs,' but is a noun. *And* is a typical *heteroscrip* as is *dog*. Neither describes anything with an obvious connection to itself. *Nonselfreferring* is not a heteroscrip by this definition. In fact I think it is a parascrip. It defines something opposing what it itself is. This does not deny Mr. Pollock's line of reasoning; I just think that this system of definition is more powerful. Whether it is the best is another matter.

Certainly, as described so far it does not eliminate paradox. *Heteroscriptive* is plainly a parascrip, *autoscriptive* is arguably auto-, para- or heteroscriptive; i.e., no obvious contradiction results from attributing *any* of the three qualities to it. *Parascriptive* is neither better *nor* worse, i.e., regarding it as self-referring leads to no ambiguity, but does lead to paradox. Only heteroscription applies to it without contradiction. In cowardice I recommend that, in order to avoid paradox and ambiguity, the definition of the three terms be based on an algorithm until less empirical theory evolves. A modest suggestion follows:

1: Select the aspect(s) of its own nature to which the word is to be considered to apply.
2: Consider the word as an autoscrip and as a parascrip in turn. If exactly one of the two terms applies, apply that term as a definition and go to step 4.
3: If each case or neither leads to contradictions, or neither applies clearly, apply the term "heteroscrip" as a definition.
4: Stop.

I also take tentative issue with limiting the field to nouns and adjectives. I grant that gerunds and participles were included by implication, in that the classification of *nonselfreferring* was mooted, but why exclude pronouns, e.g., *it*? In this sentence, if *it* is not an autoscrip (twice), what is *it*?

What, that, and *which* are similar cases, while *they* is a para-scrip, unless one is careless about antecedents or allows a shareholding definition as in: *What* and *they* (*they* and *they?*) are pronouns aren't they?"

Pronouns may be a bit close to nouns, but what about adverbs? *Here* is an autoscrip, *there* a parascrip, unless you stand far away from the page when you read this. Of course, you may say that *here* is always here to itself, while *there* is never there. Obviously their status as auto- or parascrips is context-sensitive. Facultative autoscrips?

Prepositions are less satisfactory. I am not convinced that say, *between* is a facultative autoscrip even if it is be-tween quotes. Does it have any meaning by itself, or must it be read in context? If the latter, it is necessarily heteroscriptive. Similar thoughts apply to articles. Is *an* autoscriptive? Is *a* parascriptive—or *the* heteroscriptive? If *you* don't know, I don't (and if you do, I probably disagree!). Interjections are mercifully heteroscriptive, unless one classes expletives such as *curses*, as used in comic books, as autoscriptive.

Another critical point is: to what aspect of itself must a non-heteroscrip refer, to qualify for inclusion in the category? E.g., one might consider the concept (as opposed to the term or the letters), *abstruse* as being abstruse, or *abstract* as ab-stract, in which case they are in fact autoscrips. Now note: they are then language–independent. The Dutch *Afgetrokken* is abstract and the Swedish *svarfattlig* is abstruse. *Term* is interesting, as it refers to itself as a term, but is language-independent (as long as the concept *term* occurs in a given language's vocabulary, that is). *Useful* refers to itself as a term *and* a concept and is a language-independent autoscrip. Eng-lish, French, etc., are language–dependent autoscrips, being parascriptive in all languages but one, as a rule. In this case the aspect referred to is the language. "Correctly-spelt" refers to itself as a string of letters forming a word, and is in this sense a language-dependent autoscrip.

There is no reason, I think, to separate the autoscriptive aspects of phrases, sentences or other utterances from those of words. Certainly the distinctions would be rather arbitrary. (Compare *correctly-spelt, correctly spelt,* and *This is correctly spelt.*)

This question of what aspect is referred to is rather im-portant. For example I can think of no autoscriptive verb unless one regards such cases as *spells* or *sounds* as autoscrips. Here the aspect described is surely just the character string or phoneme string. Cases such as *exists* are altogether too difficult. Certainly *exists* may be called autoscriptive in referring to itself as a term or a character string; but as a concept? Do concepts *exist*?

Also, a word can be autoscriptive, parascriptive, and heteroscriptive simultaneously, depending on the aspect one chooses to apply it to. *Abstract* is concrete in the sense of the string of letters (and therefore parascriptive), abstract as a concept, and heteroscriptive in that it neither correctly nor wrongly describes its own length or language.

Then one considers how trivial nonheteroscription can get. How about *printed, italicised, purchased, vibrating, spoken, erased, bold-face,* etc.?

I suspect therefore that the concept is little different from the existing problem in logic of self-referring statements and as such is of no importance, practical or theoretical, except as a mental excercise. However, that is important enough for me!

Jon Richfield
Cobham, Surrey

I was interested to see Gary S. Felton refer to *Murphy's Law* in his "Exceptions to the Rule" [IV, 1]. Perhaps he and your readers would be interested to hear the complete Murphy's Laws from the country of their origin.

- (1.) In any field of scientific endeavour, anything that can go wrong will go wrong.
- (2.) Left to themselves, things always go from bad to worse.
- (3.) If there is a possibility of several things going wrong, the one that will go wrong is the one that will do the most damage.
- (4.) Nature always sides with the hidden flaw.
- (5.) If everything seems to be going well, you have obviously overlooked something.
- (6.) Mother Nature is a bitch.

In pondering on these profound truths, Mr. Felton might bear in mind *Hosey's Law*—In any compilation of exceptions to the rule, no additional information, however useless, may be ignored.

Seamus Hosey
Co. Laois, Ireland

Robert Fowkes' article "Esrever Hsilgne" [III, 2] has already provoked considerable comment, but none of it directed at what is, to me, the most interesting question it raises—namely, the origin of the American term "english" as used in billiards and other ball games. (The English are satisfied with the simple word "side.") For a long time I have cherished the hypothesis that it comes from a mispronunciation of "anglish," since the ball always rebounds at an erratic angle when put under spin. I even thought that investigation might uncover a French culprit in the woodpile, i.e., *anglé*, 'angled,' easily confused with *anglais*, 'English.' (Compare, for instance, the now discredited derivation of *cor anglais*, 'English horn,' from **cor anglé*.)

Professor Fowkes prompted me finally to look into the matter. Imagine my disappointment at learning (from the *OED Supplement*, quoting the *Sunday Times*, 5 April 1959) that the billiard term, traced at least as far back as Mark Twain's *Innocents Abroad* (1869), supposedly comes from a banal proper name:

> The story goes that an enterprising gentleman from
> these shores travelled to the United States during
> the latter part of the last century and impressed
> the Americans with a demonstration of the effect of
> 'side' on pool or billiard balls. His name was English.

I say 'supposedly' because the quoted etymology still strikes me as very possibly apocryphal, whether or not my own is closer to the mark.

At any rate, even assuming the shadowy Mr. English to be responsible, after a little reflection it occurred to me that the two hypotheses might, in fact, come together rather neatly. The English, after all, stem from the Angles, who, we are told, took their name from their original homeland in Schleswig, whose shape was that of a fishhook (*angul*). If so, we have what would amount to a stunning etymological coincidence. Considering the immense number of possible proper names an itinerant billiard-shark might have, we could easily be referring today to 'reverse smith,' 'reverse jones,' 'reverse shapiro,' 'reverse urdang,' etc., none of which staggering array of possiblities would have anything whatever to do with the 'angle' that so expressively describes the trick shot involved.

Norman R. Shapiro
Wesleyan University

Five laws which excerpt the characteristics of the Intergalactic Conspiracy to Deprive You of Your Right to Happiness:

Jenkinson's Law—It won't work.

Pudder's Law—Anything that begins well ends badly.

Borkowski's Law—You can't guard against the arbitrary.

Sattinger's Law—It works better if you plug it in.

Murphy's Law (of which Mr. Felton quotes only a portion:)

> (1.) Nothing is as easy as it looks.
>
> (2.) Everything takes longer than you think.
>
> (3.) If anything can go wrong, it will.

Two contributions to help explain the workings of bureaucracies:

Oeser's Law—There is a tendency for the person in the most powerful position in an organization to spend all his time serving on committees and signing letters.

Dow's Law—In any hierarchical organization, the higher the level, the greater the confusion.

Two comments about The Present State of Affairs:

Price's First Law—If everybody doesn't want it, nobody gets it.

Kitman's Law—Pure drivel tends to drive off the TV screen ordinary drivel.

The next three Laws are the only rational observations of which I am aware about the so-called quantitative "social sciences":

Hart's Law of Observation—In a country as big as the United States, you can find fifty examples of anything.

The Law of the Perversity of Nature—You cannot successfully determine beforehand which side of the bread to butter.

Dibble's First Law of Sociology—Some do, some don't.

(Under this category is Felton's "Third Law of Experimental Psychology," which I have known as "Harvard Law" and attributed to A. S. Sussman.)

Under the well-known category of "Miscellaneous," I offer the *Law of Probable Dispersal*—Whatever hits the fan will not be evenly distributed. (Also known as—*The How-Come-It-All-Landed-On-Me Law*), and my own contributions, both of which are probably plagiarized:

Chamberlain's Laws—(1.) The big guys always win, and (2.) Everything tastes more or less like chicken.

Finally, *Laurence Peter's Les Miserables Metalaw:* All

laws, whether good, bad, or indifferent, must be obeyed to the letter. (A Metalaw is a law about laws.)

Jeffery F. Chamberlain
Rochester, New York

P.S. I have seen Ormly Gumfudgin's "People never go there anymore; it's too crowded" attributed to Yogi Berra. This reminds me of the venerable oxymoron, "good hitting always stops good pitching, and vice versa" which is supposed to have been said first by the well-known dentist, Casey Stengel.

Cripps Law—when travelling with children on one's holidays, at least one child of any number of children will request a restroom stop exactly half way between any two given rest areas.

The Fudge Factor—a physical factor occasionally showing up in experiments as a result of stopping a stop-watch a little early to compensate for reflex error.

Mervyn Cripps
St. Catharines, Ontario

Frank Schulman's article *"The Sinister Side of the Language"* [IV, 1] *left* one amused but not very well instructed in the *right* forms to use in the Romance languages to which he refers.

In the first place, 'left' in Portuguese is *esquerda*, not *esquierda*, and 'right' is *direita* (or, in some cases, *direito*), not *derecho*. In the second place, one would have expected a bit more consistency on the part of the author in his handling of genders. For some reason, he regularly used the feminine form in translating *left* and the masculine form in translating *right*. One hesitates to level the charge of linguistic male chauvinism at Mr. Schulman but has little choice after absorbing his ideas about the inferiority of the *left*. When referring to *right* or *left* as a direction, the feminine form is correct in French, Spanish and Portuguese, since the word 'hand' is inferred, which is feminine in all three languages (*main, mano,* and *mão*, respectively). It is not proper to use the masculine forms *droit, derecho,* or *direito* standing alone as meaning 'right,' but only when they are modifying a masculine noun.

Daniel N. Swisher
Woodside, California

From *The New England Journal of Medicine*, Jan. 20, 1977: PLAIN WORD FOR "PASSED FLATUS"

To the Editor: The number of letters (N Engl J Med 295: 1204-1205, 1976) in response to the article on a flatulent patient (N Engl J Med 295: 260-262, 1976) prompts me to add what I consider an interesting phenomenon.

There seems to be a curious omission on this subject both in the literature and in the English language. I do not recall any relevant treatise in the psychiatric literature and I do not know of any commonly used single word in the English language that means "pass flatus"—with the exception of a four-letter word.

This four-letter word is "fart," which is both a verb and a noun. Such awkward phrases as "passed flatus" or "excreted gas" are always used instead of "farted." And a "fart"—as a noun—can be visualized on x-ray.

It is also curiously interesting that concerning the other (upper) end of the gastrointestinal tract, the language does have usable single words: to belch and a belch, as well as to eruct and an eructation. The word "fart" appreciably arouses more feelings of disgust than the words "expelled flatus" or "belch."

The matter gets curiouser and curiouser in our wonderland, and I am awaiting etymologic studies on these words and psychologic studies on a suitable patient.

Robert J. L. Waugh, M.D.
Dunlap-Manhattan Psychiatric Center

LeMoyne Farrell of Ithaca, N.Y., referring to VERBATIM [IV, 1], wonders whether the converted *bird in the hand-me-down* is a duck-shooter's old insulated jacket.

". . . Such mismatches [between a text and the skills (language and otherwise) of the reader] are of particular interest as sources of difficulty in learning to read and write for children *whose language and culture are different from the majority*." [Our emphasis.]—From the errata sheet accompanying *Basic Skills Research Grants Announcement*, Summer 1977, published by the National Institute of Education, HEW. The halt leading the blind?

Words Across the Sea: the British Crossword Comes to America

Jack Luzzatto
Bronx, New York

The puzzle you see in VERBATIM is a British-style crossword in pattern and clues, but the idiom is American.

The difficulty one has with a British crossword puzzle on this side of the water is not in the ingenious brilliance of the clues, though they are clever: any bright word-minded person can figure them out once he gets the hang of it. Rather, the difficulty is with British references to cricket, soccer teams, English place names (Portland Bill and Tolpuddle have shown up recently in *New York Magazine* offerings from the London *Times*), and other insular items strange to Americans. Since about half of the letters are unkeyed, it takes insight to complete the crossword. (It may well be that when VERBATIM's Anglo-American crossword puzzle reaches London, it will baffle the British.)

In 1941, when I was still making American crosswords, I saw my first British puzzle in an American magazine, the now defunct *Blue Book*. I had seen other British puzzles in English publications, but I hadn't really understood them. Now I decided to try to find out what they were all about. The *Blue Book* puzzle was by-lined, "Edited by Albert H. Morehead." My cunning little mind said, "Ah, *edited*!" So I wrote to Mr. Morehead, offering my services as a fellow who could construct a crossword. [The one concession Morehead's British crossword made in its American debut was its pattern; it had the standard American style, meaning no unkeyed letters. But the clues were British style and certainly baffling to those of us to whom such clues were new.]

Mr. Morehead invited me to his office. At that time he was bridge editor for *The New York Times*. Because he played bridge with Mr. Edwin Balmer, writer and editor of *Redbook*, and because he was a most persuasive man, Morehead sold the idea of the British crossword to Balmer, and soon they were published in *Blue Book* and *Redbook*. If you know anything at all about the timorousness or conservatism of national magazine policy, you will realize that Morehead pulled off an astounding feat.

Morehead had first discovered the British crossword while covering a bridge tournament in London and had fallen in love with it. Though a bridge editor and card expert, he told me his life's ambition was to be a lexicographer (and so he was to become, abandoning his lucrative *Times* bridge column in later years). During that first visit with him, I was delighted to have him accept my offer to supply crossword puzzles, even though he said he would create the clues. I still relish the first clue he threw at me: "Wearing inside outside." Answer in seven letters. *Tedious*. Neat, to say the least. Well, I caught on fast and started an association with him which lasted until he died, in the summer of 1966. I salute him as the pioneer of the British puzzle in America.

By now, *New York Magazine* has offered enough London *Times* crossword puzzles so that the unkeyed pattern is readily accepted here. For many years, though, American puzzle editors were circumscribed by the set of rules made by the 1924 pioneers of crosswords in this country: Hartswick, Buranelli, and Petherbridge (this last member of the trio is the illustrious Margaret Farrar). These rules called for, among other things: no unkeyed letters, not more than one-sixth of the squares to be black, and not more than one word at a time in a space. The British crossword puzzle violates all of these rules. No American crossword editor, from 1930 to about 1960, violated them, however—except Margaret Farrar, who permitted Marc Connelly, the playwright, to make a few British-style crosswords for the Sunday *New York Times*.

The great advantage of the British crossword is the elimination of "junk" puzzle words such as those that pertain to Philippine trees, Hindu arcana, and extinct flora and fauna—words that are useful because they "fit." Now, all answer words can be good, the clues can be witty, tricky, even naughty, but always they are amusing or delightfully baffling. The solving of this type of puzzle gives mental stimulation and is a source of satisfaction, once it has been mastered. The solver, then, knows he has won a battle of wits. It's the only kind of puzzle I care to solve, for its interest never palls, provided the clues are good.

Do not approach these puzzles thinking the clues will prove to be too hard. Each clue carries an honest definition for the word it identifies; it but cloaks the word in a clever disguise. The disguise is a sentence, which, if you analyze it, gives you a blueprint of the answer.

Bring your powers of reasoning into the fray, and you, too, will look forward to each new puzzle with joyful and eager anticipation.

EPISTOLAE

As a mathematician, I found A. J. Pollock's article on "Self-Referring Words" [IV,1] an interesting example of re-discovery. The fact that the concept of 'nonself-referring' can lead to paradox has been familiar to some mathematicians and logicians since, roughly, the beginning of the present century. It is a pleasure to find the paradoxical nature of the concept recognized in a linguistic setting.

Various logicians, among them pre-eminently Bertrand Russell, noted that the antinomies of logic tended to contain the concept that Mr. Pollock calls 'nonself-referring,' and which in mathematics is usually called 'impredicable,' as contrasted with 'predicable.' (Perhaps a more accurate pair of terms would be 'self-impredicable' and 'self-predicable.')

Some apparent paradoxes can be resolved. That of the Spanish barber, e.g., (who, you may remember, shaved everyone in his town except those who shaved themselves) can be settled by denying the possible existence of such a person. Similarly, when Gonseth (1933) suggested the difficulty facing a librarian who wished to compile a bibliography of all bibliographies which did not list themselves, we can counter by saying that such a task cannot be carried out.

But other paradoxes cannot be so resolved, since part of the paradox shows the existence of the 'product' in question. In Russell's terminology, the question whether the word 'impredicable' is predicable or, alternatively, is impredicable (after all, it ought to be one or the other, right?) is a genuine antinomy: we cannot simply deny the existence of the word.

Research into this type of question—the subject being generally called 'metamathematics'—continues apace. Not too long ago, Gödel showed (roughly speaking) that within any discipline of logic or mathematics, theorems could be validly formulated which could not conceivably be proven true or proven false. The prototypical such theorem is the famous, "This theorem cannot be proven true," which poses obvious difficulties to someone trying to prove or disprove it. The theorem quoted is simply a formalization of the similar one, "This sentence is false," which opens Mr. Pollock's article. Gödel's work is taken as demonstrating that mathematics is intrinsically 'incomplete' in that questions may be posed which cannot be answered.

There is a related question: is mathematics consistent? That is, having proven some theorem, say, Theorem X, are we sure that the antithesis of Theorem X, say, Theorem anti-X, cannot be proven? It would be unfortunate if we could deduce both X and anti-X from valid argument. But there is now reason to believe that a proof of consistency cannot be achieved—not simply that we do not know one at the moment, but that one cannot conceivably exist. As someone said, "We know God exists, for mathematics is consistent; but we know the Devil exists, for we cannot prove that consistency."

Alan A. Grometstein
Stoneham, Massachusetts

Anglo-American Crossword Puzzle
No. 2   by Jack Luzzatto

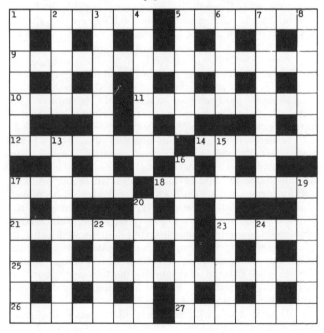

ACROSS

1 Miss Ice is rather shocking behind that cool façade. (7)

5 CB broadcast is the spot to croon out of tune in the farmer's ear. (7)

9 "Hi! See no SALT game!" White House-Red Square phone call. (1, 7, 7)

10 Just the oldtime girl for the temperance poster. (5)

11 Got in a shiver because of sly surveillance. (9)

12 Out of the running despite a great exploit indeed. (8)

14 A figure of doggone speech, to mess it up. (6)

17 Hear the charge of vice in words as ordered. (6)

18 Sees the cross borne by men and women. (3, 5)

21 Do we wrongly follow an addled brain because he's so colorful? (9)

23 Opposite of unite. (5)

25 Watch Dad get his gun now, in struggle to save the union. (1, 7, 7)

26 Tried and cast off as seedy. (7)

27 LSD in a bad trip shoots one full of holes. (7)

DOWN

1 Take to the saddle with the hundred in it when things have got too hot. (7)

2 A case of hard cheese on wry. (5)

3 Madam in a loose role makes quite a thriller.(9)

4 Warmed cold ones with comforters. (8)

5 Burden put on to curb me. (6)

6 USSR and the mysterious East are full of tricks. (5)

7 To make such exchanges may or may not be Women's Lib. (6, 3)

8 Brat she raised has unseemly aspirations. (7)

13 Whip the flames from the upper windows. (9)

15 Led astray (or by the nose?) by a not quite full-grown young lady. (9)

16 There's a short notice in the shower from that dogged peeper. (8)

17 Champ of the waves is the top. (7)

19 Hammers heavily, and the ship breaks up around the reef. (7)

20 This knocks us down and out, in knightly combat. (6)

22 Weirdly flighty, to say the least. (5)

24 Experiment with error. (5)

ANSWER to Anglo-American Crossword Puzzle No. 2

ACROSS	DOWN
1. S-e-ISM-ic	1. S-c-ALDED
5. C-ornco-B	2. Irony
9. A HOTLINE MESSAGE	3. M-elo-D-r-AMA
10. DRY-ad	4. C-ons-OL-e-D
11. O-versi-G-h-T	5. CU-m-B-e-R
12. DE-feat-ED	6. RUS-e-S
14. t-MES-i-S	7. CHANGE s-EX
17. Syn-tax	8. BR-e-AT-hs
18. THE SE-x-ES	13. Fanlights
21. RAINB-o-WE-d	15. MIS-guided
23. UNTIE	16. SH-ad-OWER
25. A SHOTGUN WEDDING	17. SURF-ace
26. ES-sa-YED	19. S-ledge-S
27. rid-DL-e-S	20. s-WO-u-ND
	22. Batty
	24. Trial

EPISTOLAE

I found "The Encompassing Circle" [IV, 1] well written and very informative. There· was, however, one error which I have seen often repeated elsewhere. The slang term *gringo*, applied to Americans by Mexicans, stems not from the first words of a song, but from the American's mispronunciation of the Mexican's term of contempt for them. The Mexicans called the Americans *griegos* or 'Greeks' because they could not understand the American's speech (speaking English or Spanish)—it was Greek to them! I'm sorry I can't quote learned references, but as a psychoanalyst and an ex-soldier I find it hard to believe our bold troopers would be singing "Green grow the rushes, oh!" (not *lilacs, oh!*)—and not a more bawdy song.

Anyway, if that were the case, we should all be called *gringoes*.

Henry Kaminer, M.D.
Tenafly, New Jersey
[Similarly, from D.E. Schmiedel
Las Vegas, Nevada]

Referring to "Charmed and Other Quarks" [VERBA-TIM III, 3], I wonder whether Mr. August A. Imholtz, Jr., is not—however amusingly and imaginatively—running around Robin Hood's barn to find a non-Quark?

It's perfectly true that Joyce's words are compounded from many languages—but why settle on German (except that one may know it better than half a dozen other equally implausible candidates) when the closest one can come to any appropriate sense is a mess of white-curd cheese, rubbish, or trifles? Poppycock (see etym)!

Has not Mr. Imholtz rather easily daffed off the known English senses or past uses of *quark*? That the West Highland frogs gurgle and quark does not require that Joyce's birds gurgle (though some birds do) merely because they quark. Joyce was quite clearly enjoying onomatopoeia in this phrase, and we should listen carefully.

For an Englishman, the *r* in *quark* would be merely graphic, indicating length on the *a*: the gulls would be not *quarking* but *quaaking*. But for Joyce the *r* most surely counted for itself. And gulls do not merely *quack*; they have an added quality, prolonging the resonance of their call, which is well represented by *r*. *Quark* is very exactly the sound the gulls were making.

Whether Joyce was already playing in his mind with *Muster Mark* and therefore heard the gulls rhyming with it, or whether he heard the *quark* first and that led him rhymingly to *Mark*, must remain an irresoluble mystery. But—let us rejoice—one need not go stravaiging from the sea-coast of Ireland to that of Bohemia to be charmed by the gulls of Joyce quarking for Muster Mark or to be gulled by the charms of Germanic etymology. In any case, when Irish gulls talk about cottage cheese, they have the decency to call it bonny-clabber.

Frederic G. Cassidy
DARE
University of Wisconsin

VERBATIM®

THE LANGUAGE QUARTERLY

Vol. IV, No. 4   February 1978

EDITOR: LAURENCE URDANG

Regional Report No. 1
—The Bay Area

Jean Montgomery
Mill Valley, California

I n San Francisco and its suburbs, a whole generation has grown up giving voice to a kind of English that is, if not broken, at least oddly bent. In the Bay Area, the farmer 'tills at the soil,' our country is the 'most favorite nation' and we have 'no truck for other countries.' A real estate dealer is a 'realator,' and *et cetera* becomes 'essetera.' 'Dippity,' we say, and 'Klu Kluck Klan.' 'In view of' becomes 'in lieu of,' and an action may not resound to someone's credit. *Sure* turns into 'sheer,' and *actually* becomes 'acksh'lly,' in a nasal rasp that could drill through plate steel. Common usage gives us 'deteriate,' and 'high arky' (as contrasted, presumably, with 'low arky' and an 'arky' in between). 'Respitory' ailments often keep company with a fever, which is shown by the 'merkurry' rising in the 'thermomaner.' To 'hannel' a high 'tempature,' doctors 'avocate' bed rest and 'aspirn.' Essettera.

To be 'bummed out' is to be discouraged. But around here, someone who is 'bummed all the way out' heads for the railing of the Golden Gate bridge.

Part of the responsibility for our bent language rests with the print media. Our newspapers carry ads for raincoats "dry cleaned and repelled" and for a detergent that comes in a "mini-giant" box. A politician's former wife is quoted by one newspaper as saying, "I loved my husband very much and wanted to accommodate. After a while I realized I was chasing a windmill." The *Chronicle* reports that the San Francisco Police Department is revising its manual because the old rule book has become too "large and topsy." A splendid new category of crime is cited by one paper: the "ultra-heinous crime—a fatal arson attack"; another reports that privacy is "trounced upon" when telephone lines are tapped.

Some newspaper columnists run on and on and on. This haunting thought appeared in a column in the weekly *Mill Valley* Record: "You should never look over your shoulder or somebody may be gaining on you if you don't tow the line." The county daily, *Independent Journal,* not to be outdone, offers headlines such as HARMONY PERVADES AT DEBATES FOR CANDIDATES, and THEATER GROUP BATTLES SURVIVAL.

A movie reviewer in the *Journal's* Sunday supplement merits special attention. Recently, he wrote that a film had a "series of mishaps upon the like of which many a petard had been hoist." The actors failed to sparkle in the clutches. Even worse, they turned the playwright's "Saroyanesque flibberty-gibbeting in a mundaneity that is almost tragic."

We are equally innovative in our oral communication, supported and proclaimed by the broadcast media. It is from radio that one can learn about the gentleman who has been "laid low by prostrate trouble" and the car driver who unintentionally" stepped on the exhilarator." Talk show guests have referred to "unwrinkable garments" and "recycable articles." Unruffled by the pitfalls of her subject, one guest hastens to explain why people are unable to make their meanings clear when they "commucate together": "It's the ambigitty of language," she says. A Berkeley school teacher has another explanation: "Nobody talks to each other any more."

In the ambigitty of talk-show conversation, one can hear about "wheel chairs and other types of illnesses"; of "back-watering" when a boat's course is reversed; of a suicide that was "self-inflicted"; of an event that "really irates" the speaker and gets his "dandruff up"; and of a bird with its wings akimbo. [The meaning of *akimbo* is probably lost forever. The caption that accompanied a recently published newspaper photograph of a parachutist floating down in an awkward position said that he had "both arms and legs akimbo."]

Some talk-show ambiguities are sheer (not 'sure') delight: "It's easier than shooting a barrel of monkeys"; "He cooked the golden goose"; "Why hang yourself by shooting in the dark?"; and "It happened kind of out of a bolt of blue."

A newscast commucator reports that Oakland has been given the anchor of the carrier *Oriskany* as a "massive momentum" of that city's favorite ship. A trial lawyer, it is said, kept his client off the witness stand so that the client "would not be pillaged by his enemies." Nor is the Reverend Mr. Spooner without his followers. A "keace-peeping" force soon showed up to prevent the pillaging. Once, when a cabinet officer resigned, we heard that in his job he had been the eye of many a storm. And one newsman, in particular, appeared to be especially well satisfied with the quelling of a recent high school disturbance: it had been, he smirked, "nipped on the vine."

In electronic adland a clothing store burbles about a bargain "so fantastic it's unreal." "Glad is what happens" on another commercial. The ad itself, though, has turned into a *this*. Now 'this.' More news after 'this.' Listen to 'this.'

Verbosity and pretentiousness abound. The University of California at Berkeley, for instance, announces the hours during which its business office "may be accessed." A teacher in Mill Valley has drawn up a "prioritized list of all components of the school program." Our people are busy *critiqueing, leafleting, scapegoating, conferencing,* and *pickpocketing.* One San Francisco appliance dealer boasts of a stove which will not only roast and broil, it will also *rotisse!*

Conversely, our most banal remarks are tagged with cringing little pleas for encouragement: "Hospitals are for sick people, right?" and "Like, I'm into macramé, okay?"

We 'relate' to steaks and 'munch out' on sandwiches. We enjoy "authentic early-English pizza." And after dinner, lolling about on a 'chase-lounge' and enjoying the euphoria that accompanies a full stomach, any one of us like feels majooberized (*majooberized* is a nonce word used in these parts for 'pleasantly relaxed').

The San Francisco police have just announced a new program for "carrying out crime and punishment." Rather than be caught up in critiqueing that one, I shall join the others in the country whom "apathy has by the throat." That means, I'm into believing this piece is finished. I mean, it's the end, right?

How to Turn a Baseball Phrase

Jack Luzzatto
Bronx, New York

When I read John O. Herbold II's article on baseball "To Understand America (and Americans)" [IV, 1], it sped me on to do my own pet thing on baseball. The locutions of the game announcers are little short of entrancing (at least, the first time around). Here are a few I have collected.

The impetus for this collection was supplied by Ralph Kiner, who, along with Lindsey Nelson and Bob Murphy, is a Mets broadcaster. I love them all dearly, but that doesn't prevent me from being amused at what they say. Ralph's gem came when he described a first baseman holding a position different from normal when holding a runner on first base and still being ready to field a ball. He said, "There are quite a few innovations that have come out of baseball, some of them old and some of them new."

However, my point is that if anyone wants to announce baseball games, he needs a stock of phrases. If a batter hits safely between the shortstop and second, or second and first, the announcer will call that "a seeing-eye base hit." If the outfielder can throw a "strike" from far away to any base or home plate to nail a runner, he has "a howitzer of an arm." A hitter who can send that ball out of the park, like Willie Stargell, Greg Luzinski, etc., has "awesome power." A baseball that is pitched and almost catches the batter full in the guts is said to be "in his kitchen." Base-stealing speedsters are characterized by the words "he can fly," or "he has a world of speed."

A ballplayer who is not an infielder, outfielder, or pitcher, and is thus doomed to be a catcher, wears "the tools of ignorance," catcher's gear. (If it starts to rain, the crowd dons "foul-weather gear.")

Batters inspire various locutions. If a hitter at the plate is given to lashing his bat in circles while waiting for the pitch he is "cowtailing his bat around." If he is at bat during a long "dry spell," waiting to get a hit, the sportscaster may say "he comes up wearing a size 19 collar," meaning he has failed till now and may be about to fail for the 20th time. If the batter gets a little foul ball to preserve his turn at bat on the third strike, then he "got a piece of it." But if Lady Luck smiles and he hits a homerun, then he "got all of it." One of my favorites is the phrase for a towering pop fly that shoots straight up to the sky and comes down in the same area, usually caught by the catcher. The announcer says, "He could have hit that ball in a silo." A homerun that becomes a well-traveled ball, going some 500 feet or more, is called "a tape-measure homerun."

Pitchers also inspire the poets of the mike. One like Nolan Ryan, who can throw a baseball at 100mph-plus, is said to be "throwing smoke." When his fastball gets a third strike that catches the hitter "looking," then "he blew it right by him with a blazing fastball." Sometimes a pitcher, who has been victimized by a hitter who scored a homerun his last time up, resents it bitterly. This pitcher is not squeamish about firing a fast one right at the batter's body, anywhere— arm, leg, torso, or head. About such a pitcher the man at the mike may say, "He'd hit his own grandmother if she was up there with a hot bat." When a relief pitcher comes in because the starter is beginning "to dig a big hole for himself" (putting men on base with walks and hits), he is called a fireman who must "put out the fire" his predecessor started. Sometimes this will result in a mixed metaphor. The announcer may say the reliefer fireman "came in and slammed the door," that is, he got the necessary third out and prevented any scoring. Of course, just the opposite may happen. He may be unfortunate enough to release a "nice fat pitch, right over the heart of the plate," thus giving the batter a chance to get it all. If a homerun results, this is called "a gopher pitch," because the batter surely can go for it. When a strikeout occurs, usually on a perfect pitch that the batter does not go for, this pitch is said to be "right down the pipe."

Some phrases belong to individual players, as with the Willie Mays "basket catch," a method of snagging fly balls by holding the glove and ungloved hand to form a basket low and in front of one's body. And Brooks Robinson, Oriole third baseman, earned the sobriquet of "the vacuum cleaner" because he sucked in everything that came his way. We all know that Babe Ruth was "the Sultan of Swat," and Jimmy Wynn, a more or less diminutive hitter with homerun potential, is called "the toy cannon."

Umpires earn vituperation simply because no decision can please both sides. When members of the team at bat, who are sitting in the dugout, grow vociferous about balls being called strikes against their teammate, they may hoot and holler at the umpire, implying he is blind, biased, or unfit for his job. This is called "heat from the dugout." If the umpire can't take it anymore, he may approach the chief offender and tell him to shut up. Further offense may make the umpire flare up enough to eject the culprit summarily from the game. Such an umpire is said to have "a short fuse."

There are many more colorful locutions, of course. I do want to say that all the above are superior to a cry of "Holy cow!" On that note, I'll be "Going, going, gone," as I run all the way home.

Moribund Metaphors Rise Again

Sam Hinton
La Jolla, California

Though language has been described as "a cemetery of dead metaphors," many of the corpses are still used in what was once a secondary sense, their metaphoric context forgotten. The earlier figure of speech was often in a language not understood by present speakers, and only by patient research—or by consulting the results of such research in an etymological dictionary—can the nature of the original metaphor be known. Nevertheless, today's users of a language frequently invent new words or phrases in which they unconsciously repeat the hidden comparison.

There are many reasons for creating a new expression—to make the language more vivid, to signify a concept not adequately described by an older term, to disassociate an expression from undesirable connotation, to provide an in-group recognition signal, and so on. Neologisms are always current among young people, as one manifestation of the revolt that is necessary if the young are to accede to their culture's dominant positions. With equal universality the elders resist being deposed, and one manifestation of this resistance is their anguished cry that their language is being polluted, degraded, bastardized. The elders of my generation have come up with a metaphor of their own to express the terrible danger they see: "The English language is an endangered species!"

A typical example of this attitude appeared in "Curmudgeon-at-Large," Cleveland Amory's regular column in *Saturday*

Review (2 Oct. 1976, p. 51), although Mr. Amory was more restrained and more humorous than many writers on the same subject. "Young people nowadays," we are told, "intend to go through life using only five expressions," which are " 'Right on,' 'With it,' 'Far out,' 'Get it all together,' and 'Let it all hang out.' " He then goes on to say that he has conducted a small poll and concludes that to these young persons " 'Right on' means 'With it,' 'With it' means 'Far out,' 'Far out' means 'Get it all together,' and 'Get it all together' means 'Let it all hang out.' " There is no doubt that some young folk don't always express themselves very clearly to us elders, but even a confessed curmudgeon might find some surprisingly pleasant affinities with his youthful informants if he would listen to how they really use their terms. He might even realize that they are working under the same traditions that shaped the "standard" language, and that he and they—and their common remote ancestors—are pretty much the same sorts of people.

Right on is most often heard as an exclamation of hearty agreement, used as a Member of Parliament would use "Hear! Hear!" The same metaphor, using a precise spatial location to represent verbal accuracy, is found in older expressions, such as "Very much to the point!" or even "You've hit the nail right on the head!" A statement that is *right on* in a clever way is officially known as an *epigram* from Greek -*gram* 'writing' plus *epi-* 'on.' (Please, may I say "write on?")

With it has several meanings and is by no means new. I heard it in the 1930s when working for a carnival; a person who was *with it* was a fellow-carny, a *compeer*—which comes from an earlier word for with—Latin *com* 'with' plus *par* 'equal.' The 'with' roots are widely used in a figurative way, as in *sympathize* ('suffer with') and *compatible* ('endure with'). The most usual use of *with it* is in application to a person who is deeply immersed in some activity, and an expert in it; our ancestors had a very similar metaphor in mind when they coined the word *accomplished*—'filled with.'

Far out, like *right on*, often occurs as an exclamation of approval and could be replaced by any number of standard words with the same idea of being "outside" of ordinary experience. *Extraordinary* can be analyzed as 'beyond that which is ordinary'; the roots of *exceptional* mean 'taken out,' and *exquisite* comes from 'seek out.' *Superior* and *superb* also denote something that is far out, this time in an upward direction, while *delightful* uses not 'out' but the similar 'away,' and means 'enticed away.'

To *get it all together* is to attain a state of composure,

and *composure* is from French words having the sense of 'put together.' The person who has *got it all together* is *collected* ('gathered together'), and not *distraught* ('pulled apart'). This term more often refers to someone who is operating at peak efficiency—that is, who is *coordinated* ('arranged together') and *competent* ('together in seeking'). When applied to the head—"I've got to get my head together"—the expression indicates a desirable state of mental *integrity* ('entireness') and *health* (from a Germanic root meaning 'wholeness'). All these carry the same implication of 'being together' in one piece—the opposite of unhealthy *schizophrenia*, or 'split mind.'

Someone with a real mental problem is said to be *off his rocker*, which is not very different from the literal meaning of *delirium*—'out of the furrow.'

Let it all hang out is an admonishment to be natural, *uninhibited*—which itself means 'not held in.' *Unconstrained* ('not bound together') and *unconfined* ('not imprisoned') are in the same family of metaphors. To *let it all hang out* can also mean to be forthright, to be *explicit*—'folded out.' This usage also implies honesty—a word having the same meaning in Latin and said to have been derived from the name of a plant whose transparent seed-pods disclosed the seeds within.

There are many other interesting words in the bright lexicon of youth. One is the adjective *cool* as applied to someone displaying *sang-froid* ('cool blood,' of course) or *nonchalance*, which is literally 'not hot'—in other words, *cool*!

At the other end of the temperature scale, young people are likely to feel *burned up* where one of their elders would be *incensed*, from Latin *incendere*, 'to set on fire.' Another word relating to fire can signify delight, as in the phrase "That just stokes me out of my gourd!" Without using slang, this could be rephrased as "That kindles in me a feeling of ecstasy!" *Kindles* is obviously related to *stokes*, while *ecstasy* ('standing outside of myself') is not very different from the rest of the phrase. The word *gourd* is a synecdochic use of a metaphor for the human head, which has cognates in a good many languages. Early Latin had the word *testa* 'a jug' which became a Roman slang word for 'the head' and eventually the standard word for the organ in several Romance tongues. The German *kopf* probably arose in the same way.

Sometimes a new term is created to replace an old one whose literal meaning is implied too faintly. *Goodbye* has become an automatic expression indicating the end of a human contact, and can be used peremptorily or angrily, its original derivation from 'God be with you' completely forgotten. Many young people have therefore discarded it, preferring *have a nice day* as possessing a conscious context of well-wishing. And even the not-so-young may be heard to say *bye-bye*, which no modification of tone or emphasis can render unfriendly.

One sad thing about the language of youth is the rapidity with which a good expression becomes obsolete. At one time the Haight-Ashbury population used *to run with* 'to understand and agree' to be *au courant* ('running with') with someone. I think it a pity that so vivid a term is no longer used. Do you *concur*? (Latin *con* 'with' plus *currere* 'run.')

"DO YOU LIKE MY HAIR?
IT'S AN 'APHRO.'"

Bleep
That Slur!

Andrew E. Beresky
New York, New York

Within the past few years, several American dictionaries have found fit to squeeze in a new derogatory entry which has no place in lexicons already crowded with derogatory terms. The word is *honky*, the latest of ethnic slurs which won its quick acceptance mainly through the medium of television.

On practically every TV situation comedy, crime series, and talk show, as well as on news shows, the discriminatory term has been bandied about indescriminately to apply to all white people. Even so-called liberal whites have cutely picked it up to show that they are "right-on" with the cause and are "telling it like it is." This is simply not the correct usage of my personal pet derogation. Not every white person can qualify as a honky.

I, for instance, am a honky by nature of birth, albeit second and one-half generation. But not by the wildest stretch of the imagination could I consider President Carter to be one. Henry Kissinger need only utter a few words to be dubbed, rather erroneously, as a honky. Meanwhile, former special Watergate prosecutor Leon Jaworski may not sound like one, but the mere signing of an autograph is a dead giveaway.

Ace TV crime fighter Karl Malden and band leader Lawrence Welk both look like honkies—and are. On the other hand, Boris Karloff had the distinctive air of a grand honky—but wasn't, though his fellow bogeymen Peter Lorre and Bela Lugosi were.

It is believed that *honky* was started on its way to biased faddism several years ago when Rap Brown used the term in front of TV news cameras. Mr. Brown may have been an astute political activist, but he hadn't learned his prejudices well. Or perhaps he learned them too well. It's highly implausible that the word, as used by Brown then and by all others now, stemmed from *honky-tonk* which my dictionary describes as 'a cheap, sordid saloon, cabaret, etc.' Heaven knows, every race and ethnic group has its share of honky-tonks.

No, I maintain that *honky* was, and is a deliberate mis-pronunciation of *hunky*, one of white Anglo-Saxon America's most popular ethnic (but not racial) slurs that gained wide usage during the era of this country's most impressive growth and development. Of the latest dictionary editions that list *honky* for the first time, only *Funk & Wagnall's Standard College Dictionary* (1974) apparently agrees. It states, parenthetically, that the word is "possibly derived from hunky."

The Random House College Dictionary (1975) merely states "origin uncertain." Curiously, while neither *Webster's New 20th Century Unabridged* (1976) nor *Webster's New World Dictionary of the English Language* (1972) makes any mention of the term, *Webster's New Collegiate* (1976) lists two alternate spellings—*honkie* and *honkey*—but offers no etymology except to say that it is "usually used disparagingly."

Most dictionaries are in accord that *hunky* is used to describe 'an unskilled or semi-skilled workman of foreign birth; especially a Hungarian.' True, the word may have its roots in the application by white Anglo-Saxon Americans to immigrant Hungarians. But in fact it was also applied to those foreign-born, regardless of skill or profession, coming from other middle and eastern European countries, especially Poland, Russia, Czechoslovakia, Lithuania, Yugoslavia, and so on. Foreigners with other accents or heritage, such as Germans, Italians, Jews, Scots, Swedes, etc., could not earn that distinction. They inherited their own ethnic slurs. But whatever the accent of the non-honky, he quickly learned to apply the term.

My maternal grandfather, for instance, often told the story of his working as a water boy for a work crew building a railroad near Pittsburgh shortly after he came to this country as a youngster from Czechoslovakia, more than a century ago. On the job, he befriended a Scottish-born timekeeper who delighted in applying a double epithet to my grandfather. In a strong, inherited burr, the timekeeper would call my grandfather, rather redundantly, "my little gr-r-reenhor-r-rn hunky." Perhaps what delighted my grandfather most in retelling the story was the fact that the young Scot was Andrew Carnegie.

Before a new TV season is upon us, I personally hope that *honky* will not again be inserted in scripts as freely as *whitey* and *Mr. Charlie* were tossed about a few years back. But at least these terms were original, not borrowed from other derogations. To borrow the discriminatory term of *honky* to denote any white person is a cop-out on discrimination.

Diplophrasis

My letter in the February 1976 VERBATIM, listing phrases in our language in which synonyms are joined by *and* (*aches and pains, alas and alack, bits and pieces*) and other examples of hendiadys and merism elicited many additions from readers. These contributions, and examples which have subsequently surfaced in my casual reading, appear in the list below. Many similar phrases permeate the Bible, legal documents, and the ritual language of Freemasonry.

Collectors of these "binomial" phrases have given them fond names, such as "tandems," "so and so's," "twofers," "sandwiches," and "double-deckers"; the second edition of Henry Fowler's *A Dictionary of Modern English* labels them "Siamese twins."

As acknowledgment of the interest of several correspondents who collect "threesomes," I append a few examples of "trinomials" at the end of my list.

aches and pains	*down and out*
act and deed	*dribs (drips) and drabs*
aid and abet	*each and every*
alas and alack	*east and west*
all and sundry	*ebb and flow*
assault and battery	*ever and ever*
bag and baggage	*fair and just*
beck and call	*fair and square*
before and after	*far and near*
betwixt and between	*fast and furious*
bib and tucker	*fast and loose*
bill and coo	*fear and trembling*
bits and pieces	*fine and dandy*
body and soul	*fire and brimstone*
bound and determined	*first and last*
bow and scrape	*fits and starts*
bread and butter	*flotsam and jetsam*
bright and early	*free and easy*
by and by	*friend and foe*
cease and desist	*frills and furbelows*
coming and going	*fun and frolic*
cut and thrust	*fun and games*
day and night	*fuss and fume*
decline and fall	*gall and wormwood*
ditch and delve	*good and thick*

good and tight
grace and favor
grand and glorious
great and small
grunt and groan

hale and hearty
hard and fast
head and heels
head and shoulders
heart and soul

heaven and earth
heirs and assigns
hem and haw
here and now
high and low

high and mighty
hither and thither
hook and crook
hoot and holler
hot and heavy

hot and strong
house and home
hue and cry
huff and puff
hustle and bustle

in and out
ins and outs
intents and purposes
jot and tittle
kit and caboodle

kith and kin
law and order
leaps and bounds
length and breadth
lewd and lascivious

lo and behold
long and endless
long and short
look and see
might and main

mix and match
moan and groan
near and far
nerve and fiber

new and different

nice and cozy
nice and soft
nice and warm
nip and tuck
nook and cranny

north and south
now and then
null and void
odds and ends
on and on

one and all
over and over
p's and q's
part and parcel
peace and quiet

pick and choose
pride and joy
pure and simple
quick and easy
rags and tatters

rank and file
rant and rave
rich(er) and poor(er)
right and left
right and proper

root and branch
rough and ready
rough and tumble
rules and regulations
sackcloth and ashes

sere and yellow
sit and wait
sixes and sevens
so and so
so and so's

sound and fury
spick and span
spit and image
stand and deliver
stress and strain

stuff and nonsense
tattered and torn

thick and fast
thick and thin
time and tide

to and fro
toil and moil
toss and turn
town and gown
tried and true

trials and tribulations
twists and turns
up and around
up and down
up and up

use and wont
various and sundry
vim and vigor
waifs and strays
ways and means

wear and tear
weep and wail

well and good
whims and caprices
whys and wherefores

widows and orphans
wine and dine
wit and wisdom
withered and died
[w]rack and ruin
young and old

Examples of "trinomials":
bell, book, and candle
cool, calm, and collected
deaf, dumb, and blind
dwindle, peak, and pine
eat, drink, and be merry
fair, fat, and forty

hook, line, and sinker
man, woman, and child
signed, sealed, and delivered
sugar and spice and everything nice
vim, vigor, and vitality
world, flesh, and the devil

Philip E. Hager
University of Puget Sound

EPISTOLAE

I raise the ante in the freight train (or boxcar) competition with this fragment that Fineman says he kept out of *The Physical Review* (but published in *Science*):

. . . the rare-earth local moment-free electron-like
conduction electron exchange integral compling . . .

He goes on to say that "Hyphens are generally avoided in the freight train construction except where they add significantly to the confusion."

As long as I have the editor's attention I will ask if readers know of another word, besides 'mantissa' (or mantisa), that is believed to derive from both Welsh and Etruscan?

Karl F. Heumann
Bethesda, Maryland

ETYMOLOGICA OBSCURA

What Emerges in an Emergency?

To some of us who dabble in etymology the field is an intriguing, if perilous study. It seems to undergo alternating periods of approbation and condemnation. But unawareness of etymology is, perhaps, in the main, more of a blessing than a bane. Relatively few people bother to ask themselves what the segments of words like *emergency, constitution*, or *challenge* mean. And it is just as well, or language might cease to function altogether. Still, an occasional curious cove may wonder what emerges in an emergency, while most of his fellow creatures treat it as an approximate synonym of *crisis* or *danger* or the like, and for them it remains just as opaque in formation as, say, *sycamore, identity*, or *carburetor*.

But *emergency* is obviously somehow derived from *emergence* (which has the same termination as that seen in *difference, continence, reticence*), ultimately from a Latin present participle of *ēmergō, -ere* 'come forth, rise up.' Whether this derivation occurred in old French or in learned Latin (**emergentia?*) or both is not too clear or too relevant here. Yet *ēmergō = ē* 'out of' + *mergō* 'immerse, dip, sink, plunge,' and *ēmergere* means 'rise up (like some sea monster?) out of (the deep?).' A *merg-anser* is a diving bird (literally a 'plunging goose'). The present meaning of *emergency* did not emerge or crop up until the seventeenth century, and Samuel Johnson was still condemning it a century later as "a sense not proper" (cf. E. L. McAdam, Jr. and George Milne, *Johnson's Dictionary, A Modern Selection*. New York: Pantheon Books, 1963, p. 165). It would be rash to venture a guess that the rhyme with *urgency* helped to promote the present meaning.

What happens in a *merger?* One firm or organization often becomes swallowed up (or down) and loses its identity. Yet we often act as if *merge* meant 'blend, join together, enter into a union on more or less equal terms.' Some linguists—not all—speak of *mergers* as if they were the equivalent of blends. In old legal terminology, however, the English translation of French *merger* (infinitive) was often 'drown.' Not long ago two colleges in our vast university were 'merged.' The undersigned, a member of the smaller and better one, mumbled in a faculty meeting, "Etymologically, yes," whereupon the presiding dean asked, "What was that?" and received the reply in simplified English translation, "We're being submerged!" We were, and most of us regarded it as an outrage.

Where is the *rage* in *outrage?* Nowhere, etymologically, and the same holds true for the *out.* For, although we may be "put out" and feel intense rage at what we regard as an outrage, the word itself contains neither of the two elements of which it might seem to consist. For it is from French *outrage,* cf. Old French *oltrage, ultrage* (cf. also Italian *oltraggio,* which may or may not be independent of the French). The source, then, is Latin *ultra* 'beyond' plus a suffix *-age,* reflecting possibly a Latin ending *-āticum.* The formation is therefore not unlike that of the neologism *outage* heard so frequently during recent power failures. This may have been modeled on some such word as *shortage,* with overtones of *wattage, voltage,* etc., but its formation is very similar to that of *outrage,* and there is scant cause for *outrage* at the upstart. It is, of course, hard to believe that there is no association, by popular or unpopular etymology, with *rage,* and rage is certainly reflected in reaction to outrages like outages. The pronunciation of the second element also attests to some such association (the word rhymes with *spout age* rather than with °*sproutidge*). An elementary school teacher of mine over five decades ago said, "When rage gets into us, we are enraged; when it comes out, we are outraged." She vouchsafed much interesting misinformation (e.g., "A.D. = 'after death' ") and may have kindled the spark of my interest in etymology, thus contributing to the delinquency of a minor.

It may be somewhat *discomforting* to be *discomfited* and also to find out that the words are not related, except in their prefixes. A glance at an etymological dictionary will reveal their actual sources. A bold knight once *demeaned* himself bravely in combat, discomfiting all he encountered, in fact. I think of a page in Chrétien's *Lancelot* where the two words occur in close proximity, and the English translator used *demeaned* and *discomfited* as their equivalents. But the analogy of *debase* has probably caused *demean* (cf. its derivative *demeanor*) to assume the sense of *de-* plus *mean* 'base.' Hence apparent etymological transparency results in new semantic directions with usurpation and replacement of the old. This does not always happen, of course. For, although the *clan* may seem *destined* to hold *clandestine* sessions, no etymological connection between that word and *clan* or *destine* can be made, nor does a fancied one impart any new sense to signifier or signified.

Sometimes old folk-etymological association prevails, and its venerability lends an acceptance long after the process is forgotten. *Obliterate* once meant to wipe out a letter *(litera)*; but association with two unrelated words *oblitum* 'blotted over' and *oblītum* 'forgotten' has extended the meaning in such a way that a merger has obliterated the "real" etymology and relegated it to oblivion. In examples like *aggravate, transpire, lackadaisical* (and maybe the wretched *viable*—for I seem to share some of Edwin Newman's prejudices) similar processes no doubt occurred. When we are old enough to have witnessed the processes, we feel revulsion—once a mistake for *repulsion*, perhaps. When they happened ages ago, we bow in veneration, blissfully aware that veneration has some connection with Venus, but not pedantic enough to confine it to one deity.

If we were not endowed with etymological oblivion, we could never (etymo)logically board a train, or sail on a steamer, or play a silver woodwind in a dilapidated wooden hut, experiences we might not want to miss. Or would we?

Robert A. Fowkes
New York University

EPISTOLAE

Willard Espy wonders [IV, 2] at the inability of Frenchmen to *bend over backwards*. The equivalent expression in French is *se mettre en quatre (pour)* . . . . It means, literally, 'to transform oneself into four parts,' and is used typically as follows: *Je me suis mis en quartre pour lui faire plaisir* 'I bent over backwards in order to please him.'

Jacques C. Richardson
Paris

Similarly, from Viviane de Charrière, Paris; Joseph G. Foster, McKeesport, Pennsylvania; Donald E. Schlesinger, Bronx, New York.

Since writing [my letter] [IV,2], I have received a number of ingenious suggestions for "wishwords," or words that we regret not having said at the party we just left.

The best suggestion by far was relayed to me by Mr. Daniel Pomerantz of Lexington, Massachusetts, who told me that his mother had heard the late great Dorothy Parker use *departee* for 'staircase wit.'

Martin H. Slobodkin
Cambridge, Massachusetts

. . . I have used *departee*. The name of its originator, alas, can no longer be recalled.

John W. P. O'Brien
Flushing, New York

. . . I'm inept at repartee but good at *departee* . . . It appeared some years ago in *Saturday Review* (Goodman Ace, maybe?).

Bill Solomon
Shawnee Mission, Kansas

. . . I suggest *postpartee*. Many years ago, *The New Yorker* contained a witty article in which the author composed *prepartee* before a social event. Of course, the necessary remarks were never made, leaving him bereft of *repartee* and frustrated by *postpartee* afterward.

Mrs. D. C. Mullery
San Mateo, California

. . . In England a person who has failed in this way often confesses to being *after-witted*.

Philip Arthur Walles
Mawgan Porth, Cornwall

I have one or two suggestions . . ..
1. *Treppe* equals 'stairs/staircase' not 'steps'
2. The French say *l'esprit d'escalier* not "les paroles d'escalier."

J. Gombinski
London

. . . How about *post-riposte*?

Alden Stahr
Columbia, New Jersey

. . . From the late 1920s or early 1930s, I have known that as *cab wit* . . ... My guess is that it came out of the Round Table at the Algonquin. If that guess is correct, then I also guess that Winchell gave it currency.

Virgil Quinlisk
Wichita, Kansas
Similarly, from Pyke Johnson, Jr., Old Greenwich, Connecticut

An English equivalent might well be *after words* or *afterword*.

Frederick W. Cropp
Santa Barbara, California

. . . An obvious [suggestion] . . . is *whistler*. I offer this based on the story, possibly apocryphal, that tells of Oscar Wilde's admiring a mot of Whistler's: "I wish I had said that," said Wilde. "You will, Oscar. You will."

Alden Stahr
Columbia, New Jersey

Unconsciously Appropriate and Inappropriate Metaphors

Donald Hawes
North Wembly, Middlesex

Mixed metaphors have often been collected and commented upon, as in Eric Partridge's *Usage and Abusage*. "Little warning," wrote Fowler in *Modern English Usage*, "is needed against [mixed metaphor]; it is so conspicuous as seldom to get into speech or print undetected." But what has less frequently been observed is the unconsciously appropriate or inappropriate metaphor, which has a certain affinity with the "Freudian slip." Here are a few examples of what I mean.

The artist has allowed his imagination *to run riot*. [Caption to a picture of the Gordon Riots in London, in The Open University Course A202, Unit 2, p. 69]

If, to broaden the canal to take, say, twenty per cent more traffic, it's necessary to halve the dividend, this will gain little favour with shareholders—that is, until such time as a rival appears, and then shareholders may prefer *to ditch* the canal and buy the rival's shares. [The Open University Course A202, Units 5 and 6, p. 60]

She has even taken a look at Boulez's music; but in charity I will not dwell on the mess of inaccurate facts and insensitive comments she produces *on that score*. [Book review in *The Times*, 25 August 1977]

Fine weather brought out the traffic in the South-east

yesterday as many people drove to the coast. Heavy traffic started in mid-morning. An RAC patrolman said: "It was as though *the floodgates had been opened.*" [*The Times*, 30 August 1977]

She has been "deliberately resting" while the surgeon has sorted out her knee. "You don't want *to make a great song and dance about it,* though, people think you're falling to pieces," she says . . .. [*The Observer,* 28 August 1977]

. . . the establishment of Ruskin College began (though surely *to a smaller degree* than he suggests) to change things for those like Jude. [*The Times Literary Supplement,* 9 September 1977, p. 1070]

I have noticed many more in recent years, but unfortunately I have not made a note of them. Their prevalence can be estimated by the fact I collected four of the above examples in two weeks' normal reading of periodicals. Perhaps correspondents to VERBATIM will be able to supply more and better examples. I would call this usage as much a fault as using a mixed metaphor, since it usually has a paradoxical effect of incongruity. On the other hand, I must admit that I sometimes welcome the amusement it gives me, especially when I find it in a tedious or grandiose piece of writing.

ADDENDA

I enjoyed Clair Schulz's whimsical article, "We Shall Know Them by Their Roots" [Verbatim, IV,2]. However, my roots in the youth culture demand that I point out three inaccuracies in Mr. Schulz's classifications.

First, I suggest that *The Beatles* properly belongs in the category of band names inspired by music itself, not by insects. Second, the group name *Ars Nova* is not a reference to a type of star, but rather, to the style of music composition characteristic of the fourteenth century in France and Italy. This group's music had a decided medieval flair. Finally, the name *Procul Harum* certainly does not refer to a variety of living quarters for women (in which case the latter word would have been spelled *harem*), but instead consists of two Latin words. These two words translated mean "at a great distance/of these": a mysterious name for a group whose music was considered by some teenagers back in the sixties to be of the "mind-bending" variety.   Deborah Storms
Evanston, Illinois

. . . Some of the names were rumored to have secret meanings. For example, *Three Dog Night* was supposed to be an Eskimo expression: the coldness of the night was measured by how many dogs were needed to keep warm. *Lovin' Spoonful* was usually explained as a junkie term for heroin heated in a spoon before being injected. *Moby Grape* was the punch line to an old riddle, "What's big and purple and swims in the ocean?" In the category of suggestive names, I would place *Wild Cherry, Queen, Kinks, Kiss* (The Seat of Affections), *Hot Tuna, Soft White Underbelly, Cream, The Tubes,* and *Badfinger.* Punning names include *Harper's Bizarre* and *Mothers of Invention.* Among my favorites are *It's a Beautiful Day, Commander Cody and the Lost Planet Airmen, Prairie Oyster, Steppenwolf,* and *Buffalo Springfield.*

Elizabeth Johnson Tsang
Oakham, Massachusetts

Clair Schulz's article reminded me that I used to be heartened when teaching in Liverpool during the '50s by the puns which appeared in pop groups' names. Apart from the *Beatles,* there were the *Fourmost* and a variety of more or less erudite groups like *Troy Dante and the Infernos, Johnnie Kidd and the Pirates, Mark Antony and the Avengers, Dave Sherwood and the Foresters, Bee Bumble and the Stingers,* and *Peter Jay and the Walkers* . . . .   Ken Smith
Lydney, Gloucestershire

EPISTOLAE

Since the article "The Seat of Our Affections" in VERBATIM [IV, 1] cites one allusion to the nose, I thought I should mention that the customary expression for "X became angry at Y" in Old Testament Hebrew is, literally, "X's nose burned at Y." For example, in Genesis xxx 2, And Jacob's anger was kindled against Rachel . . ., and in many other places.

(Note the *correct* usage of "literally.")

Stefan M. Silverston
Nashua, New Hampshire

BIBLIOGRAPHIA

LEXICON OF BLACK ENGLISH, by J. C. Dillard, The Seabury Press, New York, 1977, xiv + 199 pp. $12.95.

TALKIN AND TESTIFYIN: The Language of Black America, by Geneva Smitherman, Houghton Mifflin Company, Boston, 1977, 291 pp. $8.95.

Despite major differences in focus and approach, these two recent additions to the ever-growing literature on Black English share certain basic assumptions about that much-debated dialect. In terms of its historical development. both authors hold to (indeed Dillard is identified with) the Creolist theory, which traces the present-day Black English vernacular to a Plantation Creole, to a plantation-maritime pidgin, to an African origin. Both consequently also refute and attack the positions of those who hold that language borrowings and influences moved only in one direction—from the dominant to the suppressed culture; and both are eager to cite words in the White English lexicon whose not merely Black but African origins have been well documented, primarily through the work of David Dalby (e.g., *okay, hip, cat, badmouth*).

More significantly perhaps, particularly in the case of Dillard, is their insistence on the importance of dealing with Black English within the context of Black social and cultural life. Dillard organizes his work around "sociolinguistic domains" and stresses the importance of discourse over sentence as the primary carrier of meaning. Smitherman calls "style" that whole dimension of communication beyond syntax that conveys the message. Each believes that the main source of communication dysfunction between Blacks and Whites lies not in a difference of syntax nor in a difference of lexicon (though these differences are real) but in a difference of discourse style—those patterns of personal linguistic interaction integral to Black life but foreign, frequently unsettling, and sometimes frightening to Whites. The simplest example of this style is the sometimes spontaneous, sometimes formulaic or ritualistic interaction between listeners and speaker that is characteristic of Black discourse. Most White speakers would be insulted and distracted by precisely the behavior that tells the Black speaker his hearers are really with him—shouts, calls, interjections—all manifestations of confirming or condemning comment, some linguistic, some kinesic.

Thirdly, both Dillard and Smitherman condemn those "remedial programs" based on the assumption that Blacks are "linguistically deprived." The notion that Black children suffer from a paucity of verbal interaction they see as patent nonsense. Blacks come rather from a culture rich in oral tradition, one that uses that tradition as a continuing acculturating medium whose wide store of tales and folk heroes is still known to most Black children (tales whose African and Caribbean analogues Dillard cites). Each sees Black English as richly metaphoric and imagistic, its speakers adept at creative compounds and the double entendre, frequently extraordinarily skilled in traditional verbal battles and games which are integral to their world, a world in which the baddest dude is often the one with the best rap. (A word, by the way, whose meaning in Black English differs from the meaning it took on when assimilated into White English.)

Having said all that, it remains to be said that these two books are radically different and that none of the above constitutes the main argument of either.

J. C. Dillard's *Lexicon of Black English* is not the inventory of words and definitions the title might suggest, but rather an apologia for a lexicon, an attempt to justify the need for and the legitimacy of such a compilation, yet to be made. It is at the same time an implicit presentation of guidelines, clues, and caveats for the would-be researchers and compilers.

Arguing that vocabulary differences will be greatest where cultural differences are greatest, Dillard places heavy emphasis on the significance of conjure and root-work in the Black experience, noting its pervasive manifestations in blues lyrics and in folk trickster tales. Though linguistic transfer is greatest in areas with a high degree of interracial contact, such as prostitution, narcotics traffic, and music, he warns against and laments previous over-emphasis on these areas where the yield of words of demonstrable Black (i.e., Afro-Creole) origin is small. Too much study has focused on inner-city "jive talk," ignoring the reality that great numbers of Black English speakers do not know the hustlers' terminology.

In his own research for this preliminary lexicon Dillard relies heavily on early blues lyrics, on the work of folklorists and anthropologists, and on unpublished materials of the Louisiana WPA project. The writings of Black authors are naturally of particular interest; their comparative reliability is assessed for the future lexicon-makers (with Richard Wright coming out on top). Dillard's direction is always toward the roots of the Black experience and away from the cultural crossover points.

These roots he finds in the sociolinguistic domains of conjure, religion, folk tales, sexual practices, and music, each of which he focuses on separately, while carefully noting ties among them. In each he finds a significant number of words peculiar to the Black lexicon. These may be words unknown to White English, or shared words whose meaning or usage differs in Black English. Of more than passing cultural interest is his finding that numerous sexual terms which White English reserves for the male, Black English applies indiscriminately to male or female (e.g., *nut, grind, grinder, rider, getting one's ashes hauled*).

The work is of value for those interested not only in language, but in culture—of any color. It succeeds in being both readable and scholarly—no mean feat, particularly in the field of linguistics. Documentation is thorough and accessible, hypotheses clearly stated as such, and even those presentations which do get a bit convoluted for purposes of proving his point manage to contain nuggets that make the meandering worthwhile. You don't have to buy the whole argument or be a linguist to enjoy the book.

Geneva Smitherman's *Talkin and Testifyin: The Language of Black America* suffers from several serious weaknesses, chief among them a lack of focus and direction. Its attempts to cover everything about Black English from history to syntax, to lexicon, to its reflection of the "African world view," to discourse modes, to the identity crises and cultural conflicts of its speakers, to teaching techniques in inner-city schools make for much superficiality and little substance. Moreover, although there is no indication that any of its chapters appear elsewhere previously, the book reads like a hastily pieced-together pastiche of parts of earlier essays: it is marked by overlapping, repetition, shifts in tone and style, lack of coherence, and failure to develop any central argument.

Despite these drawbacks, it might provide the novice a good introductory survey to the subject, were it not for other failings. Ms. Smitherman digresses to the point of distraction on subjects whose relevance to Black English is never made clear. Her tone varies from an emotional, attacking one to a condescending cutesy one, with a bit of textbook chattiness ("Now let's look at," "Check it closely") thrown in for good measure. Frequent incorporations of Black English into her expository style usually fall flat. And she asks us to take a great deal on faith. Each chapter has footnotes, but specific statements do not. Trying to pinpoint the source for great numbers of her claims regarding a Black or African origin for words and phrases is maddening (and also, I think, impossible). Often her implicit criterion seems to be that she's heard an expression all her life among Black people: hardly different from the attitude of Whites who reject out of hand African origins of what appear to be Americanisms of long standing.

Illustrative support is amply provided but it is frequently too weak to support her argument, valid though that argument might be. She tells us, for example, that many Black speakers are verbally clever and linguistically creative; most language-sensitive people who have frequent contact with Blacks would agree. Then in support she offers prosaic, trite sayings, retorts, and sallies that don't begin to do justice to the vitality of Black English. No nonbeliever will be led to the linguistic light through her preaching.

Ms. Smitherman is at her best in the book's final chapters, when she deals with language attitudes and the role of the schools. She exposes the horror of the "educationally patronizing and linguistically stultifying" drill exercises being foisted on Black children in the name of providing them with the dominant dialect so they can "get ahead." She does a good job of taking language teachers to task for their obsession with correctness and unconcern with effectiveness. She's right on target with: "The public school is the main institution that continues to perpetuate myths and inaccuracies about language" [p. 191], myths that linguistics research has long ago exploded. Educators and language teachers might well attend to her comments on the problems inherent in bi-dialectalism and to her suggestions regarding primary-level reading instruction.

Overall, however, the book remains disappointing. It looks distressingly like an attempt to cash in on a burgeoning market. Black English and its speakers deserve better.

Nancy LaRoche
Hartford, Connecticut

EPISTOLAE

I've always been curious about the origin of the goodby wave *Toodle-oo*.

Now I know. The other day I heard an English friend say, *À tout à l'heure!* It came out, *Toodle-oo!*

Michael Berry
New York, New York

Humpty Dumpty's World

Francis Griffith
Port Washington, New York

Until a few years ago eggs were graded as small, medium, and large. Today, search as you will, you won't find small eggs in any supermarket.

Small and medium are pejoratives in the lexicon of advertising agencies. Giant, monster, and mammoth have taken their place. The small tube of toothpaste is now the giant economy size, a community gathering is a monster rally, and a garage sale is a mammoth event. Hens now lay only medium, large, extra-large, and jumbo eggs.

Porno movies intended for emotionally and intellectually stunted adolescents are labeled "for mature audiences." *Permanent* means 'temporary,' as in *permanent wave*. Comic strips are dull, sadistic, or just plain stupid, but comic they are not. Ginger ale, once a tawny liquid with a taste of ginger so sharp it made your eyes water, is now a pale insipid mixer which contains about as much ginger as a welsh rabbit contains a rabbit.

Sex, once the property of living things only, is now ascribed to inanimate objects. A car is advertised as a sexy import, a shaving cream is described as masculine, and perfume as intensely feminine.

Builders who invade a pleasant countryside, bulldoze its trees and shrubs, cart away its topsoil, construct hundreds of jerry-built look-alike homes, smear the earth with blacktop, and erect garish billboards advertising their depredations are called developers and the scarred landscape they leave behind is called a development.

Liberal once meant 'humane' as opposed to 'doctrinaire.' A liberal was one who espoused the rights of the weak, defenseless, and poor who were incapable of speaking for themselves. In today's world a liberal is one who advocates the destruction of the unborn, the senile, and the incurably ill because they are in the way.

Totalitarian oligarchies officially call themselves *democracies* as, for example, the Democratic Republic of East Germany or the People's Republic of China. A *terrorist* is a freedom fighter if we agree with his aims. Bombing civilian populations is called *pacification.*

Gay is another word whose pristine meaning has been reversed. Once a synonym for innocent joy, it now connotes the morose homosexuals who, humorless and tense, gather in

585

sleazy bars and other public places in a mood anything but joyful and innocent. It has taken on such a homosexual connotation that teachers avoid it in their classrooms. Wordsworth's "A poet could not but be *gay* in such a jocund company" causes today's kids to hoot and holler.

Even the BBC avoids *gay*. When the British ambassador to Ireland was assassinated a couple of years ago, his friend Sir Christopher Soames paid a spontaneous radio tribute to him. "He was gay . . ." said Sir Christopher in innocence and truth. The broadcasting officials were stunned and dropped the awkward word when the tribute was rebroadcast.

The long-haired young people who proclaim that they are *doing their own thing* are doing everybody else's. Fearing to be different, they dress alike, think alike, speak alike, act alike. Their common uniform is a pair of ragged denims, a soiled T-shirt, and shabby sneakers, and they wouldn't be found dead wearing a clean shirt, necktie, or bra. They all listen to the incessant pounding of the same rock bands and the nasal shrieking of the same vocalists, and they hold the same opinions on every subject from abortion to Zen.

Every language changes as time marches on. Words are created, acquire new meanings, thrive by use, and die from disuse. A linguistic system perishes when it no longer helps us to see the world around us as it really is.

Many of the verbal changes occurring today obscure reality. Unlike those that have gone before, they are planned, the result of a conscious effort by an individual or group to manipulate attitudes and beliefs. They are calculated perversions of truth, intended to mislead and deceive. Old words are clothed with new and entirely opposite meanings, as in the nazi and fascist national anthems which extolled liberty and justice.

During the course of centuries some words have taken on antithetical meanings. *Let*, for instance. Hamlet's threat when Marcellus and Horatio try to prevent him from following his father's spirit, "By heaven, I'll make a ghost of him that lets me," is meaningless unless we understand that in Shakespeare's time *let* meant 'prevent,' the opposite of what it means today except in the restricted tennis sense of *let* ball, which the naive believe to be an illiterate corruption of *net ball*, a variant.

Another example is *fast*, a word which is a bundle of contradictions. A man is fast if he is tied to a stake and unable to move, and he is fast if he runs a hundred yards in ten seconds. No matter whether he is a tightwad or a spendthrift, he is fast. If he abstains from eating and drinking, he is said to fast, and if he eats and drinks to excess he is said to be leading a fast life.

But the forces which brought about the semantic alterations of *let* and *fast* over the years are not the same as those that have reversed the meanings of so many words today. *Let* 'to hinder' has a different etymological origin from *let* 'to permit.' *Fast* developed new meanings gradually without conscious effort on anyone's part, following a natural order. Its original meaning was 'firm,' which suggested strength and persistence in movement. This led into 'to run fast', that is, to run without slackening, which in turn introduced the notion of rapidity. 'Living too fast,' a later development, followed almost logically from the preceding meanings. The resulting contradictory significances were unplanned and normally developed.

But many of today's reversals are deliberately contrived. In advertisements, editorials, headlines, and in fact in any place where language is used to influence opinions and actions, instances can be found without too much effort. When *large* means 'small'; *economy* 'waste'; *mature* 'immature'; *permanent* 'temporary'; *develop* 'destroy'; *democratic* 'totalitarian'; *gay* 'glum'; *liberal* 'inhumane'; *doing your own thing* 'following the crowd,' our language is setting the world on its ear. The mind reels at such semantic reversals.

We are living in a Lewis Carroll topsy-turvydom, an environment in which language does not always correspond with reality and where things are not always what they seem to be.

If our image of the world is sometimes like a distorted image in a wavy mirror, the fault, dear Brutus, is not in our stars but in our language.

BIBLIOGRAPHIA

THE WAY WOMEN WRITE, by Mary Hiatt, Teachers College Press, 1977, vii + 152 pp., $5.95. Paperback. [Available directly from the publisher: 1234 Amsterdam Avenue, New York, N.Y. 10027.]

This is an important, informative book that reports on the results of the author's systematic investigation of 50 books written by women and 50 written by men. The conclusions, stated in the briefest way, are that women's writing is different from men's, but not for the reasons commonly adduced (i.e., word selection and tone). As readers of VERBATIM may already be aware, I am more concerned with style and appropriateness of language than with "correctness," and *T3W* provides an excellent, readily understandable example of stylistic analysis that ranges from the study of such features as sentence length, choice of adverbs, adjectives, verbs, etc., to that of more subtle characteristics like structural balance, rhetorical effectiveness, and use of similes.

The book is important because of its conclusions and informative because in its exemplary analysis of style it is a paragon of clarity and organization. The analysis of style is not a simple subject, and I know only of Louis T. Milic as the leading academic researcher in the field. Professor Hiatt, author of *Artful Balance: The Parallel Structures of Style* (Teachers College Press, 1975), which is not familiar to me, has provided not only a study that is revealing but a readable introduction for any who are interested in how style can be analyzed: I have not seen such a clear exposition of polysyndeton, asyndeton, and other rhetorical devices since reading Barr's Introduction to my textbook copy of *The Orations of Cicero* (where all the examples are, of course, in Latin).

T3W makes a substantial contribution to the subject of male/female differences (*Vive!*)—if that is, indeed, a "subject"—and to language analysis, both of which are often approached by either stodgy or hysterical investigators. The only other sane approach I have seen is *Words and Women*, by Casey Miller and Kate Swift [reviewed: III,2,9]. Now I must read *Artful Balance*.

[L. U.]

EPISTOLAE

I was amused by Gary Felton's article in the May edition, and should like to contribute some of my favourites to the codified, and sometimes indistinctly perceived, laws to which we are subject, and against which we sometimes stub our toes:

Cook's constant (my version)—A variable by which an experimental datum has to be multiplied to result in an answer acceptably close to the theoretical.

A *glitch*—is an inherent, built-in, organic fallibility in a design, plan, equipment or any human contrivance.

Finagle's laws: First—The likelihood of a thing happening is inversely proportional to its desirability.

Second—Once a job is fouled up, anything done to improve it only makes it worse.

Murphy's first law (corollaries)—

(1.) It is impossible to make anything foolproof because fools are so ingenious.

(2.) Any wire or tube cut to length will be too short.

(3.) After any machine or unit has been completely assembled, extra components will be found on the bench.

(4.) After the last sixteen mounting screws have been removed from an access plate, it will be discovered that the wrong access plate has been removed.

Lowery's law—If it jams, force it. If it breaks, it needed replacing anyway.

Zumwalt's first law—The probability of failure is directly proportional to the number and importance of the people watching the test.

Dobbins's law—When in doubt, use a bigger hammer.

Everitt's form of the second law of thermodynamics—Confusion (entropy) is always increasing in society. Only if someone or something works extremely hard can this confusion be reduced to order in a limited region. Nevertheless, this effort will still result in an increase in the total confusion of society at large.

Jones's law—The man who can smile when things go wrong has thought of someone he can blame it on.

Matsch's maxim—A fool in a high station is like a man at the top of a high mountain—everything appears small to him and he appears small to everybody.

Apart from my personal contribution, all the other laws, etc., are quoted from *Malice in Blunderland* of which the name of the author and publisher escape me.

K. B. Weatherald
London, England

To Elaine Von Bruns' "Illicit Threesomes" can be added *Gaza Stripper*   inhabitant of the Gaza Strip.

David L. Gold
Haifa, Israel

Elaine Von Bruns's "Illicit Threesomes" [IV,1] were not only amusing but pregnant. As I looked at them, they gave birth to others, right in front of my tongue:

down and outspoken   recommended dress for Plain
Janes
world warpaint   general international mobilization
to hell and gonorrhea   last stage of Byronism
tertiary stagecoach   third one of the day
venerable sagebrush   old bushes
snail's pacemaker   yet another triumph of medical
science
horsehide and seek   minor league baseball

Also, like political opinions when closely examined, some of Ms. Von B's originals changed form as they coupled and tripled, producing new variations. I hope the lady won't mind these changes, which are not necessarily improvements:

bottlenecktie   worn by St. Bernards in the Alps
bird in the handshake   an unsigned agreement
scotch on the bedrocks   alcoholic refreshment during a
marital quarrel
draw and quarterdeck   stacked cards
threadbare knuckles   John L. Sullivan in old age

More examples could be given, of course, such being the agglutinative nature of the language. I shall stop here, however, lest someone accuse me of being a wordplayboy.

Calvin K. Towle
W.W. Norton & Company, Inc.

I found Elaine Von Bruns' "Illicit Threesomes" addictive. Because I couldn't dropkick the habit, I'm sending along the following:

Hero and Leander sandwich   snack for passengers
crossing the Hellespont
hot dog in the manger   food given grudgingly to
members of the Holy Family
quid pro quo vadis   answering a question with a
question
fife and humdrum   uninspired music
Koechel listing to the portside   playing Mozart while
the ship goes down

income-uppance tax   penalty for not paying the tax in
                      the first place
with might and Main Street   movie about a small-town
                      librarian who enlists in the Marines
the Infra-red Army   Soviet spy system
three-quarter time and tide   a waltz that waits for
                      no man
pen and inkling   a written hint

Josef Brand
Brooklyn, New York

CORRIGENDA

Volume IV, Number 2, "We Shall Know Them by Their
Roots":
1. *Taj Mahal* is a person, not a group.
2. *Runaways* is not "an all-female band" (unless the
   drummer has been to a Danish surgeon lately).
3. *Booker T. and the M.G.'s* bears no reference to automobiles since *T.* is *Booker T. Washington's* middle
   initial and *M.G.'s* are members of the Memphis Group.
4. *Fleetwood Mac* is not a Cadillac on a hamburger but
   a hybrid name taken from the band's rhythm section,
   drummer Mick Fleetwood and bassist John McVie.

Joe Fusco
Menlo Park, California

The *Sopwith Camel* rock group is named after a World
War I biplane, and should be listed among the methods of
travel rather than among the wildlife.   Victoria Nowell
Chilliwack, British Columbia

Mr. Schulz had better brush up on his Latin if he thinks
the name *Ars Nova* an astronomical reference. It means,
quite simply, 'New Art.'   Andrew Baird
Princeton, New Jersey

Schweppes, le 'drink' des gens raffinés

Myrna Knepler
Chicago, Illinois

Why is it that a high priced condominium is advertised in American newspapers as a *de luxe* apartment while French magazines try to sell their more affluent readers *appartements de grand standing*? Madison Avenue, when constructing ads for high priced non-necessary items, may use French phrases to suggest to readers that they are identified as super-sophisticated, subtly sexy, and privy to the secrets of old world charm and tradition. In recent years French magazines aimed at an increasingly affluent public have made equally canny use of borrowed English words to sell their wares.

The advertising pages of the *New Yorker* and the more elegant fashion and home decorating magazines often depend on blatant flattery of the reader's sense of exclusiveness. Time and time again the reader is told "only *you* are elegant, sophisticated, discriminating and rich enough to use this product." Of course the "you" must encompass a large enough group to insure adequate sales. Foreign words, particularly prestigious French words, may be used to reinforce this selling message.

French magazines often use English words in their advertising to suggest to potential consumers a slightly different but equally flattering self-image. The reader is pictured as someone in touch with new ideas from home and abroad who has not forgotten the traditional French arts of living, but is modern enough to approach them in a completely up-to-date and casual manner.

Of course, each language has borrowed words from the other which have, over the course of time, been completely assimilated. It is not these that the advertiser exploits but rather words that are foreign enough to evoke appealing images of an exotic culture. When the French reader is urged to try "Schweppes, le 'drink' des gens raffinés" or an American consumer is told that a certain manufacturer has "the *savoir faire* to design *la crème de la crème* of luxurious silky knits," the foreign words do not say anything that could not be as easily said by native ones. What they do convey is something else. They invite the reader to share in the prestige of the foreign language and the power of the images associated with that language's country of origin.

In each country a knowledge of the other's language is an important sign of cultivation. Today, English is the language studied by an overwhelming majority of French students, and the ability to speak it well is increasingly valued as a symbol of prestige as well as a marketable skill. Despite the decrease in foreign language study in the United States, French has maintained its reputation as a language people ought to know. Adding a few obviously foreign words from the prestige language not only increases the prestige of the product itself but also flatters the reader by reminding him that he has enough linguistic talent to understand what is being said. As in the "only-*you*-are-elegant, -sophisticated, -discriminating-and-rich-enough" appeal, the advertiser must be careful not to exclude too many potential customers, and the foreign expressions are usually transparent cognates or easily understood words. A French reader may be urged to buy cigarettes by being told that "partout dans le monde c'est YES à Benson and Hedges" while the *New Yorker* reader can consider a vacation on "an island [off the coast of South Carolina] where change hasn't meant commercialism, and tranquillity still comes *au naturelle.*"

Even monolinguals are not excluded from this flattery. The word can be given in the foreign language and then translated; the reader is still in on the secret: " 'goût' is the French word for taste and Christolfe is the universal word for taste in vases."

The prestige of a foreign term and its possible ambiguity for the reader may serve to disguise a negative fact about the product. A necklace of Perle de Mer advertised in an American magazine is not composed of real pearls made by nature in the sea but of simulated pearls produced by a large American manufacturer. By the same token, when a French advertisement for a packaged tour offers "aller et retour en classe coach" the prestige of the English word *coach* disguises the fact that it is the less luxurious form of airline transportation that is being offered.

But the most important function of borrowed words in advertising is to project an image of their country of origin in order to create for the reader the illusion that the product, and by implication its user, will share in the good things suggested by that image. French names like *Grand Prix, Coupe De Ville,* and *Monte Carlo* attached to American car models help the advertiser to get across the message that the car is luxurious, sophisticated, and elegantly appointed and that driving such an automobile reflects positively on the taste of its potential owner. In almost all cases French names are reserved for the more expensive models while American words are favored for small meat-and-potatoes cars like *Charger*, *Maverick*, *Pinto* and *Bronco*. Similarly, the French reader is likely to encounter a large number of American technical terms in ads for appliances, radio and television equipment, cameras, and "gadgets de luxe," since the manufacturer benefits by associating American mechanical skill with his products. An advertisement for French-made hi-fi equipment appearing in a French magazine spoke of the product's "push-pull ultra linéaire, 6 haut-parleurs, 2 elliptiques et 4 tweeters . . . montés sur baffle."

Images, which are used again and again, are often based on myths of the other country's culture. Words like *tomahawk* and *trading posts* are used in French advertisements to evoke images of a western-movie America of naturalness, freedom, and adventure in order to sell products like "Chemise de 'cow girl,' " "bottes Far West," and vests in the style of "Arizona Bill," irrespective of the real West that is or was. The name *Monte Carlo* attached to an American-made car trades on the American consumer's image of a once-exclusive vacation spot, now available as part of low-cost travel packages. Thus the name *Monte Carlo* can convey to an automobile a prestige that the real trip to Monte Carlo has long since lost.

Those images that are not completely mythic are usually gross stereotypes of the other country's culture. Few Americans would recognize the image of American life presented in French advertising—a new world filled with eternally youthful, glamourously casual, up-to-date men and women devoted to consuming the products of their advanced technology. Similarly, few French men and women would recognize the nation of elegant and knowing consumers of food, wine, and sophisticated sex pictured in American ads.

The image of France as a nation of lovers, bold yet unusually subtle in their relations with the opposite sex, is often called upon to sell perfume and cosmetics, sometimes of French origin but packaged and advertised specifically for the American market. An ad which appeared several years ago in the *New Yorker* showed a bottle of perfume labeled "voulez-vous" implanted next to a closeup of a sexy and elegant woman, her face shadowed by a male hand lighting her cigarette. The text: "The spark that starts the fire. Voulez-vous a new perfume." *Audace, Robe d'un Soir*, and *Je Reviens* are other perfumes advertised in American magazines with pictures and copy that reinforce the sexual suggestiveness of the prominently featured French name on the label.

It may be surprising for Americans to learn that English

names are given to perfumes sold in France to enhance their romantic image. *My Love, Partner,* and *Shocking* are some examples. Advertisements for French-made men's cosmetics in French magazines may refer to products such as *l'aftershave* and *le pre-shave*. Givenchy's *Gentleman* is advertised to Frenchmen as an eau de toilette for the man who dares to appear at business lunches in a turtleneck sweater and has the courage to treat love in a casual manner.

The recent swelling of the list of Americanisms used in French advertising and in French speech has pained many Frenchmen and has even caused the government to take action. For a number of years the leader in this "war against anglicisms" has been René Etiemble, a professor at the Sorbonne. Etiemble, through magazine articles, radio and television appearances and his widely read book, *Parlez-vous franglais?*, struggles vehemently against what he most often refers to as an "invasion" of American terms. He does little to disguise his strong anti-American sentiments. American words are rejected as agents of a vulgar American culture and both are seen as threats to the French way of life. According to Etiemble "[the] heritage of words [is the] heritage of ideas: with *le twist* and *la ségrégation, la civilisation cocolcoolique,* the American manner of not living will disturb and contaminate all that remains of your cuisine, wines, love and free thought." It would be difficult to find a stronger believer in the power of words than Etiemble.

In response to the concerns of Etiemble and others, a series of committees composed of highly placed French scientists and language experts were charged with the task of finding Gallic equivalents for such popular terms as *le meeting, le marketing, le management,* and *le know-how.* The recommended replacements are: *la réunion, la commercialisation, la direction,* and, of course, *le savoir faire.* The replacements do not seem to have taken root.

At the end of 1975 a more radical step was taken. The French National Assembly passed a law banning the use of all foreign words in advertising in those cases in which a native alternative has been officially suggested, and instituting a fine against violators.

Both Etiemble and the government purists rely strongly on the "logical" argument that most loan words are not needed because there already exists a native equivalent with exactly the same meaning. Yet a look at the advertising pages of French and American magazines will show that borrowed words are used again and again when there are obvious native equivalents. Certainly the English words in "c'est YES à Benson and Hedges" and "Le 'drink' des gens raffinés" could be translated without loss of literal meaning—but they are not.

It is precisely because of the connotations associated with the culture of its country of origin, not its denotations, that advertisers find the borrowed word attractive.

ETYMOLOGICA OBSCURA

Public Servants

The names of our governmental institutions are too opaque. Almost every one of them is Latin in origin, the real meaning hidden in that utterly alien speech. This gives them a false grandeur. We have a president. What's that? The first man of a company, a college, the country. But where does it come from? From *sideo, sidere* 'to sit,' and *pre-* 'in front.' We really have a Sits-in-Front. Just another chairperson.

We have a city of Washington, where he does his ruling. This city is known to everyone who presides over a TV set as The Nation's Capital. A resounding phrase, and meant to be. But what's its origin? *Nation*: from *natus* 'to be born, to be a native.' *Capital*: from *caput* 'a human head.' The Headplace of the Natives. Just what explorers were constantly finding in nineteenth-century Africa.

One day a year, to keep our leaders modest, all governmental names should be rendered into English. Then we would remember that a *senator* is nothing but a *senex* 'an old man'—and *Congress* itself just a bunch of old folks shuffling along. *Con* 'with' and *gradi, gressus* 'step.' The 95th Step-Together. An *ambassador*, for all his diplomatic immunity and social pretension, we would recognize as own brother to the butler. The word comes eventually from Gothic *and-bahti* 'service' cognate with Gallo-Latin *ambactus* 'a servant or vassal.'

Most of all, we could reflect on the FBI. *Federal*, from *foedus*, a league or treaty. *Bureau* from French *bureau* now meaning an 'office' but once meaning an 'office desk,' and before that a 'cloth to be spread on a desk.' It in turn from Old French *burel* 'woolen cloth,' and that from Latin *burra* 'a shaggy garment, sheep shearings, coarse hair for stuffing.' *Investigation*, from *vestigare* 'to track.' (*Vestigium* means a 'footprint.') The League of Desk Cloths Used for Tracking Down.

Noel Perrin
Dartmouth College

My Grandmother's "Spaghetta"

Charles L. Todd
Hamilton College

My Grandmother Todd, who died at ninety-one in 1944, was no bigot, but like many Yankees who settled in New York State's westernmost county, Chautauqua, she was uncomfortable with words and proper names that sounded "foreign" to her, especially when they originated with the Italians and Poles who settled in that rich grape-growing area. For instance, words ending in the short Italianate "i" she would "prettify" with a broad "a." Whenever she cooked up a "mess" of spaghetti or macaroni, it immediately became "spaghetta" and "macarona" (that word "mess," by the way, was usually associated with the bullheads I brought in from the Cassadage lakes, or the dandelion and cowslip greens I picked in the early spring). Oddly enough, the nearby towns of Laona and Fredonia, became "Lay-ony" and "Free-dony," just as Cousin Sarah and Aunt Louisa became "Sary" and "Louisy." I have long pondered these little linguistic aberrations of my grandmother, and I finally, somehow, reached the conclusion that those broad "a's" she reserved for the foreign words and names were part of the ethnocentricity which often crops up in rural (especially Yankee) America—an attempt to elevate the speech of the newcomers. While Benito Mussolini was making Italian trains run on time and seemed like a respectable, though noisy, fellow, he was "Mr. Mussolina" to Grandmother, but when he began to act up in Ethiopia, and became a pal of that man Hitler, she went back to "Mussolini"—hitting hard on the "eenie." We had a young "Eye-talian" boy, named Luigi Petronelli who used to help out during the haying season. He was a good hand at "mowing away," and Grandmother always had a glass of ice cold, pure Concord grape juice waiting for us between loads. Luigi, however, would retire to his old Model A where he had stashed away a bottle of wine. Having a keen sense of smell, Grandmother soon caught on, and would go to the back door and call out "Luiga Petronella—you come in here and drink what's good for you!" Luigi never tried to straighten her out about his name, but he was adamant about the unfermented grape juice. Grandmother was very fond of the "Opry" programs which came to us via radio on Saturday afternoons, and one of her favorite singers was "Giovanna

Martinella." Not even the mellifluent Milton Cross, whose Italian came so trippingly off the tongue, had any effect on her determination to make those "Eye-talian" names more elegant.

The same treatment was accorded the Polish people who moved into nearby Dunkirk to work in the steel mills, and who occasionally went into vegetable farming in Chautauqua County. She liked the morning polka hour on Buffalo's radio station, WGR, sponsored by Dom Polski (a national Polish group), but Dom Polski invariably became "Dom Polska." I might add that she was delighted to learn that Polaski, N.Y., where Cousin Sary lived was prounounced Polas-sky, "the way it should be." My friend, Ed Roski, whose father was injured in the steel mill, became "that poor Rosk-eye boy."

We had few people of French descent in the area, but they had long accepted the fact that all "er" endings, as far as Grandmother and her fellow Yankees were concerned, sounded just like that—and nothing more. "Neighbor Bellanger," for example, tried hard for a few years to hang on to "Bellan-jay," but it was no use. The same thing happened, of course, to that "Frenchy" actor Charles Boyer, whom Grandmother used to see occasionally on the movie screen in Fredonia, and also to that other Frenchy, "Morris Chevaleer," of whom she disapproved. Some of her Fredonia friends had been to "gay Paree" and knew better—but Grandmother said they were "putting on airs." All this made life difficult for me when I returned from my college French classes and told her her new silk crepe scarf that she wore over her hat was not called "Georgietta," but rather "Georgette." She would immediately remonstrate that "Georgietta" was the more elegant way of saying it, and it often reminded me of the way in which she crooked her little finger when she lifted up her cup of tea. I am told by one of my linguist friends that this might be called "hyperurbanism," but I'm not sure that it isn't simply linguistic ethnocentricity, or perhaps even a form of xenophobia. I strongly suspect that native Cape Codders and Nantucketers are similarly affected when the mainlander folks stream in during the summer months. I also recall vividly the nudging and grinning that went on when I spoke in the Morganville, Kansas, town hall one night and came out with "to-mah-to" instead of "ta-may-ta," and got equally careless with my "eithers" and "neithers." I should have been more careful since the chairman of that meeting had informed me previously that the town was founded by one Morgan, Captain of a Yankee Clipper, who chose his future residence because it was "the futhest place in the good old U.S.A. away from both the oceans."

I think what actually got me started on all this is my name "Lafe," pronounced as in "safe." Most of the letters I get from strangers who don't know any better are addressed to "Lief" Todd, indicating sound Nordic origins. But, alas, this isn't true, for "Lafe" is what my Yankee forefathers contrived out of Lafayette, who visited Fredonia, New York, during his triumphal tour of the Eastern states in 1825. My grandmother's mother was invited onto the platform after he spoke; managed a graceful curtsey, and had her hand kissed by the gallant Frenchman. Great-grandfather, I am told, got the giggles and kidded her about it for years, but Great-grandmother was overwhelmed, and named her first boy child after the General—a name inherited by my father and myself and several others in the family. Naturally, Lafayette, as a "Frenchy" would pronounce it, couldn't survive in Yankeeland, so it became "Lay-fay-ette"—with, thank heaven, no final broad "a" as in "Georgetta." But that final "ette" sounded too feminine for a boy-child, so it was quickly reduced to "Lafe." The same vowel transformation took place in most small villages named after the great Frenchman, though oddly enough most big city streets and hotels bearing the name went unscathed. Try asking a Throughway attendant how to get to "Fye-etteville" in New York State! It has always been a great boon to me incidentally to know that the State of Arkansas boasts a town named "Lafe," but I am less happy when I read regional novels, mostly about the southwestern mountain country, and find the village idiot named "Lafe." Why not Zeke, or Luke?

The city-bred mother of a great-uncle of mine went the whole hog, as Grandmother put it, and named a son, "Marquis de Lafayette Todd," with all the right sounds in it. Years later, however, he was reminded by his congressman out in California that titles of nobility are not used in democratic America. My great-uncle, totally unperturbed, went to court and had his name changed to Marcus de Lafayette, frequently shortened to "M.D.L." Todd. But Grandmother taught me to call him "Uncle Lafe," and I did.

I once got up the courage to ask Grandmother why she said "spaghetta" and "macarona." She looked puzzled for a moment, and then exclaimed, "Why, Land o' Goshen, I guess I just spleen against eating those Eye-talian sounding things!" As for "Georgietta" she simply allowed it sounded silkier and prettier that way! I must have been at least ten years old, by the way, before I learned that her favorite expletive wasn't "Atlantic Ocean!"

&JEERS

Have you noticed how advertising copywriters have recently been attracted to the "clever" use of *double entendre*? Some of the visual and textual puns are apt, others emerge as what we must call "bent metaphors." To wit:

'Who could make light of themselves better?" [Benson & Hedges 100's Lights.]

"Get a leg up." [*Time*; accompanying a picture of flamingos, one with its leg tucked up.]

"Get the Big Apple and the Big Avocado in one bite." [*New York/New West*; no amount of research has turned up any evidence that California is ever referred to as "the Big Avocado."]

Christmas jeer: "In the holiday spirit of giving, Barney's is happy to give you Sundays 'til Christmas to shop." [Advt. in *N.Y. Times*.]

"Custom Calibration—exclusive technological breakthrough enables the wearer to personally accurize the watch to one's own unique lifestyle to an accuracy of less than 10 seconds per year . . . without the use of tools or the need to open the case." [Advt. in *Wall St. Journal* by Hammacher Schlemmer for a solar-powered watch; that is, if your lifestyle calls for getting up an hour after you should, arrive 45 minutes late for appointments and 15 minutes early for cocktails. —Daniel James, Ivoryton, Ct.]

EPISTOLAE

Eric Partridge is doubly mistaken in his "A Dictionary Of Catch Phrases" [IV, 3].

The correct wording of the catch phrase is *not* "After you, my dear Alphonse — no, after you, Gaston." It is "After you, my dear Alphonse—no, after you, my dear Gaston."

It is *not* Canadian in origin. It originated in a Hearst (King Features) comic strip called, "Happy Hooligan." The cartoonist was F. Opper. It appeared all through the 1920s and into the 1930s.

Alphonse and Gaston were two supporting players in the strip's cast of characters. They were very dapper Frenchmen (top hats, frock coats, moustaches and imperials like Napoleon III). So courteous were they that in moments of extreme danger to themselves they would forgo escape in order to invite each other to go first.

Opper originated another phrase that had a short vogue just before the 1920s: "And her name was Maude." Maude was a mule in one of his strips.

And *you*, I regret to say, are mistaken in calling *Where was Moses when the lights went out?* an early 20c. riddle. It can be found in "Huckleberry Finn" by Mark Twain (Chapter XVII), a novel copyrighted in 1884. And it reads as though it had originated long before that.

Walter Newman
Sherman Oaks, California

In Eastern Virginia, in Mobjack Bay country near Williamsburg, where the York River meets the Chesapeake Bay, is a small band of folk known as Guineamen who speak a dialect that is said to be similar to Elizabethan English. The legend is that these people are descendents of deserters from Cornwallis' army at the time of the surrender. H. L. Mencken, in *The American Language, Supplement Two*, gives a similar explanation (p. 224). The difficulty with this theory is that there are no Hessian or German names in the community, as would be expected if the persons who came to Guinea were the rank and file of Cornwallis' army, who were mercenaries from Hesse.

In Michael Pearson's book *Those Damned Rebels,* a history of the Revolutionary War from the point of view of the British, an interesting fact was noted (p. 397). When Cornwallis found that help was not going to arrive because the French fleet under DeGrasse had barricaded the British from rescuing him and his army, he decided to make a forced march north to join up with other British troops. He assembled boats and his choice of the assembled troops, and the assumption here is that the troops chosen to accompany him would be primarily British. They attempted on October 16, 1781, to cross the York River to Gloucester to head north but "a York River storm came up" [having been in several York River storms, I know that they can be devastating] and many of the boats were blown down the river to the area that is now Guinea. The men in these boats would have been British and would have had a community of interests to hold them together.

Cornwallis sued for surrender the next day. The troops at Yorktown were soon moved to Williamsburg and subsequently west into the Valley of Virginia, where the security seems to have become lax. Many of these troops remained in the valley, especially in the Charlottesville area, and there we do find some German dialects and many German and Hessian names.

The British soldiers who landed at what is now Jenkins' Neck, in Guinea, had no difficulty in settling down. Having a common background, similar interests, and a probable fear of being taken as prisoners of war, they are assumed to have remained in the area and to have maintained in this isolated part of the country their dialect, which they brought from England. As the county government became more organized and was able to demand payment of taxes from these people, they paid them in the coin with which they had been paid by Cornwallis: guineas; hence they became "Guineamen."

The principal surnames of those who still speak this dialect are Brown, Smith, West, Jenkins, Hall, Robins, Rowe, Belvin and Shackelford. With the advent of the central school system, radio, and television, the dialect is fast disappearing and probably not more than two or three hundred people speak it today.

Raymond S. Brown, M.D.
Gloucester, Virginia

Anglo-American Crossword Puzzle No. 3 by Jack Luzzatto

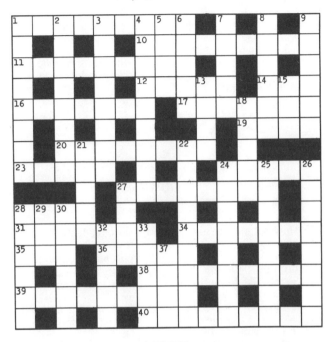

ACROSS

1 Undetectable toupee? (3, 6)
10 Good for a ring of fire. (5, 4)
11 Sheep's clothing for dirty dogs, at times, under cover. (4, 5)
12 Tennis action returning East from Colorado park. (5)
14 A hot spell. (3)
16 A few well-chosen words for the poor heap around the pit. (7)

17 The ephemeral dollar or something really green and durable? (7)
19 The slam is an odd place for the welfare of the poor. (4)
20 Muddled picture about nothing. So much for Dunkirk! (4, 4)
23 Cries for tears in silken ensemble. (5)
24 Wise old Greek returns to pose a moral problem. (5)

27 Get bail in dire need when it could have been withheld. (8)
28 You've heard this before! (4)
31 Opposite of handbook for a thief? (7)
34 Marked with symbols, but not at editor's discretion. (7)
35 Just dandy! (3)

36 Sounds tolerable enough to be heard. (5)
38 Disorderly clutter around the UN makes it all so bellicose. (9)
39 Lots in the game let orgies develop. (9)
40 Concerning the ghost who treats every*body* with consideration. (9)

DOWN

1 How dates are made by blondes. (8)
2 Office-seeker on the primrose path. (8)
3 Sounds like former radio nuisance is now very happy. (8)
4 Wearer of short jockeys in jockey shorts. (9)
5 Note taken from skeleton at the old fraternity. (4)
6 A fastidious state of mind. (5)
7 Morning practice to entertain. (5)
8 Hoover and Smith collaborate on a book of the simple things. (6)
9 Extorts money from the French in strange beds. (6)
13 Time to get up and get out. (4)
15 How cockney sailor handles the tiller. (3)
18 Go headlessly to the fray. (5)

21 With navigator I plot the course. (5)
22 Jack of all trades. (5, 4)
24 Subtly concealed being both a brute and an ass! (8)
25 Let's beat the accident rate with safety measure. (4, 4)
26 Rode wildly into trap hidden by hunter. (9)
27 Backward praise has double value. (4)
28 Suffered mostly by overflowing. (6)
29 See sweet nothings written here. (3)
30 Dreamers of a posher way of life. (6)
32 Cap in blowup causes quite a scare. (5)
33 Red to turn into the loving kind . . . (5)
37 . . . despite the impulse for beheadal of the old Stalinist policy. (4)

ACROSS	DOWN
1. Top secret	1. T-owh-EADS
10. Alarm bell	2. PROMISER
11. Wool socks	3. EC-STATIC
12. E.stes	4. Racehorse
14. Bee	5. ELKS (skel minus eton)
16. E-pit-APH	6. Taste
17. eph-EMERAL D-ollar	7. AM-use
19. ALMS	8. Herb-Al
20. EPIC R-o-UT	9. B-le-EDS
23. SERIC	13. emiT
24. AESOP, pose A	15. 'elm
27. DEN-iabl-E	18. (t)ravel
28. Echo	21. p-I-lot
31. Foot-pad	22. Union dues
34. Not-at-ed-itor's	24. A-b-S-tru-S-e
35. Fop	25. S-eat b-ELT
36. Aloud	26. PR-ed-A T-or
38. truc-U-le-N-t	27. DUAL
39. SOR-t-I-le-GE	28. EFFUSE (SUFFE-r-E-d)
40. Re-specter	29. C-OO
	30. HOPERS
	32. PANIC
	33. DOTER
	37. (p)URGE